The Classic Vision

Murray Krieger

Visions of Extremity in Modern Literature

A mammoth variation-piece of lamentation . . . broadens
out in circles, each of which draws the other resist-
lessly after it: movements, large-scale variations,
which correspond to the textual units of chapters of
a book and in themselves are nothing else than series
of variations. But all of them go back for the theme
to a highly plastic fundamental figure of notes, which
is inspired by a certain passage of the text.

THOMAS MANN, *Doctor Faustus*

Volume II

The Classic Vision

The Retreat from Extremity

The Johns Hopkins University Press   Baltimore and London

The Johns Hopkins University Press, Baltimore, Maryland 21218
The Johns Hopkins University Press Ltd., London

ISBN 0-8018-1312-3 (clothbound edition)
ISBN 0-8018-1551-7 (paperbound edition)

Excerpts from T. S. Eliot's "Burnt Norton," *The Cocktail Party*, and *Murder in the Cathedral* are reprinted by permission of Harcourt Brace Jovanovich, Inc., and Faber and Faber Ltd. from *The Complete Poems and Plays of T. S. Eliot*; copyright 1935 by Harcourt Brace Jovanovich, Inc., copyright 1943, 1950, 1963 by T. S. Eliot.

Excerpts from Robert Penn Warren's *All the King's Men* are reprinted by permission of Harcourt Brace Jovanovich, Inc., and Eyre & Spottiswoode (Publishers) Ltd.; copyright 1946 by Robert Penn Warren.

Excerpts from William Faulkner's *Light in August* are reprinted by permission of Random House, Inc.; copyright 1932 by William Faulkner, copyright 1950 by Random House, Inc.

Originally published, 1971
Johns Hopkins Paperbacks edition, 1973

To my wife, Joan,
and my children, Catherine and Eliot,
for their classic gift

Contents

Contents

Preface

I recall quite clearly my awareness, even before I had finished with *The Tragic Vision*, that *The Classic Vision* would have to follow it in order to right the balance. Indeed, I felt that the seeds of the classic were immanent in my treatment of the tragic, although —as but seeds—only implicitly there and in need of being distinguished from what I called the "ethical." In that earlier volume I tried to convey an awareness of a mild, other-than-ethical alternative to the tragic, in dealing, for example, with Frau Schweigestill and Serenus Zeitblom, and their attitudes toward Adrian Leverkühn, in *Doctor Faustus* (pp. 108–13 in *The Tragic Vision*); or with Melville's defense of the homely catnip against the encroaching amaranth in *Pierre* (p. 197); or with Lizaveta Epanchin in *The Idiot* (p. 227); or with the specially conciliatory role of Ishmael in *Moby Dick* (pp. 249–51). Finally, there was the brief discussion of the roles of Lena Grove and Byron Bunch in *Light in August* (referred to and extended in Chapter 11 below) with which I concluded *The Tragic Vision*—by bringing that vision out of itself and asking that we look beyond it.

These foreshadowings meant that I had come to look at *The Tragic Vision*, in its entirety, as a promissory note that could be redeemed only by the present volume. Such redemption has taken ten years, during which I have, of course, written other things but have kept this study very much alive and at the center of my thinking and sensibility. I have never before spent this long mellowing an idea and a book, but the classic, by its very nature, would seem to call for such a relaxed development, such maturation, more than most subjects. (I am tempted to pursue the appropriateness of "Ripeness is all" as one of the great classic mottoes, but that sort of discussion is too substantive for the dimensions of a preface.) Now that this book is completed, I see that doing it has helped clarify, ex post facto, the reaches and the limits of the earlier one. It is as if examining the areas beyond the tragic vision has provided me with a new awareness of the boundary beyond which the present study is to move. I might hope that, if this study could serve its reader's understanding as it has served mine, then even such an alien time as ours could turn out to be the precise moment when such a study is most timely.

Yet superficially it would seem that, however good the reasons for the time consumed in producing this book, the delay has turned out to be very unfortunate because it has carried me to a point in history that would appear frightfully unfriendly to my interests here. If ever there was a moment antagonistic to the classic spirit, this would appear to be it. Indeed, I must confess that it takes something of a classic sense even to conceive of a study like this one in a world of extremes like ours. Even if it is an act of daring to ask that others still take the classic seriously—most of all now—nevertheless this fact would be one reason why such a book as this may be desperately needed. I must confess that I myself came close to suggesting the exclusive reality of the tragic these days when I wrote, in *The Tragic Vision* at the conclusion of the initial chapter on "Tragedy and the Tragic Vision,"

> *in our time, driven as it is by crises and "arrests" and*
> *blind as it is to the healing power and saving grace of*
> *tragedy, the tragic has come, however unfortunately,*
> *to loom as a necessary vision and—or so it*
> *seems to the sadder of us—as one that can be neither*
> *reduced nor absorbed. Or is it, perhaps . . . that*
> *our world has itself become the tragic visionary, in its*
> *unbelief using self-destructive crises to force itself*
> *finally to confront the absurdities of earthly reality—*
> *those which have always been there lurking beneath*
> *for the visionary who would dare give up all to*
> *read them?*

The possibility, alas, seems far more persuasive in 1970 than it did in 1960.

Is the classic vision, then, obsolete? If so, this book becomes only an observation of a quaint and antique disposition in our literary tradition, one no longer available to us. It is already clear that I must hope and suggest that such is not the case. Let it be granted that the classic's profound acceptance of the human lot and human foibles, its retreat from extremity, may appear to be a maddening complacency—if not a maddening condescension toward vigorous activism—to a world too easily maddened. (We can at once imagine hearing such a vision referred to as a "cop-out.") But can we engage in action without the classic visionary's broadly receptive sense of human history, of the destiny of the race, except at our peril? Can we think in extreme terms or commit ourselves to extreme actions without some awareness of what extremity costs our humanity? Obviously, contemporary history shows that we can—but also that we pay the price for doing so. On the other hand, we can allow the classic sense, to the limited extent that it may be available to us now, to enrich our attitudes, as we allow the rich historical sense bestowed by earlier generations to soften us. The most remarkable part of these generations and their history (which is our history) is, after all, their literature, which bears this classic sense. I like to think that, in freeing its vision in my critically discursive way, I am using our literature to free us all, even from ourselves. Is that not what literature, finally, is for?

There are some details concerning terms and methods that are worth a word of preliminary explanation or justification. I should say something about the use here of the term "classic" rather than "comic" as my alternative to the "tragic"—short of admitting that in my earlier study "romantic" should have been used rather than "tragic." There seems to me good reason to avoid the obvious antithetical partners, either "tragic" and "comic" or "romantic" and "classic." The term "comic" is related to comedy in a way I wish to avoid. It is true that the classic can be comic, but it is not coextensive with the comic. It can be—and often is—other things, so that calling it the comic might distort its focus, and mine. Thus there are examples of the comic (we shall examine two of them in Chapter 8) which—whatever their virtues—are not examples of the fully earned classic vision, although on the other hand it must be acknowledged that all the works I see as classic are in some sense, whether superficial or profound, comic as well. What I mean to emphasize in using the term "classic" is the sense of restraint, of acceptance, of coming to terms with limitations self-imposed—as well as the awareness of the alternative one rejects in turning away from self-indulgence.

Further, I still defend the use—as counterpart to the classic—of "tragic" rather than "romantic," not because there are not major romantic elements in the tragic vision (indeed, there clearly are), but because I mean to emphasize the relation of that vision to the wholeness of tragedy, as I tried to make clear in the first chapter of my earlier volume. One could complain also of the hopelessly messy haze of possible meanings surrounding "romantic," but I fear that its counterpart, "classic," is not often used with any more precision, although this fact has not precluded my adopting it here. Still, I'll hold to the imperfect terms tragic and classic, only because—whatever my difficulties with them—they seem to circumscribe their subjects more adequately than any alternatives, though as I pair them each term forgoes its usual antithetical partner.

One feature of my discussions of the literary works themselves should be pointed out: they are meant to reflect a variety of literary approaches, as my treatment is adapted to what the work appears to require, given—of course—my own special interest. Not that I am suggesting any eclecticism on my part; quite the contrary, since I fear that—as always—my commitments are all too evident, and constantly so. What *is* monolithic is my attempt to uncover the reductive metaphors as they are both developed and denied. But I have meant to vary the approach to the task at hand in accordance with the nature of the work or author involved. So, for example, there is considerable concern about the history of ideas in my treatment of Pope, concern about the extensions of verbal play in that of Sterne, concern about the manipulation of archetypes in that of Faulkner, concern about the Aristotelian sense of plot architecture in that of Austen and Warren. With Wordsworth I must pay attention to his contemporaries and predecessors, relating him to their ways of disposing of the philosophical and existential problems he had to come to terms with. Wordsworth also is the author who most required the examination of a corpus of works rather a single isolated text, such as characterizes my discussion of many other writers here from Sterne to Warren. (In treating Wordsworth, by the way, I apologize for my neglect of that dominant work *The Prelude*: I feared to dip into it lest I be submerged without a chance to escape unless I were to overextend what was already the longest chapter in the book.) In other authors too (Pope,

Johnson, and Swift in particular) I seek corroboration or extension of my claims beyond a single work.

It is unfortunate, I should add, that this volume does not reveal similar corroboration beyond English and American literature for the case it tries to make. After the largely Continental scope of *The Tragic Vision*, I am myself surprised by this restriction to works in English. I hope this is attributable less to my parochialism than to the special receptivity of this literature to this vision. It would be tempting to argue for the specially classic nature of the English literary tradition, if not the British temper. I am convinced of a similar receptivity in many non-English works as well, but a preface is hardly the occasion for one to seek to apply his findings to new materials.

Let me also say a word about one of my stylistic mannerisms, but only because it is expressive of the more important matter of tone, and even reaches to my own vision itself. A recent commentator on my work complains about the poignancy reflected in my habitual use of the "even as" construction (something is true, *even as* something else—apparently contradictory—is also true). The observation is a just one: the occasions on which I use "even as" pile up, and only I can be aware of how many additional times I have used an alternative phrase while the sense of "even as" resounded in my mind. I am thus seen as accumulating qualifications, as taking back with one hand what I give with the other—while sighing, alas, wistfully at such doubleness. But for me literature (and literary theory after it) may be seen to arise out of such difficult balances, so that I feel obliged to trace these balances, however indecisive they make me appear, however they may detract from the "clarity" of the argument. To deny the "even as" of literature and our existence is too much to pay for a clarity that is really pretty cheap. Such is my style of humanistic temperament, though I understand that others may find it quite uncongenial. I enjoy adding that such poignancy—if that is what it is—is probably evidence of my own attachment to the classic vision.

All that remains is the pleasant task of thanking those to whom I have incurred obligations in the course of this lengthy project. I am grateful to those who published earlier versions of some of these materials and are permitting me to include them here. Chapter 3, which appeared originally in *Eighteenth-Century Studies* (3 [Fall 1969]), and Chapter 12, which appeared in *The Shaken Realist: Essays in Honor of Frederick J. Hoffman*, ed. Melvin J. Friedman and John B. Vickery (Baton Rouge: Louisiana State University Press, 1970), have been altered only slightly. Portions of Chapter 1 appeared in "Mediation, Language, and Vision in the Reading of Literature," in *Interpretation: Theory and Practice*, ed. Charles S. Singleton (Baltimore: The Johns Hopkins Press, 1969), and portions of Chapter 2 appeared in "The Continuing Need for Criticism," *Concerning Poetry* (1 [Spring 1968]). I wish also to thank *The Centennial Review* for permitting me to quote extensively from my essay, "The 'Frail China Jar' and the Rude Hand of Chaos," which first appeared in that journal in Spring 1961, and Princeton University Press for permitting me to quote from pp. 209–13 of my book *A Window to Criticism: Shakespeare's* Sonnets *and Modern Poetics* (copyright © 1964 by Princeton University Press).

Two fellowships contributed substantially to the writing of this book. I am indebted to the John Simon Guggenheim Memorial Foundation for the award in 1961–1962 that allowed me to get started on this project and to the American Council of Learned Societies for the award in 1966–1967 that put me well on the road toward its completion.

Among my colleagues and intellectual comrades with whom I have shared the ideas in this book, there is none whose responses have influenced me as have those of Rosalie L. Colie. As a reader of the manuscript, her keen perceptions improved, in large ways and small, each of the many areas she lighted upon. For her patience and her helpfulness I am deeply thankful; for my inability to bring the book to the high levels of her hints and her hopes I am equally regretful. I should mention also a large number of students in several classes who suffered with me as I tried out some of these notions on them. Their acute responses at times encouraged me, at times persuaded me toward crucial changes or toward rethinkings that later led to such changes. Further, among those who helped transform my words first into a manuscript and then into a book, I should single out Mary Gazlay, Frances Foster, and Jean Owen for contributions that were especially generous. Finally, I must once more pay tribute to my wife, whose name once more appears on the dedication page. How much more appropriate this dedication is here, in the classic vision, than it was in the tragic! Indeed, it is the special warmth of her intelligence that has kindled whatever humanity glows through these pages.

The Classic Vision

Introduction

1

Theoretical: The Tragic Vision and the Classic Vision

But where will Europe's latter hour
Again find Wordsworth's healing power?
· · · · · · · · · · ·
The cloud of mortal destiny,
Others will front it fearlessly—
But who, like him, will put it by?
　　　Matthew Arnold, "Memorial Verses April. 1850"

I begin by admitting that I can get to the classic vision only by way of the tragic,[1] a vision which I have spent a volume trying to define and demonstrate. When I opened *The Tragic Vision* with the assertion that "the tragic is not the only vision projected by our serious literature and philosophy, nor is it necessarily the profoundest vision," I was trying even then to leave room for the alternative of the classic. If much of that earlier volume concerned itself with distinguishing the tragic as an authentic vision from what I saw as aesthetically (and existentially) deceptive or self-deceptive pseudo-visions, I must open this volume by preparing for a distinction between what I see as two authentic (if mutually exclusive) visions.

I must get to the classic by way of the tragic because I see them both as responding to the same data of our moral experience, or rather (to shift to a more honest language, less suggestive of naïve realism) because I see them both as proceeding from a similar, if not identical, construction upon the data of our moral experience. They are alternative, though not quite antagonistic, responses, although the stimuli to which they are responding are viewed in a single way in both cases.

[1] See my Preface for my attempt to justify the use of the "classic," rather than the "comic," as my term for the alternative to the "tragic."

They both turn upon a view of the existential trap *as* trap, of the face of reality as fearfully and maddeningly Manichaean; a view of routine existence as a mask behind whose teasing placidity lurks extremity. The classic is no less ready to recognize extremity than is the tragic, since the inauthentic pseudo-vision has been defined as that which evades such recognition, and these two visions, though alternative, are equally authentic.

But while the tragic confronts and even embraces extremity—at all costs—the classic is enabled to "put it by," as Arnold says of Wordsworth; it is enabled, that is, at once to see it as extremity and not to choose it. Knowing what extremity is and means, the classic vision chooses to reject it, to turn, in mature acceptance, away from it toward the wholly compromised human condition. It is far more difficult to argue for the authenticity of so unheroic a claim to vision and to distinguish it from the ersatz visions of a willed blindness. How to show the retreat from extremity to be an authentic movement, one controlled by a force more affirmative than a failure of nerve? It takes some borrowing of classic spirit even to ask and approach the question. But all this is to move too quickly and to get ahead of an argument which, because of the objections that it obviously and from the first arouses, must be retraced to the start and allowed to move slowly.

1. Literary Stress as Liberating Force

I dealt at some length in *The Tragic Vision* with the union in older (especially Greek and Renaissance) literatures of the Apollonian and Dionysian spirits which Nietzsche saw as one in Greek tragedy. My earlier discussion defined tragedy as the transcendent form which at once exposes the unrelieved tension of the tragic vision, resolves it aesthetically, and yet leaves it thematically unrelieved. Thus the Apollonian and Dionysian motives—which is to say the classic and tragic visions—are seen as unified, and therefore as finally reaffirming the Apollonian principle in the teeth of the Dionysian challenge which the Apollonian absorbs even while preserving it intact. The two can be seen as a single, unbroken realm extending from epic through tragedy. In epic as well as tragedy we sense a containing wholeness, both formal and thematic, whether the finally soothing quality is in the spirit of Ithaca or in the spirit of Colonus. For, in both, the Apollonian and Dionysian come to be at peace with one another.

Consequently, I claimed (after Nietzsche) that the Apollonian and

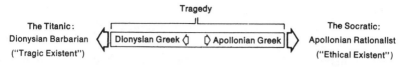

Dionysian motives could be defined only in terms of each other and would become seriously corrupted when not maintained dialectically, in an opposition that is a tensional union. This falling apart is indicated in the diagram.[2] Once there is a disruption of the union that produced the Dionysian Greek and the Apollonian Greek as two sides of a single consciousness, the two deteriorate. The Apollonian, on its own and without opposition, becomes what Nietzsche called the Socratic, the thinly rational, the anti-existential worship of order for its own sake, without concern for whether that order reflects the depths of human need and response: in short, it becomes the "ethical."[3] The Dionysian, on its own and without the overpowering imposition of a transcendent order, becomes the Titanic worship of the unrelieved darkness of chaos, unredeemed tragic existence free of its containing frame in tragedy and defined by the state of Kierkegaardian despair. Hence, in modern (i.e., post-Renaissance) literature, we too often find painful alternatives: on the one hand the projection (however guarded) of the ethical in didactic celebration of propositional order with its moral imperatives, and on the other hand the projection of the demoniacal (but often equally didactic) celebration of chaos in the dark night of the anti-soul.

In the best of the literature of the tragic vision, however, I claim to find a new, less satisfying, but still aesthetically coherent version of the motives of Apollo and Dionysus, of order and dark disorder. I find this aesthetic coherence in the unyielding tensions that create the

[2] This is the first of several diagrams, for whose presence in this chapter I ought to apologize. Even one would be too many for my taste. But I fear that I must resort to such crude and unsatisfying devices in my attempt to simplify materials that, I confess, can use any simplification that I can provide.

[3] Throughout this study I use the term "ethical," as I did in *The Tragic Vision*, in Kierkegaard's sense, as the subsuming of the particular within the unyielding moral universal (see *The Tragic Vision: Variations on a Theme in Literary Interpretation* [New York, 1960], pp. 11–13). We must remember that, in Kierkegaard, this use and this definition were directed against Hegelianism, whose universalism was especially ponderous in its impositions. Surely, we must hope, there is a more tentative, more flexible ethical, free of such excesses and their accompanying blindness. But, as I hope to suggest by the end of this chapter, such a light-footed ethical is precisely what the classic can help produce.

dialogue between the tragic and the ethical domains, between the Dionysian turned self-indulgently and drunkenly destructive in a flight from all universals and the Apollonian turned shallow in a flight from authenticity. The two motives are not—as they once were— transcended or absorbed into a higher union that grants both aesthetic and thematic satisfactions; they merely are held in tentative suspension in their shabbier states, each suffering the isolation from the other. For the merely ethical can be maintained only if one is willfully blind to the Manichaean face of reality, and the merely tragic can be maintained only if one demoniacally refuses to surrender the uniqueness of his drives to any universal and binding claim. The two seem, as each is held at varying moments in our literature, to be mutually exclusive, with only the acrobatic writer—if he still can be aesthetically astride his materials—able to maintain them both, now in alternation, now in surges of claims and self-distrust, now in the simultaneity of belief and counter-belief displayed through the perilous balance of irony. Thus I offer the second preliminary diagram, which illustrates how far I had come by the end of *The Tragic Vision*.

I have maintained that in the successful literature of the tragic vision two orders of existence, what I have called the tragic and the ethical, are aesthetically sustained by the encompassing vision of the writer who creates them both, but creates them both as inadequate since, as dialogist, he is existentially committed to neither. Nevertheless, he acknowledges the duplicity that characterizes our moral experience when we dare confront it (or ourselves in it) with naked honesty, even if he must resist the most reckless response to that duplicity. He must even more strongly resist the urge to turn aside— for the sake of his sanity—from his recognition of what duplicity there is and what contradictions that duplicity must carry with it into the moral life. Thus the tragic vision, even if it precludes action by

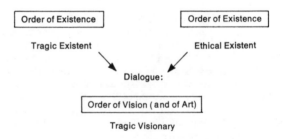

6

using each of the two orders of existence to destroy any conceivable commitment to the other, urges the fullness of all we may *see* in spite of the limited vision imposed on us by what we must decide to *do*. Hence the primacy of the orders of vision, of dialogue, over the orders of existence—and the greater authenticity (or honesty) of confrontation given us by the tragic vision (in the totality of the literary work), in contrast to the partial awareness given us either by the tragic existent or by the ethical existent, each with his own blinders. The given in an experience that makes possible the tragic vision must subvert all institutional (or anti-institutional) morality by seeing beyond it to all that gives it the lie.[4] Thus the work fulfills the fundamental obligation of literature to undo our commitments, if not to undo the very possibility of commitment, to subvert allegiance by liberating us *from* action, liberating us *for* total vision.

So far, then, I have assumed a common "given" of experience for modern literature, a "given" characterized in its most extreme form by a driving, or merely driven, quality that demands either confrontation or evasion. I have dealt with one mode of existence, the tragic, which confronts extremity and embraces its consequences, and with another mode, the ethical, which chooses not to see it, which chooses the blindness which permits confident, self-righteous action and the moral judgment of others actions. The first mode of existence, the tragic, claims to be authentic, although we can be persuaded of its authenticity only through a visionary who sees, dialogistically, beyond. But if we condescendingly dismiss the ethical as inauthentic in its visionary consequences, what other vision and what other mode of existence can we claim that accepts the same given, acknowledges the same extremity, and yet sees more than extremity and acts not to confront it and embrace its consequences? How, out of the tension produced by the simultaneous needs to confront existential absurdity and to live socially and sanely, can we find a reconciliation: not a recon-

---

[4] This distinction between orders of vision and orders of existence leads to the distinction between the tragic existent (character or portion of character) and the tragic visionary (the consummate author or at best, his narrator, as with Marlow or Ishmael—see *The Tragic Vision*, pp. 252–54, and *A Window to Criticism: Shakespeare's* Sonnets *and Modern Poetics* [Princeton, 1964], pp. 20–21). This distinction (between tragic existent and tragic visionary) is one which I failed to urge systematically in *The Tragic Vision*, where I too often use the single term "tragic visionary" to refer indiscriminately either to the consummate author (whom I now, with more care, call "tragic visionary") or to the all-committed tragic existent.

ciliation that dissolves the elements of tension, but a reconciliation to the unresolvable facts of tension? How, that is, can we find an affirmation in the unswayable balance of antagonistic forces instead of joining with chaos in tearing them apart as they endlessly tear at one another? This volume is to argue that we can claim such a vision. In attempting to define and demonstrate the classic vision, I mean to defend it as an authentic vision, distinguished both from the destructive authenticity of the tragic vision and from the sane inauthenticity of the ethical vision.

2. The "Given," Vision, and the Whole Work

Before proceeding further, I must pause to examine the nature of the "given" in moral experience as it is assumed by the thematic genre I call the tragic vision. Then we can see how that "given" achieves aesthetic form and thus vision in the literary works being claimed for this genre. At a time when "visionary" critics are in the ascendancy, it is clear that I cannot use the word "vision" as a central term without trying to set off my sense of it from the sense it has commonly been given of late—especially since its common meaning would separate it from the work's totality while I try to identify the two.[5] I must see the work not as a projection of a pre-existing vision, formed in the self behind it, but as a dialogistic entity that comes into being out of the dramatic conflict of the forces and the language that constitute its finished form. With a similar objective, Leo Spitzer used "vision" as a pre-aesthetic category that characterized how the author saw rather than how the poem meant, reserving his aesthetic claims for what became of vision when the whole went to work on it by becoming a "work." Though in the spirit of Spitzer, I prefer to use "vision" for what comes out rather than for what goes in.[6]

But it is the construction upon the "given" that creates the forms of a vision that (to be tautological) creates, and is created by, its form. Still we must begin once more with the "given," since it is all that is outside the circular relations among form, vision, and work. In *The*

---

[5] Perhaps it is for this reason an error for me to employ the term "vision," and indeed I might have searched for an alternative, had I known when I began *The Tragic Vision* what the contemporary and subsequent use of "vision" was to do to the word.

[6] Leo Spitzer, *"Explication de Texte* Applied to Three Great Middle English Poems," in *Essays on English and American Literature,* ed. Anna Hatcher (Princeton, 1962), especially pp. 216–19.

Tragic Vision I attempted to expand upon the common assumption in tragic literature that our routine (which is to say pre-tragic) existence depends upon the universalizing veils that our social and moral necessities force us to hold between ourselves and the brawling chaos—the jumble of unique instances—that is actually out there (and within us) ready to show its Manichaean face to any who dare thrust the veil aside to look.[7] And it is that forced confrontation with extremity—the unpalliated series of ineluctable consequences which practicality normally persuades us to shun—that creates the tragic existent and sets him on his tragic course.

If we assume, then, the existential immediacy of the Manichaean face of reality as irreducibly there for the stricken existent, we assume also the multi-dimensionality contained in the unique particularity of this experience, now viewed without the universalizing veils that comfort normally and automatically used to impose. In its particularity this experience is thus inaccessible to the reducing or abstracting habits of our usual linguistic apparatus, of our rational—or at least propositional—responses which we have so well and universally learned. In its uniqueness it resists all but its own unrepeatable, flowing, unadaptable self. For it is instantaneous—not just an instance, but an instant. It is utterly closed, shut off, because nothing else is like it; nothing else can explain it, its conjunction of impossible coordinate or simultaneous aspects. But—and here is the Bergsonian paradox—it is also and at the same instant utterly open, because, being instantaneous, it is not even an entity; rather, denying itself any discrete instance, it flows into all other instantaneous non-instances and has them flow into *it*.[8]

Well, then, inner experience, as flowing instantaneity, is impervious to language. We are trapped in the linguistic shadow-world of the subjective, so-called phenomenological critic (really observer and voice-catcher more than critic), the participating commentator who tries to match his introspective, impressionistic language to the elusive structures of mental experience before him. We note his necessary

[7] See also my attempt to put this conflict between the universalizing veils and particularized actuality in the context of contemporary criticism in "The Existential Basis of Contextual Criticism," *The Play and Place of Criticism* (Baltimore, 1967), especially pp. 246–49.

[8] This is similar and related to the paradox of the literary work which recent critics, from contextualists to Northrop Frye and even Ihab Hassan, have had to see as at once uniquely closed and yet open. This latter is a paradox we shall examine later.

antipathy to form as the objectifying enemy. Such a literary observer tends to see an unavoidable dichotomy in the options open to all literary observers, so that each must choose either the subjective or objective aspect of the work.[9]

The literary work, for Georges Poulet, is the representative of the author's thought if we but conceive this thought as a physical place, a home for its constituted objects. Thus conceived, the work, like the thought, may seem to those of us not attuned to interior distances to be related most obviously to its objects, to those things of the outside world which it presumably is about. Being most obvious, the relation gives rise to "objective" criticism as the most usual sort. But the work, again like the thought, with those entities which it houses so commodiously, is related more crucially, if less obviously, to the thinking subject, the self, that has "redisposed" those objects, now newly created by mind. This "interior distance" between subject and his thought or work, thus conceived, and the redisposition of the objects in accord with the housing demands in this inner space, give rise to the less obvious but more urgent sort of criticism which must be practiced if the study of literature is truly to be humanized. This criticism brings to light the dark side of the moon, the Cartesian *Cogito*. What it can give us are the unmediated, subjective forms of consciousness instead of the frozen mediations that are the forms of external objects —including the poem itself as object.

But we cannot help noticing that, in this open choice of an antiformalist criticism, Poulet too easily disposes of all formal matters by ranging them on the side of the "objective" features, as if formal features were of the same order as the external objects which thoughts or works presumably are *about*, external objects to which, in other words, thoughts or works would seem to the naïve critic to refer, objects which—to use the most naïve notion—they would appear to "imitate." Poulet blandly sees the "objective aspect" of literature as including both "formal" elements (the word "formal" apparently meaning no more than generic, the "contours" that lead us to "poems,

[9] These claims may be found almost anywhere one looks in the work of Georges Poulet. Nowhere does he put them more briefly or precisely—or in more extreme terms—than in his one-paragraph preface to *The Interior Distance*, trans. Elliott Coleman (Baltimore, 1959). Many of his fellow-critics and followers make similar or related claims. These have recently been receiving considerable attention. For the most compact and useful discussion of the group, see J. Hillis Miller, "The Geneva School," *Critical Quarterly* 8 (1966): 305–21.

maxims, and novels, plays") and referential elements, "accounts" or "descriptions" of "objects." And he promises to turn from both to the subjective side. It is a promise he keeps all too faithfully.

But, if Poulet disposes of all properly formal matters by lumping them indifferently with what we used to call objects of imitation, referring to both as equally "objective" features, then perhaps he should be asked to "redispose" his notion of form (as, after Mallarmé, he has the mind in its "interior vacancy" "redispose" its world of objects) in order to make it (as good critics usually have made it) into something more than flat categories so dully externalized. Must we choose between the ineffably subjective and the naïvely objective? Such a choice is insufficiently subtle. The external object does not stand in the same relation to the poem as its form does, unless we are restricting ourselves to what has long been an obsolete eighteenth-century notion of form as universal generic mechanics. Clearly, such a notion is too flattened out and externalized for it ever to allow form a vital existence; it can conceive of form only as that which would deaden through abstraction the particular living work to which it is applied.

What else has literary criticism been about since Coleridge and before, if not working toward a notion of organic form that would enable us to talk formally about a work without adapting it to stale generalities, but finding instead a form that is uniquely its own, expressive of its own unrepeatable characteristics? This effort has led to examinations of the special properties of poetic discourse and its ways of meaning, which permit it to open vistas of vision which normal discourse, with its limitations, seems determined to shut off. The critic has had to show how the literary medium, though still only the words that we all, like Hamlet, contemn most of the time, manages to free the subjective even while freezing it into a permanent form; to make the poem an *im*mediate object rather than a mediate one. For the medium is at war with itself in literature: language refuses to serve as it normally does. But it shows him who can master it how thoroughly it can master the most inward folds of our experience. Still, though a medium rendered immediate, a poem's language works to make the poem an *object* and to that extent external and communicable, and in need of more than subjective observation. The dark side of the moon *is* what we are given, but this firm mastery gives it to us in a way we can hope to secure—for ourselves and others. It is a formal way, though of course "formal" here has so many other-than-formal elements in it if we define the term in the manner of an archaic formalism, as Poulet does.

All of which returns us, but, I believe, newly armed, to the matter of vision and the way it gets into the literary work. For I mean to claim here that we need not see our inner experience as being, after all, impervious to all language once we remember the inward immediacies which our great poets can force their language to embody. Let me recapitulate. We can begin, as I have begun, with the special sort of "given" which I saw the tragic vision assuming in moral experience: we can characterize it in its extremity as unadaptably unique, at once an indissoluble lump among innumerable other equally autonomous but dissimilar lumps in the chaotic stream of particulars and yet at the same time the stream itself, always becoming but never having become, and thus never hardened to a lump. But this is to begin by seeming to put such a "given" and such experience beyond the generic, freezing powers of language. It is this sort of formulation that leads to Ihab Hassan's apocalyptic assault on the word, out of his fear that subjective "outrage" may be fatally compromised by culture's dedication to a mediating "object," with the consequence of abstraction, death. He does not permit the word, or its order of beauty, to be in any service but death's, nor does he suggest that language can ever be tortured into an object that preserves immediacy and existential vitality—that, for all its fixed eloquence, language can be forced into a form which is discursively silent.[10]

If I am to qualify such fears about the existential incapacities of language, I must first recall that these limitations refer only to the "normal" powers of language, so that we can—if we are prepared to look—find a very abnormal series of possibilities in the history of our great literary works. The subjective flow of the self's awareness of its experience must somehow be preserved, even while being preserved in a fixed object. The death-dealing immobility of the spatial impulse must yield to the dynamic, moving vitality of the temporal, while yet creating that which must persist in an unchanging form. I maintain this need despite those champions of unmediated consciousness who

[10] See "The Dismemberment of Orpheus: Notes on Form and Antiform in Contemporary Literature," in *Learners and Discerners*, ed. Robert Scholes (Charlottesville, Va., 1964), pp. 135–65; and "Beyond a Theory of Literature: Intimations of Apocalypse?" *Comparative Literature Studies* 1 (1964): 261–71. See also the work of Hassan's philosophical master, Norman O. Brown.

claim—against all objectivity—that the ever-changing vitalism of our inner experience must be retained as inviolate. Despite all that contemporary personalism and existentialism have taught us about objectification (the making into things) as the murderer of the unique, I believe the critic must claim to have found in the abnormalities of poetic language the one way of having his object without surrendering the immediacy of its data.

There is in the work, as in the "given" of experience, both the instance and the instant or even instantaneous, with the strange etymological and semantic coincidence of opposition and identity between these: on the one hand, the absolute and irreducible instance, which demands discreteness, a continual awareness of and pausing over the boundaries that constitute it as discrete, cutting it off from all that is not itself; and on the other hand, the absolutely instant or instantaneous, which denies the existence of bounds, of the entity-hood of the moment, to get on with the movement, the flow of the moment becoming the next without pausing to be marked. It is the role of poetic discourse to manage both of these at once: it must undo the generic tendencies of normal discourse and must complicate the context with contingency until it creates that language context as its own unique body. Moving dynamically in time, the poem must yet become transfixed into a spatial form.

Hence what I have elsewhere termed the ekphrastic principle is the poetic principle in that it invokes "still movement" (in both the Keatsian and Eliotic senses of "still") as the special grace with which poetry is to be endowed.[11] In this mood we can speak in many varied metaphors of the miraculous doubleness of the critic's and the poet's job when we say that it is the critic's job to locate—as it is the poet's job to produce—the spatial orders within the temporal. We can speak of creating the circular principle within linear progression, or the logical within the chronological, or the still-recurring within the still-moving, or the freezing principle within the free-flowing, the emblematic within that which resists all spatial fixity. We can speak too of creating the causal and the casuistic within the casual, which is another way of speaking of creating the closed system of an internally related language within a language which, like language generally, is propelled outward toward reference. And finally, to move toward the-

[11] See "The Ekphrastic Principle and the Still Movement of Poetry; or Laokoön Revisited," *The Play and Place of Criticism*, pp. 105–28.

matics, we can—by hardly changing our terms—speak of creating the extremities of experience within the compromising muddles of the uncommitted middle.

Language, the medium of literature, seeks to follow its natural (which, paradoxically, is to say conventional) paths—its "naturally" conventional paths, as it were. As it does so, language seems to be either only casual and free (in its "ordinary," unsystematic modes) or only causal and frozen (in its non-poetic systematic modes). The poet must struggle against this very nature of language if he is to have it as both at once: he must create the language as *his* medium by fostering in it the multiple capacities that transform the word to terminal entity, to body, to effigy, to emblem, even as that language clearly seems to function still in the semantic and syntactic ways that words have as their wont. So the "given" is found in the work, preserved in its density and contingency and not reduced to any conceptual formula, but yet preserved and intact by being an utterly formed object once and for all for one and all. It has a form but is not a formula, is constitutive but not conceptual; that is, it gives the forms for our reality but not concepts about it.

If the poem, then, in accordance with pure formalism, should reduce itself to fixity and only stand still, it would reduce itself to the frozen death of the spatialized discourse of non-poetic systems, as, alas, all too many poems do. It would thus lose the empirical dynamism of movement, the flowing vitality of experience; it would lose these because it would be subservient to universality, to the Platonic archetype that levels particularity. But is it enough for the poem to do the opposite? For it can, as a Poulet would have it, force itself to be still moving, though only in the sense of always moving, so that it would give up the paradox of unmoving movement at the heart of the stillness of the Keatsian urn. But this is for the poem to deny utterly its character as object by yielding, without restriction, to the boundless, ceaseless flow of our experience. We would be no better off for art, for this art would have given over its proper nature in its worship of imitative form (or formlessness). It is a form that decries form and cries for formlessness in its attempt to imitate a chaotic welter of experiences.

My distrust of unlimited subjectivity, with its defiance of all forms, dictates that I use the term "vision" in a way that is systematically distinct from the way it is used by our explicitly visionary critics, who seek in the literary work signs (often related to signs found in other works) of the author's grasp of his reality as that constituted reality relates to the grasping self. I rather seek no vision behind or before the work, though I do seek the vision that comes to be created in the work, *as* the work.[12] Perhaps, if I may borrow a notion from Eliot (a notion by now much overused), it is that the visionary correlative I seek is objective, not subjective, although the fact that it is objective makes it in the end no correlative but the thing itself. In its concern with vision my study is still within the discipline I have called thematics; by this I mean the formal study of an aesthetic complex, a study which becomes more than formal because the complexities which it unifies, as unresolved tensions, reflect the tensions of our pre-propositional and extra-propositional experience.[13]

If, unlike Poulet, I insist on the work—for all its elusive, subjective churning—as an object, I nevertheless share his fear that the dead hand of objectification can destroy its unique voice by adapting it to alien structures or classes. But my anti-structuralist, Crocean antagonism toward all literary classification carries with it difficulties that seem to strike at my very enterprise here. Since I claim a discontinuous uniqueness among works, each of which is coextensive with its special vision, what generic possibilities can there be for me to exploit in order to create the common areas of vision that would allow for *The Tragic Vision* and the current study? I must somehow defend the usefulness of thematic genres created by the critic even as I defend the uniqueness of the work and its vision. But I believe my formulation shows how we may evade this dilemma. We need only admit frankly that these thematic genres, like others, operate for the critic, indeed are largely invented in the act of criticism. It is the critic's role to distort works somewhat as he serves his thematic-historicist, as

---

[12] In Coleridgean terms, I seek in the work a direct reflection of the secondary imagination, which in its workings with language I must claim to be discontinuous with the primary imagination, "the prime agent of all human perception." Instead of merely being an "echo" of the primary, the secondary "dissolves, diffuses, dissipates" our reality as envisioned for us by our generally constitutive power, the primary, and creates it anew. In chap. 13 of the *Biographia Literaria*, Coleridge uses both descriptions—that of echo and that of creator—to make up an almost contradictory definition of the secondary imagination. I choose to see it only in its character as creator, not in its character as echo, since the latter would not allow to the work the unique, organic quality Coleridge proposes for it.

[13] See *The Tragic Vision*, pp. 242ff., for my original definition of "thematics," together with a discussion of the consequences of that definition.

well as his formalist, interests. Of course, his obligation to literary works requires him to guard as best he can—which "best" is never good enough—against intruding universal categories upon any work's uniqueness, even as he works outward toward similarities he claims to find among their visions. It is a painful trial for him to honor his literary obligation to that vision by disdaining to reduce it to an historicist "vision" extrinsic to it even while he performs his thematic-historicist function.

So I must maintain the usefulness and theoretical possibility of my scheme. I do not mean my categories, my orders of existence and of vision (or the over-simplified diagram which contains them), to limit the characterization of any work; nor are they meant to be ideal norms toward which the work ought to be directed. They are not to reduce the work to themselves, seeing themselves as universal potentials to be realized by individuals and making such a realization the basis of judgment. From my anti-universal viewpoint here, this would be a cardinal sin. Rather, my categories and the diagram that relates them to one another are only rough guidelines to help us mark off the common ground from which characters and their actions in single works can diverge as they pursue their singular movements. These guidelines can help these movements make existential sense for us. They may not characterize any individual works, but they can constitute a vocabulary of modern possibilities for vision and existence—no more than this; but even this can be valuable for critic and reader as they seek to work outward to existence and history. As it may be the role of the critic to project such guidelines, however individual works may elude them, so it is the role of the poet to mess them up, as he messes up all categories, in tending to his own special movements. But it may be helpful for the historicist-critic to have these heuristic universals in mind as he tries to chart those utterly differentiated and unchartable voyages taken by our great—which is to say our uncategorizable—works.[14] Our interest as critics, then, must be not in the categories themselves and in how we place what in them, but in those splendid works that move, each in its own way, out from them in a

---

[14] See the title essay of *The Play and Place of Criticism*, pp. 3–16, where I discuss at greater length and more graphically the place of the critic's semi-existential categories in trying to capture the existential-contextual dynamics of the aesthetically self-contained work.

discursive blur, leaving them and us behind with our inadequate measuring instruments.

3. Extremity and the Reductive Metaphor: Its Self-Denial and the Classic Impulse

How does the work achieve its unique vision, its objective formulation of all in the "given" that in its dynamics resists formulation? This is to ask, how does the infinitely variegated flow of experience achieve an aesthetically transcendent unity? In the midst of experiential chaos, endlessly divisive, we look, as desperately as Gerard Manley Hopkins did, for an aesthetic inscape that will satisfy our thematic craving.

> All things counter, original, spare, strange;
>   Whatever is fickle, freckled (who knows how?)
>   With swift, slow; sweet, sour; adazzle, dim;
> He fathers-forth whose beauty is past change.

A secular theorist would allow the miraculous metaphor of poetic incarnation to substitute for Hopkins' theological Word made flesh. As I have argued elsewhere, figuratively (that is, in terms of the *figura*) the Trinitarian paradox is the very model of the poet's farthest claim for metaphor as transubstantiating miracle, with its union-in-duality of tenor and vehicle.[15] So there is the aesthetic need and the thematic need to freeze experience, but only in order to feel its flow most immediately. With the subjectivity of experience behind and beyond, the work must be created formally as its emblem, a total object; and the work must be created existentially as its vision, the word "vision" bestowing upon the work the spatial fixity of a thing seen.

How, then, is the poet to play the casual casuist? How is he to realize and master the muddled flow of the confused center of our experience through an aesthetic-thematic symbol? I speak of our experience in its subjective confusion as the "center of our experience" because it resists the purity of definition, the a fortiori clarity, of the polar extremes. Experience at its hard edges is no longer confused, though in

---

[15] *A Window to Criticism* rests almost wholly on an attempt to demonstrate the contextually sustained metaphor as the secular substitute for a theologically sustained transubstantiation (see especially pp. 200–204).

its extremity it is not where we dare live it unless we ourselves are to become polar creatures, tragic existents. For, as my examination of the tragic vision was intended to demonstrate throughout, the existent cannot embrace either pole at all costs without having it transformed into its antagonist (as, for example, in the confounding of puritanism and sensual debauchery in many works in this thematic genre). Better the safe sanity, the ethical probity—if the visionary blindness—of the inconclusive, compromised middle.[16] But the poet dedicated to aesthetic resolution has to un-muddle the middle through a casuistic play that leads him to summon up and cultivate the extreme. However uncommitted existentially, however aesthetically committed to dialogue alone, he vicariously nourishes the extreme. His method of capturing the extreme (and, with it, all the impurities of the middle he has bypassed and yet, like the alchemist, distilled) is that of converting the endlessly variegated muddle into the terms of his extended metaphor for it. The critic's hypothesis of the work's form is his best guess about what this extended metaphor is, based on everything in the work that feeds it.

The repetitive patterns I have spoken of, which give stillness to the movement by freezing subjective freedom, must be read by the critic into his hypothesis of the form of the work, as he makes it a reductive metaphor—an emblem, a constitutive symbol—for all its moving life and liveliness. The metaphor, while excluding so much of the middle in its reductive, extremist purity, is at the same time all-inclusive in its emblematic fullness. The hypothesis tests itself by its capacity to account for every aspect, aesthetic and experiential, that is stuffed into the work (if the hypothesis is not being imposed by the over-anxious critic). At once puritan and catholic, the reductive metaphor must gather within itself all of middle existence which it passes by in its pursuit of extremity, as it must gather within the holistic form determined by its vehicle all the varied possibilities sloppily assembled in its tenor. Thus the reductive metaphor, while it must exclude as it reduces, must attain an all-inclusiveness at once existentially (or thematically) and aesthetically (or formally).

---

[16] This was the anti-tragic, anti-Dostoevskyan, anti-Kierkegaardian plea which the late Philip Blair Rice saw Thomas Mann making: a plea for experience of the center rather than experience at the polar extremes. See "The Merging Parallels: Mann's *Doctor Faustus*," *Kenyon Review* 11 (1949): 199–217.

It may be helpful at this point to quote at some length from the extended discussion of the reductive metaphor as both single and double, closed and open, in *A Window to Criticism*:

> *The author plays the casuist, dedicated to extremity,*
> *by committing himself in the work absolutely to a*
> *reduction of one sort of experience to another, to a*
> *transfer of properties of one to those of another, a*
> *transfer to which every element in the work lends itself*
> *totally. Experience of a normal sort—messy, pre-*
> *poetic, of mixed and uncertain tendencies, veering in*
> *this direction and in that, impure in its continual*
> *compromise with the totality of definition—is viewed*
> *under the aspect of an extremely delimited sort of*
> *experience that threatens, momentarily, within*
> *its context, to reduce all experience to itself and to*
> *read life within its own awesome terms as unbearable*
> *and—to a common-sense reason that needs life as*
> *mixed—as irrational, even impossible.*
>
> *Thus, in Mann's Doctor Faustus, for example, all*
> *forces lend themselves to reveal the generally accepted*
> *world of artistic dedication and controlled artistic*
> *creativity exclusively under the aspect of the world of*
> *disease, to reveal the world of decent austerity and*
> *harsh asceticism exclusively under the aspect of the*
> *world of license. But the total transfer of properties, the*
> *total reduction, is deceptive. The terms I have used in*
> *my hasty oversimplification of these worlds should*
> *indicate that even as the extremes are poetically equated*
> *they remain polarized. In furnishing us a very*
> *paradigm of the functioning of extremity, Mann*
> *allows no mediation between extremes, but forces one*
> *to support the other, even to reflect the other, finally*
> *to become a mask for the other. Mann's extreme*
> *necessarily bears its opposite within itself by the very*
> *nature of its seemingly singleminded purity. The*
> *ill-defined, mixed components of the life he deals with*
> *follow the path of their most dangerous tendencies*
> *to extremes that are at once polar and reversible,*

> *opposed and identical. For the equation of the two*
> *worlds, the reduction of one to the other, becomes a*
> *substantive metaphor. As such it turns on itself,*
> *asserting for common sense the duality of its terms, the*
> *distinctness of their properties, even as it works the*
> *miracle of transubstantiation. Everything in the work*
> *—character, incident, language, style—contributes*
> *to the collapsing of the broad and mixed world to the*
> *narrow and pure one and thus to the creation of the*
> *work as a total metaphor, except that, even as the*
> *transfer becomes dramatically complete, the separate-*
> *ness of elements asserts itself to our rational, less totally*
> *committed selves.*

I could go on from *Doctor Faustus* to discuss the reductive meta-phors, at once transubstantiating and skeptically self-denying, in others of the novels I treated as fully tensional bearers of the tragic vision. Here, for example, is an oversimplified characterization of Gide's *The Immoralist*: there is the drive to assert the freedom of the self from the bonds of ethical restraint, but all forces lend themselves to transfer this drive to its appearance exclusively under the aspect of a total enslavement to the senses. Or Malraux's *Man's Fate*: here there is the ethical drive to merge the self with the struggle for social better-ment, but all forces lend themselves to transfer this drive to its appearance exclusively under the aspect of the demoniac drive to vio-lent, uninhibited self-expression. Or Melville's *Pierre*: here there is the moral devotion to well-meaning self-sacrifice, but all forces lend themselves to transfer this devotion to its appearance exclusively under the aspect of a total perversion guided by monstrous desires. In each of these cases too—just seen in *Doctor Faustus*—the hope for synthesis proves a delusion, since the polar extremes will not yield up their exclusiveness and their purity. The drive to order and to reck-lessness in *The Immoralist*, the drive to the expression of self and of social-political ends in *Man's Fate*, the drive to self-sacrifice and to the fulfillment of inner need in *Pierre*—each set of extreme alterna-tives holds out the happy hope of a solvent merger. But, in each case, these drives lead only to a pair of one-way streets going in opposite directions, even though—curiously—each can accommodate either of the opposed drives.

So the humanistic transcendence created by the promised compromise in each case proves only self-deception, fatally so (witness Leverkühn, Michel, Kyo, and Pierre). And only the special sort of reductive metaphor can begin to reveal the extremity-driven world that springs from the ashes of the failure of all synthesis. Finally, and in similar terms, we can consider Kafka's *The Trial*, in which all forces lend themselves to transfer the amoral routine of cotidian existence to its appearance exclusively under the aspect of blind and unmitigated, moment-by-moment guilt. Of course, the half-innocence in K.'s stumbling half-pursuit, his essential ignorance, proclaim the absurdity of this absolute transfer of properties even as they help us marvel at the nothing-left-out character of Kafka's contextual inclusiveness that allows him to "work" his metaphor. But so it is with all of these and other examples. Always the transfer is complete; the "aspect" under which we are forced to see *is* imposed exclusively. And yet, and yet . . . the polarities rebound; the muddled center reasserts itself; despite our utter captivation by the Word, our sensible selves skeptically reassert the recalcitrant world that resists all transfer and insists on doggedly, dully remaining itself. Still, the magic is never quite dispelled. We have it and we do not, we believe it and we do not, are hypnotically trapped and yet move freely in and out.

To return to the passage from *A Window to Criticism*:

> *I see Mann's version of extremity as a paradigm*
> *that allows us to consider the poet's casuistry more*
> *broadly, so as to turn it into a generic literary strategy*
> *that can serve us with lyrics as well. To use another*
> *obvious example . . . I can cite Donne's lovers in*
> The Canonization, *whose absorption by earthly love—*
> *which is shown in its normal state to be woefully mixed*
> *and incomplete in its nature—we are forced to view*
> *under the aspect of the total and unworldly dedication*
> *that earns sainthood. Everything in the poem, in the*
> *fullness of its contextual interrelations, works to*
> *bring off the equation, to complete the metaphor in*
> *its transfer of properties from tenor to vehicle (from*
> *earthly lovers to saints), even though the tenor*
> *and vehicle seem opposed to one another. Nevertheless*
> *this step-by-step extension of the metaphor carries*

*along with it the covert guide of rationality that asserts
the absurdity, even the speciousness, of this extension.
It is not that the identity produced by the
metaphor is being denied, since such a denial would
lead us outside the context and its mutually dependent
terms, but that the miracle can be asserted as
miracle only by continually recognizing its impossibility,
by continually acknowledging the intransigence of
the materials and oppositions being mastered, though
they are never destroyed.*

*Such a miracle of substantive identity should of
course not be viewed as a propositional truth claim
(A is B) any more than it is a dramatic demonstration of
a propositional moral claim (A ought to be B).
With its context totally working to create it, it is
rather a total and totally committed incarnation, an
effigy of mixed and intransigent experience which
has been substantively transferred into, or rendered
within, an extreme, unmitigated reduction of one
pure and narrow aspect to whose sway all cooperates or
conspires in order to make the transfer complete—
even as the miracle asserts itself as such by urging an
awareness of its denial. Like Shakespeare's Phoenix and
Turtle, like his mirror and window, like the in and
the through of contextualism, but perhaps most like
Clarissa's scissors which the baron manipulates in*
The Rape of the Lock, *the miraculous metaphor divides
even while it joins. [That miraculous poem itself works,
like the scissors, to divide as it joins, if we consider
how thoroughly it creates its vision of the
heavy prosaic world of flesh and blood under the aspect
of the airiness of the pure world of absolute play.]*

*In its simultaneous performing of its dividing and
joining functions, its opening-out and closing-in
functions, the dual nature of the extremity that leads to
miracle—but a special sort of miracle at once assertive
and denying—can correct an unfortunate over-
emphasis that has for good reason bothered students
of recent criticism. From Aristotle onward, critics,*

*in insisting on the unity of the literary work, have
insisted upon its convergent movement toward a
unitary, sharply pointed conclusion and conclusive
meaning. The* Poetics *traces, in the development of the
literary work, the gradual, inevitable elimination of
the multiple probabilities with which it began until,
when the climax turns the complication into the
denouement, only the one way that—though hidden to
us and to the protagonist—has been inescapably
there all along is left and is pursued to its end. It has
been hard to improve upon this classic formulation
in its convergent simplicity. Thus it could not help
seeming dangerously perverse to find recent critics
[perhaps our best or most extreme example here would
be William Empson] rather emphasizing almost
exclusively the divergent meanings of literary works.
While also insisting upon unity, they dwell upon
the organic nature of that unity, upon the variety which
is being unified. They celebrate the ambiguous instead
of the unilinear, the unresolved tensions among
centrifugal forces instead of the crowning assertion
of the all-dominating centripetal force. At their more
reckless moments they may seem to be claiming for
the work no more narrowly unified a precision than that
of a shotgun blast. And yet they have on the whole
been persuasive about the many voices with which
even an apparently simple poem may often speak.
I am suggesting that literary extremity and its miracle,
with the completeness of their absorption of alien,
resistant, and incomplete materials together with
the completeness of the unbridgeable separateness of
these elements, can allow for the combined emphasis on
the divergent and convergent natures of literary
movement and meaning, the density and plenitude on
the one side, the rarity and the order on the other.
It can insist on the centrifugal thrust of a work only
while placing its control within the pressing and
uncompromising union of its finest and most centered
point. The impossible combination of identity and*

> *polarity can make a total view of the object possible: the*
> *perspective is reduced to a single point even as, at the*
> *same time, the range of possibilities multiplies*
> *endlessly—thus the consequence of the object as both*
> *single substantive world and as bodiless reflection of*
> *multiple worlds beyond.*

I claimed at the start of *The Tragic Vision* that the thematic reconciliation produced by Hegel's "ethical substance" (the metaphysical projection of the Hegelian synthesis) had to be denied if the tragic vision was to exchange the soothing notion of catharsis for the continuing lacerations of unresolvable tension (between the ethical and the tragic). For what converts reconciliation into unyielding tension is the refusal of a polar extreme to melt into its antagonist by way of synthesis. In effect, my version of the tragic vision thrives on the rejection of Hegelian synthesis.

The model of Hegelian synthesis is obvious and well known. Here is the culmination of Goethean humanism, man's increasingly inclusive (and creative) containment of the forces within him of order and chaos, of the moral and the brute natural. The mutual denials existing between *A* and *Anti-A* convert into the affirmative obliteration brought about by the mutual transcendence of the *New A*, the obliteration of warring particulars yielding to the inclusive harmony of the embracing universal. Thus the following diagram.

THE HEGELIAN DREAM OF SYNTHESIS
AS THE UNIVERSALIZING SOLUTION TO EXTREMITY

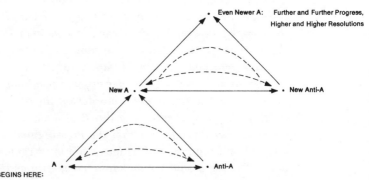

Even Newer A: Further and Further Progress,
Higher and Higher Resolutions

New A   New Anti-A

A   Anti-A

CYCLE BEGINS HERE:

24

But even as Mann's *Faustus* is created in reaction to the deceptions of Goethe's, so modern man must live with his awareness of the false promise of humanistic synthesis, with his consequent awareness of poles that do not synthesize, that—instead—sustain each other in the purity of mutual repulsion, thus mutually reinforcing each other's particular (and polar) identity. This is, essentially, Kierkegaard's response to Hegel, the mutually exclusive, ineluctable "either/or" that proclaims the utter autonomy of the particular in its defiance of the falsely imposing, "both/and" claims of the universal. Thus we shall have to extend the diagram to eliminate the false promise provided by its claim to mediate the polar antagonists.

Let us first, however, pursue the diagram further in its Hegelian hopefulness. Granted that *A* and *Anti-A* begin in the tension of unending collision, the antagonistic line between them somehow—through the pressure exerted at either end—bends upward (the broken curved lines) until antagonism miraculously breaks through to the synthesis won at the apex of the inverted V. (Note how the direction of the arrows has reversed itself, and they now move from alienation to mutual reinforcement.) This synthesis then engenders its own antagonist, becoming the *New A* to a *New Anti-A*, whence another twin-directioned arrow between them again bends under the doubly exerted tension of antagonism, until extremity again yields to the affirmations of centrist synthesis, an *Even Newer A*. And so it is to proceed, ever onward and upward, in a movement dedicated to the glories of the man-god in conquest of his opposing principles, ever converting subversion into higher humanistic orders.

But if, with Kierkegaard and later with Mann, we dwell instead on the fraudulence of the humanistic dream of synthetic transcendence, then the poles—instead of merging—exaggerate their mutual extremity. (See the diagram on p. 26.) What promised a synthesis of the center provides only a momentary meeting place for extremes once again moving apart to their old poles, though with apparently reversed positions. Here is a profound change in our model. The line of opposition hardly bends, and it is never broken. The arrows on the two ends go through the mid-point only on their way to reasserting their polar—if reversible—identities. It is true that *A* and *Anti-A* have criss-crossed, that they appear to have traded places. Each has become the mask for the other and thus together they prove the interchangeability of the poles, seeming to urge the radically paradoxical claim that ties polarity to

Introduction

THE TRAGIC DENIAL OF SYNTHESIS BY EXTREMITY

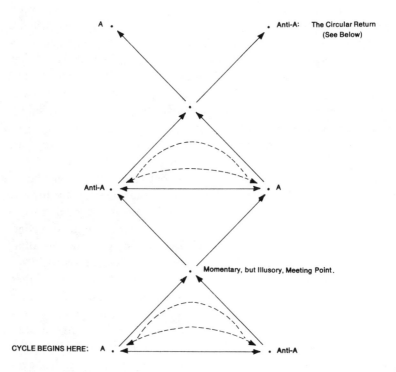

identity. The pole cherishes its private, particular extremity, narrowly presses it, and yet the methodology of extremity makes it one with its opposite. Austerity and license, health and disease, enslavement and freedom, guilt and innocence, in the Gides, the Manns, the Kafkas, the Conrads, and the Melvilles, as I have treated them, are refined in their dualities until each purifies itself by wearing the face of the other. The destruction of the center preserves the hard edges of the poles, even as the identity of either one is concealed beneath the disguise of its contradictory partner.[17] Thus we are trapped in the decep-

[17] Can we help but be reminded here of those endless debates in *The Magic Mountain* between Naptha and Settembrini, with the interchangeable polar roles each plays in them? (See *The Tragic Vision*, p. 105.) Or, as we acknowledge the prophetic powers of Mann, can we help but be reminded of the roles of left-right extremism in more recent political behavior? See also his *Doctor Faustus* and my discussion in *ibid.*, especially pp. 91–97.

tive politics of extremity, the continuing Manichaean subversion of the ethical as *via media*, and the recognition of the false promise of each would-be synthesis. The movement continues, always unprogressively; for the only upward thrust is an illusion of my two-dimensional representation in the diagram. Behind that illusion, the particulars—refining and defining themselves by mutual opposition—remain ever more narrowly themselves though wearing their contradictory masks, remain ever more narrowly themselves though the intolerable masquerade keeps playing itself out.

Or we can illustrate the strange commingling of closedness with inclusiveness, of extremity with its paradoxical coupling of opposition and identity, by shifting to another, simpler diagram altogether: the ancient, maddeningly imponderable figure of the circle. This would reflect what has been my continuing concern with what I have called the hard edge of experience (the circle itself along its circumference) and its resistance to the soft center of experience (the broad expanse of space enclosed by, but not including, the circle). Here we could see the polarities literally as poles, at opposite ends of the circle. But the circle is a moving, turning figure: that is, there are no isolable points on a circle to slide around it, along its circumference. Without fixity there can be no polarities whose opposition can retain a pointedness. Yet each point tries to become purely defined, tries to convert itself and its opposing point into poles on which the circle can rotate. But the circle will not fix, not even to become a sphere; it rather continues to assert its mere circularity along its moving circumference, emphasizing its pointlessness. Oppositions thus run into one another even as, being trapped on the circle rather than in the more open area enclosed by it, they retain their extreme character.[18]

So the extremities are doomed to trace the circle, at once trying to retain their distinguishing point-hood and yielding to their need to flow into other points, annihilating the very possibility of distinctness. (In this they carry out the paradox of "instant" and "instance" which I have several times introduced here.) Their one restriction is that they cannot leave the circumference to merge into the rich heart of experience which the circle includes and encloses as its soft center, even as the circle itself can only remain the hard edge of that experi-

---

[18] Of course, what seems to be a more open, freer area deceives us, since the circle is always, equally, there to restrict any apparent freedom or openness. The circle limits—indeed, defines—that openness by enclosing it.

ence, its extremist bound. To that bound the experience inside tends to advance (or to retreat, to shrink) as it tries to purify and define itself, even as—once on the fine line of the circumference—it must lose itself in undifferentiated extremity. So the figure of the circle also demonstrates the impossibility of the momentary gains of human synthesis; it can never allow for extremes that can annihilate their extremity by merging with the synthetic compromises of the center. Rather, the center is the amorphous, inconclusive heart of experience, at once in search of and in fear of definition. And it is that definition, the fine-line extremity, the precision-without-goal along the perimeter, that contains and defines—by enclosing—the rich softness of experience. Thus the circle becomes the ideal figure to describe the closed, conclusive, the ultimately defining and thus the extreme nature of the reductive metaphor.

The reductive metaphor can in its closedness open an *im*mediate access to reality's figures, which is to say the way reality becomes "figured" for us, "figured" in the double sense of Auerbach: at once the concrete symbol of the single instance, instantaneous, and—while holding to this character—the *figura*, its ultimate human meaning for us, its allegorical representativeness that exceeds itself, but only by being thoroughly itself. Hence emerges the vision, but not any vision that existed before the work in an individual psyche or in a culture's "*humanitas*" or in a normative structure held in its potentiality for individual entities to fulfill; rather, the vision that is attained figurally by cutting so fine a verbal figure *as* the work. Yet it *does* become the culture for the moment, and for the minds that, metaphorically, so constitute it. The extremity of total transfer, of metaphor, becomes a window to the reduced moment of vision which characterizes the reality created for a culture (created *as* the culture) by its most symbolically gifted seer-makers.[19]

The hypothesis of the work's reductive metaphor thus becomes the

---

[19] For an expanded treatment of this cultural function, see my discussion of Eliseo Vivas' terms, "subsistence," "insistence," and "existence" (from "The Object of the Poem," *Creation and Discovery* [New York, 1955], pp. 129–43) in *A Window to Criticism* (pp. 59–63, 214–15). This discussion is central to my attempt to relate the poetic context to the existential context: "For it is this metaphor, this total substitution, that allows us to see what an historical moment, in the privacy of hidden, personal inwardness has, in its most daring creations, in the total metaphors of its single, reduced moments of vision, dared to make of its world."

formal opening to the work's existential vision. All of its direction-less (because multi-directional) experience of the center, all of its "dappled," "pied" beauty, utterly ungraspable, is reduced to the emblematic unity that enables us to grasp its varied movements in a vicarious moment of condensed vision. We are given this extreme way (which neither precludes nor contradicts other ways) of seizing upon the experience as an entity we may perceive in its discrete entity-hood. It neither precludes nor contradicts other ways because it gives us no propositional claim about the experience, which would reduce it in an other-than-metaphorical way, a logical way that would cheat it of its uniqueness and integrity by making it serve a universal law, thereby reducing it to a cipher, an enslaved particular that is therefore particular no longer. Instead, the metaphorical, visionary grasp gives us all the particularity which the *poesis* helps us see as *one*, but as no more than one and as translatable to no others. Thus the metaphor, as the formal enabling cause of our vision—its source and its mouth—in the self-enclosure of its extremity, resists all propositional extrapolation, its persistent drama countering every would-be propositional claim with its antagonistic counter-claim.

The very reductive and yet all-embracing nature of the metaphor claimed by the critic's hypothesis must bear within itself the rational denial of its absolute nature. The metaphor must force us to see nothing less than an identity between the muddle of its tenor and the pristine extremity of its vehicle. But the equation it proclaims as a self-enclosing metaphor it must proclaim in awareness of our skepticism. To be metaphor it must insist on the miracle by which things change their nature, become other than themselves, their substance dissolving into other things. So as the metaphor exerts the equal pressure, the unrelenting tightness of a total aesthetic control everywhere within its domain, it creates the vision of the messy center of our experience *becoming* its own purified reduction at the hard edge. For our vision the metaphor assumes a guise that alters the thing itself, thus proclaiming, however irrationally, the destruction of discrete entities, the blurring of the bounds, the limits, that create the property and propriety of entity-hood. And it achieves the fullness of capacity that (in Sigurd Burckhardt's terms) corporealizes itself, attaining the totality of definition possible for metaphor.

But, despite all such seeming magic, discourse remains only discourse. No matter how dedicated metaphor may seem to be to subverting its nature, discourse seeks to remain an open structure that leads us in and out, relating to other discourses and to the world that comes before and after all discourse (or so we assure ourselves in our naïve realism, our common sense of how things go with us). And we as prosaic users of discourse—even as we are victims of the subversive perfection of its involutions in poetry—stubbornly retain the openness of our relations to discourse and the world, persisting in an anti-Kantian confidence that sees us and our world as pre-existing our symbols, as being objects for those symbols to point to. Consequently we must find in the poem that which seems comforting to our anti-aesthetic resistances, to our recalcitrance to the miracles of language fully if too trickily endowed. The poem's turnings upon itself end by allowing a part of us to turn on *it*, or to turn it against its most contextual or corporealizing pretensions. Our more rational selves find hidden within the poem, for all that would make it a new word, the comforting assurances that our prosaic sense for distinction and for property (which is to say propriety) may yet be preserved—nothing less than the comforting assurances that it all has been but a verbal game. Consequently, we try to set at rest that apocalyptic challenge to make the word into the Word, which is to say the fleshly world.

But of course this challenge, so persuasively urged by the closing, all-reducing action of the all-inclusive metaphor, still remains to possess us. This is to say that the rational covert guide which threatens to undo the mask by revealing it as no more than mask undercuts the miracle of metaphor by proclaiming it not as equation but as miracle, with all the inspiration of awe—and of skepticism—that the notion of miracle engenders. It is no fact; it is no proposition; indeed fact and proposition flatly deny it. It is but an *im*position upon our vision, sanctioned only by the daring leaps sponsored by the delicate play of language. As no more (but no less) than miracle, it can be held only in the teeth of all rational denials. For it goes without saying that if we can believe in it as a rational possibility, it is no miracle. By definition, its very existence for us as miracle depends upon that part of us which knows it cannot happen—except in a way that passes understanding, an understanding we cannot altogether yield up.

Thus it is that, even as the enclosing metaphor captures the motley variety of experience's soft center within the hard edge of its extremity, thereby reading all of life within its own closed visionary system, there is a counter-metaphorical motion at work as well: in the skeptical denial that restores distinction (that restores our sense of duality where there are two entities), there is an opening outward beyond the miracle (beyond the metaphor, the work, and the world of its words) to the world we know and what that world refuses to permit. An ironic self-doubt arises from the state of dialogue in the work that comes to terms with itself and yet, on the sly, proclaims itself as play; this self-doubt finally can lead beyond the still-limited dialogue of the tragic vision. For the simultaneous fact of the miracle together with its denial can make the total and uncritical confrontation of extremity and the embracing of its consequences (as by the tragic existent) less than finally acceptable to the critical temperament forged out of the dialogue that it continues to pursue. This dialogistic temperament, bent on joining dialogue to dialogue in an accumulation of self-conscious awarenesses, can make the classic vision ultimately more appropriate to our fullest aesthetic demands than the tragic. For the tragic seeks always to break the dialogue at last by converting the Manichaean to the single-mindedly demoniacal and, thus, by keeping the existential world hopelessly, endlessly closed.

The dual awareness that I have been urging, the dialogistic sense that returns with a furtive openness to what has been closed, may seem to echo the claims for the anti-poem of neoromantic apocalyptic critics like Hassan:

> *Literature recoils from the withering authority of*
> *the new Apollo, but it does not surrender itself wholly*
> *to the frenzy of Dionysus. It only feigns to do so. It*
> *employs self-irony and self-parody, as in the novels of*
> *Mann and Camus; it develops, as in the works of*
> *Beckett or Genet, forms that are antiforms. . . .*
> *Literature, in short, pretends to a wordy worldlessness*
> *and participates in the Dionysian denial of language*
> *not with its own flesh, but with the irony of its divided*
> *intelligence.*[20]

If Hassan would concede more to what closed form can permit, this might seem a helpful way to indicate the Janus-faced character of the work. The very closedness of the work, its absolute commitment to a metaphorical reduction, its compression into a constitutive symbol as

---

[20] "The Dismemberment of Orpheus," pp. 148–49.

its emblem, all are accompanied by that in it which prompts our common-sense denial, by that which dissolves its miracles and drags it to earth.

All poems must covertly contain their anti-poems, must transcend themselves and their closed limits, transform themselves into *genera mixta*. I restated earlier my claim that those traditions which characterize poetic form as convergent (as in Aristotelian unity) must be reconciled with those which characterize it as divergent (as in Empsonian ambiguity). The centripetal emphasis on an exclusive unity and the centrifugal emphasis on an inclusive variety, simultaneously asserted, are further reflections of the strange commingling of openness in the aesthetic closedness of the literary object. The reader should be reminded here of the discussion of the paradoxical coexistence of openness and closedness in our discrete experience viewed at once as instant and as an instance. Having insisted on the union of the open and the closed again, as I have from the start, I must move on to define what is meant by the vision that newly reopens our thematic world, the classic vision, as I add to the preliminary diagram of the dialogue outlined as summary of the tragic vision.

4. CLASSIC ACCEPTANCE AS AN AUTHENTIC AFFIRMATION

The extreme situation is that which, forgoing the ameliorations of the center, forces confrontation at the edge of our experience. All right, then. The extreme situation is that which forces confrontation; but the existent who would confront is also the creator of the extreme situation. Buried in this circularity is the notion that the mess at the soft center of our experience is a mess that we create in order to muddle ourselves and preserve our sanity, to keep going as social animals who do not want to look too deeply into mirrors, or into another's eyes. Our pursuit of endlessly diversified experience, veering in its infinitely various and self-aborting directions, our blunting the points we have sharply shaped, our lurching and starting and slowing and gliding and leaping, by turns, these are ways we hide from confrontations of what we dare not confront. In Kafka's *The Trial*, we must accept the ambiguous duality of K.'s having been seized for arrest gratuitously *and* K.'s having chosen the state of being arrested; so in this literature generally we must acknowledge both that extremity is there beckoning for him who would cast off all palliative veils to confront it and that extremity in a creation of those so willful as to choose the confrontation. The visionary courage—which is to say, the metaphorical courage—of those whose fear of blindness will not permit their confronting impulse to be diverted must be matched by the self-conscious insanity that forces them to wrestle with casuistic phantoms instead of joining the rest of us in the center, going round and round the dizzying dance of life. As we stop to look at them as our surrogates, if we observe closely enough, we find their struggle to have the purity and perfection of ballet. After such a vision, with what self-consciousness, with what new and corrective sense of our aimless heavy-footedness, do we return to make our motions?

Cast in this framework, authentic existence would seem to belong uniquely to our tragic existent, who buys it at high cost and, unable to talk for himself, must depend on a tragic-visionary author—too much like the rest of us not to be trapped in dialogue—if his story is to be told. Our own dependence on the tragic-visionary authors is our confession of our own inauthenticity, of the cost of our own willed blindness, and our desire to *see*, if (like Conrad's Marlow) only vicariously and without undergoing the awesome risks of vision. An acknowledgment of vision—indeed, the very word—implies a something-there-to-be-seen, which suggests that in our tragic mood we *are* ready to attribute an existential actuality to the Manichaean face of experience that is revealed under the aspect of extremity. Such an attribution implies, as corollary, that the moral universals we live by to keep disruptive particulars in their place have *no* actuality but are only pleasing fictions invented by our failure of nerve: we would rather hold onto its trim idols than face, without a mediator, the chaotic horde of unleashed, sovereign particulars.

We move from literary theory to ontology by obvious steps, then: if the poem, as uniquely particular, does give us access to a face of reality to which no other discourse can lead us, then this face of reality, in its particularity, must slip through the universals constructed by our normal propositions. Consequently, our propositions and the moral universals they express cannot be referring at all adequately to the reality we experience. How much of a step beyond this is it to maintain that the reality we experience is a mass of raging particulars that resists all propositional meaning, since such meaning would only serve to preclude their particularity? And how far from here to maintain that our experience itself has no rational grounding, makes no sense, that it requires the services of the poet or else remains hidden from the vision of those of us who do not ourselves wrestle with it in the darkness of its extremity? Thus literary theory can serve to authenticate the absurd in our experience. The poet is licensed this far by an existentialist theory of the tragic vision.

But the poet can do many things, whether we license him to do them or not. Even so he can manage to move to a dialogue beyond dialogue: he can return even from the absurd, can return from the tragic, possessed of a bleak vision that ensures authenticity, and can renew (literally re-new—on new terms) the affirmation of an existence before rejected as fraudulent. We have seen so far the poet as tragic visionary conducting the dialogue between the tragic existent and the ethical existent. As a creature of vision and of dialogue, he is rescued from the too committed or the too complacent orders of existence by the aesthetic orders of vision: he can join neither the tragic order of existence, which in its cult of singularity cannot descend to the universal even enough to speak with one's fellows, nor the ethical order of existence, which preserves its bloodless universals by deserting authenticity for blindness. So the poet-tragic-visionary is, after all, only a vicarious and partial tragic visionary in that he can choose the tragic as his order of vision and of art but still cannot rest in it as an order of existence.

Indeed, it is fortunate that for us the poet, less a participant than even a Marlow, need not have more than an order of vision and of art; as poet he is only creator and not creature. But a Marlow does instruct us that the vicarious and partial tragic visionary must, when he comes to choose an order of existence, choose the ethical, however warily and skeptically. He chooses the veil of falsely imposed universals—as Marlow chooses "the fixed standard of conduct"—knowing the universals to be no more than veil, and aware of the brawling turmoil they seek to cover. But he sees through the falseness of their pretension and now knows enough to prevent this shabby order of existence from being projected into an order of vision. For he understands that how he finally must act is sadly out of keeping with what his darker vision has revealed, even as he understands that—as a vicarious and partial visionary only—he dare not act in accordance with that darker vision. That is, he dare not partake of the tragic order of existence even if he borrows its vision from it. He knows, then, of the bizarre fracture between vision and action, the impossibly unsound basis in what he sees for what he must do. Almost paralyzed by his state of dialogue, he can finally choose his ethical mode of action. He *can* move, but only tentatively, and with self-distrust as his constant companion.

By contrast, the tragic existent he chronicles embraces the consequences of the extremity he confronts, and the chronicler (an author like Mann or a character-narrator like Zeitblom or Marlow or Ishmael) dare not evade the vision even if—unable to rest in the paralysis of dialogue—he may finally have to choose an existence that retreats from it. But, as I have said, the poet always has more tricks and turnings than we suspect or would know enough to license; so he can move beyond dialogue to return to community—by way of further dialogue.

We have seen the author as tragic visionary move almost at once beyond the tragic—which he could entertain only vicariously through his surrogate, the tragic existent—to a dialogue with the ethical; so we observe him now broadening his dialogistic role, becoming a classic visionary who can reject the confrontation of extremity even while acknowledging the authenticity of its threat, of the awesome pull toward immersion in its recklessness. In this rejection, however, what is being denied is the existent's answer—narrated by the visionary— to the data of the tragic vision, but not the data themselves. Indeed we shall see that these can be affirmed even as they are willfully evaded by the classic visionary.

Unless there is in him an awareness of these data, the classic visionary would be open to the charge that he is not classic at all, but merely returned to being an ethical visionary. This would be to charge that his vision—as inauthentic—would not have cast aside the fraudulent veil of universals, imposed upon existence by society to deceive itself into functional sanity; that he would be blind rather than maturely courageous; that, in other words, his vision would prefer to surrender his (and our) always errant particularity to the dominant universal, out of fear that such a vision could not otherwise return affirmatively from the negations of the tragic. Now the classic vision cannot exist without affirmation. But how can the visionary earn a right to affirm while he maintains a capacity to see? Can he keep from surrendering the one out of his desire for the other? How can we know that he is no longer just ethical, but has become classic; that he has had a success of vision and has not just suffered a failure of nerve?

This volume is written to demonstrate that there is an authentic classic—as well as the cheaper ethical—affirmation, and that our profoundest authors have attained to it. It will claim that the tragic visionary has too simple a dialectic—leading to too limited a dialogue —if his antagonist to the tragic existent is only the easily assailed straw man composed of unyielding universals drawn from the Babbitt-like ethical realm. Hegelianism has probably been our sole enemy for too long, and we must force our visionaries to be more subtle. A less parochial view of our literature reveals alternatives to the tragic other than the ethical: it reveals ways to return to the living without denying all that the tragic has revealed, without yielding up the primacy of the uniquely particular that was established by the existential trauma which led to the tragic. Let me, then, list and distinguish among the kinds of affirmation in order to discover those that, even from the tragic perspective, can be viewed as authentic.

It is important first to accept the claim, for which I argue from the start and through the course of *The Tragic Vision*, that the tragic (though not the art-form "tragedy") is the great denier, the negation of all order—cosmic, moral, and aesthetic. As the outlawed and solitary, unabsorbed Dionysian, as unrelieved Kierkegaardian despair, it can affirm only the denial, only chaos; and this is the self-denying contradiction in that it precludes the order needed to affirm anything, even the existence of the tragic state itself as an entity. So the tragic is not really a state so much as it is power—raw, nay-saying, destructive power—the release of naked force, the flow of self-governing sensation. It is an unmediated embrace of the extremity that the existent has confronted and which, simultaneously, has stricken him. For the tragic is what follows upon, what comes out of, the final, if sudden, irreparable rupture of what one, ethically, has been (the constellation of universals which are one's attachments, that to which one's living frame has been attached). But what has been destroyed, when one has been arrested and wills the arrest, when the trauma and its radical discontinuity have hit, is not a single ethical constellation only, but the very possibility of having such a constellation, of substituting another one for it. It is, as Kierkegaard has said, the ethical stage itself that is now gone beyond. This is why the tragic existent cannot be the unmediated narrator of his own tale, why he has need of an author who creates the aesthetic order which can contain his vision and his existence (even as this author frequently needs the mediating presence of a dialogistic narrator). And it is why I have called the author (or his narrator) only a vicarious and partial tragic visionary—because he is other things too.

(a) *Aesthetic Affirmation.* Thus the first and most obvious sort of affirmation to be maintained in the face of the tragic data is the aesthetic. The task of the author as tragic visionary, the reason he must retreat from the realm of existence to that of vision, is that he must resolve into a unified, comprehensive, aesthetic order the divisive, order-defying materials with which he deals, the materials which allow him his vicarious vision. But in giving despair a voice—as Mann's Zeitblom puts it—he is taming it to the dimensions of human symbol, indeed, is creating it through human symbol, and so is transforming it from the existential to the visionary, "rendering" the existential (in the several senses of "rendering") so that it is domesticated as the visionary. To the extent that the author creates it as a measurable entity, trimmed to the dimensions of human perception, within the categories of form that human perception creates, he works an aesthetic resolution (implying an aesthetic affirmation) upon his recalcitrant materials. His aesthetic monad contains, indeed is constructed out of, the ineluctable thematic duality engendered by the nay-saying principle of opposition; that is, he has forced into a perceptual union the cleavages which, in existence, remain asunder. Whatever appearance of wholeness there may be—and *must* be if the materials are to be seen as *a* work, aesthetically sound in that it comes to terms with itself—is appearance only, since thematically the universe is forever cleft.

Of course *aesthesis* is nothing but *Schein*, as I have elsewhere said, borrowing from old aesthetic tradition, so that appearance may be enough—for aesthetics. But as *thematics* it is an aesthetic delusion, since the wholeness has not dissolved or resolved or even relaxed the ineluctable tensions that the vision of the work has generated. However we may persuade ourselves that what the orders of the work manage to generate is rightly thought of as catharsis, all that was to have been purged is still naggingly there. And however we may persuade ourselves—through a comfortingly inflated doctrine of *Logos*—

that a symbolic universe so totally rendered as orderly system in itself guarantees the existence of order as a cosmic principle, the anaesthetic skeptic within reminds us ruefully of the merely rhetorical powers of the momentarily reductive metaphor that is the work; he insists that —finally—the word really is not the world, cannot draw the world to its shape. We have several times seen already that the miraculous metaphorical closedness yet insists on being accompanied by skeptical, common-sense, anti-metaphorical openness. So while as affirmation the aesthetic is convincing enough and suggests nothing of inauthenticity, it is from the thematic standpoint only a mock-affirmation: it does not return us to the world soundly renewed, except as we are ready—as aesthetes—to retain the world permanently as a work of art. This is a difficult pose to hold for long, to say nothing of permanently. So, still world-weighted, let us rather move to more lasting and substantive affirmations, though these are likely to prove even more difficult to earn—and to sustain.

(b) *Thematic Affirmation.* From the viewpoint I have been representing, it is clear that what I would term thematic affirmation or resolution must be seen as beyond the reach of aesthetically (or existentially) authentic drama. If all the motions and counter-motions, motives and counter-motives, that create the tensional structure of a work are to be resolved, if all that appears to our propositional consciousness as incipient contradictions are at last to be harmoniously synthesized, then the work would have to give up the existential waywardness—the heart of its aesthetic particularity—in order to surrender to the universals of the ethical realm. And we would be back where we were before being confronted by this literary work—back behind the veil, deluded and hiding from the face of reality—secure in the oneness of our universals standing against the Manichaean forces of opposition. But we would have paid the price of having the aesthetic unity of the work intruded upon by those outside, propositional forces that held sway before, during, and after it.

There is, then, this major difference between aesthetic and thematic affirmation: aesthetic affirmation supervises, through its unified awareness, the awesome fracture between vision and existence, a fracture which its own unity comprehends but does not, cannot mend; thematic affirmation dares to claim the final substantive union of the orders of vision and existence—a synthesis of the ethical and the tragic, but a synthesis that bifurcates the aesthetic. For the price of an affirmed thematic oneness—that testifies to the adequacy of universals —is the sacrifice of the aesthetic monad. So thematic affirmation is the converse of aesthetic affirmation; for in speaking of aesthetic affirmation, I have maintained that an organically self-sufficient union can be sustained only while the principle of opposition, which is the source of the thematic duality we have termed Manichaean, is recognized and acknowledged.

If the vision from the tragic perspective cannot authenticate any final thematic affirmation, then clearly it has, on the way, precluded a world in which actions and the possibilities for action seem to be rationally grounded—to have a grounding, that is, which can live up to, or be measured by, our propositional sense. The tragic perspective need make no ontological denials, for it knows nothing of the metaphysical, can see it only as leading to pretensions that evade the face of our reality.[21] But addressing itself to the physical and not the metaphysical, to the existential and not the ontological, this perspective can find an indispensable revelatory role for literature. The tragic mind is defender of the literary mind in that it would preserve the existential as exclusively the domain for literature, a game-preserve with no poaching by the propositional. Its defensiveness, though tautological (the literary is the existential because the existential is the literary), leads it to deny literary (and existential) authenticity to all cosmic and religious affirmations. It can see these only as heady extensions (Northrop Frye's "existential projections") of thematic affirmation. What is seen as fraudulent about thematic affirmation at large would be only aggravated by the transcendent version that would claim a religious resolution of the tensions engendered in the literary drama. A propositional moral claim, which ends by subordinating the drama and collapsing dramatic tensions to its universal truth, seems only the more ruthless if it is seen as a reflection of cosmic planning. Such a claim reduces existential to rational order, uses it as a micro-

---

[21] For the literary mind is a radically empiricist mind: it is concerned at the level of human drama with actions and language in which changes can be observed as being earned, as being probable, in some Aristotelian sense that sees the post hoc as being related to the propter hoc. Even miracles of metaphor must—if only in a strange, literary sense—be earned through a step-by-step movement, if such a mind is to accept them. They cannot appeal to, or be dependent upon, metaphysical or propositional leaps. See A Window to Criticism, pp. 5–16.

cosmic proof of its transcendent ground—a procedure most offensive to the anti-ethical perspective.

(c) *Religious Affirmation.* There is an alternative sort of religious affirmation, that of the Kierkegaardian Christian who cries "Yea!" not because he sees a transcendent order reflected in the existential, but because he sees (as does the tragic visionary) a complete lack of reason in the existential to which he chooses to respond by a leap of faith. Here the data are the same as they are for the tragic visionary, except that a final paradox somehow dissolves the tension between the world of experience and the Christian's response, which flies in the teeth of that world. He accepts the notion of all turbulence below, from which follows (but what greater non sequitur could we conceive?) the serene union with a transcendent splendor from above. Here is a higher reason that passes understanding, a reason that bears upon its face only an absurdity that defies understanding. But again we are in the realm of the metaphysical, here most of all, where the transcendent betrays no slightest sign of itself in the existential. Here most of all can the tragic visionary, whose eye can never move from the maddening face shown him by his experience, fear some fraud in a conclusion so willfully unearned.

We saw earlier that the tragic visionary could simply assume that the orthodox thematic affirmer had seen his experience shallowly but that, given what he had seen, his metaphysical conclusions were inevitable. The breach of vision between the two is awesome—so great that there hardly seems to be a common humanity between them. But the Kierkegaardian sort of affirmer is one who begins with the very confrontation of absurdity to which the tragic visionary was led by the tragic existent. Thus the unearned leap of faith, despite all that the tragic visionary and the Christian existentialist see in common, seems to the former a more offensively unearned affirmation than any other. For the tragic visionary insists upon nothingness from nothingness; to seize transcendence from nothingness is, for him, too magnanimous a gesture to an absurd universe. Whatever our judgment of this quarrel, as literary men we must maintain that—while we need not judge the metaphysical issue—so long as the leap cannot be earned dramatically, so long, that is, as the metaphysical does not touch the existential, this sort of Christian affirmation is an external imposition that does not allow for aesthetic authenticity. The leap is, by definition, unearned; being discontinuous with prior experience, it is in violation of the need for aesthetic continuity. This problem, for example, constitutes our difficulty with *Billy Budd*[22] and, given several turns, it constitutes the dialectic around *Murder in the Cathedral* that, in the last chapter of this volume, gives my own argument its final turn.

In the recent development of our culture we have moved from the bankruptcy of dogma to a disbelief in the possibility of dogma and then to the despairing irrationalism that leads to the worship of the absurd, the disbelief—in effect—in the possibility of sane living. Thus, in a way parallel to the movement traced here, we record the death of the ethical and the rebirth of the tragic as a mode now divorced from the grandeur and transcendence which were essential to it when it had its home in tragedy. But what return out of Dionysian despair to mere living is there—and has there been? How can we account for the simple human joy, the hallelujah chorus of affirmation —however modest—that fills some of our best literature? Must such high literary moments be outlawed as fraudulent, aesthetically unearned comfort-seeking? Obviously not. We must not, it is clear, distort our literature to protect a grim theory. How, then, to make theory serve such moments? How to hold these moments within a framework that preserves the existential basis of the theory which still sees literature as defying the propositional—and the ethical?

(d) *Classic Affirmation.* Yet, from the perspective that has moved beyond the ethical, where can we find the possibility of affirmation? Nowhere else than in that mild and moderate affirmation that I here term the classic. Melville saw it in the homely attractions that were unfortunately ignored by the heaven-aspiring (but hell-bent) tragic existent, Pierre. His warm defense of the neglected catnip, as it is overcome by the ambitious amaranth, is an effective call for classic existence, even as it is an acknowledgment of its unheroic modesty, which allows it to be abandoned by all zealots:

> But here and there you still might smell from far
> the sweet aromaticness of clumps of catnip, that dear
> farm-house herb. . . . that plant will long abide,
> long bask and bloom on the abandoned hearth. Illy hid;

[22] See my discussion in *The Tragic Vision*, pp. 260, 263–64.

> *for every spring the amaranthine and celestial flower*
> *gained on the mortal household herb; for every*
> *autumn the catnip died, but never an autumn made*
> *the amaranth to wane. The catnip and the amaranth!*
> *—man's earthly household peace, and the*
> *ever-encroaching appetite for God.*

Yet in the classic the tragic reading of the data of experience is not denied. There is no ethically willed blindness to the Manichaean face of reality, for the classic can see as far, and as darkly, as the tragic does. If it is to be an earned vision, the classic must move through and beyond its experience with the tragic: it must acknowledge that extremity is there to be confronted and inviting our embrace, but the classic refuses to choose it. It rather wills a retreat from it to an all-too-human acceptance that accepts also the significance of that retreat. Yet its movement is a positive and knowing one, a willed affirmation and no mere failure of nerve. The difficulty in making these discrete differences stand up is not easily overcome by the theorist. The balance of this volume is devoted to this delicate attempt.

Once more, as with the tragic, there must be a distinction drawn between the existent and the visionary, this time between the classic existent and the classic visionary. This dictates another return to the diagram I began with, this time in order to add to it in the classic direction. In this form it can represent the entire spectrum of the thematics of modern literature conceived as dialogistics.

Now that the diagram has been supplemented, we find at the two extremes two orders of existence, the tragic and the classic, whose

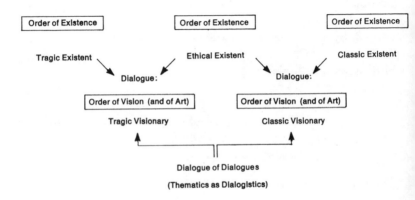

protagonists are so pure in their status as existents that they cannot themselves give voice to the vision implied by them. In dead center is the ethical, which is a necessary order of existence for him who may vicariously share the tragic or classic vision. As dialogist, he must choose his order of existence as his compromise with the compromising social forms. Of course, those who are blinded to the Manichaean face of reality would also want to claim the ethical as their order of vision; but as such it is seen as profoundly inadequate, as a surrender of authenticity, of individual uniqueness, to the over-riding universal. The visionary may be forced to accept the ethical as the only order of existence which his aesthetic commitment to dialogue (and, consequently, to non-commitment) leaves him—with irony and self-distrust —to pursue. But he can never accept the visionary consequences of the ethical order of existence; he sees its fraudulence and so is kept from self-deception only by his cynicism as regards the sphere of action. Thus he rejects the ethical vision as an utter failure even while accepting the ethical as his order of existence, however compromised, however grubby. So the visionary, torn between his vision and his existence, between what he sees and what—in view of what he sees— is left to him in the sphere of decision and action, chooses either the tragic or the classic as an order of vision that provides aesthetic satisfaction and moral paralysis. These are the questionable compensations for his necessary failure to accept the consequences of what he sees; instead, he must keep what he sees and what he does—or sanctions doing—apart. What he has really chosen is the impossible order of dialogue—or, perhaps more honestly—of schizophrenia. But it is a schizophrenia of the man that is the freeing of the artist.

The left side of this diagram was described earlier as a summary of all that I tried to demonstrate in my earlier volume; the right side remains to be explored here. But before breaking the two sides apart, I must comment upon the analogies in the relations between the two visionaries and the less eloquent—if more extreme—existents for whom they must seek to account. The contrast between the tragic existent and the tragic visionary is the contrast between the living out of the tragic vision through a total commitment to its existential consequences and the vicarious sharing of the surrogate's vision, which the "secret sharer," through his withholding of total commitment (since he remains existentially within the ethical), can only partially glimpse. The price of the visionary's being *our* sharer, as well as the tragic existent's, the price of his return to society through the dialogue that permits a fidelity to the aesthetic order, is paid in the partial and momentary—rather than the total and continual—nature of his glimpse of "the horror."

From what our authors and their narrators have shown us, we can accept the notion that for the tragic existent himself there is no return to dialogue with the ethical, no renewable acceptance of social responsibility, except, perhaps, if one is not provided with his Marlow. Then one can choose to become his own narrator, like the Ancient Mariner or the André Gide of *The Immoralist*, in which case one must—for the occasion—put his own tragic existence within the dialogistic context that makes him his own visionary, furnishing critique as well as apologia. More usually, the vicarious and partial tragic vision, ready for aesthetic projection, comes only to one who is already proof to tragic existence even as he sees the bankruptcy of ethical vision, so that for him the state of dialogue is there from the start; nor can that ambivalent state be relaxed enough to permit the totality of commitment, the giving away of oneself or the absorption of everything into oneself (as two parts of the single act). Instead, for the mere visionary, the self stands apart, in contemplation of its own separateness (and thus of its relation to the demands of others), lending itself and withdrawing itself by turns, in awareness of the impossibility of its integrity either in isolation or in union with others.

It is this habit of self-conscious awareness that similarly disqualifies the classic visionary from being a classic existent. For the classic existent, we shall see, can have even less of critical self-consciousness in him than can the tragic. Leech-gatherers or Michaels or Lena Groves, they are, in effect, Dostoevsky's peasant women of simple faith who know not what remarkable things they are. These unsophisticated creatures, utterly identified with their kind, lack any awareness of their existence as separate selves, just as the tragic existent lacks any awareness of the existence of any other self which can command the submission of his own. In either case, the existent can be the sort of existent he is only insofar as he cannot transcribe the vision that sanctions his existence; for he cannot—as the visionary must—see beyond his existence, lest he lose the purity required to realize that existence in the un-self-consciousness that permits its polar quality, whether at the pole of utter self-alienation or at the pole of utter loss of selfhood.

The visionary character of the dialogist can even make it most difficult—at times instructively difficult—for him to distinguish the tragic from the classic; and it may make it profitable to see them as overlapping. (Think, for example, of Ishmael.) Thus my analytical purposes here may tend to suggest more rigid demarcations in the middle portions of the diagram than literary experiences would justify.

With this much of general comment, we can examine the several stages of the diagram separately and in their interrelations. The ethical that stands so dominantly in dead center need not by this time detain us long. It is, at the least, an order of existence, one to which both the tragic visionary and classic visionary will have to resort despite their visionary awareness of its untenability. Despite what they see, they retain with sanity their social role by falling back, if with irony, upon society's universals. But, of course, for "ethical man" the ethical is an order of vision as well as an order of existence. He believes defensively, and at times aggressively, in the guiding universals to which his actions are meant to be attuned, though they deny him his particularity and deny his actions and decisions—in their very decisiveness—the vision that grants particularity to anyone else.

His assumptions—assumptions that the existential vision sees as blind—are, first, that there is *a* way and, secondly, that he can act disinterestedly in the service of it. The first assumes the validity of the universal to absorb particulars to itself by denying their particularity; and the second assumes his own capacity to suspend the uniqueness, the drivenness, of his person as a particular, in order to become the trustworthy representative instead of the distrust-worthy individual. The danger, as I traced it repeatedly in *The Tragic Vision*, always is that the self-righteousness stemming from the lack of self-distrust can lead to a self-absorption that converts the would-be ethical man into the demoniacal creature ready for tragic existence. Always seeing only the veil of universals that he has interposed for his rational comfort between himself and existential reality, and concentrating upon that veil in order to protect himself from worrying about what lies behind, he can perform cruelties in its behalf, as he preserves its preservative qualities. He thus transforms all persons into things, into the ciphers they trace upon the veil. And he can act absolutely and indifferently upon them all, until—or unless—a sudden guilt-ridden awareness of what he has performed forces him to strip existence of the veil he has imposed upon it. This would propel him, like a Kurtz or an Ahab, through the veil and into unmitigated tragic existence.

This leads to the left side of the diagram, from which we can move quickly toward the right. The tragic existent is he who lives the consequences of the tragic vision even if he cannot himself enunciate it. He has pierced the veil and rushes to embrace the consequences of confronting existential extremity. His order (or rather disorder) of existence, shared by no one but himself, is witnessed or rather apprehended—even comprehended—by one for whom the tragic is only an order of vision, one who must resort for his order of existence to the ethical and to the order, both aesthetic and moral, that it sanctions: this one is the partial and vicarious tragic visionary. Conducting his dialogue between the tragic and ethical, this visionary yet remains, though most critically and qualifiedly, within the ethical. He is aware of its limitations because his own veil of universals has been torn by the clawing violence behind. The tears have made holes in it, and through the holes he can see through to existential reality. His slightest awareness of the holes gives him certainty that the veil is only a veil and nothing more: it is not reality, for reality rather lies behind, momentarily perceptible through the holes. At once licentiously attracted and austerely faithful, he dares both to peep through the holes and to remain loyal to the veil, refusing to remove it even as it proves increasingly flimsy. He steadfastly tries to concentrate on the areas between the holes that remain in the veil, though he never evades his awareness of the gashes that lie between and among them. But in his doubleness and his self-consciousness, he can never be more than voyeur—and raconteur.

Easily confused with the tragic visionary, in many ways overlapping him but still differentiated from him according to my scheme, is what I term the vicarious and partial classic visionary. He has earned his way back toward acceptance, not by living through the tragic (any more than the tragic visionary did), although, like the tragic visionary, he has seen the possibility of the tragic. That is, the classic visionary has also seen beyond the ethical, so that he shares the data of experience seen by the tragic vision. But, seeing the possibility of the tragic, seeing the extremity waiting there to be confronted, he traces the consequences of choosing not to confront it. While the tragic visionary also turned aside from the existential consequences of confronting extremity as he turned to his dialogue with the ethical, he never denied the authority of extremity's demand that it be confronted; he never stopped using the tragic existent as his surrogate, even as he never dared surrender so completely from humanity as to join him. (Again we may recall the examples set by our narrators who used their creatures as vicarious sources of vision: Marlow with his Kurtz, Zeitblom with his Leverkühn, Ishmael with his Ahab.) But the classic visionary, as I see him, does deny the authority of this call to confrontation by extremity (thus differing from the tragic visionary). Nevertheless, he does acknowledge not only that such extremity exists, but that his awareness of this existence must work a revolution on the order of his moral universe as it pre-existed this awareness. (In this way he differs from the ethical visionary just as the tragic visionary did.) He is rejecting the conclusiveness, not merely of tragic existence, but of the tentative tension generated by the dialogue I have been calling the tragic vision. He is rejecting that order of vision together with that order (or rather disorder) of existence. He cannot, like Marlow, counter the attraction to Kurtz with the retreat to a "fixed standard of conduct," returning with his fidelity to society even as he remains loyal to the vision of "the horror."

In ways that should become clear only as this volume proceeds, the classic visionary moves, not to an acceptance of the ethical, but to the acceptance of something more catholic—embracing the entire race—and less doctrinal: the very opposite of the persistent, aggressive puritanical commitment to righteousness that is at the heart of ethical imposition. And somehow its very catholicity is not, in any binding sense, universal. There is always, in the classic visionary, an underlying assumption of the barnyard imperfection of the race. But instead of seeking to subdue the stinking animal (in himself as well as others) by organizing the race in accordance with ethical universals, he suffers imperfection to be lived with in rejection of the "either-or" considerations that could drive it, and him, and us all, into the extremity that sanctions demonism.

If the tragic vision generates the unyielding tension of mutual impossibilities, in which all is polarized into extremes and all extremes are faced doubly (through the totality of ethical imposition and the totality of demoniac secession), the classic is the vision that is utterly relaxed and unexclusive, where everything is possible *except* the extremes. The visionary at once sees the veil and sees through the holes in the veil; but he also keeps the veil at sufficient distance to view it with the detached irony born of knowledge that this and all veils are unfortunate and, in their impositions and visionary distortions, dan-

Introduction

gerous. Seen but as a mask that threatens to deprive the race of its
humanity—an all-too-human humanity at once degrading and joyous
—the veil may be either dropped or still held, for nothing is done in
violence. But his allegiance is rather proclaimed—no, quietly affirmed
—to an all-embracing illusion, an always opening "canopy": "this
most excellent canopy, the air, look you, this brave o'erhanging firma-
ment, this majestical roof fretted with golden fire."[23] And we may add
the protective sense of Shakespeare's Sonnet 12: "When lofty trees I
see barren of leaves, / Which erst from heat did canopy the herd."

Beyond all veils, then, and in silent recognition of the unspeakable
possibilities in existential reality, the classic visionary can quietly
affirm the canopy without disputing its illusory quality. For it is an
illusion he sees as fostered by the bond of our common humanity in
our common history. The canopy is seen as covering all the herd, protecting it from extremity: a herd of classic existents who must never
claim to be more than members of the herd, of the natural human
community. The single, simple line from Tennyson's "Tithonus"
seems to bear this entire notion within it: "Man comes and tills the
field and lies beneath." Here is the plea for the natural, routine march
of generations made by the one man (Tithonus) doomed to be exceptional and thus separated from the routine. This one line traces the
common course of life for the classic existent, with the way of death
seen to be as natural, as accepted, indeed as voluntary (if as unquestioned) as the way of life: the coming, the ritual tilling of the field,
and then the cooperative, similarly ritual descent beneath that field,
man's field of work and his eternal home worked by those who follow
in the same ritual pattern. For unexceptional man, all is active, ongoing, even as it takes place in a passively welcome continuity. How
different is this unhindered, almost automatic march of generations
from the fate of Tithonus, or from Keats's vision of death as the
weapon of inimical time, which men—each a would-be exceptional
man—rush over each other to escape. Addressing the immortal nightingale, Keats' un-classic visionary envies its exemption from the desperate doom of man: "No hungry generations tread thee down."
Coleridge's Ancient Mariner, rather like Tithonus, envies—as the

[23] *Hamlet*, act 2, scene 2, ll. 311–13. But the tragically driven Hamlet, who
falls far short of any classic acceptance, must undercut this vision as he
adds, "why, it appeareth no other thing to me than a foul and pestilent
congregation of vapours."

homeless outsider—the natural universe of unalienated entities responding instinctively and properly to the natural law, the law of the routine of the hearth, from which he has been excluded. The narrator provides us with this marginal gloss: "In his loneliness and fixedness he yearneth towards the journeying Moon, and the stars that still sojourn, yet still move onward; and every where the blue sky belongs to them, and is their appointed rest, and their native country and their own natural homes, which they enter unannounced, as lords that are certainly expected and yet there is a silent joy at their arrival." The Mariner thus also points the way to classic affirmation under the canopy.

If classic man is unexceptional man, at one with the race, how can he still be preserved as unique? The uniqueness of the person, as seen in the classic vision, is protected from ethical universality, not by the assertion of his unique rights (which is the way to the demoniacal assertion of the ethical), but by a modest, if paradoxical, acknowledgment of his common uniqueness. All-yielding and all-embraced, the oppressive "Burden"-some history of the race liberates (as it does Robert Penn Warren's Jack Burden) rather than suffocates (as it does William Faulkner's Joanna Burden). And the herd of classic existents can thus be liberated. Still, remnants of the veil, together with an awareness of the reality behind the veil and of the illusory nature of the canopy, remain to remind our merely vicarious classic visionary of his selfhood, of his separateness from the un-self-conscious herd of classic existents. He too remains a creature of dialogue, indeed of a dialogue of dialogues, a dialogue compounded: the "infinite resignation" of Kierkegaard asserts itself, but it is at the same time modified and sustained by recognizing not only the collision of the ethical with the Dionysian state of despair, but also the further collision of both with itself. Still he remains resigned: as consistently as he may acknowledge extremity, he rejects it.

But the classic visionary does make a forward as well as a backward movement. He turns from extremity toward a mature—if imperfect—acceptance of the human condition. I find at least four, often overlapping, grounds for this acceptance. These constitute the major divisions of the present study: (1) the rejection of extremity through the worship of bloodless abstractions, (2) the rejection of extremity through the embrace of the natural human community, (3) the rejection of extremity through reconciliation with the depths of the human barnyard, and (4) the rejection of extremity through the posing of an alternative to sainthood.

The purity of the classic way can be lived only by the un-self-conscious classic existent. Since he is not a visionary, we cannot expect of him a visionary's articulateness. We cannot expect him to have an awareness of the relation of his order of existence to alternative orders of existence or of vision: to the ethical or the tragic. Indeed, he may be serving a local universal, a community's ethical imperative, and thus may be confused by us with an ethical existent; and in his naïveté surely he cannot make the distinction between the veil and the canopy. But the distinction is there and is made articulate for us through the vision of the classic narrator who, trapped by dialogue, remains existentially one of us. The existent, though not the visionary, has an immediate identification with the anti-extreme, anti-exceptional, anti-heroic history of the race in its routine aspect of mere generation and endurance. Suffering is the role, historically ordained. What is suffered, among other things, is the fate of having to exist within the veil of social law in its many historically conditioned manifestations. But, always beyond (or always prior to) rebellion, the classic existent must accept the veil, as he must everything else, because he can see it only as one with the canopy, as if it were a microcosmic reflection of it. Social life is for him a good, and the local version of it is to be accepted if he is to join the routine march of history's generations. Still, any ethical acceptance is for him accident and not substance; nor can he assume any role as aggressive defender and imposer of ethical universals. Whatever delusions he may be under about the innocuous role of the ethical, however he may confuse the ethical with those resplendent reflections from the canopy that bind man's life to itself, these are for the classic visionary to show to us, even as the classic existent himself blithely moves along his historically ordained way in innocence—and ignorance.

My diagram would seem to move, from left to right, from the extreme of individual self-assertion and alienation to the extreme of integration, of oneness with the race. It moves, that is, from the aggressive insistence on one's absolute role as exceptional man— endowed with exceptional needs and exceptional rights—to the passive acquiescence in one's routine role as unexceptional man, part of the herd which is the natural human community. This latter is man seen as part of nature, as in nature. Paradoxically, it is the self-assertive extreme that is destructive of self, that in self-hatred fails to honor the self any more than it honors the others it must violate; and it is the selfless extreme that preserves the self, preserves the unique person that is the self by rejecting any self-imposition, by claiming nothing for the self that it would not claim for others. The refusal by the classic to intrude the ethical upon another person makes possible the respect for the uniqueness of each person—the common uniqueness, as it were, of the person as herded in racial history. This dedication to man's historic barnyard role rejects the exceptional man who would make special claims for himself or on behalf of his favorite ethical set. So the classic existent loses the self in order to save it, as the tragic existent destroyed the self by over-asserting it. The movement from the tragic to the classic, then, is not from all self to no self, even if the converse is also too simple. After all, only the ethical, in dead center but reaching both ways, is dedicated without reservation to the obliteration of the unique person.

The diagram is deceptive in another way too. As two-dimensional, it has, of course, the weakness of all diagrams in that it tries to capture complex nuances in crude categories, which it then relates to one another in the simplified graphic terms of a flattened symmetry. Thus, although it can show the parallel relations between the tragic and the classic orders of existence and of vision on either side of the ethical, it cannot reflect the way in which the classic vision—even as it is analogous to the tragic—also includes the tragic awareness within itself, involves itself with the tragic dialogue while it broadens that dialogue to include the further dialogistic possibilities opened up from its own point of vision. So while there is a coordinate symmetry among alternatives, there is also something cumulative as we move from left to right, from the limited dialogue of the tragic vision to the relaxed dialogistic inclusiveness of the classic. All this intimates a hierarchy among these orders of vision and existence, a notion that would require the diagram to have vertical as well as horizontal directions.

As the existents are the surrogates for the visionaries, so the visionaries are *our* surrogates. The critical reader of the visions of modern literature, creating *his* vision of modern literature, must create his own dialogue of dialogues fed by the tragic and classic dialogues of our literary visionaries. Out of these balanced tensions comes what literature does for us all in the significance of its grapplings with modern existence, at once filled with impossibilities *and* persistence. By partaking of the dialogues and standing atop them, thanks to our visionaries who worked through them, the critic pursues his literary discipline of thematics, which becomes another term for dialogistics. It is the way literature gives us vicarious breadth, both existential and visionary, as it undoes our fanaticisms. We ourselves, even less bold than our cautious literary visionaries, dare not give up the ethical as our order of existence; but we are forever newly broadened by our dialogistic visions and the dialogue *we* conduct among them.[24] As we return to walk our ethical path, we walk the more tentatively as our sadness becomes the more certain: our forbearance rises as our expectations fall. Softened by vision, we tread with a light foot and a heavy heart.

[24] This is the return to the ethical which I intimated in note 3 above: an ethical less objectionable than the Hegelian ethical assailed by Kierkegaard. This acceptance of the need to accept the ethical after all is a lightening of the ethical. By introducing such a likelihood, I mean to prepare for the acceptance of the burden of history in chapter 10 below and for the lightening of the burden of history in chapter 11. Thus is the ethical related to human history. The consequences of this relationship open us to the opportunity for the vision which this book is all about.

2

Historical: The "Drab" Vision of Earthly Love

I think of the two visions, the tragic and the classic, as post-Renaissance visions. So it would make sense to look for their early manifestations in the late Renaissance. And it is in the Renaissance that I find, almost side by side (sometimes, as with Sir Philip Sidney, for example, in the work of a single poet), some examples of a unified vision in which these two visions do not appear in separable forms and some examples where such unity has broken apart. For the tragic and the classic, as I have defined them, can become discrete visions only when the extremity of man's earthbound condition can no longer achieve an aesthetic-metaphysical transfiguration, only when man's earthbound condition must be either violently confronted (as in the tragic) or blandly—if maturely—accepted (as in the classic). In the Renaissance, such transfiguration still characterizes many of our greatest literary achievements—where the catholicity, the total human breadth of the epic voice still speaks, or where full tragedy still triumphs over the merely tragic, or where even the tiny lyric still attains an earthly-heavenly union under the dominion of an all-embracing metaphor. But also in the Renaissance the unitary vision falters, so that—in retreat from totality and in the face of an extremity which we can no longer transform—the tragic and the classic formulate their separate natures.

Since my study proper is to begin with poems of Pope, Johnson, and Wordsworth, it may be worthwhile for us to trace reflections in poetry of the break-up of vision that creates the tragic and the classic as discrete alternatives. My work in *The Tragic Vision* concentrated on the visionary implications of fictional and dramatic forms. In my introductory discussion in that volume and in the first chapter here, I have suggested that, while many Greek and Shakespearean tragedies transformed the tragic vision into a transcendent affirmation that could countenance no separation of the classic from the tragic, the drama and fiction outside these aesthetic-metaphysical moments of delicate balance fell in disarray between tragic and classic alternatives. This is the split, lamented by Nietzsche, that followed upon the disintegration of Apollonian-Dionysian unity. In this way, one might claim to see—say in Webster and Marston—the pursuit of separate possibilities seen as indivisible in Shakespeare's greatest plays, whether tragedies like *Lear* or romances like *The Tempest*. But my interest here is, first, to trace something like this di-vision (bifurcation of vision) within the development of the magnificent lyrics of the same general period, and, second, to pursue the classic vision as I pursued the tragic vision in my earlier volume. As we observe what happens to metaphor and language, we uncover what happens to vision. And we are on our way to the special kinds of discovery I want to make about Pope.

In order to trace the break-up of the transfigured vision, let me first distinguish crudely between what I choose to call monistic and dualistic Renaissance poets. Others might prefer the opposing terms to be Neoplatonic and Platonic, respectively. The distinction to which I mean to point would find on one side (the monistic or Neoplatonic) those poets who would drive all earthly-spiritual polarities upward into a transcendent synthesis that is earned in vision, in metaphor, and in the achieved union of what I have elsewhere called a miraculous language ("miraculous" in that it defies, through transubstantiation, the limiting properties of words). On the other side (the dualistic or Platonic) would be found those poets who modestly accept that downward movement which preserves both the discreteness of the earthly and the verbal limitations of mere language. In terms of my scheme, the monistic poet represents the unitary vision (prior to the break-up into the tragic and the classic), while the dualistic poet is the tragic or the classic visionary. It is the classic version of dualistic poet who will primarily concern us here. But first it is worth expanding the general contrast between monistic and dualistic poets.

The monistic poet strives to break through the drag of the sublunary—to make finite experience into a "figure" of archetypal experience and to extend the verbal reach of words to the substantive element that creates body. He bends all his efforts to achieve a victory over the tragic, downward pull of material reality by dissolving its discrete entity-hood; and he does this by means of his victory over the limiting definitions of words that—through metaphor or phonetic accident—are now made to grow beyond their bounds. Thus he tries to create—as he discovers—a golden union of inspirited substance. In the lyric he subjects himself to the extremity of finite experience and triumphs over it—in a manner not at all dissimilar to the way I have claimed that the writer of tragedy triumphs over the tragic vision.[1]

The dualistic poet, in consciously refusing to press earthly (and earthy) realities beyond their natural limits, reveals a classic tendency that evades the cosmic pretension or the existential ambition which could involve him in the tragic. Aware of the potential dangers of any attempt to transform the modestly transient stuff of his experience, he has made himself proof against the restlessness that would deprive him of his classic willingness to dwell on the riches of his world as he exploits them. This persistent involvement often leads him to embrace the comic as the classic. On those occasions when he is serious and concerns himself with all that the City of Man excludes, he is likely to be metaphysical rather than existential, philosophical rather than poetic, coolly postulating abstractions rather than vibrating with particulars. His living reality finds and expresses itself in the trivial enclosure that his immediate experience makes available to him. And though as an existent he may long for more, his classic sense keeps him from asking for it. His is the mood that Thomas Nashe's Unfortunate Traveller, Jack Wilton, freely wayfaring rogue, venerates in a work written against gravity, against puritanism, and against novelistic form. Wilton and his tale must resist and defy all moral and aesthetic impositions that would inhibit his sense of the random, mark of freedom, a freedom to wander and to play—all over the face of the "civilized" world, but not for a moment beyond it: "Now I beseech God love me so well as I love a plain-dealing man; earth is earth, flesh is flesh, earth will to earth, and flesh unto flesh, frail earth, frail flesh, who can keep you from the work of your creation?"

In the Renaissance lyric, it is most clearly the love poems that betray such lustily classic notions. The arena of love play is neatly circumscribed, and the game of pursuit of the mistress is worked out in its own terms. The mistress herself, as an object of pursuit, is no more than that, enjoyed in the chasing and once caught—even more, of course—in the tasting. But nothing more is made of her, and she in turn makes nothing more of the poet. The game requires that both

[1] See *The Tragic Vision*, chap. 1 ("Tragedy and The Tragic Vision").

equally accept this limitation, indeed, that they embrace it, rejecting any more pretentious alternatives.

It is just such alternatives that prompt the enormous ambition—visionary and verbal—of the love poetry that creates the monistic tradition in the Renaissance. Here we have the Neoplatonic conventions of Courtly Love rather than just plain earthly love. The Petrarchan mode itself, with its sources in Courtly Love, serves to institutionalize a symbolic form consecrated to the transformation of earthly love to spiritual. Thus this became the dominant mode which the monistic poet found for his purposes. The union of bodies is made to blur into the union of essences; and for the best of these poets this union of unions is created by breakthroughs in the language, as words also overflow their bounds and dissolve into one another. The mistress herself, both agent and object of transformation, becomes ritualized beyond her material and historical reality. As idolatry merges with typology, the metaphorical play on the divine-human paradox of Christianity fuses the mistress into an eschatological figure.

Elsewhere I have treated Shakespeare's entire sonnet sequence in terms of a figural reality achieved by analogy to the Trinity and the Second Coming, and in language that—celebrating paradox—unites essential oneness with physical division.[2] Entities are forced to blend into identity, as tragic separateness in existence and in death is overcome by verbal magic or by faith (is it religious or merely poetic faith?) created by the Petrarchan ritual. Material reality that maddens, as it depresses, the faithful is not denied, is indeed encouraged to assert its *apparent* sovereignty, even as language opens outward and upward to allow a transcendent reality to dominate over appearance. Is this not similar to what, at the outset of *The Tragic Vision*, I saw as the indulgence of the tragic vision by the full tragedy that yet triumphed over it by keeping it in its metaphysical place?

For example, Shakespeare's frequent use in his sonnets of the language of the marketplace (of lawyers, accountants, merchants), which he insists on applying to the profoundest matters of love's fidelity, emphasizes the conflict between the worldly drag and the supernal thrust. And the triumph of the latter must be earned by the conversion of the crass currency of a counter-language to heart's gold—and this by way of the alchemy of language! For it is the lowest word itself that is made to serve by keeping and yet changing its meaning,

[2] In *A Window to Criticism*. See especially pt. 2 ("The Mirror as Window in Shakespeare's *Sonnets*"), pp. 71–190.

remaining true to one world as it opens the way to another. Thus, to cite just a couple of obvious examples, words like "dear" (Sonnet 87, "Farewell! thou art too dear for my possessing") and "true" (Sonnet 72, "O, lest the world should task you to recite," or Sonnet 113, "Since I left you, mine eye is in my mind") insist upon the mundane requirements of marketplace reality—for all the doubts such requirements cast upon Neoplatonic ambition—even as the words themselves stake the claim in the name of that ambition.

Similarly, I have pointed out[3] that the spectacular double sonnet, 30–31 ("When to the sessions of sweet silent thought"), raises up precisely what drags it down as it joins in single (though double-meaning) words the language of the earthling and of the sublime lover. The books of the speaker's lamentations cannot be made to balance, as the "expense" of the "losses" of those who are "precious" can never be "cancell'd" or "paid": they remain beyond the capacities of the (in two senses) teller. The transience of earthly reality persists in asserting itself to the mourner, with whose more-than-material needs such transience is incommensurate. Beyond his capacity to measure, he must use what measuring tools he has, carrying on as a futile accountant of human sentiment. Suddenly, in the couplet of Sonnet 30, the interjection of his present beloved friend miraculously restores all "losses" and ends all "sorrows," performing what it was beyond all of his reasonable instruments to perform for him. This victory over earthly (and deathly) sorrow is extended and explained in Sonnet 31, which introduces a different, transfigurational burial and, with it, a magical form of arithmetic, one that turns subtraction into addition, producing a different sort of "interest," a different sense of what is "due" to the dead and the living. Out of these arises a special —and, from the limited view of the auditor's usual reckoning, a shocking—equation: "Their images I lov'd I view in thee, / And thou —all they—hast all the all of me." Love, through its magical additions, produces a totality ("all . . . all . . . all") that allows an infinite fullness to grow from the privations which threatened to bring nothingness in the first of these sonnets. The terms themselves (whether the terms of language, the terms of life and death, or the terms of debts and repayments) are transformed as they are transcended. But, however they are altered, the worldly terms are not denied: they are faced, even as they are faced down.

[3] *Ibid.*, pp. 179–87.

Even a self-consciously anti-Petrarchan poet—so long as he is monistic or Neoplatonic—must, in spite of himself, end by being essentially Petrarchan in his claims. Thus, in the most obvious cases like that of John Donne, the material limitations of earthly love turn out to have spiritual consequences as microcosm converts to macrocosm. However prosaically such a poet may dismiss sweet Petrarchan extravagance, he only in the end reinforces and—if anything—extends that extravagance by bringing a seemingly antagonistic, hard-headed logic to affirm it, if necessary by denying its own logic. Thus, as in Shakespeare (despite the difference in surfaces and strategies), poets like Donne use language and reason to justify what it is their proper business to refuse to countenance: the blurring of categories, of entity-hood, of the routinely limited laws of time and space.

A poet like Sidney may be a less obvious case, although I find him an important one. The brilliantly discursive manner of many of his Petrarchan sonnets usually reveals anti-Petrarchan intentions. However, these lead to attacks directed not against the claim of the naïve Petrarchan monist who would transcend the world after submitting to its rigorous limitations, but against his failure to recognize that such a claim cannot be justified unless he faces his linguistic and rational incapacity to express them or account for them. Sidney's tough-minded conversations with himself lead through arguments and counter-arguments, in which he ponders love, its costs and its impossibilities, its unavailability for reasonable and moral man—only to persuade himself to make the impossible and the unavailable both possible and available. Words, burdened with all they can mean and limited by what they cannot be extended to mean; reason and virtue, defined by the rules they have created—all are strained to defy their nature and, thus, to defy nature itself. So in many of his best sonnets Sidney feels free to "admit impediments" to "the marriage of true minds" (to use the language of Shakespeare's Sonnet 116): the impediment of conventional language and, through it, the impediments of reason and of sexual passion, of reason confused with passion, and in the end of a reason transformed magically (that is, through the magic of Stella, of trying to reason about Stella) into a justification for a transfigured passion. Such is the pattern of unarguable argument in sonnets like *Astrophel and Stella* 4 ("Vertue alas, now let me take some rest"), 5 ("It is most true, that eyes are form'd to serve"), 10 ("Reason, in faith thou are well serv'd, that still"), 19 ("On *Cupid's* bow how are my heart-strings bent"), 28 ("You that with allegorie's curious frame"), 34 ("Come let me write, 'And to what end?' To ease"), 44 ("My words I know do well set forth my mind"), 47 ("What, have I thus betrayed my libertie?"), 71 ("Who will in fairest booke of Nature know"), and 74 ("I never dranke of Aganippe well").

Let me use *Astrophel and Stella* 35 as a heightened example of what occurs in many of these sonnets.

> *What may words say, or what may words not say,*
> *Where truth itself must speak like flattery?*
> *Within what bounds can one his liking stay,*
> *Where Nature doth with infinite agree?*
>   *What Nestor's counsel can my flames allay,*
> *Since Reason's self doth blow the coal in me?*
> *And ah what hope, that hope should once see day,*
> *Where Cupid is sworn page to Chastity?*
> *Honour is honour'd, that thou dost possess*
>   *Him as thy slave, and now long needy Fame*
>   *Doth even grow rich, naming my Stella's name.*
> *Wit learns in thee perfection to express,*
>   *Not thou by praise, but praise in thee is rais'd:*
>   *It is a praise to praise, when thou art prais'd.*[4]

The speaker, aware of the absurdities of words in their normal uses, has a proper distrust of language as names, although here this distrust yields its own anti-nominal system. What we have in the poem is a series of collisions within what seems to be a simple and direct language, although the statement ends as more extravagant and—in the Petrarchan sense—more pious than the more conventional ones poets usually give us. The sense of controlled reasonability governs a string of outrageously irrational compliments. From the confession of the incapacity of words in the opening line, the verbal paradoxes ensue. Each key word denies its own meaning; each abstraction obliterates itself by being itself in a way that identifies it with its opposite. The very possibility of language has been precluded by the reason-defying perfection of Stella. Yet it is reason itself that justifies the impossibility ("What Nestor's counsel can my flames allay, / Since Reason's self doth blow the coal in me?"). The infinite reach of nature deserves a desire sanctioned by reason itself. Here is the reverse of the usual

---

[4] In this and other poems quoted in this chapter, spellings have been modernized.

condemnation of a reason that serves desire—seen, for example, in the judgment delivered by Shakespeare's Adonis upon the arguments used to advance the lowly desires of Venus, whose "reason is the bawd to lust's abuse." Sidney's speaker, rather, accepts the help of reason as it blows the coal in him, so extraordinary is the source of that desire.

This is, then, the Petrarchan sonnet to end all Petrarchan sonnets. Impelled by the need to utter unique praise with nothing at his hand but common words and conventional claims, the speaker manages the highest possible compliment to her who teases him (and us all) out of thought. The unsubstantial nature of words even makes Sidney's usual pun on his lady's actual married name (Rich), which might ordinarily be seen as no more than a species of "false wit," especially appropriate here. It serves as a master stroke, revealing the final bankruptcy of words in their usual naming function: "long needy Fame / Doth even grow rich, *naming* my Stella's *name*." The poet has forced the nominal to take on substance. The naming act becomes the en-Rich-ing act: Stella has forced the poet to create a world in which names are no longer an "accident."

The couplet is the speaker's final gesture, with its too repetitive insistence on "praise" (a form of the word is used five times), as he triumphs over his rhyme-enforced need to raise praise. Here is the paradox in which personified praise, rather than Stella, is praised by the act of praising her, so that it is she who overcomes even praise in their competition of mutual elevation, as one last time the personified abstraction is outdone (and undone!) by the fleshly reality of her presence. Her unique immediacy has negated language, but it has become its own language—the language of *this poem*—which has transcended the emptiness of a general language that mediates particulars.

Out of the mutual blockages of normal language, then, the speaker has broken through to his own language, with meaning newly restored out of the accumulated verbal wreckage of conventional meanings. Having achieved his riches beyond "rich," honor beyond "honour," a praise beyond "praise," he has been responsive to his reason beyond "Reason." He has, for this poem and this lady, arrived at the absolute, substantive language of poetry's and love's transformations through their mutual finality. In concert these two, poetry and love, act upon normal language as eschatology acts upon history, both ending and transcending it. We are on the threshold of the world of *The Phoenix and the Turtle.* So are many of Sidney's sonnets, and in much the same way. Such sonnets reveal to us the visionary possibilities of love and reason in this Renaissance world. But if they are to do so, they must, in a shrewd, hard-headed manner, reveal the shabby limitations of our usual language and the common world to which it points. Here, on the wings of a language liberated in spite of itself, we are brought to a transcendent "golden" vision. "What may words say, or what may words not say" indeed, when the poet has thus forced them to take flight, opening to an ultimate, all-unifying vision.

The earthly has denied itself by using itself—and using itself up. In so doing it has transfigured itself, proclaiming Stella as its unique voice, its uniquely transcendent figure even though she is, after all, but of earth herself. This is how the poem enters the eschatological mode, the use of language to end language and the very possibility of language as, this one last time, it is dedicated to final, earthborn perfection.[5] It is as if, through her, language—always until now half a failure—can at last achieve true referentiality, but only because it becomes Stella, and she—as the final particular—can point only to herself.[6] The monistic poetic temper can go no farther or higher in its

[5] The poem has thus discovered a much more profound way to overcome language (by allowing it so thoroughly to realize itself!) than the apocalyptic denial of language suggested by Hassan.

[6] It is in this way too that Thomas Campion's "Rose-cheeked Laura" unites female grace with all the arts, visual and oral, spatial and temporal, as the transcendent object that combines flowing and stillness in her own liquid being—that she proclaims the synesthetic aesthetic which she embodies. She, like her poem, is the harmony that reveals our discord, as, for Sidney, Stella—with her poem—is a language that bankrupts the language of the rest of us.

> Rose-cheeked Laura, come,
> Sing thou smoothly with thy beauty's
> Silent music, either other
>   Sweet gracing.
>
> Lovely forms do flow
> From concent divinely framed;
> Heav'n is music, and thy beauty's
>   Birth is heavenly.
>
> These dull notes we sing
> Discords need for helps to grace them;
> Only beauty purely loving
>   Knows no discord,
>
> But still moves delight,
> Like clear springs renewed by flowing,
> Ever perfect, ever in them-
>   Selves eternal.

transcendently ambitious absorption of all that would otherwise lead to the tragic implications of finitude.

It is this finitude, with a muted sense of its tragic implications, which casts forth the assumptions out of which those I have termed the dualistic poets create their love poems. Often their grudging worldliness leads to a bitterly self-conscious assault on the Petrarchan pieties that would transfigure the mistress. Instead, the mistress is reduced—but not, for all that, enjoyed the less. Indeed, perhaps freeing her from metaphysical obligations permits her to be enjoyed the more, provided that her physical limitations are embraced instead of magically wished away through tricks of the lover's mind and a lover's specially empowered language. Plain speaking and a general distrust of extreme metaphor create an anti-Petrarchan style to match the anti-Petrarchan attitude, as discreteness comes to be cherished over synthesis, with the instruments of man clearly separated from the instruments of God.[7] The former are far, far below, but not without their pleasurable compensations if our modesty will but permit us —unambitiously—to accept them for what they are.

Such dualistic practices are about as old as the sonnet tradition in English, beginning with Wyatt (who of course produced many orthodox Petrarchan "translations" as well). Let me comment upon one of his most quietly modest sonnets, whose directness and unadorned simplicity underline its anti-Petrarchan vigor. Its straightforwardness misled even Douglas Peterson, a sympathetic champion of Wyatt's plainness, into underestimating its richness of implication.[8]

> Divers doth use, as I have heard and know,
> When that to change their ladies do begin,
> To mourn and wail, and never for to lin,
> Hoping thereby to pease their painful woe.

---

[7] It must be acknowledged that Sidney himself is the dualistic kind of poet in some sonnets—though not, I think, in his best—sonnets that I have avoided mentioning or discussing above. In a dualistic mood he is capable of lines of such unmitigated skepticism as, for example, his conclusion to *Astrophel and Stella* 52: "Let Virtue have that Stella's self; yet thus, / That Virtue but that body grant to us." Or see the downward, anti-cosmic movement of the comic 76 ("She comes, and straight therewith her shining twins do move"), concluding: "But with short breath, long looks, staid feet and walking head, / Pray that my sun go down with meeker beams to bed."

[8] Douglas L. Peterson, *The English Lyric from Wyatt to Donne: A History of the Plain and Eloquent Styles* (Princeton, N.J.: Princeton University Press, 1967), pp. 105–6.

> *And some there be, that when it chanceth so*
> > *That women change and hate where love hath been,*
> > *They call them false, and think with words to win*
> > *The hearts of them which otherwhere doth grow.*
> *But as for me, though that by chance indeed*
> > *Change hath outworn the favor that I had,*
> > *I will not wail, lament, nor yet be sad;*
> *Nor call her false that falsely did me feed;*
> > *But let it pass and think it is of kind,*
> > *That often change doth please a woman's mind.*

What is at once apparent is the no-nonsense reasonableness of the speaker. His calm, good sense, and patience—just on the tolerant side of exasperation—are evident from the start: from the unrushed line-and-a-half interruption that splits the idiomatic "use . . . To" construction. It is evident also in the metrical regularity (so rare for Wyatt!) which he seems almost to insist upon, whatever padding may be necessary. It is as if Wyatt, showing he can write proper iambic pentameter when he wants to, is emphasizing the all-passion-spent acceptance that produces the untroubled pattern, suggesting that his more uneven rhythms and imperfect rhymes elsewhere serve other moods. (Of course, the knowledge that this *is* Wyatt's work, as well as our awareness of his usual metrical irregularities, is central to our sensing this effect.)

The speaker's reasoned acceptance is a dominant feature of the mature realism of the sonnet's anti-Petrarchan mode (and mood). The knowing calmness of tone reflects the sad truths which he, somewhat distantly, acknowledges. The truths he acknowledges are clearly universal, a common occurrence with men, as the "divers" assures us. How foolhardy and immature, then, are the Petrarchan lamentation and complaint, described in the first two quatrains as the common response of other men and rejected in lines 11–12, with one line referring to each quatrain. We can note how, in the opening quatrain, the speaker momentarily adopts the Petrarchan's alliterative jargon ("pease their painful woe") as in keeping with the mourning and wailing which he personally and simply rejects in the sestet ("But as for me"). He turns away from lamentation as he turns away from making charges against her who provokes the lamentation; but he turns away without denying the facts of female behavior which by convention provoke lamentation and charges. Indeed, he affirms these facts as undeniably applicable to him, as to all men. For he has made his peace with them, in a most un-Petrarchan fashion.

The unruffled surface of this painfully won peace, however, rests on an absurdity of its own, all the more shocking for its being unquestioned: there is the single *unchanging* fact of women's *changing*. The fickleness, the caprice, the unpredictability in the behavior of each one is, when seen in the behavior of all, a general law; far from capricious, it is inevitable in members of the species. Instead of wailing over woman's changeableness as an irrational or immoral response to kind treatment, the speaker simply sees her as a changing creature: he expects her to change almost as though it were a physiological necessity ("When that to change their ladies do begin"). The unchanging fact of change, the persistence of change, is pressed upon us with the repetition of the word. It occurs four times, once in each of the three quatrains and once in the couplet. Twice there is also the curious juxtaposition of "change" with the cosmically crucial, and yet maddening, doctrine of chance ("When it *chanceth* so / That women *change*" and "by *chance* indeed / *Change* hath outworn"). It is more than juxtaposition, though; it is almost an internal rhyme; indeed, it is just a shade short of identity, "chance" with "change." So change, though universal, is the product of chance, is one with chance. This mutability sonnet does not, after all, proceed in accordance with reason, although the speaker's bland acceptance may put us off so that we accept absurdity as if it were reason. Still, in defiance of all that is reasonable, the sonnet actually proceeds in accordance with caprice.

In view of woman's disregard of what man's behavior has earned and, consequently, in view of the causeless, chance-y change from one strong feeling to its opposite ("and hate where love hath been"), it is no wonder that the speaker has lost confidence in the firmness of words as names. (We recall that Sidney suffered a similar loss of confidence in words, except that he presses his language to a transcendent triumph over its limitations as the more modest and sensible Wyatt would not.) Not only does the speaker here slip from "chance" to "change" almost as though they were interchangeable, but in consequence he recognizes the instability of even as fixed a term as "false," leaving himself unable to "call her *false* that *falsely* did me feed." Of course, the poet is wittily assured that the entire sonnet stands as his proclamation of her falseness, whatever his disclaimer here. Yet the fact of chance-y change from hate to love persuades him, despite his implicit proclamation of her falseness, to dissociate himself from those uncomprehending Petrarchans who call their ladies false (see line 7), so that he can insist that this strange cosmology of anti-love must force moral judgments and ordinary words to lose their meanings. Thus, though she *has* fed him "falsely," he must not *call* her "false." Instead, he must see this acknowledged disparity between fact and nominal judgment. For woman's *mind* is answerable to woman's *kind* (a superb rhyme). Hence he arrives at her falseness as a falseness induced by change which is at the mercy of chance (although chance universally produces the same sort of change, so that chance and its change may be raised to the level of a cosmic law of the woman's world, the world of anti-love). In acting falsely to him, she is being true to her kind, with her kind defined by the absurd and amoral general law ("But let it pass and think it is of kind, / That often change doth please a woman's mind").

So the price of the speaker's non-Petrarchan acceptance is his reduction of women to the less-than-moral. From his own superior, human, moral position of rational understanding—of a constancy and a sense of what is deserved that would require *like* to respond to *like* —he condescends to these absurd, senseless creatures, mere tropisms, in their predictably capricious behavior. Far from joining the Petrarchan in placing the lady on a pedestal as an object of worship, he has placed her well below man as a subhuman, submoral creature.

This "drab" vision of a degraded love's fickle fortune is profoundly at odds with the transcendent "golden" vision we examined earlier.[9] The "drab" opens the way to the twin awarenesses that become the tragic and the classic visions—depending on whether finitude is aggressively confronted or indulgently accepted—while the "golden" would merge them into a transcendent union. If Sidney's was a world of limits defied, Wyatt's is a world of limits sadly but wisely embraced for what—in their limitations—they could offer. If Sidney offered a language that was struggled against and transcended as reason was transcended, Wyatt also sees his language as an incapacitating instru-

[9] The terms "golden" and "drab" are borrowed, of course, from C. S. Lewis, who employs them as central alternatives in his discussion of Renaissance poetry in *English Literature of the Sixteenth Century, Excluding Drama* (Oxford: Clarendon Press, 1954).

ment, changing like love with chance, though he succumbs to it in its caprice. If Sidney created a breakthrough, Wyatt finds a moral, manly victory in resigning himself to a breakdown.

As we free ourselves from the tight context of the Wyatt sonnet, we can use it to enter or at least to reinforce his vision elsewhere. Thus in the delicate sonnet "Whoso list to hunt, I know where is an hind" we can be newly aware of the relation between lover and mistress as one between wearied but faithful man and maddeningly evasive animal. Or we can renew our receptivity to that remarkable, and remarkably complex, poem "They flee from me," where the gentle, tame, and meek collection of lady-pets has now turned wild, using their naked feet, which used to stalk in his chamber, to run away from their lover. The sense in which they are—to use the language of "Divers doth use"—feeding him falsely is heightened ironically when we are told that they had taken bread at his hand. How differently, "They flee from me" assures us, he as the kindly human keeper fed them! Now freely ranging, "Busily seeking with a continual change" (here once more that notion of "change," and "continual change," that we have noted), they are serving him "kindly" in return, the speaker tells us with bitter irony. So, kind for kind: what is kind in them (true to them as womankind, though hardly true to what is kind in the moral world) is returned for what is kind in him (true to mankind as morally kind beings). No more here than in "Divers doth use" is their creaturely kindness, to which they are true by being unkind, a source of the speaker's lamentation. The "fashion of forsaking," however "strange" to man, is natural to them. One should have expected nothing more—even despite that one, unique moment ("once, in special") separated from all the rest as a precious, particularized human occasion, almost dreamlike in the perfection of its singular display of affection.

What is constant in the dualistic poet is his condescending attitude toward the woman's world as an arena of conflict and disappointment, though one that yields a temporary pleasure. But the pleasure is sufficient—all that one might ask—and worth the discomforts the playthings cause, provided that man in his maturity understands their nature and the finite—if irrational—cosmos that controls them. How different a use is made of animal comparisons by a monistic poet like Spenser, who turns every device into a revelation of his lady's metamorphic magic. Thus *Amoretti 67* creates a delicate mythological air in which the mistress—who, unlike Wyatt's, has been pursued and won—is seen as a deer, a transformation which, in Ovidian fashion, elevates rather than degrades her. There is no explicit effort to apply the deer-like terms metaphorically to her (except for the obvious pun on the word "deer" itself); only its gentlest, most abidingly attractive qualities are presented. And, without needing to "extend" his image in the obvious way, the poet finds the animal to have *become* her, as she becomes his. The simile is left incomplete, except that we never miss the fourth term, the transfer from animal to lady.

> *Like as a huntsman after weary chase,*
>   *Seeing the game from him escap'd away,*
>   *Sits down to rest him in some shady place,*
>   *With panting hounds beguiled of their prey:*
> *So after long pursuit and vain assay,*
>   *When I all weary had the chase forsook,*
>   *The gentle deer [dear?] return'd the self-same way,*
>   *Thinking to quench her thirst at the next brook.*
> *There she beholding me with milder look,*
>   *Sought not to fly, but fearless still did bide:*
>   *Till I in hand her yet half trembling took,*
> *And with her own good will her firmly tied.*
>   *Strange thing me seem'd to see a beast so wild,*
>   *So goodly won with her own will beguil'd.*

The hushed moment of her surrender beguiles *us*, puts to sleep the hard-headed questions the skeptic in us would ask, the distinctions he would want to insist upon. The effect is much like that in the *Prothalamion*, where the inversion of the Leda story permits bride and bird to be confounded. The swans (as birds and brides) lend their pure whiteness as well as their divine associations (with Venus as well as Jove) to elevate and ritualize the masque-like ceremony.

If even animal comparisons can lead the monistic poet upward toward the divine, rather than downward, then everything points heavenward while the mistress performs her role as goddess and star (witness the very name, Stella) and raises her earthbound poet-lover through *her* miraculous, transforming powers. The briefest glance at Sidney's *Astrophel and Stella* 74 reveals the "vulgar," prosaic, stammering, almost tongue-tied lover converted to "golden" sonneteer—

converted not by fidelity to the Petrarchan convention ("I am no pick-purse of another's wit") but by Stella's kiss, which honeys his lips and the words they speak. Indeed, that kiss is said to *inspire* (to provide the very air for) those honeyed words.

> *I never drank of* Aganippe *well,*
> *Nor ever did in shade of* Tempe *sit:*
> *And Muses scorn with vulgar brains to dwell,*
> *Poor Layman I, for sacred rites unfit.*
> *Some do I hear of Poets' fury tell,*
> *But (God wot) wot not what they mean by it:*
> *And this I swear by blackest brook of hell,*
> *I am no pick-purse of another's wit.*
> *How falls it then, that with so smooth an ease*
> *My thoughts I speak, and what I speak doth flow*
> *In verse, and that my verse best wits doth please?*
> *Guess we the cause: "What, is it thus?" Fie no:*
> *"Or so?" Much less: "How then?" Sure thus it is:*
> *My lips are sweet, inspired with Stella's kiss.*

We note that Stella's kiss performs the very muse-like function that Aganippe has not performed for the speaker. It converts him to poet, one who speaks his thoughts in verse "with so smooth an ease" that it pleases the "best wits." And we watch the conversion take place in the poem itself, in the almost too sharp, melodramatic contrast between the self-consciously awkward, broken lines with their prosy, staccato words ["But (God wot) wot not what they mean by it"] and the lines of smooth Petrarchan ease which reach their climax in the golden affirmation of the last line. So if, thanks to his "vulgar brains," he has had to forgo the profession of poet, his profession of lover converts him to poet after all. But it is not the distant tradition of poetic language so much as his immediate embrace of Stella that has so converted him. In the spirit of incarnational ritual, the true and substantive word is founded in the flesh rather than in the emptiness of other words. So he trades the figurative inspiration of the waters of Aganippe for the literal inspiration that flows from Stella's kiss. I wish to stress the notion of ritual because Sidney does: while as a "Poor Layman" he is "unfit" for the "sacred rites" of the traditional poet—rites associated with Aganippe and Tempe—the rites of love perform the sacramental function for him. Though a confessed lay-man of poetry, the speaker is an initiate of a love which produces its own poetry out of its own "sacred rites."[10] Although his lightness of tone makes it clear that the poem is, in part, only a highly sophisti-cated mockery of Petrarchism, nevertheless I believe the notion of Stella's lips as his Aganippe is worth taking seriously. Such are the extravagances which the monistic poet has prepared us to accept.

How much less the dualistic poet, ripe for the modesty of the classic vision, asks of us—or of his subject. Ben Jonson, in his well-known "Drink to me only with thine eyes," insists on and presses the distinc-tion *between* the sacramental and the earthly, between the wine and the kiss, Jove's nectar and the lady's.

> Drink to me only with thine eyes,
>   And I will pledge with mine;
> Or leave a kiss but in the cup,
>   And I'll not look for wine.
> The thirst that from the soul doth rise
>   Doth ask a drink divine;
> But might I of Jove's nectar sup,
>   I would not change for thine.

The brilliant strategy of rhyming "wine" with "divine" and "thine" carries the argument by reinforcing the metaphysical effects Jonson is rejecting and the merely physical effects he is embracing when he turns from the wine (as divine) to her. Hers is an alternative to the "drink divine," whether seen as sacramental wine or as Jove's nectar; and the speaker accepts the difference between them and her, holding onto the earthly as her province, and his, forgoing the transcendental reaches of what is beyond his grasp. He confesses that "The thirst that from the soul doth rise / Doth ask a drink divine"; but (and the "But" is his) he cuts short this upward yearning ("The thirst . . . doth rise") by replacing the longing of the soul with the longing of the body. He thus acknowledges the monistic tendency from which the dualistic poet retreats in his modesty. Her nectar is not Jove's, her kiss not wine; but it will do. It will serve as his nectar and his wine, and

[10] I cannot help thinking here of Shakespeare's own impatience with "the perfect ceremony of love's rite" in his Sonnet 23; see my discussion in *A Window to Criticism*, pp. 75–79.

she will serve as his heaven on earth, only because he will not look beyond earth. So the effect is to split her from the heavenly and to distinguish between words which the monistic poet would drive together: the "thine" does not here grow into the "divine" but is kept distinct from it, is indeed a come-down, or let-down, from it. Unlike the monism of *The Phoenix and the Turtle*, which produces a resurrection out of the ashes of the "distincts" that have died, here the "distincts" are preserved. In neither language nor vision is there the claim to a union that blurs the sense of distinctness, the limiting definition of an entity, and thus that defies reason itself.[11] For Jonson's speaker is above all reasonable and properly impressed by the limits of his world and its mistress.

Within these unexaggerated limits, of course, she affects him totally, and in ways that he is now free to exaggerate—though mockingly. Having traded away all claims to divine agencies in return for what issues from her mouth, he chooses to attribute pseudo-divine effects to her breath while it performs its usual worldly function.

> *I sent thee late a rosy wreath,*
> *Not so much honoring thee,*
> *As giving it a hope that there*
> *It could not withered be.*
> *But thou thereon didst only breathe,*
> *And sent'st it back to me,*
> *Since when it grows and smells, I swear,*
> *Not of itself, but thee.*

The speaker is forced to maintain ("I swear") that in the course of casually rejecting his flowers (supposedly sent to her, as to heaven, in order to immortalize them), she has bestowed her substance upon them, thus performing the sort of miracle for which sacramental wine is required. Still, the exaggeration of the delicately turned compliment is obvious enough in view of the firm distinction between her kiss and the wine (between "thine" and "divine," in other words) which the first stanza manages. He thus emphasizes that this false attribution of divine power to her is no more than his graceful refusal to receive her rebuff. The prosy reality of what has in fact happened dissipates the elegance of the overdone compliment. So the force of the poem—its

[11] See *A Window to Criticism*, pp. 150–54, for a longer discussion of *The Phoenix and the Turtle*.

first stanza and the facts behind the implied narrative in the second—
serves to deny her power to perform what he must "swear" she performs. The difference between what has really happened and how the
poet is sworn to interpret it reinforces the un-divine nature of his
earthly love.

We have already seen more than once that the relation of the mistress to the heavens is the key to her divinity and to her control over
the poet's world. The Petrarchan poet presses his language and metaphor upward to turn her into a star (his Stella), giving her a star's
attributes—including influence over human destiny. And, of course,
for the anti-Petrarchan such glorification can be the source of parody.
Instead of an upward thrust of metaphor from earth to heaven, from
mistress to star, we can have a downward movement, in which true
cosmos dwindles into the arbitrary micro-world of the mistress. The
poet-lover forsakes the rational controls of the sublime order for the
irrational, fickle control of love's order under the mistress.

Here is such a poem by Fulke Greville, a philosophical poet whose
serious use of cosmic imagery in other poems makes his inversion of
it here, as a lesser foil to the greater Myra, all the more striking.

> The world, that all contains, is ever moving;
> The stars within their spheres for ever turned;
> Nature, the queen of change, to change is loving,
> And form to matter new is still adjourned.
>
> Fortune, our fancy-god, to vary liketh;
> Place is not bound to things within it placed;
> The present time upon time passed striketh;
> With Phoebus' wand'ring course the earth is graced.
>
> The air still moves, and by its moving cleareth;
> The fire up ascends and planets feedeth;
> The water passeth on and all lets weareth;
> The earth stands still, yet change of changes breedeth.
>
> Her plants, which summer ripes, in winter fade;
> Each creature in unconstant mother lieth;
> Man made of earth, and for whom earth is made,
> Still dying lives and living ever dieth;
> > Only, like fate, sweet Myra never varies,
> > Yet in her eyes the doom of all change carries.

Introduction

I have reproduced the entire poem so that its persistently downward movement can be traced by the reader. The four quatrains move from far off to near, from stars to man, affirming everywhere the universality of change. Far more explicitly than in Wyatt's "Divers doth use" we are given here a mutability poem, as we follow the unchanging fact of change as it descends from the planetary universe under the aegis of nature herself to the earth with its time and place under fortune (its "fancy-god") to the four elements that constitute earth and, finally, to all earthly creatures and to man himself. As the quatrains close in upon private human destiny, the poem turns theological, almost apocalyptic: "Man made of earth, and for whom earth is made, / Still dying lives and living ever dieth." Clearly, all of the natural world—the world outside the stasis of God—has the character of endless change, the character, in effect, of Wyatt's submoral woman's world: "The earth stands still, yet change of changes breedeth." And man himself is of earth, indeed its most prominent creature, changing and the victim of change—like the rest.

After these four quatrains dedicated to total process at all levels, the comic anticlimax (or is it?) of the concluding couplet converts the poem. "Only" "sweet Myra" is the exception to the universal law we have seen exhaustively applied: she herself "never varies." She is the exception because, in mock-Petrarchan fashion, she is allowed to rule over all of nature and thus to transcend it. It is the pagan world she controls, "like fate." She "never varies" though "her eyes"—in proper Petrarchan fashion—carry "the doom" that universal and endless change involves. Like a Petrarchan mistress, she seems to be the goddess of the world of the poet (and of everyone else too). But unlike the Christian analogy so often appealed to in Petrarchism and the tradition of courtly love behind it, this goddess is a sub-Christian one, an indifferent pagan fate dooming with her eyes. Thus, like Wyatt's mistress after all, she is the source and cause of all change—unchangeably so. And the world she dominates—even as, like God or fate, she is strangely unaffected by it—is a cruelly amoral one inexorably subject to undeserved change, to a fickleness that is part of Myra's fixed nature.

It is this inversion of the relation between his mistress and the stars that accounts for the poet's striking condescension toward the heavens in another poem: this one moves downward to earth only to find a strange microcosm of love which then becomes (for him) the amoral equivalent of the macrocosm that has been allowed to dwindle.

> *You little stars that live in skies*
> *And glory in Apollo's glory,*
> *In whose aspects conjoined lies*
> *The heaven's will and nature's story,*
> *Joy to be likened to those eyes,*
> *Which eyes make all eyes glad or sorry;*
> > *For when you force thoughts from above,*
> > *These overrule your force by love.*
>
> *And thou, O love, which in these eyes*
> *Hast married reason with affection,*
> *And made them saints of beauty's skies,*
> *Where joys are shadows of perfection,*
> *Lend me thy wings that I may rise*
> *Up, not by worth, but thy election;*
> > *For I have vowed in strangest fashion,*
> > *To love, and never seek compassion.*

The poet's direct address to the "little stars" at once diminishes them; and when he directs them to be grateful, as lesser entities, to be compared to the greatness of her eyes, their subjugation (like the poet's inversion of stars and mistress) is complete. Once more we find that it is the mistress, rather than the heavens, who is the source of control over human life: her eyes "make all eyes glad or sorry" and "overrule" proper religious thoughts ("thoughts from above") with thoughts of love. Here is a universe of Platonic dualism where the earthly dominates the spiritual, and with no confusion between the two—except that the proper hierarchy has been inverted. We move again from the Christian to the pagan world, from rule by heavenly thoughts to rule by love (Cupid). And the world of love is apparently ruled by Cupid not in response to moral values but out of the caprice which finds some chosen and some not. Thus the speaker asks to borrow Cupid's wings to "rise / Up, not by worth, but thy election." What we have, then, is a sort of Calvinist doctrine of election, with or without merit, which persuades the speaker "To love, and never seek compassion." This is to act in the "strangest fashion," a most un-Petrarchan fashion, somewhat reminiscent of Wyatt's condemnation of the "strange fashion of forsaking." But what is the point of lamenting when this world of love, and of love's fickle fortune, operates by laws which claim no relation between what one gets and what one ought to get?

Love's replacement of worth with election and the speaker's refusal to seek compassion are echoed also in the explicit anti-Petrarchan poem that begins,

> *Away with these self-loving lads,*
> *Whom Cupid's arrow never glads.*
> *Away, poor souls that sigh and weep,*
> *In love of them that lie and sleep;*
>   *For Cupid is a meadow god,*
>   *And forceth none to kiss the rod.*
>
> *God Cupid's shaft, like destiny,*
> *Doth either good or ill decree.*
> *Desert is born out of his bow,*
> *Reward upon his feet doth go.*
>   *What fools are they that have not known*
>   *That Love likes no laws but his own?*

This self-enclosed, self-justified world of love has no morality, no sense of desert: all is caprice, the product of chance. "Desert is born out of his bow," which projects "Cupid's shaft": it thus operates as destiny does, decreeing "good or ill." So here too one is victimized by chance-y change, a fickleness that must be accepted because it exists, continually asserting itself in this unelevated and unelevatable world.

> *The worth that worthiness should move*
> *Is love, which is the due of love.*
> *And love as well the shepherd can*
> *As can the mighty nobleman.*
>   *Sweet nymph, 'tis true you worthy be,*
>   *Yet without love, nought worth to me.*

This utter circularity precludes extramural meaning or purpose. All things turn back on themselves, are mutually reinforcing. The joys of this lowly microcosm of Cupid never lead beyond themselves—nor does its value (its "worth"). But these joys are cherished *for* themselves, as if the other, higher world with another god and demanding another theology—unrelated to human desire—might require an earnestness beyond human reach. For the world of earthly joys, under the strange whims of the mistress and—through her—under the capricious laws of love (the "meadow god," Cupid), is implicitly juxtaposed to the Christian world under its God and with its ascendant morality. And the unambitious poet-as-lover, in the classic vein, makes the modest choice and exploits what is here to be exploited, accepting its strangely amoral terms.

In a serious sonnet Greville explicitly juxtaposes the two worlds, this time in a Christian mood that would seem to elevate the one to the other as a monistic poet might.

> Fie, foolish earth, think you the heaven wants glory
> Because your shadows do yourself benight?
> All's dark unto the blind, let them be sorry;
> The heavens in themselves are ever bright.
>
> Fie, fond desire, think you that love wants glory
> Because your shadows do yourself benight?
> The hopes and fears of lust may make men sorry,
> But love still in herself finds her delight.
>
> Then earth, stand fast, the sky that you benight
> Will turn again and so restore your glory,
> Desire, be steady, hope is your delight,
> An orb wherein no creature can be sorry,
> > Love being placed above these middle regions
> > Where every passion wars itself with legions.

What is immediately noteworthy here is Greville's use of identical rhyme words in the three quatrains.[12] The fact that these words are applied to the world of religion in the first quatrain (earth vs. heaven), to the world of love in the second (desire vs. love), and to both (two lines to each) in the third would appear to work for the union of the two worlds in the sonnet, in Neoplatonic fashion. But actually this repetition of the words emphasizes the gap between the two worlds, since the words are applicable to them in such differing ways. It is

[12] Or, really, identical in all but one case, since "bright" in the first quatrain varies from "delight" in both the second and third. This is the only exception. Greville also makes use of this device elsewhere. See, for example, the sonnet "The earth with thunder torn, with fire blasted," where the repetition of rhyme words in the first and second quatrains serves a similar dualistic purpose: that of distinguishing the world of religion from the world of love, even as it relates the two.

clear that the words "glory" and "benight" can be applied *literally* to the astronomical materials of the first quatrain and the first half of the third, while they can be applied only *figuratively* to desire and love in the second quatrain and the second half of the third. And the figurative does not merge with the literal. It is true that we can see desire as the product of our flesh—and hence of our "sinful earth" (as Shakespeare puts it)—so that "fond desire" (line 5) can be seen as an outgrowth of "foolish earth" (line 1), to which it exists in parallel; nevertheless, the language of the poem does not play upon this overlapping of meaning so as to extend it toward a metaphorical identity between the two worlds. The merely figurative is not pressed beyond itself, so that when desire is transformed by hope into "An orb" (line 12), we do not probe the meaning of the word too seriously or feel that its astronomical sense has been earned.

The incapacity of the language of the poem to stretch itself to cover these diverse worlds reminds us of their diversity. By so restricting the applicability of the terms of his vehicle to the tenor of the poem, the poet—despite his Neoplatonic hopes for his heavenly "love"— proves his essentially dualistic temper and vision. His language breaks apart—respecting the limits of its meaning and the propriety of its application—thus reflecting the discreteness of the two worlds. Despite the appearance given by the repeated rhyme words, there is no aggrandizement in them: they do not, finally, exceed their proper territory. Of course, as it is used in the poem, "love" may seem to exceed its limits, if we define these as the domain of Cupid that we have observed as its exclusive domain in the other poems of Greville I have treated here. But love as Cupid, or as Cupid's whim—as the product of fickle fortune—exists in "these middle regions" only; in short, such love is the desire against which this poem is directed. On the other hand, Platonic love, "above these middle regions," has heavenly virtues attributed to it which are to elevate desire. This would be a monistic hope at odds with the spirit of Greville we have seen elsewhere. But the breakdown of language and the failure of the analogy to gain the identity (of tenor and vehicle) of true metaphor keeps the hope a merely pious one; and the poem closes, starkly, with "these middle regions / Where every passion wars itself with legions."

Greville's sonnet successfully imposes its dualistic vision after all, despite its forlorn monistic hopes. It means its language to fail to achieve the union of tenor and vehicle; and it uses the identity of rhyme words to shout out the differences of the worlds to which they are being applied. For the poem, in its fullness, lives down here with us in "these middle regions," with a metaphysical hope that is not existentially sustained. And the stark close of the poem reminds us of our darkness, which it reinforces. What has happened here is that Greville, in attempting to press beyond the classic satisfactions of this world ("these middle regions"), which he can embrace in other poems, succeeds—not in reproducing the monism that yields a transcendent union—but in revealing the tragic vision as the alternative to the classic in this fractured universe.[13] For where there are tragic implications to be confronted, there is the earthy classic vision that can be affirmed in retreat from them. But one can reject the retreat as well.

It is this existential undercutting of monistic metaphysical confidence that can create tragic implications even in Greville's strictly philosophical (and theological) poems. He will not dispute the essential doctrines of reality, but he will dispute the efficacy of those doctrines in alleviating the agonies we suffer down here. From the moving "Chorus Sacerdotum" let me quote only the first half-dozen lines and the last.

> *Oh, wearisome condition of humanity,*
> *Born under one law, to another bound;*
> *Vainly begot, and yet forbidden vanity,*
> *Created sick, commanded to be sound.*
> *What meaneth nature by these diverse laws?*
> *Passion and reason self-division cause. . . .*

[13] I could trace a similar existential darkness—coexisting, or at least alternating, with the classic grasp of earthly joy—in Sir Walter Ralegh's work. There is in it the recklessness of "Now what is love? I pray thee, tell"; but there is also the fearsome acceptance of this world's utter enclosure. We need look only at that incredible line from "The Nymph's Reply to the Shepherd" which marks the shift in that poem ("Time drives the flock from field to fold"), or at the closing line of "Like truthless dreams" ("To haste me hence to find my fortune's fold"), or at the final lines of that matchless poem "Nature, that washed her hands" ("Who in the dark and silent grave / When we have wandered all our ways / Shuts up the story of our days"). But it would take at least as long to argue adequately for Ralegh's place among these poets as it has for Greville. And then many other poets would beckon as well.

> *We that are bound by vows and by promotion,*
> *With pomp of holy sacrifice and rites,*
> *To teach belief in God and still devotion,*
> *To preach of heaven's wonders and delights,—*
> *Yet when each of us in his own heart looks*
> *He finds the God there far unlike his books.*

This shocking conclusion leaves us with the dark god in the private heart, the inwardness, of each existent. And the true God's nature stands condemned for the contradictions it permits between the properly ontological and the immediately existential: "Nature herself doth her own self deflower, / To hate those errors she herself doth give." Or "If nature did not take delight in blood, / She would have made more easy ways to good." The Augustinian on the verge of Manichaean sacrilege, such a priestly speaker cannot forgo his "wearisome condition" even for the abstract, bookish commands he is sworn to uphold.

Such insistence on remaining responsive to man's existence in "these middle regions" seems to foreshadow Alexander Pope's similarly tragic description of man as a "middle nature" in the opening lines of Epistle II of his *Essay on Man.*

> *. . . A Being darkly wise, and rudely great:*
> *With too much knowledge for the Sceptic side,*
> *With too much weakness for the Stoic's pride,*
> *He hangs between; in doubt to act, or rest;*
> *In doubt to deem himself a God, or Beast;*
> *In doubt his Mind or Body to prefer;*
> *Born but to die, and reasoning but to err;*
> *Alike in ignorance, his reason such,*
> *Whether he thinks too little, or too much:*
> *Chaos of Thought and Passion, all confused;*
> *Still by himself abused, or disabused;*
> *Created half to rise, and half to fall;*
> *Great lord of all things, yet a prey to all;*
> *Sole judge of Truth, in endless Error hurled:*
> *The glory, jest, and riddle of the world!*

Is this a tragic or a classic vision? What we can be certain of is that it is a dualistic vision in which the chasm between the *is* and the *ought*, earth and heaven, is not to be leaped by the magic of metaphor or language. And it is a vision continuous with the one that speaks through Greville's "Chorus Sacerdotum," which I have used as a dialectical conclusion to my survey of Renaissance poetic dualism. Once the inherent experiential stubbornness of the "modern" world asserts itself as the existential thinker's extension of brute empiricism, then the magnificent, all-embracing pretensions to metaphysical monism tend to fade into obsolescence. But without the living myth of metaphor, the essentialist abstractions tend to lose their hold, their immediate responsiveness to increasingly desperate human need. And the top or heavenly half of the dualism tends to drop away as a source of human comfort. The tragic and the classic, as I have defined them, may then offer themselves jointly or alternatively—depending on whether we choose to confront what we have lost and what we are left with or whether we choose to retreat from the consequences of what we fear we know so that we may cherish what we most immediately have.

It is the retreat that concerns us here. So grim an awareness of the immediate and inward particularities of our experience—the agonies of a finitude that can no longer open upward—can cause a flight from the existential that leads to the worship of the bloodless abstractions which we (and our metaphysical or religious tradition) interpose to shield ourselves from having to confront those particularities unrefined. But we remain aware of what we choose not to confront. The god in our heart still challenges the abstract God of our books. In this way Greville's "Chorus" (or even his "Fie, foolish earth") can, in its divided vision, lead to Pope and even (let us recall the description of man as "Vainly begot, and yet forbidden vanity") to Dr. Johnson himself.[14] As the Metaphysicals do not, the profoundest of neoclassi-

---

[14] If we see Greville's "Chorus Sacerdotum" as his essay on man and move from it to Pope's *Essay on Man*, it is worth reminding ourselves to distinguish them both from George Herbert's verse essay "Man," one of the highest affirmations in the monistic tradition. The upward movement and the synthetic aggrandizement are everywhere apparent:

> For man is ev'rything,
> And more: he is a tree, yet bears no fruit;
> A beast, yet is, or should be, more . . .

cal writers do extend the vision of the more "modern" of our Renaissance poets, those who are more skeptical about the powers of man and language. But the gift of these successors, their group name tells us, is a classic gift—as we shall see. It was left for *their* successors among the Romantics to explore the tragic alternative.

> *Man is all symmetry,*
> *Full of proportions, one limb to another,*
> *And all to all the world besides . . .*
> *His eyes dismount the highest star;*
> *He is in little all the sphere . . .*
> *Oh, mighty love! Man is one world and hath*
> *Another to attend him.*
> *Since then, my God, thou hast*
> *So brave a palace built, O dwell in it,*
> *That it may dwell with thee at last!*

Clearly we must skip across this culmination of the monistic vision to move from Greville to Pope and beyond.

I

The Retreat from Extremity

Through the Worship
of Bloodless Abstractions

3

"Eloisa to Abelard": The Escape from Body or the Embrace of Body

"No pulse that riots, and no blood that glows"

It is in the perspective of the preceding chapter that I want to consider the work of Pope and Johnson and the relation of their visions to the dominant notions of their period. I believe I can consider the dogmatic structures of eighteenth-century rationalism as the god projected by its "books." We must wonder how this god (to continue with the language of Greville) is undermined by the god seen in men's hearts. The eighteenth century, in its monolithic pretension, may have felt impelled to try one last time for the affirmation of an orderly, over-arching structure; but its best sensibilities may well have come away existentially empty after such intellectual self-indulgence. Yet their distrust, thrust upon them through the merest glimpse at the extremity behind the period's cocky universals, led their classic dispositions to reassert the grounds for sanity.

A desperate moment in a culture well on its way to losing its metaphysical assurances, the neoclassical period willfully created a naïvely essentialist doctrine totally dedicated to the objective and the universal. In other words, it was as little as possible responsive to the private demands of the person. Thus the need of philosophic man—derived from his "metaphysical pathos"—to believe in his extravagant, all-assuring, all-answering construct was matched by the subjective need of the particular existent to answer to the fears and anxieties generated by his awareness of his finitude. And this latter need led to doubts that undercut his metaphysical need to believe. The poets, as usual, were among those who most intimately exposed the visionary consequences of these contradictory needs.

I. Through the Worship of Bloodless Abstractions

I turn to Pope with the admitted objective of finding such exposures —half-conscious or perhaps barely conscious at all—that are normally not looked for. And I acknowledge the danger, to which the critic must always be alive, that what I think I have found I may have looked for too hard and too ingeniously. A central difficulty in treating Pope's work, it seems to me, lies in the distractions caused by the fact that he seems to subscribe so uncritically to the neoclassical pseudo-vision, what I call its bloodless abstractions. His would seem to constitute a total institutional allegiance that would inhibit the private person's freedom to move beyond the rhetorical in poetry and the "ethical" in vision. The unqualified, dogmatic "universal frame" would seem to be an unfortunate substitute for the truly classic affirmation, a self-deceptive alternative to authentic vision.

But this difficulty with Pope, I suggest, may be ours rather than his. Our too-knowing historical awareness of the eighteenth-century ideological monolith may preclude our seeing through the seeming allegiances of its subscribers to comprehend the full array of their private responses. And I shall insist here that it is so with Pope. The joyous task of living intimately with his work should uncover how truly free he could become within the discipline he accepted—free for an authenticity far more revealing than the neoclassical commonplaces which, without denying, it transcended. These neoclassical commonplaces are what I have termed bloodless abstractions. To call the abstractions bloodless, like Greville's book-ish god, is to draw attention to the blood-filled heart that contains its own god. So I begin, in Pope, with the body of the man of flesh and blood and its claims against the disembodied, the bloodless. And this leads me, though with some indirection, into the heart of "Eloisa to Abelard."

Many critics have called attention to the striking influence of *Paradise Lost* upon some of the poems of Pope, especially—by means of parody—in "The Rape of the Lock." What makes the influence striking, of course, is the enormous difference between the two poets in temperament, style, and affiliations—religious, political, poetic. So it is no wonder that the influence seems to make itself felt in reverse, by parody.

There is, however, one echo of Milton in Pope that bounces back directly and right side up, even if its effect is comic in "The Rape of the Lock" and only rather quizzical—if not downright uncertain—in *Paradise Lost*. What Pope does is to accept the absurdities implicit in Milton's material treatment of his immaterial gods and to press the

absurd consequences that flow from it. It has frequently been remarked that the fun in the inconsequential mock-battle between
beaux and belles at the end of the "Rape" ("Like Gods they fight, nor
dread a mortal Wound") derives from Milton's self-conscious, even
embarrassed, struggle to make credible and sensible the battle in
heaven among his supernatural creatures. In his derivative battle between the sexes, Pope extends to a pseudo-literalism the life-and-
death (or love-in-death) exaggerations of the archaic Petrarchan love
conceit still alive in contemporary love songs; but he does so with the
borrowed inflations of the heroic rhetoric which Milton has used for a
battle just as unsubstantial in its actions, a battle with as little literal-
ism in which to ground its merely metaphorical characters, characters
as disembodied as Pope's were to be.[1] It is in this sense that I speak of
Pope as merely pressing, for his mock-heroic purpose, an absurdity
latent in Milton's heroic precedent.

But there is a more subtle, if less commonly noted, exploitation by
Pope of Milton's need to involve his disembodied creatures in physical
activity. In Book Eight of *Paradise Lost*, Raphael's speech reflects the
need to relate the disembodied angels to love even as they remain
firmly identified with chastity. Raphael answers Adam's questions
about how the angels make love and what the nature of their enjoy-
ment of it can be with a self-conscious evasiveness that echoes
Milton's description of heaven's war. Is Raphael's blushing embarrassment also a reflection of Milton's, or at least a reflection of the
absurdity of both their attempts? Adam's questions are direct enough:

> "Love not the heavenly spirits, and how their love
> Express they, by looks only, or do they mix
> Irradiance, virtual or immediate touch?"
>   To whom the angel, with a smile that glowed
> Celestial rosy red, love's proper hue,
> Answered. "Let it suffice thee that thou know'st
> Us happy, and without love no happiness.
> Whatever pure thou in the body enjoy'st
> (and pure thou wert created) we enjoy
> In eminence, and obstacle find none
> Of membrane, joint, or limb, exclusive bars;

[1] See my essay, "The 'Frail China Jar' and the Rude Hand of Chaos,"
Centennial Review 5 (1961):176–94 (collected in *The Play and Place of
Criticism* [Baltimore: Johns Hopkins Press, 1967]).

> *Easier than air with air, if spirits embrace,*
> *Total they mix, union of pure with pure*
> *Desiring; nor restrained conveyance need*
> *As flesh to mix with flesh, or soul with soul.*
> *But I can now no more. . . ."*

How vulnerable is this Platonism to the skeptical realism of as worldly a reader as Pope! Is it not this absurdity of both having and not having one's sex that prompted Pope's outrageous, if disarming, suggestion, in his dedicatory epistle to Arabella Fermor, the real-life Belinda, that sylphs were innocent, disembodied creatures that offered the maiden a safe, chaste embrace? "For they say, any Mortals may enjoy the most intimate Familiarities with these gentle Spirits, upon a Condition very easie to all true *Adepts*, an inviolate Preservation of Chastity." Here's love with the fun but without the cost, love with a disembodied airy essence. But can it, for lowly humankind, produce satisfaction, or only frustration, the frustration of a ritual without substance? What are the chances for one to delude himself in the interest of gratification? In the "Rape" Ariel proposes—for all maidens concerned with "honor"—precisely such a chaste substitution of the disembodied lover for the "earthly lover." And, curiously, it is that telling word "embrace," the ambiguity of which we should recall from the passage from Milton, above, that at once gives Ariel's game away and insists on its innocence through its rhyme with "chaste," the word that recalls Pope's words to Miss Fermor: "Know farther yet; Whoever fair and chaste / Rejects Mankind, is by some *Sylph* embrac'd." Ariel thus warns Belinda against seduction, but with a pseudo-seduction of his own. We must remember that Ariel, airy sylph, appropriately assumes, for Belinda, a form that holds a sexual promise, however unfulfillable:

> *'Twas he had summon'd to her silent Bed*
> *The Morning-Dream that hover'd o'er her Head.*
> *A Youth more glitt'ring than a* Birth-night Beau,
> *(That ev'n in Slumber caus'd her Cheek to glow). . . .*

No wonder he warns her of "Man," that full-bodied creature; no wonder he works against the baron as his rival and is rendered powerless only by viewing her desire—"An Earthly Lover lurking at her Heart."

Most important in this poem, the rape itself has the double character of both the disembodied and its sexual equivalent. It is a doubleness similar to that revealed by the "wigs" and "swordknots" doing their mock-battles with their painted, "cosmetic" goddesses. The mixed and uncertain relation of the rape to the hair and the body of Belinda ("Oh hadst thou, Cruel! been content to seize / Hairs less in sight, or any Hairs but these!") reflects Pope's concern, on the one hand, for the drag of time-bound, earthly reality with its costly history (Clarissa's world) and, on the other, for the humanly unsatisfying, empty promises of disembodied, airy, artful perfection (the Ariel-Belinda world).

If we transpose this concern over the conflict between the crudely actual and the aesthetic to the serious religious conflict between the sensual and the ascetic, we are led to the central concern of Pope's "Eloisa to Abelard." I think the poem can be profitably approached from this direction. As we consider Eloisa in her relations both to Abelard and to God, we again ask—in both cases!—how to embrace the unembraceable, how to be intimate without sexuality, how to encompass the body of the disembodied? Of course, for sexual purposes, the emasculated is equivalent to the disembodied. Or is this to utter the sacrilegious claim that, for Eloisa, Abelard is the same as God? It is precisely on the question of possible sacrilege that the poem founders, if indeed it doesn't fall—or at least fail.

It would appear to be clear that, at the level of its rhetoric, its apparent argument, the poem sees Eloisa forced to choose between God and Abelard, between religious and earthly love, as we follow in her what Pope terms "the struggles of grace and nature, virtue and passion." And the poem, as a conscious rhetorical structure, works toward the virtuous resolution of Eloisa's ardor for Abelard, as it becomes submerged in her ardor for God. The peace and the aesthetic distance of the final verse paragraph, with its sadly quiet vision after death and into the future, are to be seen as an appropriate postlude to the all-passion-spent acceptance that Eloisa has achieved. She is to have subdued the rioting pulse and the glowing blood by her submission, even as she has seen—in the line I quoted as the epigraph to this chapter—that Abelard's emasculation had subdued *his* pulse and blood.

I. Through the Worship of Bloodless Abstractions

The rhetorical structure of the poem can also be traced through the modulations of the imperative verb "come." Eloisa moves to the present moment by tracing the history of the lovers, which brings her to the acknowledgment of the falseness of her vows and her continuing fidelity to love and Abelard ("Not grace, or zeal, love only was my call, / And if I lose thy love, I lose my all," ll. 117–18). This leads to her first summons to him ("*Come!* with thy looks, thy words, relieve my woe; / Those still at least are left thee to bestow" [ll. 119–20]). The hint of licentious vulgarity in this first call to him to come and lead her to love is made explicit as she asks him to lead her again through the sensual pleasures of drinking, panting, pressing. She arrives, almost coarsely, at a pseudo-consummation: "Give all thou canst—and let me dream the rest" (l. 124). The "Ah no!" which opens the next line (l. 125) finds her turning against love for the first time as she asks Abelard to help her reject him ("And make my soul quit *Abelard* for God"). He has been, after all, her priest as well as her lover and so can serve her ambiguously now. She must have recourse to both sides of his duplicitous service, now alternately, now —however sacrilegiously—at the same time. Addressing him in his priestly role ("Ah think at least thy flock deserves thy care"), she recalls the simple austerity of his pious workings. But by line 152 she is turning once more toward his office of lover, seeing it grow out of his other office; and she beckons him once more to "come."

> Come *thou, my father, brother, husband, friend!*
> *Ah let thy handmaid, sister, daughter move,*
> *And, all those tender names in one, thy love!*

The language in the passage that follows is replete with the conventional contemporary jargon of poems of passion as Pope, like others, adapted it to his heroic epistle: "dying gales that pant" or "lakes that quiver." As she moves toward awareness of the unbearable division in her between desire and enforced religious obligation, she summons him yet again, but this time to lead her, not to love, but to God: "Oh *come!* oh teach me nature to subdue, / Renounce my love, my life, my self—and you" (ll. 203–4). The comparison of the virgin's dreams with her own leads her to love instead, even as Abelard's absence and —more devastating—his emasculation reinforce her sense of unending frustration. Still she calls to him again, though half in scorn: "*Come Abelard!* for what hast thou to dread? / The torch of *Venus* burns not for the dead" (ll. 257–58). She swings back from love to religion, however, and by line 281 beckons Abelard one last time, beckons him doubly and defiantly:

> Come, *if thou dar'st, all charming as thou art!*
> *Oppose thy self to heav'n; dispute my heart;*
> Come, *with one glance of those deluding eyes,*
> *Blot out each bright Idea of the skies.*

This passage is her last desperate gesture to the service of love, as she sees the impending victory of religion. The passage concludes with her plea to Abelard to prevent this victory: "Snatch me, just mounting, from the blest abode, / Assist the Fiends and tear me from my God!" But it is a final desperation, so that at once she turns from love to religion, and for the last time. For the first time she changes her plea, but with an explicit consciousness of polarity. "No, fly me, fly me! far as Pole from Pole" (l. 289). And immediately "come" is joined to the negative: "Ah *come not*" (l. 291).

The major turning point has been reached, and there is to be no significant backsliding or re-turn from here on. The imperative is next spoken *to* her by the dead spirit: "*Come*, sister *come!*" (l. 309). Eloisa's decision to die, the final victory of religion over love, is yet another variation on the same verb: "I *come*, I *come!*" (l. 317).[2]

It would appear, then, that the variations in the poet's use of "come" constitute the major device through which the rhetorical structure of the poem is manipulated. The increasing tension between earthly love and religion, derived from the increasing frequency and intensity of the alternations from pole to pole as we move from "come" to "come," moves us toward the resolution of the issue in favor of religion. And, rhetorically, the resolution would seem to be achieved following the climax that occurs as "come" changes—by way of "Come, if thou dar'st" (l. 281)—to "fly me, fly me" (l. 289) and then to "come *not*" (l. 291). After these, the movement to "Come, sister come!" (l. 309) and "I come, I come!" (l. 317) is part of the fall-

---

[2] The repeated "I come" may very well, as Tillotson suggests (Twickenham ed., 2:284), be derived from the *"venio, venio"* of the *Dido* of Ovid, who was the author, after all, of the original source of the heroic epistle. Tillotson points out also that the Sherburne translation, beginning with the line "I come, I come," made the words even more directly available to Pope. I have italicized all the occurrences of "come" in these quotations in order to call attention to them as I go through the poem.

ing action as the resolution is secured. Only the calm retreat remains, that which carries us beyond the picture frame to the perspective of the future's version of this tale as the distant past, as history.

It should become apparent later, when other elements of the poem are introduced, that I have, at this early stage, purposely oversimplified the operation of the rhetorical structure, picturing it as swinging back and forth from pole to pole before it settles upon one and reinforces that settlement. I have so oversimplified it at this point in order to exaggerate Pope's *apparent* intention to overcome "passion" by "virtue," to reduce Eloisa's ill-advised emotional rebellion to painful but calmly reasonable acceptance. In effect, this exaggerated view sees Pope as overriding her unruly fervor with his classic calm, as imposing his rage for order upon her rage.

If this rhetorical intention is reflected in Pope's imposition of a structure of polar alternations that stop when the right side has won, may not this rhetorical structure be further reflected in his imposition of the brilliantly fashioned heroic couplet upon what should be the spontaneous effusions of Eloisa's heart? There should be no blinking the fact that, at the most superficial level, the poem as a fiction is absurd. Presumably this is a letter written at the height of Eloisa's passion, not in detached contemplation of passion after it has been spent. There are passages in the poem (for example, ll. 13–14: "Oh write it not, my hand—The name appears / Already written—wash it out, my tears!") which show her clearly struggling with herself as she writes. Thus the poem represents at once a finished letter and a letter that, apparently finished, is actually in the stormy process of being written. We witness not just the dead product of a living hand. Rather, we watch, over Eloisa's shoulder, her struggle to compose the letter as she composes herself. If such is the case, what could be more *in*appropriate than to use Pope's most polished version of that most finished verse-form, the heroic couplet, to convey such immediacy? Pope's perfection of the couplet is a syntactical masterpiece of studied, self-conscious artifice. Its grammatical precision reflects its rhetorical precision: it achieves an epigrammatic completeness through the pair of end-stopped lines, each broken by medial caesuras, often allowing a four-part structure controlled by parallels and antitheses. We are brought up sharply by each brilliantly fashioned two-line unit and find it hard to sustain the unbroken sweep of emotion. Surely there is an insufficient sense of riot, or even of more moderate passion, in so

obvious a series of well-wrought contrivances. The incongruity between the spontaneity represented and the artifice of the manner of
representation could not be greater. If, as justification, we appeal to
the accepted forms of the pathetic mode and the conventional diction
of contemporary heroic epistles, we can explain, but we do not lessen,
the absurdity.

But I am concerned about more than the incongruity of verse form
to the central fiction. I am asking a more crucial question: are the
rhetorical structure that arises out of varied repetitions of "come" and
the resolution to which that structure seemingly leads equally incongruous with the dramatic "given" and the emotional complexity of
Eloisa's predicament? For I must wonder whether there are other elements in the poem, manipulations of words and images, which undercut the rhetorical intention and betray a far richer poetic intention.
Such a poetic deepening of the rhetorical structure must depend,
clearly, upon complicating the relations between the poles of Abelard
and God, upon the systematic blurring of the discreteness of these
poles. But, of course, if there should be such a blurring, shall we
ascribe it to a poetic "system" or merely to the uncertainty of the
poet?

To begin with, it is surely a misleading oversimplification, as I have
suggested, to find in the structure of the poem only an alternation
from pole to pole that finally is halted at the propitious moment, with
victory assured for the preferred pole. The two poles do not remain so
neatly distinct. Eloisa's desperation increases as she moves from her
consciousness of the past to her increasing awareness of the impossibilities of the present, from the lost physical realities gone by to the
precluding of all physical realities ever again. She moves, that is, from
present dreams of past sensual joys to a present that offers only
dreams of what can never again be sensed. It is all a matter of "ideas,"
that fine Lockean term: the remembrance of sensation with the stimu-
lating object removed. The heat that *her* senses still feel can respond
now only to "ideas," the "idea" of Abelard as she has known him, the
"idea" of Abelard as he is now, the "idea" of God both in Himself (as
incipient bridegroom) and in His representative, the priestly-sensual
Abelard of before and the enforcedly ascetic Abelard of now. Eloisa's
increasing consciousness of how it is now with Abelard, and how it
would now be with them, accompanies her seeming movement from
Abelard toward God, and in such a way as to suggest an awareness

that Abelard has been purified by his emasculation, that he is ahead of her, above her in finding his way toward God and His angels:

> For thee the fates, severely kind, ordain
> A cool suspense from pleasure and from pain;
> Thy life a long, dead calm of fix'd repose;
> No pulse that riots, and no blood that glows.
> Still as the sea, ere winds were taught to blow,
> Or moving spirit bade the waters flow;
> Soft as the slumbers of a saint forgiv'n,
> And mild as opening gleams of promis'd heav'n.
>
> (ll. 249–56)

But by the end of this passage we are given more than a mere comparison: Abelard himself in this poem is to become the "saint forgiv'n" to whom "promis'd heav'n" presents "opening gleams." This promise is realized in Eloisa's beatific vision near the close:

> In trance extatic may thy pangs be drown'd,
> Bright clouds descend, and Angels watch thee round,
> From opening skies may streaming glories shine,
> And Saints embrace thee with a love like mine.
>
> (ll. 339–42)

So she sees that they (Eloisa and Abelard) are far from together, that he has been purified and is on his way, while she is still dragged down by her "pulse that riots" and "blood that glows." Thus her heat *is* hers, not his. It is caused by her "idea" of him as he was rather than by how he is. It is true that he, as a sensual reality, was the source of that "idea"; but thanks to his absence from her *and* his emasculation, which makes their relation the same whether he is absent or present, he has now no reality beyond that of the "idea" ("let me dream the rest"). It is Eloisa's increasing awareness of this truth about Abelard (and about her true aloneness in her sensual craving) that enables her, as she moves to the final acceptance of the religious alternative, to see—not that she has chosen God over Abelard—but that Abelard himself has moved toward God's realm, that his own present reality (or rather unreality) permits a synthesis between Abelard and God. And the conquest by religion can be presented, now less painfully if more figuratively, in the language of love.[3] But so mild a complication of what I have called the rhetorical structure—that Abelard's change allows a language which forces one pole to lose itself in the other—really calls for no more than a pseudo-synthesis which still treats the issue as finally static. The best of both poles is to be arrived at through the distillation of sense into beings emptied of body and metaphor emptied of literal meaning. I fear that the full meaning of the poem is more dynamic—and messier—than such a resolution by spiritual synthesis.

The fact is, of course, that Abelard himself has from the start been a representative of both poles. As God's surrogate ("of Angelick kind, / Some emanation of th'all-beauteous Mind"), he has the austerity to raise "hallow'd walls" and "such plain roofs as piety could raise." Yet he also represents the polar extreme of uninhibited sensuality:

> Guiltless I gaz'd; heav'n listen'd while you sung;
> And truths divine came mended from that tongue.
> From lips like those what precept fail'd to move?
> Too soon they taught me 'twas no sin to love.
> Back thro' the paths of pleasing sense I ran,
> Nor wish'd an Angel whom I lov'd a Man.

> (ll. 65–70)

In examining the poem we will also come to the point of wondering whether, perhaps through her initiation at the hands of Abelard, the "idea" of God does not also represent both poles for Eloisa, whether it does not—like Abelard—reflect her sensual desires as well as her spiritual needs. We would then come to worry about the profound sacrilege in the poem: we would come to worry about the unhealthiness of the subterranean basis for Eloisa's religious fervor, her "enthusiasm," as she yields to her role as "bride" of God.

In his present state, Abelard is like God in his relation to Eloisa: her

[3] The fine essay by Brendan O'Hehir, "Virtue and Passion: The Dialectic of *Eloisa to Abelard*" (*Texas Studies in Literature and Language* 2 [1960]: 219–32), strives effectively to argue for just this notion: that Pope succeeds in synthesizing the polarity between God and Abelard. Although I agree (and indeed have been taught by his essay to agree) that the simple alternation of poles is better seen as a synthesis that sees them as merging (or, rather, effectually removes one of them), I must not stop with this formula either. For, rather than finding them to merge, I find the poles to cross one another and become confounded with one another.

rival lover, he is also physically absent and physically incapable of a sexual response to her passion. Like Milton's angels (of which Raphael spoke) or like Ariel in the "Rape," he is a disembodied, chaste lover. Though possessed himself of "No pulse that riots, and no blood that glows," Abelard can produce a rioting pulse and glowing blood in Eloisa as Ariel could produce them in Belinda when he came to her in a dream in the form of "A Youth more glitt'ring than a *Birth-night Beau.*" Abelard also becomes the product of dreams, of sexual visions both at war with religious visions and in danger of becoming identified with them, as his "idea" both struggles with and becomes blurred with God's. Recognizing Abelard's incapacity, whether he is absent or present, to do more than inspire dreams, Eloisa early in the poem calls upon him—as we have already noted—to give sensually all he can ("Still on that breast enamour'd let me lie, / Still drink delicious poison from thy eye, / Pant on thy lip, and to thy heart be prest; / Give all thou canst") "and let me dream the rest." Clearly it is the sexual consummation itself which she must dream for herself, since Abelard —physically reduced to "idea"—cannot help. It is a serious and sinful playing out of the mocking fantasies of the "Rape" and of the evasive uncertainties of Raphael in *Paradise Lost*.

These, then, must be the dreams of Eloisa to which she refers, a shameful contrast to the "visions" of the "blameless Vestal"; "Far other dreams my erring soul employ, / Far other raptures, of unholy joy" (ll. 223–24). The un-rioting, calm obedience leads the virginal nun to a far different dream of marital consummation from Eloisa's:

> For her the Spouse prepares the bridal ring,
> For her white virgins Hymenaeals sing;
> To sounds of heav'nly harps, she dies away,
> And melts in visions of eternal day.
>
> (ll. 219–22)

This idyllic love-death is a dying-away, a consummation strongly in contrast to the passionate one Eloisa dreams of with Abelard. Even close to the end of the poem, as she looks forward to her own calm dying-away at last, she has a momentary reversion which would damn Abelard into usurping God's role by partaking of her own orgasmic dying: "See my lips tremble, and my eye-balls roll, / Suck my last breath, and catch my flying soul!" (ll. 323–24). She then returns at once to the classic acceptance that Pope has tried rhetorically to earn ("Ah no—in sacred vestments may'st thou stand"), but a good deal has been given away which the rhetoric of the poem can never persuade us is recaptured.

The "Spouse," the "bridal ring," and the "*Hymenaeals*" remind us that Pope makes considerable use of the metaphor of the nun as the bride of God. It is a metaphor which permits a further confounding in Eloisa's tortured mind of God with Abelard, who acted the role of her husband more literally. In viewing the rivalry of God and Abelard as her lovers, Eloisa views herself as engaged in a deceitful marriage to God: "Ah wretch! believ'd the spouse of God in vain, / Confess'd within the slave of love and man" (ll. 177–78). Thus it is that when she calls upon Abelard to act the role of generous, altruistic lover by giving her up to her other lover, her language is most suggestive: "Fill my fond heart with God alone, for he / Alone can rival, can succeed to thee" (ll. 205–6). But what sort of succession is this to be, we must ask, as we recall the literal sort of lover that Abelard has been? The war between the "ideas" of Abelard and God can go on only as polarity strangely, if momentarily, is confounded with identity. Again, just before the climax, when Eloisa summons Abelard one last time to win her from God, she does it in language that confounds the two kinds of love she should be at pains to distinguish: "Come, if thou dar'st, all charming as thou art!" / Oppose thy self to heav'n; dispute my heart" (ll. 281–82).

Eloisa immediately returns to the mutual contradiction of the "ideas" in conflict, restoring the polarity that is less troublesome to the rhetoric of the poem's movement: "Come, with one glance of those deluding eyes, / Blot out each bright Idea of the skies" (ll. 283–84). These lines suggest that the essential opposition is not between two "ideas" so much as it is—in Platonic style—between the deceptions of sensuous reality ("one glance of those deluding eyes") and the truth of the spiritual idea ("each bright Idea of the skies"). But, we have seen, Abelard is now *doubly* an "idea" only: in his physical absence and his sensual incapacity. And though his "idea" *is* for Eloisa one that awakens her senses, it is one that can be blurred with God's "idea" because of his past priestly function as God's surrogate and his present asceticism, his enforced purification through emasculation.

Here is the central critical problem of the poem, it seems to me. The neatness of the would-be argument of the poem requires that the opposition of Abelard to God be a Platonic opposition between the illusory joys of present sense and the lasting presence of idea; at the same time the poem also reveals a full awareness of Eloisa's predicament—her hopeless state and Abelard's—in which there is a collapsing of all sense (as mere history) into "ideas," ideas with properties that are at once alternative and interchangeable. The poem, we must remember, opens with Eloisa kissing, not Abelard, but his name (l. 8). Thus sense and non-sense. The lines that follow remind us that even the name cannot achieve full sense, cannot—thanks to her vow of silence—be spoken, cannot appear on those very lips that have kissed it ("Nor pass these lips in holy silence seal'd"). The name, hidden in her heart, can lead, then, not to his body, but to his "idea": "Hide it, my heart, within that close disguise, / Where, mix'd with God's, his lov'd Idea lies" (ll. 11–12). This latter line springs the poetic—if not the rhetorical—problem upon us fully. Once Abelard is disembodied through his name to his "idea," he is no longer simply opposed to God as he came to be in body; he is—through his "idea"—"mix'd with God's" idea. Eloisa can never again consistently sort them out, so bizarrely "mix'd," confounded, are they. Consequently, in the letter that follows, the relations between Eloisa and God do not merely use the *language* of lovers and of marriage, as metaphors empty of body; these relations take on some of the *properties* of lovers and of marriage which justify that language. In spite of the cool and rational demands of "virtue," the heat of sexual "passion"—with all the impertinent suggestions of sublimation—persists in being applicable to Eloisa as she turns to her God. Thus the religion of the mystics intrudes itself appropriately, in this sensual medieval tale, upon Pope's reasonable neoclassical intention, springing out of the controlled precision of his heroic couplets.

The rivalry between the "idea" of God and the "idea" of Abelard returns us to the concern with which we began this view of the poem: the relation of physical love to a disembodied object. The problem with which Milton struggled, it is also what initiated the hilarious rivalry between Ariel and the baron in the "Rape," even as this rivalry permitted the metonymic implications of the hair to function as a playful extension of the question of the chaste embrace. In "Eloisa to Abelard" these duplicities lead to the multiple dimensions of the love-death. Nowhere is the use of the language of love to describe the leap of religion more telling than in the transposing of the nun's death into a consummation, the ultimate meeting of the bride with her spouse. Pope has probed to the initiating impulse at the source of that overworked pun on "die" (as both the end of life and the sexual climax), so dear to modern criticism.

It is still the marked inconsistency in Pope's treatment of the relation of the disembodied to love that confounds the relations of God to Abelard and of both to Eloisa. Again and again we observe the slipperiness with which we seem to move from the merely figurative to the literal and back again. Or have we moved at all? Have we really had both at once, with one the deceptive mask for the other, and sometimes the other way round? In Eloisa's subverted mind is the metaphor of the bride of God literally meant, even as our sense for propriety (and hers!) dictates that it not really be meant? Perhaps it is that her habit of sensuality causes it to apply too well, so that it destroys the rhetorical opposition between religion and love, "virtue" and "passion," as well as the promise of a synthesis between them that would absorb the second of each pair into the first.

The metaphorical dimensions of other elements in the poem become similarly troublesome, as we try to balance Pope's rhetorical perspective and Eloisa's passionately existential confusions. For the metaphorical strives for the identity of those very polar elements which the rhetorical tries to keep opposed. The repeated use of water, fire, and cold sometimes appears to serve only a flatly prosaic purpose, but sometimes it seems to strain toward a complex sensual-ascetic religious symbolism. Eloisa's tears, of course, are everywhere: they can be caused by sorrow for what sensual joys she has lost, or (more promising to "virtue") they can spring from her deep shame at her way of life with Abelard, or (most promising of all) they can act as religious absolution, a self-baptism. It is in this last sense that she tries to wash out Abelard's name with her tears or later sees that "stern religion quench'd th'unwilling flame" (l. 39). But "flame" occurs probably at least as often as "tears" in the poem, and again with a range of meanings running from the heat of sensual desire through the glowing blush of shame to the purgation of holy fire. The opposition of flame sometimes to cold and sometimes to water compounds the difficulties.

It would be foolish for the critic not to allow Pope in the main to be the sort of poet he clearly means to be: we must acknowledge that these images, for the most part, serve the rhetorical pattern in a one-dimensional way. For example, it is clear that, toward the end, the flames have been purified of their sensual heat when Eloisa speaks of her heavenly destiny "Where flames refin'd in breasts seraphic glow" (l. 320). This line fulfills the earlier promise of fire turned spiritual and merely figurative: "But let heav'n seize it [her soul], all at once 'tis fir'd, / Not touch'd, but rapt; not waken'd, but inspir'd!" (ll. 201–2). It is in this way that love can achieve a condition as de-sensualized as its language is de-literalized. The product of "flames refin'd," a cool fire, this condition is what is required "Ere such a soul regains its peaceful state" (l. 197). This development of rhetorical image and rhetorical argument, with entities distinguished and at war with each other, accords with Pope's usual practice as poet and thinker. We move, in a Platonic fashion that is a flight from true metaphor, from the literal to the merely figurative use of flame that reflects the movement from physical to purely spiritual love.

But, despite this normal practice, these images—of tears as well as flame—can be seen to join the other elements we have examined in subverting the apparent plan that, in its rhetorical clarity, depends on keeping distinctions distinct. And again we come upon blurrings, over-runnings of bounds, polarities momentarily becoming identities or, worse, half-identities (whatever these might be—and our normal discourse would never permit us to define them).

There are two splendid and related passages in which opposed elements become merged and/or interchanged. The portion of the poem constituted by them clearly becomes its metaphorical climax. First fire and cold:

> *Come* Abelard! *for what hast thou to dread?*
> *The torch of* Venus *burns not for the dead;*
> *Nature stands check'd; Religion disapproves;*
> *Ev'n thou art cold—yet* Eloisa *loves.*
> *Ah hopeless, lasting flames! like those that burn*
> *To light the dead, and warm th' unfruitful urn.*
>
> (ll. 257–62)

Here is the total realization of the doubleness in their situation, that which emphasizes her heat and his cold and—through him as through God—her own cold heat. Thanks to his emasculation as well as his absence, her love has had forced upon it the cold quality of religious asceticism as well as the heat of desire. And both are equally endless, since she is to be as permanently unsatisfied as he is permanently incapable of satisfying—except, that is, through the "idea," as disembodied. We have seen that Abelard's reality is different from his "idea," that his reality is cold and purified, while his "idea," in the shape of Eloisa's memory of past sensations, is the stimulus for continuing—if unfruitful—heat. Hence the brilliant union, in the last quoted couplet, of desire and death, flames and the unheatable, urn as womb (the receptacle of the procreative flame) and urn as tomb (the receptacle of the destructive flame).[4] Here is the consequence of that Petrarchan paradox, cold flame, the objective correlative of the frustrating impossibility of their relationship, indeed of all attempts at a disembodied love ("Give all thou canst—and let me dream the rest"). One might claim that, as emasculated and absent, Abelard is as unattainable as God; that in some crucial way he reflects God now even more significantly than he did at the start of their relationship when he was God's austere surrogate. The physical reality of Abelard, always as God's shadow, has moved from cold austerity to sensual flame to an enforced austerity that—because of the persistence in her of his "idea" as memory—is still the source of heat, though unfruitful. Now more than ever can he be viewed as God's image for Eloisa, and his sensual relation to her—reduced to the status of "idea"—no less a preparation for her reception of God than his asceticism had been, or now once more is. God-Abelard (now seen as being one as well as two) must serve her desire as well as her deprivation.

From the passage in which fire and cold fruitlessly merge, the heat of the confession builds once more. When the liquid element, drawn from the many uses of tears, is added, the religious equivalent of the sexual climax is attained:

> *What scenes appear where'er I turn my view!*
> *The dear Ideas, where I fly, pursue,*
> *Rise in the grove, before the altar rise,*
> *Stain all my soul, and wanton in my eyes!*
> *I waste the Matin lamp in sighs for thee,*
> *Thy image steals between my God and me,*

[4] My expansion of this "urn" image in this and other poems can be traced in my essay, "The Ekphrastic Principle and the Still Movement of Poetry; or *Laokoön* Revisited," *The Play and Place of Criticism*, pp. 105–28. Pp. 111–12 and 116–18 refer explicitly to "Eloisa to Abelard."

I. Through the Worship of Bloodless Abstractions

> *Thy voice I seem in ev'ry hymn to hear,*
> *With ev'ry bead I drop too soft a tear.*
> *When from the Censer clouds of fragrance roll,*
> *And swelling organs lift the rising soul;*
> *One thought of thee puts all the pomp to flight,*
> *Priests, Tapers, Temples, swim before my sight:*
> *In seas of flame my plunging soul is drown'd,*
> *While Altars blaze, and Angels tremble round.*
>
> (ll. 263–76)

The last three of these lines bring the flames and tears apocalyptically together, fire and water creating the "seas of flame" to drown Eloisa's soul in its downward ("plunging") movement. The "idea" of Abelard has caused the sacrilegious plunge that follows the soul's rising to the "swelling organs."[5] It has been pointed out elsewhere that these lines make literal sense once we grasp Eloisa's vision as coming, distortedly, through her tears and the flicker of the tapers.[6] These produce "seas of flame" as things she seems to see, though they become more as well. It is just this united moment of vision—in which Priests, Tapers, Temples swim and Altars blaze and Angels tremble—that produces the poetic earning (from literal through metaphorical levels) of the symbolic merger of the polar opposites, fire and water. For Eloisa sees the religious objects as distorted both through the tears springing from her sexual deprivation and through the tapers which are part of the religious ceremony itself. In this grandly climactic moment, in which all barriers collapse, her reality is transformed. And the medium of such profound, if momentary, transformation is a blend

[5] I can barely resist the reckless Empsonian (or Freudian) temptation to make an utterly unwarranted comment upon "swelling organs" and "rising," though by thus recording my resistance I suppose I have meant to further the overwhelming impression of language exploding beyond all bounds in this passage. For whatever kind of organ is swelling, Eloisa is being raised toward apocalypse or orgasm, indeed apocalypse *as* orgasm. The organs swell and her soul rises; then the "seas of flame" are produced in her which drown her soul in its descent. The spent, "prostrate" aftermath follows.

[6] By Brendan O'Hehir, in the essay referred to above. These climactic distortions are in keeping with the apparent nature of everything else she sees (or dreams) in her confession. We are presented with things only as she perceives them—her "ideas" of them. These "soft illusions, dear deceits" (l. 240) make up her dreamy reality, momentary protection against dead fact.

of fire and water, "grace" and "nature." For this fire is holy even as it is of the substance of the flames of desire; and the tear confesses guilt in its being "too soft" even as it is of the substance of the sacred water of absolution.

The orgasmic nature of this apocalyptic moment of vision is further indicated by what follows it: the exhausted, post-climactic, self-condemning aftermath, with Eloisa on the ground: "While prostrate here in humble grief I lie" (l. 277). The rhetorical turning point is shortly to follow, and the falling action after that. In these the poles are to be sorted neatly out once more and properly put (and, despite some lingering resistance, kept!) in their places. But after witnessing so highly ambivalent a scene, together with the language that opened it up, can we help feeling doubt about any attempt at resolution? Can we be persuaded of her contentment with watching "dying lamps" (l. 307) or of her fire transmuted to "flames refin'd" (l. 320)?

When we think back to the language and vision that restlessly subvert the poem, building to their own metaphorical climax, we may be impressed more with Eloisa's rejected vision of her orgasmic death ("See my lips tremble, and my eye-balls roll, / Suck my last breath, and catch my flying soul!") than with her more acceptable, hallowed vision of her death, with Abelard as her proper priest. Our disbelief in the final, purified relation between the lovers which she postulates even grows to embarrassment when, seeing heaven opening to Abelard after her death, she prays that—with him in "trance extatic" in which his "pangs" are "drown'd"—"Saints embrace thee with a love like mine." As we recall Pope's use of "embrace" elsewhere (and Milton's before him), we must feel uncomfortable at the language of this apotheosis in spite of ourselves. After all, how disembodied or spiritual an embrace or a love has hers been? So even here, this late in the poem, when the resolution should have removed the tendency of language to face toward both the literal and the metaphorical, such two-facedness is still there to taunt our understanding. The love-death, with its consequent double meaning of what it is to die, remains a will-o'-the-wisp. But if it eludes us, it has deceived Eloisa—and perhaps Pope as well.

For all its richness of possibility, the poem, in its intention and its structure, remains unhappily divided, perhaps because it is a vehicle that eludes Pope's classic insistence. There is the poem that Pope as rhetorician seems to have meant to write, and there is the poem that tried to come to life under his hand, in response to the existential demands of the persona's situation and of a language striving for plasticity. We have already noted the glaring inappropriateness of Pope's epigrammatically contrived heroic couplet to the would-be spontaneity of Eloisa's outpourings. Nor can references to Pope's poetic habit and to the contemporary heroic epistle make the couplet any less inappropriate for us. Further, the use of the common language of contemporary poems in the pathetic and erotic mode only makes us more aware of the stylized character of Eloisa's laments that make up her couplets.

So we can see the impropriety of form as symptomatic of Pope's general problem in the poem: his classic need for order must override whatever chaotic tendencies there may be in his materials, however existentially resistant they prove to be. Thus he would serve his rhetorical need to keep the demands of spirit and the demands of body distinct by forcing this need to override the confusions of a messy human psychology that finds these demands to be identical. Pope imposes his rhetorical structure upon the recalcitrant materials he has let loose from the inmost workings of Eloisa's mind, imposes it with the very rigor we find in the careful couplets that package (and inhibit) her passionate cries. In stripping her mind, Pope bares something he dares not confront fully; and he uses his rhetoric with his verse form to subdue it to the orderly entities his classic restraint can admit and entertain. If this taming of his materials means that he must refrain from indulging the existential specificity of Eloisa's torment, he will try to set his limits upon that torment. But it is true also that Pope has too sensitive a creative imagination to resist probing further than his initial categories should permit. Our sense of being misled by the poem, whichever way we read it, is caused precisely by this failure of single intention, by Pope's being drawn into character, situation, and language even as he wishes to stand safely free of them to retain an a priori, unthreatened control over them.

So I have traced the rhetorical structure of the poem, the increasingly intense alternation of the poles between which Eloisa moves. And, as I followed it to its climax and beyond, to the final acceptance in its falling action, I recognized that its one-sided resolution was inadequate to account for all that has been going on in Eloisa's mind and in her language. The rhetorical climax seemed unearned in light of the impact of the psychological and metaphoric climactic union.

The application of terms of earthly love to religious ritual and the movement of Abelard in his mutilated state toward the heavenly then suggested to me the possibility of a synthesis between the poles, or rather the subsuming of one by the other as the sensual is rendered spiritual, the literal rendered figurative. But this seemed merely a pseudo-synthesis because it still maintains the ascendancy of one pole over the other, if only by eliminating the latter. So I have tried to claim that, at the level of Eloisa's intensity and the language that sometimes sustains it, the poles manage to be at once polar, identical, interchangeable, literally themselves yet figuratively (or is it still literally?) other. In short, they move toward total metaphor. There is another climax here, perhaps a more livingly authentic one, even if the rhetorical one tries to overcome it by putting it in its place.

Of course, the poem does not maintain this metaphorical level at all consistently. Sometimes we apprehend only the merest glimmer of it, and we never find it to achieve anything like the totality of an independent system. But I believe we have seen that it is there, and with a play on the notion of the disembodied that is not altogether strange to Pope's practice, so that we cannot say with certainty that he is not aware of some of the dimensions he has released. We can, however, be certain that he is not comfortable with having so profound a threat to chaos on the loose, even if he cannot completely resist the risk. In making his poem a partial failure, Pope has opened it to a visionary excitement that enhances its attractiveness to us enormously. If the modest retreat into the distance of its closing lines suggests an uncritical confidence in the power of order, rational and poetic, to subdue what would subvert it, enough of the resistant sub-structure remains even at the end to keep our imaginations alive. Pope's classicism may seem rather sterile in the unyielding precision with which it meets any collision with alien subject matter, so that his fidelity to that classic persistence produces a poem (or, perhaps, two poems) in conflict with itself (themselves). It may be that Pope required the double-edged quality built into the mock-heroic in order to bring off the controlled or systematic duplicity that can give us the now-you-see-it-now-you-don't vision whose airiness comes to have body.

4

The Cosmetic Cosmos of "The Rape of the Lock"

If I have half (but oniy half) converted "Eloisa to Abelard" from a carefully manipulated heroic epistle to a self-revealing confession, it is consistent with my finding in so many places in Pope the playful evasions of neoclassical genres even as he indulges them. Thus I have elsewhere found the Horatian epistle in "Epistle to Dr. Arbuthnot," with its element of apologia, half converted to mock-apologia in its human awareness of the public poet's plight.[1] But, more to the point here, I have found the mock-epic in *The Dunciad* half converted to serious epic and the mock-epic in "The Rape of the Lock" half converted to a new genre of pastoral-epic fabricated for the occasion.[2] It is what I have just called Pope's "systematic duplicity" that is needed to bring off his brilliantly ambiguous relation to the genre he uses, adapts, half-parodies. It was his failure to make that duplicity systematic that accounted for the failure of "Eloisa," since it allowed an ambiguity that is more unfortunate than

[1] In "Contextualism and the Relegation of Rhetoric," *The Play and Place of Criticism*, pp. 165–76.

[2] In dealing with "The Rape of the Lock" in what follows, I am faced with the fact that I have already written on this poem at length ("The 'Frail China Jar' and the Rude Hand of Chaos," pp. 53–68). Much of what I have said there is relevant to this discussion, although my point here requires certain differences in emphasis. I can hardly carry my arguments here only by referring the reader elsewhere. So I can neither repeat the essay nor leave it alone. I suppose I must try to combine some new words with as few of my old words as I feel I can get by with. With this unsatisfactory compromise, I still must refer the reader to my other essay for detailed extensions and demonstrations of notions briefly summarized here and for discussions of exemplary passages needed to establish claims seemingly made here as mere postulations.

brilliant in that it bespeaks the poet's confusion and failure of control rather than his sitting astride, masterfully, his largely contradictory materials.

His language may lead him toward the teasing elusiveness that gives body to the airy or aerates the full-bodied. The very mention of the name Ariel suggests from the first the inventiveness which Pope resorted to in the "Rape" in order to submit that poem and its central mock-heroic action to the levitation that could double its every meaning. At every stage of this strange "rape," both the biologically real elements and the make-believe elements of social convention play, as echoes, with one another, and with such a simultaneity that we cannot tell original sound from resonance, cannot tell which is literal and which figurative. It is this "systematic duplicity" which the later poem, "Eloisa," cannot attain to, perhaps because of its singleminded seriousness, its lack of that undercutting element of mockery as its central principle of structure. Just such a principle of structure frees the language of the "Rape," while in "Eloisa" the language seems to struggle out of Eloisa's torments and free itself from the impositions of a fearful poet and his relentless convention. But the language of "Eloisa" finds no sanction, as does the language of the "Rape," in the poet's (and the convention's) own sense of play, of doubleness.

Still, as I opened my discussion of "Eloisa" by way of the problem of love and the disembodied, using the rivalry in the "Rape" between Ariel and the baron to give us a new view of the rivalry between Eloisa's unearthly and earthly lovers, God and Abelard, so now I turn back—by way of "Eloisa"—to the earlier poem to inspect the rich embroidery the mock-heroic Pope could work on both sides of his fabric. In the "Rape" his classic vision realizes itself by overcoming any alien qualities in its materials through its very catholicity. It can resort to bodiless abstractions even as those abstractions betray an awareness of all that has body which they have bypassed. The airy and the disembodied somehow—by the miracle of the totality of metaphor, a systematic duplicity—cohabit, are mutually sustaining, instead of offering the merely alternative possibilities that are never altogether blended into compatibility in "Eloisa."

I have already several times mentioned the chaste embrace as being at the heart of the "Rape" both in its relation to "Eloisa" (as I saw it) and for its meaning in its own terms. We have noted other things too: the central place given to the rivalry between unearthly and earthly lovers, pointed out by the sylph so appropriately named Ariel; the relation of the metonymic lock of hair to language and attitudes appropriate to an actual rape (together with the joining of mock rape and actual rape through those brilliantly nasty lines I quoted earlier: "Oh hadst thou, Cruel! been content to seize / Hairs less in sight, or any Hairs but these!"); the contrast between the "purer blush" of the looking-glass Belinda (created out of obedience to the "Cosmetic Pow'rs" in the magnificent dressing-room scene) and the glow of desire produced in dreams (by Ariel!) by "A Youth more glitt'ring than a *Birth-night Beau*"; and the several pseudo-Homeric, pseudo-Miltonic battles that play around the notion of the love-death, as the war between the sexes takes the mocking form of card game, Petrarchan song, and playful duels of revenge.

There are also the several metaphorical uses of the fragile drawing-room bric-a-brac, fine China, explicitly or implicitly in juxtaposition to the frailties of female virtue.[3] The following are the obvious passages:

> *Whether the Nymph shall break* Diana's Law,
> *Or some frail* China *Jar receive a Flaw . . .*
>
> (2.105–6)
>
> *Or when rich* China *Vessels, fal'n from high,*
> *In glittring Dust and painted Fragments lie!*
>
> (3.159–60)
>
> *'Twas this, the Morning* Omens *seem'd to tell;*
> *Thrice from my trembling hand the* Patch-box *fell;*
> *The tott'ring* China *shook without a Wind . . .*
>
> (4.161–63)

The specific significance I attribute to these passages is echoed in a poem written in the following decade by Pope's friend John Gay. "To a Lady on Her Passion for Old China" clearly suggests that Gay (perhaps with his friend Pope's help?) saw some of the meanings in the "Rape" which I have found:

> *New doubts and fears within me war:*
> *What rival's near? A China jar.*

[3] These passages and their metaphorical extension are the basis for the title of my original essay on the poem (see n. 2). As the quotations from John Gay's poem will indicate, the use of unbroken China as an emblem of virginity is common in the period.

> *China's the passion of her soul;*
> *A cup, a plate, a dish, a bowl*
> *Can kindle wishes in her breast,*
> *Inflame with joy, or break her rest.*
>
> (ll. 5–10)

> *When I some antique jar behold,*
> *Or white, or blue, or specked with gold,*
> *Vessels so pure and so refined*
> *Appear the types of womankind:*
> *Are they not valued for their beauty,*
> *Too fair, too fine for household duty . . .*
>
> (ll. 29–34)

> *How white, how polished is their skin,*
> *And valued most when only seen!*
> *She who before was highest prized,*
> *Is for a crack or flaw despised;*
> *I grant they're frail, yet they're so rare,*
> *The treasure cannot cost too dear!*
>
> (ll. 37–42)

Surely Pope's passages on China—both jars and vessels—resound the more meaningfully, in their emphasis on rarity and frailty, as we read Gay's implicit response to them.

But the following passage, more brilliantly than any other, sets against one another (even while providing a mutual reinforcement) the toyshop world of aesthetic play in the drawing-room and the crude world burdened by the harsh realities of biological multiplication; it justifies and gives body to those other passages concerned with "China."

> *On shining Altars of Japan they raise*
> *The silver Lamp; the fiery Spirits blaze.*
> *From silver Spouts the grateful Liquors glide,*
> *While China's Earth receives the smoking Tyde.*
>
> (3.107–10)

How shocked we become as we gradually perceive another level of meaning beneath what appears to be the absurdly inflated language of extravagant euphemism. For the euphemism is precisely what is required for the double meaning that is being denied even as it is being suggested. The mock-heroic equivalent of the epic meal, surely all this is the reduction to the toyshop world of decorum: what Tillotson has termed "the lacquer and silver ceremonial of coffee."[4] But look what else, so heavily burdened with bodies, emerges by antithesis (or even by negation) out of the words! There are "grateful Liquors," heated by "the fiery Spirits" that "blaze," gliding from "silver Spouts" into "*China*'s Earth" that "receives the smoking Tyde." A description of coitus—both emission and reception—could hardly be more graphic: the heating, leading to the "grateful" liquid pouring from the spout, the reception of "the smoking Tyde" by the flesh ("Earth") of China, that most prolific land. China's earth is thus the real China's flesh and blood in the sense of "earth to earth . . . dust to dust": it is Shakespeare's "sinful earth."

But we must cut short our verbal imagination and the implications of the double meanings it sponsors: the spouts are only silver, we must remember, the smoking tide only hot coffee, and—most crucial of all (for here is the central pun)—"*China*'s Earth" (rather than the place itself and its teeming people) is only China's earthenware, the frail China cups. The earthen, the artifact of the drawing-room, is hardly to be confounded with the earthly or—better—the earthy, natural heir (hair?) of the body. And yet the language insists that we so confound them in this ceramic masque (an asexual sexual substitute) that denies the earthy side, even as Belinda and her poem, with its metonymic rape, deny it. The world of the artificial, "purer" blush could not more pointedly celebrate its disembodied nature. In the same way Belinda, the goddess who is the cosmetic image in the mirror rather than the fleshly maiden herself, takes part in her make-believe war—whether in card game, or in the battle of revenge for her "rape," or in that "rape" itself—as the epitome of this art-for-art's-sake flight from body. Thus the timeless, if trivial, perfection of "lacquer and silver ceremonial" is celebrated only by negating what still suggests itself beneath the language: the time-bound, aging, dying world of the teeming millions pouring from flesh-and-blood "spouts."[5] China's earthenware or China's earthiness? And both as "*China*'s

---

[4] Twickenham ed., p. 117.

[5] Must not the author of *Tristram Shandy* have pondered these lines and this word as whimsically as their author did in writing them? See vol. 5, chap. 23, in that novel and my own comments in chapter 9 below.

Earth"![6] So Belinda's world and her poem choose only the timeless purity of the earthen, rejecting the urgent consequences of flesh and blood, although the language shrewdly preserves our awareness of what remains visibly there, sustained by double meanings, even if it is visibly there only by negation. The very euphemism for the coffee-pouring, in its pompousness, proclaims its irrelevance to our worka-day world. After all, "fiery Spirits" are mere flames heating coffee, "Spouts" the mere pouring devices of the silver coffee-pots, "grateful Liquors" or "smoking Tyde" the mere hot coffee itself, and "China's Earth" the frail, precious coffee cups. How many effects beyond the mere mock-heroic this extravagant euphemism achieves with the strategy of its peculiar cluster of secondary (or aren't they really the primary?) meanings. No other passage that touches on the frailty of fine China can now escape our suspicions as we seek to relate that China to the world from which it is so disengaged.

The full-bodied, full-blooded world of time and biological reality that the disembodied, bloodless world of Belinda seeks to escape is hardly an attractive one. It barely exists, just at the edges of the poem and under its language, although that existence is painfully felt in its sordid contrast to the make-believe toyshop of extravagant play. And the juxtapositions, though rare, are enough to authenticate the sec-ondary meanings that occur so frequently in the language, which gives that play its half-consciousness (or its negative awareness, an aware-ness of absence, as it were) of the world to which it is irrelevant.

The shock with which we see the real world impinging upon the fluffy play of Hampton Court indicates the force of Pope's unexpected juxtapositions. Critical comment has often been provoked by the questionable propriety with which Pope intrudes upon our social idyll the dread vision of the world in which "Wretches hang that Jury-men may Dine" (3.22). But how sure Pope must have been of his delicate creation to permit us this glimpse beyond its frame. Here is the real world's justice, the doom of its bloody judgment, with no artful counterpart in language or playful juxtaposition to lighten it. As I have said elsewhere, "This brief, terrorizing glance at the alternative should send us clutching at the innocuous grace of the 'toyshop'

[6] Or have I come to the poem too impressed by Yeats's Byzantium world, the "artifice of eternity" constructed as a carefully wrought alternative to "the fury and the mire of human veins," "those dying generations," "mackerel-crowded seas"?

where we need fear neither hunger nor execution though we may have the make-believe equivalent of each."

Early in canto 3, with the arrival at Hampton Court, Pope gives us three crucially related passages on the kinds of dooming—playful, courtly, and deadly real. We have already looked in a preliminary way at the doom pronounced by the real world upon the "Wretches" who are victimized more by time than by their crimes:

> Mean while declining from the Noon of Day,
> The Sun obliquely shoots his burning Ray;
> The hungry Judges soon the Sentence sign,
> And Wretches hang that Jury-men may Dine.
>
> (ll. 19–22)

We must note how blunt and direct the language is. There are no classical euphemisms for the sun here; and the sun's action is as immediately intrusive as it is unpleasant. The harsh realities of worldly time permit no nonsense, as the sun—an accomplice in the deadly conspiracy to accord with time's demands—joins in the dooming with judges and jurymen. This is hardly the same sun as the "Sol" who at the opening of the poem "thro' white Curtains shot a tim'rous Ray" to open the eyes of its rival, Belinda. For the sun must treat the cosmetic world and its goddess with a uniform and transcendent grace to match their own natures. Thus, in the opening verse paragraph of canto 2 Belinda is introduced with the extended simile that makes her not only the match to the sun but its representative, its goddess, shining on her world with the beneficent smiles of a universal monarch.

> Favours to none, to all she Smiles extends,
> Oft she rejects, but never once offends.
> Bright as the Sun, her Eyes the Gazers strike,
> And, like the Sun, they shine on all alike.
>
> (2.11–14)

Again, this is hardly the sort of being or behavior we find in the time-bound sun, shooting "his burning Ray" to awaken the appetites of judges and jurymen and thus to cooperate with the unfeeling dooms these help bring about.

By contrast, here is a passage, just a couple of lines later in canto 3, describing the innocuous, make-believe judgment Belinda would deliver in order to achieve dominance in a card game:

> Belinda *now, whom Thirst of Fame invites,*
> *Burns to encounter two adventrous Knights,*
> *At* Ombre *singly to decide their Doom;*
> *And swells her Breast with Conquests yet to come.*
>
> (ll. 25–28)

Belinda's victory in this mock-battle is the forecast of the doom in the later mock-battle, the Petrarchan battle between the sexes in the final canto. The playful mock-doom, the love-death of the disembodied, is visited upon lovers who rise in response to a smile as they fell in response to a frown. This mock-doom recalls us, in its negations, to the truly destructive, the cruelly indifferent doom in the time-ridden real world—full-bodied and bloodied—with its irreversible consequences.

But there is a third, yet more complex kind of doom which Pope introduces. Indeed, it precedes the other two in canto 3 as it establishes the dimensions and bounds of the two worlds, the world of "Wretches" and the world of Ombre, as well as the relations between them. This form of dooming embraces the other two: in the perfect spirit of the mock-heroic, it joins by pun and zeugma the doom of serious consequences and the doom of conventional play. The fact that the party is going to Hampton Court for their games reminds the poet of the affairs in the great world that are conducted there:

> *Here* Britain's *Statesmen oft the Fall foredoom*
> *Of foreign Tyrants, and of Nymphs at home;*
> *Here Thou, Great* Anna*! whom three Realms obey,*
> *Dost sometimes Counsel take—and sometimes* Tea.
>
> (ll. 5–8)

The yoking of "foreign Tyrants" and "Nymphs at home," both similarly foredoomed by "*Britain*'s Statesmen" at Hampton, like the yoking of "Counsel" and "*Tea*" as they are similarly taken by the Queen, effect the reduction of the serious world to the merely courtly. And, after all, isn't Hampton Court precisely the place for such a yoking and such a reduction, as the action of this poem—in its mock-heroic grandeur—testifies? The very next line of the canto ("Hither the Heroes and the Nymphs resort") expresses just such classically sanctioned heights, even as the line which follows ("To taste awhile the Pleasures of a Court") undercuts it, reduces it to its appropriate triviality. Belinda then attempts to impose her dooming power in the hope of "Conquests yet to come" and in this is like *"Britain's* Statesmen" (in their dealings with tyrants or with nymphs?), even as these lines, coming where they do, juxtapose her to those cruel worldly judges who sign sentences for hangings.

These three forms of dooming provide a key to the possibilities that the poem as a whole either embraces, merely countenances, or turns away from—but in dread awareness that all of them exist, with the claim of the most devastating perhaps the least easily escapable. There is the inconsequential mock-heroic kind of dooming involved in the major action of the poem; there is the most frightfully consequential, anti-heroic kind of dooming being performed on the Wretches just beyond the edges of the canvas (and we are permitted a brief glance at it as it goes on outside the frame); and there is, as the starting-point for it all, the heroic kind of dooming performed by statesmen and Queen that can itself be reduced to the mock-heroic kind, thus revealing the tawdry, more devastating possibilities its heroic posture may conceal. The zeugma seems to assert, to insist upon, the mock-heroic character of the contemporary world, the reduction of great affairs to the merely courtly, tyrants treated like nymphs, counsel like tea. Style, on its own, parades in indifference to substance, preserving its purity in precious emptiness. In so doing, it may preserve sanity as well—at least the sanity of an unyielding classic visionary like Pope who perhaps knows that the neoclassical is not the classical, and who may fear that he has seen the death of style in our substantial world, as witness the judges and jurymen.

This empty parade (or even charade) of style, the rejection of body for the purer blush, constitutes much of what the poem is about in its celebrations and its rejections. The several doomings we have witnessed represent the three worlds Pope addressed himself to: one he may have yearned for nostalgically even as he recognized its unattainability, one he turned away from in disgust, and one he grasped playfully, wittily, even as he knew its airiness precluded its actuality. Thus we have, respectively, the properly classical, high heroic world of substance and style in mutual accord (to which Pope paid his homage in his translations); the horribly realistic but hardly classical world of body and consequences; and the neoclassical shadow world of disembodied styles, wigs and sword knots, dancing their empty gestures, their rituals, in flight from solid reference. Perhaps Pope is in his own way acknowledging the breaking apart of style and substance in the contemporary realities that for him succeeded the archaic mythology of classical tradition. In my earlier essay on this poem I put it this way:

> As his Homer shows Pope to have viewed it, in the old and revered heroic tradition the world of serious significance and consequence and the world of high play and the grand manner were one. Actuality was somehow hospitable to decorum. But in the dwarfed mock-heroic world Pope sees about him, actuality, in becoming sordid, rejects all style: its insolent insistence allows decorum to make only a comic appearance as its pale reflection. Instead of the all-accomplishing Homeric heroes, Pope must accept either the jurymen and wretches or the wigs and sword-knots, either Clarissa's breeder or Ariel's nymph of the "pure blush."

These words turn us to Clarissa and, with her, back to time, to history, as the villain that makes substance deny itself and seek its refuge in empty, if decorous, style. And we remember that Homer's heroes, as the rational Plato would remind us, have mythic rather than historical reality.

The fact of historicity (which is to say fact-icity) is the enemy of the structural projections of the eighteenth-century imagination in its spatial, aesthetic perfection. Change the purer blush to the blush of flesh-and-blood desire and we change the cosmetic goddess to Belinda, the young but even now aging virgin in search of a husband and out to ensnare him, for marriage and child-rearing, with her locks. This Belinda is certainly a character in Pope's poem too, as his sexual secondary meanings assure us: she is indeed what I have called Clarissa's breeder and, except in the miracle of Pope's language, she would do away with the simultaneous existence of that other Belinda, the disembodied cosmetic goddess. How shrewd of Pope to add that speech of Clarissa's in which she forces this flesh-and-blood Belinda upon us, pressing us to acknowledge the realities of time that make the premises of the world of this poem an absurdity: "But since, alas! frail Beauty must decay, / Curl'd or uncurl'd, since Locks will turn to grey" (5.25–26).[7]

Pope also will confess the action of time upon Belinda's hair, but he cannot rest with Clarissa's homely truths. How clearly Pope transcends this desperate knowledge when, in the last lines of the poem, he juxtaposes his own Clarissa-like confession of Belinda's (and even her hair's) mortality with his insistence upon the timeless, eternal sameness of the glorious, resurrected look:

> For, after all the Murders of your Eye,
> When, after Millions slain, your self shall die;
> When those fair Suns shall sett, as sett they must,
> And all those Tresses shall be laid in Dust;
> This Lock, the Muse shall consecrate to Fame,
> And mid'st the Stars inscribe Belinda's Name![8]

Pope is also juxtaposing the metaphorical death caused by Belinda's Petrarchan role ("after Millions slain") with her actual physical death. (Or may "after Millions slain" be viewed as an independent construction, suggesting all those "Wretches," like ourselves, who are being literally slain constantly by such routine horrors of the real world as have been suggested in this poem? Perhaps the phrase "after Millions slain" has a duplicity that opens the cosmetic world outward into time, which now can overcome even Belinda's precious "Tresses.") So the vision of the "Tresses" "laid in Dust" serves to remind us that even the lock, after all, is related to the body, to aging flesh, and thus

---

[7] I remind the reader again of Gay's "To a Lady on Her Passion for Old China," where he reveals his indebtedness to Pope (as I read him). As Gay earlier in the poem echoed Belinda's preciousness ("I grant they're frail, yet they're so rare"), so he ends on Clarissa's note (ll. 67–70):

> Love, Laura, love, while youth is warm,
> For each new winter breaks a charm;
> And woman's not like China sold,
> But cheaper grows in growing old. . . .

[8] The name, like the lock but unlike the person, is inscribed there. Like the lock, the name is the airy symbol, the nominal substitute for the substantive creature herself, now dead.

to earth, which, as dust, must in course return to dust. Yet Pope preserves also that special cosmetic lock which symbolizes the earthen (China) and which, by being severed, escapes the body's earth and its slavery to time. Though Pope may have introduced Clarissa, as he says, "to open more clearly the *Moral* of the Poem," he clearly triumphs over this sort of morality, but only as he fully testifies to its truths, as they apply, under the aegis of time, to those of us who choose to march back out of the looking-glass into reality.

The facts of life under time, to which Clarissa draws painful attention and which she wishes to have an exclusive sway over behavior, must not be recognized as such by this company—which is why, after her speech, "no Applause ensu'd" and why the action in the balance of the poem carries out the denatured charade of the love-death in defiance of her common-sense precepts. And what defiance "grave Clarissa" has shown to life captured in the looking-glass, the life cherished by this company—not only by her speech but earlier by her furnishing that rapacious "two-edg'd Weapon," the scissors, to the baron for the act that so profoundly challenges the delicate autonomy of the make-believe world. She crudely points to the domestic social-biological reality that underlies the conventional social games of this playful company (as it underlies Pope's ambiguous language); she thus converts disembodied myth to bodied, bloodied history, converts charade to grim drama, converts the Wonderland world without time to the world where time condemns wretches, condemns us all by converting *us* into wretches. The fantastic constructs of man-made order —the order of the dressing table, of the card game, of drawing-room manners, of the hierarchy of Sylphs, of the Chain of Being notion itself—suddenly have to give way, under the crushing weight of Clarissa's revelations, to the fragmented multiplication of history's casual facts.

No wonder Pope's creatures, reflecting the desperate need for the classic vision of their creator, reject this threat to their art-world and grasp the fragile unreality of their ritual games that preserve the possibility of their sanity. It is indeed like Pope's assertion of the final metaphysical dogmatism in the two couplets near the end of Epistle I of *An Essay on Man*:

> *All Nature is but Art, unknown to thee;*
> *All Chance, Direction, which thou canst not see;*

> *All Discord, Harmony not understood;*
> *All partial Evil, universal Good.*

My comments on this passage elsewhere should serve me here:

> *Is not such a universe decorum itself, decorum*
> *erected into a cosmic principle, all the spheres and the*
> *links in the chain of being taking and keeping their*
> *places with a propriety resembling that of the sylphs,*
> *and of the drawing room? And the seeming disturb-*
> *ances within it are seeming only: the discord that*
> *is a false front for harmony reminds us of the battles*
> *in "The Rape of the Lock" that are only decorous*
> *and conventional mock-battles, war-games that secure*
> *rather than threaten the world of fashion. The*
> *dangerous casualty of flesh and blood gives way to*
> *the controlled inevitability of art.*

So, like the disembodied, anti-existential abstractions in the dogmatic, deductive metaphysics Pope's age needed so desperately, the bodiless pseudo-creatures of the "Rape" are cherished for their bodilessness: wigs instead of men, sword knots instead of swords, cosmetic blushes instead of sexually inspired ones, silver spouts and coffee instead of male spouts and their liquid, "frail China" as earthen instead of the flesh of China as earthy, the decorative lock of hair (at all different from a man's wig?) instead of the sexually functioning body, and finally that lock of hair as an eternal star instead of aging, graying tresses. But the choice is made with an awareness—sustained through double meanings, through juxtapositions, and above all through the systematic duplicity of the mock-heroic itself—of the worldly under-side, the biological under-world that is, alas, our world after all, as Clarissa's moral has demonstrated.

Nevertheless, the poem can never abandon its artificial mask (and masque) and must close with the apocalyptic testament to the lock, that artful, sexless distillate of the hairy seat of sexuality. Are we not reminded by it of the reverse, infernal apocalypse at the close of *The Dunciad*? If, at the close of the "Rape," Pope enshrines the lock in the heavens beyond the reach of men (those Clarissa-like little men of history who conduct time's destructive march), it is, at the close of

I.   Through the Worship of Bloodless Abstractions

The Dunciad, very much within the reach of the unruly mob responsible for extinguishing the stars ("*Art* after *Art* goes out, and all is
Night"). It may be too much to suggest, as I have elsewhere, that *The
Dunciad* is a Dantesque extension of the threat which Clarissa constitutes to the art-world of the "Rape," that it is the vengeance of the
forces of history, of the temporal sense, upon the neat eighteenth-
century world machine that man's rational, anthropomorphic quest
and his spatial imagination led him to project upon the stubborn
world of contingent objects around him. But I *have* suggested it elsewhere and have done little here except to suggest it no less strongly.
For I do feel it is expressive of Pope's inmost consciousness and best
accounts for the elaborately duplicitous conclusions of both poems.
Hence I use once more the language I employed in the earlier essay:

> [*The eighteenth-century cosmos*] *represents also a
> supreme act of human will, the will to order—and to
> sanity. It is finally, then, an aesthetic construct only. . . .
> Is it not, however, rather smug of us to assume that
> minds as sensitive and probing as Pope's could believe
> in their dream-world so utterly and simply? That
> they could rest so secure in an unquestioning acceptance
> of this architecturally perfect model-universe? Perhaps
> at some level of their consciousness they were alive
> to the ultimate futility of their desperate postulation.
> Nevertheless, postulate they had to in western man's
> final attempt to resist universal disintegration. But
> in this last assertion of cosmic solidarity there may have
> been the insecurity that was aware of its vulnerability
> and of the surrounding hordes of modernism already
> closing in. I am here suggesting, of course, that
> "The Rape of the Lock" is Pope's testament of the
> aesthetic universe, one that reveals a nostalgic yearning
> for it along with a critical acknowledgment of its
> impracticability; and that* The Dunciad *is his bleak
> acceptance of the chaotic forces he most feared. . . . For
> the usual picture of Pope as pure rationalist must be
> balanced by that of the subterranean Pope who is
> the pure and frightened skeptic. By the time of* The
> Dunciad, Book the Fourth, *Pope may know the dream is*

> *shortly to be smashed forever. But his was not a*
> *dogmatic slumber, or a slumber at all. It was an artful*
> *delusion—of himself and of us—by a mind too*
> *aesthetically fine to accept the universe as less than a*
> *work of art.*

How helpfully, it should also be noted, Pope's heroic couplet, so troublesome to the pretense at spontaneity in "Eloisa," serves in the "Rape." For here its insistence on reducing all the challenging dimensions of his worlds in conflict to syntactic and rhetorical sameness, to indiscriminate uniformity, is precisely what is needed to reflect Pope's classic insistence that the order of a never-never land remain imposed upon the disorderly threats and intrusions of the real biological and social worlds beneath. The disembodied abstractions or empty images that substitute for empirical personages may belie all that the existential in its contingency holds for us all; but the play of their artificial and imaginative reality must be sustained. The art impulse that sustains it also sustains the heroic couplet in its function as the equally arbitrary imposition of human form upon all that resists it. And even in *The Dunciad* the poet himself proves the incompleteness of the defeat of art and light and the properly human that he chronicles at the end of the poem by asserting the perfection of his own art in giving voice to it, in defying the chaos that dullness brings ("Joy to great Chaos!") through the magnificent couplets that give dullness and chaos their life and their false dominion. Finally, Pope's art—and, by reflection, the art-world itself, the world of light and stars—is not so fragile even if man's less orderly instincts seem to have overcome it.

Like Pope's art, like the eighteenth-century cosmos, like the China that so curiously concerned Belinda,

> *"Tott'ring ... without a Wind" by virtue of its very*
> *delicacy, Pope's aesthetic construct of a universe is*
> *unable to withstand the merest touch of the hand of*
> *reality. It now lies in the "glitt'ring Dust and painted*
> *Fragments" of "rich China Vessels, fal'n from high."*
> *But it did not only crash, though* The Dunciad
> *chronicles that it did. Thanks to Pope, we can cherish*
> *with him the very fragility that assured its perfection*
> *even as it guaranteed its destruction. For, like Belinda's*

> lock, even as it ceased being a force down here, the
> muse "saw it upward rise." . . . The poem, too, is
> inscribed there ["mid'st the Stars" where it inscribes
> Belinda's name]! And with it that illusory universe, like
> the "Beau-monde" constructed as a work of art,
> whose very artificiality testifies to the persistence, the
> indomitable humanity of its creator's classic vision—and
> to his awareness that the insubstantial nature of this
> universe could allow it to transcend all that chaos
> ground into "glitt'ring Dust."

This victory of chaos is what we witness, to our horror, in the final accession of the forces of anti-art at the conclusion of *The Dunciad*:

> In vain, in vain,—the all-composing Hour
> Resistless falls: The Muse obeys the Pow'r.
> She comes! she comes! the sable Throne behold
> Of Night *Primaeval, and of* Chaos old!
> Before her, Fancy's gilded clouds decay,
> And all its varying Rain-bows die away.
> Wit *shoots in vain its momentary fires,*
> The meteor drops, and in a flash expires.
> As one by one, at dread Medea's strain,
> The sick'ning stars fade off th'ethereal plain;
> As Argus' eyes by Hermes' wand opprest,
> Clos'd one by one to everlasting rest;
> Thus at her felt approach, and secret might,
> Art *after* Art goes out, and all is Night.
>
> .   .   .   .
>
> Nor public *Flame, nor* private, *dares to shine;*
> Nor human *Spark is left, nor Glimpse* divine!
> Lo! thy dread Empire, CHAOS! is restor'd;
> Light dies before thy uncreating word:
> Thy hand, great Anarch! lets the curtain fall;
> And Universal Darkness buries All.

The "Rape" testifies to the power of the poem, that creating word which puts "Art after Art" in the skies in the form of stars, those moving but unchanging patterns to be followed by the "*Beau-monde*."

But *The Dunciad* ends with the "uncreating word" that extinguishes "Art after Art" and even seems to threaten that grand constitutive symbol of art and the poem, Belinda's lock, whose resurrection at the end of the "Rape" was to secure its place in our heavens forever. But its brilliance remains, enough to keep the illumination which allows even the triumph of the anti-poets in *The Dunciad* to occur only within the radiance of that magnificent work. After all, the upward movement of the lock to the heavens at the end of the "Rape," we were told, could be "mark'd by none but quick Poetic Eyes." It is the quick that keeps the light of life burning even in the darkness which is the slow dullness of the dead. It assures us that the end of the "Rape" is not countermanded by the inverted apocalypse of *The Dunciad*. Instead, it provides us with the vision we need to remind ourselves of the quick poetic brilliance which remains with us reassuringly even at the end of that mockingly despairing poem. Are we not being turned toward Thomas Mann's (or rather the gentle Serenus Zeitblom's) description of the miraculous ending of Adrian Leverkühn's *Lamentation of Dr. Faustus*, in which "the final despair achieves a voice," transcending itself, changing its meaning as silence and night change their meaning because of what is no longer there, so that it "abides as a light in the night"?[9]

But this is all too serious. It is all a joke too, we must remember, for Pope. Both poems *are* mock-epics. Pope's conviction stems only from a half-belief, even if there is something of desperation (or is it mock-desperation?) in the way he clings to it. Can he fear the timely world of flesh and blood enough to settle—as unregenerate classic visionary —for the trivial world, emptied of all that is routinely pertinent? In view of the perspective I have gained from "Eloisa," I must see the "Rape" and *The Dunciad* as suggesting as much. But dare we forget, as much as I have, the silliness of the fops in the one poem and of the dunces in the other? Dare we forget, as much as I have, either the serious business of the premarital societal realities, which Clarissa points out to us is surreptitiously involved beneath the playful charades in the "Rape," or the bitterly earnest, name-calling poetic rivalry engaged in by the speaker in *The Dunciad*?

If I have so extensively forgotten or overlooked the obvious in these poems, one reason could be advanced for my doing so that

[9] Trans. H. T. Lowe-Porter (New York: Knopf, 1948), p. 491.

would constitute a more serious charge against my work than any other: that this misplaced emphasis reflects the attribution to Pope of an existential, anti-universal awareness that is foreign to him and to the mind of his time. The charge, in effect, would be that I have turned Pope into a post-Kantian.[10] But I must on my side wonder whether we really needed Kant for us to feel like so-called post-Kantians. Even before Kant, how dogmatically secure could the suffering individual existent feel about the objective reality of those universal, orderly structures that his philosophy so confidently told him were out there imposing their forms to tame all errant particulars? We shall soon see the increasing insecurities that showed themselves in the often confusing work of the magnificent Dr. Johnson, who nourished his own persistently classic vision by means of his own devices, even while he was naggingly aware of the threats to his dreams of neoclassical order.

What it may all come down to is a Pope's or a Johnson's inward failure of confidence in the power either of his own spatial imagination, or of the spatial imagination of his time, to still the temporal resistances to order by freezing them into a pattern. What is at stake is the actual existence of the securely seated "rationalist" who can constantly and consistently hold onto his confidence while he daily, momentarily, experiences the fact of time, or rather the ever-shifting facts of the movement of time. And surely man's inwardness experi-

---

[10] This is the charge a critic-historian like W. K. Wimsatt has more than once brought against my work in general, although his extension of it specifically to my work on Pope has been confined to the friendly and valued private correspondence between us. See my collection of the public record of our differences in "Platonism, Manichaeism, and the Resolution of Tension: A Dialogue," *The Play and Place of Criticism*, pp. 195–218. I believe that Wimsatt's commitment to a pre-Kantian philosophical Realism requires him to view with suspicion (if not resentment) an attempt to make skeptics even of those who wrote before the Kantian revolution. By "skeptic" here I mean one who fears that the so-called objective structures that are to order reality may be no more than anthropomorphic projections of our minds, projections imposed because we are anxious to accommodate an alien reality (which may be no more than a flow of random particulars) to the universalizing needs of those minds. The dogmatic realist, on the other hand, believes exactly in the reality, the objectivity, of that universal structure, in terms of which no particular is ever random. Without arguing his special role, I am using Kant (in talking of pre-Kantian or post-Kantian) as a symbolic name, a convenient point to mark our total awareness of the constitutive function of mind in creating the structures by which it lives.

enced these as self-consciously, as fearfully, before Kant as after him, whatever may have been the reigning philosophy to which he offered his allegiance.

The secret, existential awareness which I am attributing to Pope, then, need not involve the claim to ontological chaos instead of ontological order so much as it involves the awareness of the ungraspable transience of the fleeting moment. The eighteenth-century cosmic-aesthetic structure depended utterly on a spatial imagination that could freeze all flux into unchanging universals where time is not. But —during moments now and then—can this view, what has been called "naïve Realism," help but be seen as naïve by any human being who suffers and who knows he is to die, who feels time and the unrepeatable, unpausing passing of its unmarked instants (never an instance)? If all rushes past, how can anything but the passing-changing non-instance be phenomenally there? Is not this what makes (and has made) existentialists of us all? Long before Kant—and, since Kant, without him—we should have learned to distrust the easy metaphors of convenience invented by our spatial imagination as substitutes for those flowing temporal metaphors that elude our rational need for the boundaries making for entity-hood. So before, or without, Kant we had to wonder whether that gorgeously symmetrical imaginative structure within which the well-behaved cosmos was expected to conduct its business, that structure with its spatial completeness, was not, after all, no more than imaginative: the product of our mind, of its need for comfort, and not existing on its own out there.

In effect, we are asked to be Northrop Frye before Frye, insisting on our construct of the world as imagination would have it; but we are not confusing our construct with that glut of finite and inhuman objects which is that alien world out there, the world before mind, without mind, and indifferent to mind. It may be a gloriously humanistic endeavor to cherish the anthropomorphic projections that reshape the world to the forms of our mind, as it is sadly human to acknowledge the anthropomorphic as being what it is and no more, of us and not of the world, born of our rage for order even as the rest is mere rage.

These secret fears are what I am attributing to Pope, and the product of these fears becomes the density of his poems. So I believe that, in this density, he has revealed them—and himself—to us. Fearful of body (and who more than he had a right to be?), in love with abstractions that escaped its limits, its ugliness, its time-ridden destiny, Pope had to oppose Clarissa, if only by the frailty of that ravished and resurrected lock, metonymic symbol of the wispy world of appearance, the cosmetic powers. But all that this escapist world transcends or evades—the facts of Clarissa and of wretches in their governance by time—all this stands heavily, dully, by, with its undeniable truths, an obstacle to the willful escapism of so expensive a classic vision. Yet Pope dares hold out for it, though by the time of *The Dunciad* half vainly, to the end. So long as one knows the odds, not weakness, not even a willed existential blindness, need force us to wield the scissors with the baron. Rather we can share the joyous imprisonment under the spell of artfully controlled illusion:

> *Fair Tresses Man's Imperial Race insnare,*
> *And Beauty draws us with a single Hair.*

5

Samuel Johnson: The "Extensive View" of Mankind and the Cost of Acceptance

Dr. Johnson, both as poet and as literary critic, may be seen to be searching, as intensely as Pope, for a way of bearing with sanity the threat posed to the rational life by the disordering tendencies of runaway particulars. But there is more evidence of Johnson's willingness to recognize the stubborn fact of their existence, though he seems anxious to shut them out rather than face the consequences of admitting them as full members of his consciousness, or—even more devastating—as full citizens of the rational domain that was his intellectual construct. Still, he did assail the Soame Jenyns treatise.

If we take "The Vanity of Human Wishes" as our sample of his work, we find it is Johnson's direct and almost unceasing traffic with abstractions that buys him the placidity of temperament he needs. The poem becomes our model of the period style of the mid-eighteenth century. Its style is heavily rhetorical, in the manner one thinks of as properly "Johnsonian," filled with the syntactical symmetries of strong repetition and parallelism, the Latinate verbs as well as nouns, the abstract indirection of uncharged, conventional epithets. The lines are strongly end-stopped, and doubly so at the end of each couplet. In short, the artificial character of neoclassical poem-making is being insisted upon. The medium of poetry—that is, the poem as a mediating agency coming between man and his experience—is exploited to the maximum. The more the poem can be crammed with the lifelessly conventional, with all that is of art rather than of life, the better. It is to be as far from imitative of life's particularities, as close to the artist exhibiting himself as artful, as the poet can manage. And Johnson can manage more than most, indeed more than almost anyone else in this way. His poem, then, is not only our model of period style of the mid-eighteenth century; it is a splendid, if not unique, example of how that style can be exploited with a self-consciousness and a consistency that verge on perfection. It may seem like a stereotype, but it is one of such brilliance that it merits being called unique, even if characterizing perfect typicality as something unique seems self-contradictory. I know of no example in our language of a conventional poetry that turns out to be so remarkably self-transcendent. However we may object to the staleness of this period style in others, Johnson presses its common qualities to a power which a less consistent use of them— or a use of them less consistently aimed at an end to which they were peculiarly adaptable—could never have achieved. And, clearly, the end to which I see these qualities so successfully adaptable is one created by Johnson's adherence to his classic vision, *his* special cherishing of bloodless abstractions.

Johnson's capacity to see so broadly and generally is permitted by the loftiness of his perch. His opening couplet is ponderously, majestically, characteristic: "Let observation, with extensive view, / Survey mankind, from China to Peru." The unforceful, polysyllabic, Latinate personification as his subject ("observation"), the general but again Latinate adjective ("extensive"), the weakly static verb ("survey"), the untroubled distance of the whole passage, all are typical of his controlled, dignified performance. The distancing is precisely the key: China to Peru observed in this single survey—one has to be a good distance away, far far up above it all, to encompass all this. It is thus proper for "observation" itself—rather than any person—to be the subject, in this master stroke of indirection. If this couplet accomplishes the broad sweep of space which Johnson's generality intends, a later couplet (ll. 223–24) similarly accomplishes the equally broad sweep of time: "All times their scenes of pompous woes afford, / From Persia's tyrant [Xerxes] to Bavaria's lord" (Charles Albert). We span eighteen centuries here as we spanned the continents earlier. And even here the spatial stretch from Persia to Bavaria is an impressive one—which may be why Johnson places his rulers geographically instead of naming them.

It is also true that it is often his practice in this poem to substitute a more general description or a euphemism for the name of the personage. It is another device to hold off any too specific or limiting a concern on our part: Persia's tyrant (how many there have been!) and Bavaria's lord (which one? or all?). The words which open this couplet and verse paragraph, "All times," emphasize the universality (in time as well as space) of the vanity ("pompous woes") Johnson is describing. And the uncharged verb, "afford," like the earlier "survey," in its inactivity sets the precedent for our restraint as we make our vast observation.

The notion of "All times," of "China to Peru," permits Johnson again and again to substitute the generic for the singular, the euphemism for the specific historical name. One device we note everywhere is the use of a series of general adjective-noun combinations, introduced by definite or, occasionally, indefinite articles. Thus in the tale of Wolsey's fall,

> At once is lost the pride of aweful state,
> The golden canopy, the glitt'ring plate,
> The regal palace, the luxurious board,
> The liv'ried army, and the menial lord.

(ll. 113–16)

Or, similarly, the death of Charles XII: "His death was destin'd to a barren strand, / A petty fortress, and a dubious hand" (ll. 219–20). No names are given here, or needed. The sameness and universality assure us that the generic will do. Our precise awareness of what has happened to "The vanquish'd hero" (again the generic, since Charles's name is not used except for the perfunctory mention of it at the start of this portrait) will have to depend on the editor's footnotes or our own historical knowledge. The generically veiled narrative, all of whose happenings are indirectly implied only, is everywhere characteristic in this poem. As Charles's victories are roughly (very roughly) enumerated, we must again fly to footnotes or history books to identify Frederick IV and Augustus II in the lines "Behold surrounding kings their pow'r combine, / And one capitulate, and one resign" (ll. 199–200). Once more we can note the lack of intensity in the weak Latinate verbs. But, in view of the universal purpose of his satire and the loftiness of his perspective, does Johnson need (or want) language more charged? Even the turning point in Charles's career is given to us by implication only, through an allusion which requires us to draw upon specific knowledge outside the poem:

> Stern Famine guards the solitary coast,
> And Winter barricades the realms of Frost;

> *He comes, not want and cold his course delay;—*
> *Hide, blushing Glory, hide Pultowa's day.*
>
> (ll. 207–10)

So indirect is the manner by which the implied narrative is presented that we are kept from witnessing any palpable action. The precise historical personages are transformed into blurry silhouettes carrying on their unindividualized universal actions. All intensity is precluded, as our responses are dulled to the level of contemplative detachment appropriate to Johnson's devices—a detachment that would seem to match his own. After all, he seems to have shoved every sort of rhetorical device and universalizing indirection between us and the single historical action. The use of stale personification as just that, without any attempt to vitalize it, reinforces the distance created by artifice. "Stern Famine," "Winter," and "blushing Glory" in the passage just quoted serve as obvious examples, especially as they work with *the* unnamed "solitary coast" or with *the* unnamed "realms of Frost" or with the dropping of the unqualified "Pultowa's." No wonder the story of Charles ends with the explicit reference to its exemplary function, to the universalizing expansion Johnson has given to the name and its deeds: "He left the name, at which the world grew pale, / To point a moral, or adorn a tale" (ll. 222–23).

But such decorous use of personification has been with us since the very outset of the poem, as we should have known from the initial "observation," with its "extensive view," which served as our first, generalized subject. Subsequent personifications—either proclaimed by capitalization or working more subtly in lower case—appear continually; and they are equally rhetorical, equally undramatic, equally decorous in their behavior, never exceeding the role prescribed for them by their initial definition. The verbs through which they act are only those that lie immanently within their own nominal meanings. More than the characters whose portraits appear in the poem, the personifications follow one another in their dehumanized way— "As treach'rous phantoms in the mist delude" (l. 9), if I may adapt a line to my own purposes.

The poem achieves its greatest power, however, not where these personifications are abandoned, but—on the contrary—where they are brilliantly pressed into a rare discourse, in which the language of universal personification becomes magnificently participatory without relinquishing its universal character, where language permits the most specialized of personified dramas. A strength is discovered in the very Latinisms themselves as they are forced to triumph over their own limitations, while still remaining true to their decorous self-discipline. Is there a better example of a conventional poetry succeeding through the total exploitation, rather than the rejection, of its stylistic commonplaces? Let me cite three examples early in the poem, two brief, one longer.

> With fatal heat impetuous courage glows,
> With fatal sweetness elocution flows,
> Impeachment stops the speaker's pow'rful breath,
> And restless fire precipitates on death.
>
> (ll. 17–20)

We move from courage (naturally, "impetuous courage") to elocution to the silencing action of impeachment, and then to the startling Latinate fitness of "precipitates," especially as predicated of "restless fire." There is a full and final story here, or rather many stories, all of which go this way, projected out of a hidden morality play.

Even more brilliantly compacted is the tale springing from the abstract drama a few lines later:

> Let Hist'ry tell where rival kings command,
> And dubious title shakes the madded land;
> When statutes glean the refuse of the sword,
> How much more safe the vassal than the lord.
>
> (ll. 29–32)

In the same tone and in a similar rhetoric of striking personification, the verse paragraph concludes with the grim observation that "confiscation's vultures hover round." The conflicts of disorderly rivalries repeated through political history and their woeful consequences on the lowly individuals trapped by them—all their stories—are conveyed by inhuman words and phrases like "dubious title," "madded land," and the verbal perfection of the entire line, "When statutes glean the refuse of the sword." The line is overpowering in the awesome completeness with which it so impersonally shows history's destructive propensities. All the myriads killed in battles not their own we can infer from those who are somehow overlooked ("refuse of the sword"), indeed those who are rejected by history as worthless —if we can give that word "refuse" all the dimensions it demands. Those left standing by the sword (now seen in terms of its peaceful analogue, the plowshare, if not the inevitable scythe of the grim reaper) remain only to be cut down by the laws promulgated to kill the captive remnants of the conquered kingdom. This much is yielded by the abstract precision of that line, "When statutes glean the refuse of the sword." How much in keeping with this historical clean sweep are "confiscation's vultures," with which the passage ends.

A lengthier and even more impressive example of indirect and depersonalized narrative occurs a few verse paragraphs later. It is worth quoting in full, though my interest centers on the last eight lines.

> *Unnumber'd suppliants crowd Preferment's gate,*
> *Athirst for wealth, and burning to be great;*
> *Delusive Fortune hears th' incessant call,*
> *They mount, they shine, evaporate, and fall.*
> *On ev'ry stage the foes of peace attend,*
> *Hate dogs their flight, and insult mocks their end.*
> *Love ends with hope, the sinking statesman's door*
> *Pours in the morning worshiper no more;*
> *For growing names the weekly scribbler lies,*
> *To growing wealth the dedicator flies,*
> *From ev'ry room descends the painted face,*
> *That hung the bright palladium of the place,*
> *And smok'd in kitchens, or in auctions sold,*
> *To better features yields the frame of gold;*
> *For now no more we trace in ev'ry line*
> *Heroic worth, benevolence divine:*
> *The form distorted justifies the fall,*
> *And detestation rids th' indignant wall.*

(ll. 73–90)

Here is portraiture, though it is universal portraiture without a name attached to it. We are dealing, after all, with "Unnumber'd suppliants" who manage to "mount," "shine, evaporate, and fall." The universalizing use of the definite article (as in the relation of the "sinking statesman" to the former "morning worshiper" no longer being poured in by the door, or to the scribbler and the dedicator) is everywhere evident enough. But it is the animated drama of the replacement of the fallen man's portrait with his successor's that is so remarkable. The combination of personified subjects and Latinate diction accomplishes the grotesque, almost surrealist, masque. We note that it is in the active voice that "the painted face," no longer capable of protecting those on whom it shines, "descends" from the wall of every room. The same gold frame "yields" to a more deserving portrait, the new "palladium," now subject to the same flattery as its fallen predecessor. There is a superb, if economical, strength of implication in lines like "To better features yields the frame of gold," the grudging sense of "yield" overcome by the justification for the change in the spectacularly bitter couplet that follows. The symbol must fall with the man: "The form distorted justifies the fall." How enriched becomes the sense of art imitating life, the fall of the painting justified by the fall of its object of imitation. But the strength of the passage derives from the notion of the "form distorted" as it relates to the changed attitudes, dictated by political fortune, toward his features as they reflect "worth" and "benevolence." Indeed, the features themselves are seen as transformed (since *they* had earlier been seen as the "better features"); the "form" in the portrait has, in effect, become "distorted." Political fashion dictates aesthetic response; indeed, it creates the nature of the object itself.[1] The finality of the last line of the passage is the ultimate success of pathetic fallacy, as it effectively juxtaposes the polysyllabic ("detestation," "indignant") and the simply direct ("rids," "wall"). It is the insult after the injury, with detestation the accomplice to the indignant wall, now safely rid for good of its suddenly unwanted burden.

The drama, complete and subtle, has been consummated in these eight lines. And the personifications have carried forth its action, though always in accordance with the decorous limits of its abstract meaning. Johnson, clearly, is carrying out the principle which allowed him to justify Pope's use of the sylphs in "The Rape of the Lock": "Discord may raise a mutiny, but Discord cannot conduct a march,

---

[1] I cannot help being reminded of the bitter line in Shakespeare's Sonnet 71, in which the speaker asks his beloved to reflect the fickleness of man's destiny: "But let your love even with my life decay."

nor besiege a town."[2] Here is a literalistic theory of metaphor, one perhaps too literalistic, too limited by common sense. Whatever our feelings about its prosaism, however, we must admit that it is peculiarly—and ideally—suited to poetry with the characteristics we find in "The Vanity of Human Wishes."

If it is not difficult to justify Johnson's poem in the light of his theory governing the employment of abstractions as characters, it is indeed difficult for me to justify this sort of poetry and the theory that supports it in the light of my own assault on universality, my governing insistence on the autonomy of the radical particular. Why not simply relegate this poem, with others I *have* so relegated, to the pseudo-poetry of pure rhetoric, produced by what Yeats called "the will trying to do the work of the imagination"? The more consistently distanced the abstractions of the poem and the more consistently rhetorical its nature, the more I should reject its ethical evasion of poetry's existential function.

My point here, however, is that the brilliance and force with which Johnson manipulates the muted drama of his abstractions creates, through the willfulness of its very evasions, our awareness of the existential pressures that manifest themselves in their so rigorously enforced absence. Johnson so diligently sustains his lofty perch only because he wants to keep plenty of distance between himself and the awesome flood of individual existences. He dare not descend—and, from his perspective in the sky, it would be a literal descent—to the palpable struggles of discrete persons. From the lunar sphere he can see only the general outlines, the universalizing abstractions, of our sublunary lives which display only particularized characters and happenings. My claim is that Johnson has a need for the universal as a

---

[2] The full passage from *The Life of Pope* is worth quoting: "The employment of allegorical persons always excites conviction of its own absurdity: they may produce effects, but cannot conduct actions; when the phantom is put in motion, it dissolves; thus Discord may raise a mutiny, but Discord cannot conduct a march, nor besiege a town." There is an equally forceful passage in his *Milton*, which pronounces the same theory of metaphor: "To exalt causes into agents, to invest abstract ideas with form, and animate them with activity has always been the right of poetry. But such airy beings are for the most part suffered only to do their natural office, and retire. Thus Fame tells a tale and Victory hovers over a general or perches on a standard; but Fame and Victory can do no more. To give them any real employment or ascribe to them any material agency is to make them allegorical no longer, but to shock the mind by ascribing effects to nonentity."

bulwark against confronting the threatening particulars that loom before us asking to be confronted; it is a need amply demonstrated by the painfully inconsistent judgments in his "Preface to Shakespeare."

Calling for "just representations of general nature" and for the overlooking of "particular manners," Johnson celebrates Shakespeare's treatment of characters (moved by "general passions and principles") who are not individuals, but who represent a species. But he also pays tribute to Shakespeare's power to exhibit "the real state of sublunary nature" instead of making an arbitrary selection from it in order to satisfy an artificially exclusive sorting out of life's confounded fullness. Here is the "sublunary" or the particular as the proper object of poetry's imitation, even if its disorderliness seems resistant to the critic's lunar desire to impose the limits of human reason. For in the "sublunary," however our reasonable temperaments would have it, "many mischiefs and many benefits are done and hindered without design": it is a "chaos of mingled purposes and casualties." The "casual" replaces the "causal" which man's lunar reason, in its persistent anthropomorphism, would impose upon the "chaos" of "sublunary nature" around him. This is not the place to argue the confusing ins and outs of Johnson's criticism (and there are many other passages that reveal this doubleness).[3] But, even seen this briefly, his struggle, in his critical theorizing, with problems of particularity and universality reveals some nagging dilemmas that are reflected in the generalized, rhetorical poetry he tried so steadfastly to produce: Johnson wants to commend those works that do not stoop to particularity but treat only the generic; and yet he seems from time to time to fear that all we really have is a chaos of raging particulars and that the generic is an arbitrary imposition of a human mind stubbornly holding onto its order and proclaiming that order to be the objective principle of the moral universe. This is the Johnson who distrusts "bookishness" and, with it, the intrusions of the conventional categories that make experience too circumscribed.[4]

The question he seems unable to resolve is whether we dare look upon particular reality unless we interpose those artifices that tame it,

[3] See my essay on this precise subject, "Fiction, Nature, and Literary Kinds in Johnson's Criticism of Shakespeare," *Eighteenth-Century Studies* 4 (1970–71):184–98.

[4] We can recall also his rejection of Milton's use of mythology or his preference for Shakespeare's "forest," with its "weeds and brambles," to Addison's "correct and regular" garden.

blur individual outlines until they merge into the general, to the point where we can bear the looking. At times he feels the neoclassical tug so deeply, and then, with all the dogmatism so many associate with him, he retreats from the streaks of the tulip. But, at other times, he feels the awareness of the candid realist that all such mediation by universals robs experience of our honest vision of its immediacy. The universalizing impulse of the desperate neoclassical world that we discussed by way of Pope may have been sensed by Johnson to be a necessary preservative for a comfortable (that is, comfortably dogmatic or anthropomorphic) metaphysic, always threatened by the stubborn contingency of unfettered experience. As neoclassicist, he wanted to retain the comforts of dogmatism, so soothing to human reason; and, as terrorized individual human trapped by time, he seems to have sensed the fraudulent basis of these comforts, the terrors lurking beyond them for which they could not account and which they could not begin to obliterate. There seems, then, to have been in him a subversive nominalist who would not be convinced even by the order the neoclassicist claimed to be able to supply. Surely this is also the private Johnson we sometimes see in the pages of his biographer. I find him in his works as well.

All this is meant to account for the impression, given to me, at least, by "The Vanity of Human Wishes," that Johnson's excellently consistent management of his artificialities and his abstractions is a way of mediating the intensities of experience, of preventing himself from indulging them; that what is so studiously left out of his poem asserts its effect upon the poet by the very studiousness of his omission, by the almost excessive concentration upon the abstractions that distance his (and, one may hope, our) responses. If Latin restraint is the dominant feature of the poem, horror—though never quite glimpsed—may be its underside.

I see Johnson's need for distance as the dominant motive for his self-conscious impersonality. This impersonality, which is responsible for the meditative transcendence that directs the poem, is even more Latinate than the Latin source of the poem. Next to this "Vanity of Human Wishes," the original, the Tenth Satire of Juvenal of which this is an "imitation," seems quite immediate in the directness of its rancor and in the particular presence of the peculiar personality of its author, our biting satirist. Again and again we sense him there, in his own mocking voice. But whatever Johnson's superficial borrowings from Juvenal in organization, subjects, and even words and phrases—and these are considerable throughout—he gives us a totally different sense of voice: dignified, unmoved by specific events, the voice of a universal (almost godlike) observer who sees all and sees beyond all, and who sadly understands and accepts all he sees. Perhaps this change in voice is what makes Johnson's Christian stoicism at the end of the poem finally more persuasive than Juvenal's Roman stoicism. Whether this change in voice also suggests evasions of the special ugliness displayed by particular characters engaged in particular actions is another, if more searching, question of the sort that I have been asking all along.

So steady is Johnson's hand in commanding restraint that his slightest lapses shriek their inconsistency to us. There are two troublesome passages that reflect the Juvenalian spirit more than the Johnsonian. Curiously, that dispassionate, delicately wrought passage I examined earlier on the rise and fall of political fashion is followed immediately by a direct onslaught on British politics:

> But will not Britain hear the last appeal,
> Sign her foe's doom, or guard her fav'rite's zeal?
> Through Freedom's sons no more remonstrance rings,
> Degrading nobles and controlling kings;
> Our supple tribes repress their patriot throats,
> And ask no questions but the price of votes;
> With weekly libels and septennial ale,
> Their wish is full to riot and to rail.
>
> (ll. 91–98)

Thus, after one of the most subtle manipulations of indirection, of the implied drama of abstractions, Johnson blurts out this painfully direct attack. Here suddenly there are specific objects against which the satire is directed, which necessarily turns the satirist into a specific subject, a personality. The satire becomes local rather than universal; it is bound by the special circumstances that create the situation he inveighs against. In this way the satire, rather than being what Shakespeare called "hugely politic," becomes itself a "fool of time," as much so as those against whom it lodges its complaint. In another context, of course, the satire of reform is quite defensible. But in this poem, directed as it is at exposing the vanity (in both senses of the word) of all human wishes, the issues are beyond solution by political reform. Indeed, reform would only remove the discovery of its vanity to the next stage of our observation. And this our speaker must well know. Why, then, expend his anger over what, reformed or unreformed, is—by its political nature—the demonstrated instrument of folly?

Or there is the single couplet that comments upon the undeserved fate of learning represented by the death of Archbishop Laud: "Around his tomb let Art and Genius weep, / But hear his death, ye blockheads, hear and sleep" (ll. 173–74). The undisguised anger in this final line reminds us how rarely, in contrast to Juvenal, Johnson addresses his audience directly. Indeed, unlike Juvenal, he uses the second person (referring to his readers) or the first person (referring to himself) almost not at all. Consequently, where his words are spit out at us this way, as they are here, we recognize a serious breach of his dominant intention. I want to insist, however, that these passages of Johnson's personal and local intrusion, by their exceptional status in the poem, only demonstrate the general tone while they violate it.

How does this lofty meditation proceed from subject to subject? Johnson borrows from Juvenal the five vanities he treats and the order in which they come between the introduction and the conclusion: wealth (and the power allied to wealth), learning, conquest by war, long life, and beauty. There is not, in Johnson any more than in Juvenal, any clear argumentative connection or progression among these varied vanities. Why these five? And why this order rather than another? But, from his universalizing perch, Johnson sees these single vanities as similarly reducible to the general vanity of all human wishes. From this special vantage point the several parts of the poem achieve subtle relations among one another which they otherwise lack. The poem is a journey through time and space; it is a vain search for an unvain wish, with each of the five vanities—treated generally and in terms of historical examples—serving as a stop along the unprogressive way.

The first of the wishes treated, wealth and power, would seem most easily shown to be vain. From the standpoint of the great world and the shaky public life in it, the modest small world and the private life appear relatively secure:

> *When statutes glean the refuse of the sword,*
> *How much more safe the vassal than the lord,*
> *Low skulks the hind beneath the rage of pow'r,*
> *And leaves the wealthy traitor in the Tow'r,*
> *Untouch'd his cottage, and his slumbers sound,*
> *Though confiscation's vultures hover round.*
>
> (ll. 31–36)

In beginning with the immodest ambition of the wish for wealth and power, we are encouraged by this passage to look forward expectantly to less pretentious wishes as we move toward less patently vain subjects. (But of course we are being deliberately and dialectically misled: the modest private life seems safe from vanity only momentarily, in contrast to the obvious perils of unlimited worldly ambition. Its turn to demonstrate its own vanity will shortly come.) After dispensing with the first wish as intolerably vain, we turn with some relief to the second, to the reduced pretensions of the scholar in his pursuit of truth rather than power. It is, however, also the case that he is anxious for "renown"; and it is this thirst for fame that can lead to "grief or danger." So all is not really modest or private yet, and the vanity of the wish is to be expected. That expectation is fulfilled: the scholar's wish is no less vain than that of the seeker after wealth and its power.

The return, in the third wish, to the great and public world leads to a far more ambitious and reckless desire for self-aggrandizement, the warrior's insatiable hunger for conquest. Here to an exaggerated degree is the immodesty with which these wishes began, the polar extreme of the political drive. Its fate is predetermined by what we have seen. If the third wish is a distillate of the prideful assumptions of the first, so the fourth improves upon the second as the final, unqualified pursuit of the least imposing, most modest, private wish: "Enlarge my life with multitude of days, / In health, in sickness, thus the suppliant prays" (ll. 255–56). We are moving toward the argument a fortiori for the vanity of all human wishes, toward the end of the futile search for an unvain wish. All that is asked for is a peaceful, uninterrupted, and hence lengthy existence. It is as if, remembering the earlier claim about the safety of the vassal, with untouched cottage and sound slumbers, we are now forced to discover that his wretchedness is equal with that of the lord. It is here we find what really is the epigraph of this all-embracing, pessimistic poem: that man "Hides from himself his state, and shuns to know, / That life protracted is protracted woe."

Johnson moves to the a fortiori in two stages, revealing that, even in this minimal assertion of private desire, there are refinements in simplicity. The unqualified call for long life (in sickness as well as in health) shows on its face the grief it holds in store. And we are shown the physical and moral evils usually attendant upon "protracted life." But, to make his presentation complete and his argument truly from the strongest, he must consider even that unusual "protracted life" which is unaccompanied by these evils:

> But grant, the virtues of a temp'rate prime
> Bless with an age exempt from scorn or crime;
> An age that melts with unperceiv'd decay,
> And glides in modest Innocence away;
> Whose peaceful day Benevolence endears,
> Whose night congratulating Conscience cheers;
> The gen'ral fav'rite as the gen'ral friend:
> Such age there is, and who shall wish its end?
>
> (ll. 291–98)

"Yet ev'n on this her load Misfortune flings": this heavily laden, almost onomatopoetic line announces the futility of even this last possible wish. Even so idyllic a "protracted life" is also, according to the universal formula, reducible to the "protracted woe" from which only "pitying Nature" can sign "the last release."

We have, then, rocked from the great world to the small and back to more extreme forms of each, moving climactically to the vanity of even man's least demanding and, thus, his most promising wish. Johnson, in pursuing his generalized melancholy, has managed to create a meaningful argument out of the several wishes upon which he loftily and sadly meditates. The critic can only apologize, however, for the fact that Johnson follows this point beyond which nothing further is possible, a point reached through careful maneuver, with the anticlimactic passage on the fifth wish, physical beauty of person. The apology must rest on Johnson's too faithful adherence to Juvenal's model. It is perhaps proof of the stronger discursive sinews in Johnson's treatment of the four wishes that his section on beauty seems so much more an unfortunate appendage than does Juvenal's.

This strength in Johnson springs, we have seen, from his openly rhetorical exploitation of these vanities for his uniform and reductive generalization. One could maintain that there are not movements from particularity to generality in the poem, but only movements from one level of generality to another. There would then be no particularity except of the most obviously disguised sort, the particularity that serves only as a front for its generality and thus abdicates from true particularity. Viewed this way, three levels of generality can be distinguished, even if—since all of them finally *are* generalities—they collapse into one another. There is the openly rhetorical pure generality in which the vain wish is presented, there is the brief mention of a host of historical examples, each only barely mentioned, and there is the detailed portraiture of single personages. But as we have seen in the case of "Swedish Charles," even this furthest descent to particularity is never really particular. As we could see equally in the cases (and they are literally *cases*) of Wolsey or Xerxes, the case is to interest us only because of its exemplary function ("To point a moral, or adorn a tale"). There is never any uniqueness in the case, as we have observed in Johnson's reliance on nouns converted to the generic by the use of the definite or indefinite article but rarely the demonstrative adjective.

> At once is lost the pride of aweful state,
> The golden canopy, the glitt'ring plate,
> The regal palace, the luxurious board,
> The liv'ried army, and the menial lord.
>
> (ll. 113–16)

We are constantly given the "the," meaning "any," rather than "this" or "that" one, meaning peculiar to the historical circumstances surrounding the special instance of Cardinal Wolsey.

We can say, then, that Johnson's lofty meditative perch permits him, first, only the blurring outlines that persuade one to generalization, to the sameness of the objects under his "extensive view." Not only do all examples of a single vain wish seem similar but, at the highest level of generalization, all wishes seem similarly vain. We can, second, imagine our speaker descending a bit to make out the separate identities of historical figures, but barely: perhaps only enough to name them and speak roughly about their situations, as they blur into a group representative of the vanity of the wish. Thus the accumulation of Villiers, Harley, Wentworth, and Hyde (ll. 129–31) or of Croesus, Marlborough, and Swift (ll. 313–18). Or he may make his furthest descent to those lengthy portraits already discussed. For even these are absorbed at once into the higher levels of generality which they are to serve. As we recall the implicit, even cryptic, nature of the historical allusions that attach to them, we may even doubt that the use of the specified name is really indispensable to their function, even if we prefer the comfort of recognition. After all, how much less effective than Wolsey's or Charles's story is the generalized portrait of the unnamed universal type, such as the "sinking statesman," the "young enthusiast" of learning, or the long-lived "dotard"? Indeed, how different is the one kind from the other, except for the occasional prodding of a familiar name or allusion? Are they even two kinds? Even the detailed historical portrait, after all, is immediately referred to the next level of generality, that of other possible candidates for similar treatment, and finally to pure generality, to the abstract treatment of the naked wish itself. And this wish, in turn, is subject to the single generality which predicates the vanity of all wishes alike. The title reminds us that it is the wishes that seem to be plural, while the vanity to which they are reduced is, to our despair, singular.

This unison which overwhelms all apparent variety allows the sense of exhaustion, the helplessness and finality with which the conclusion comes upon us:[5]

> *Where then shall Hope and Fear their objects find?*
> *Must dull suspense corrupt the stagnant mind?*
> *Must helpless man, in ignorance sedate,*
> *Roll darkling down the torrent of his fate?*
>
> (ll. 343–46)

[5] I want to concede once more that the effect of exhaustion (and exhaustiveness) would be the greater if the order of the wishes (dictated by Juvenal) were altered to permit the wish, a fortiori, for a healthful long life, to be the last possible wish, the necessary end to the vain search for the un-vain wish; only after this should such an inclusive possibility as that raised by these questions be uttered. This is merely to repeat my dissatisfaction with the placement (or perhaps the inclusion at all) of the passage on beauty. Surely it is by then too late in the poem to introduce so obviously and superficially vain a wish as this one—especially after the finality of the one that has preceded it.

This un-Christian suggestion, almost worthy of a Camus, is rejected for a Christian stoicism, even though the mere posing of the questions suggests that they are the most immediate logical consequence of the futilities we have witnessed as fellow-observer with our speaker. He denies the inevitability of such a consequence and calls off any further search ("Enquirer, cease"), although the denial is hardly meant to produce a strong alternative, any more than the calling off of the search is meant to dispute the data he has produced. What is remarkable about the religious alternative is that it is not impressively useful at all, even if we are told not to deem it "vain." Finally here is something *not* vain, even if there is not much he can say about what it is good for. "Still raise for good the supplicating voice": the "Still" is powerfully, if sadly, concessive here in its acknowledgment that we cannot expect to see results. Regardless of what comes, then, we accept it as "the best"—and how crucially different is this sense of "the best" from that of Epistle One of Pope's *Essay on Man*!

Here is the classic visionary as God's justifiably melancholy man who shuns the tragic. The data he has gathered surely are suggestive of extremity, although they produce acceptance rather than rebellion. He has his dossier, as Ivan Karamazov will have his; but our meditator in the "Vanity" returns no tickets to an Augustinian God, preferring to accept His absurd rules.[6] According to these rules, we cannot make a human wish unvain, but we can put up with its and our vanity: "With these celestial Wisdom calms the mind, / And makes the happiness she does not find" (ll. 367–68). It is this need to evade the undeniable logic of the extreme consequences of his data, the need to accept the unacceptable, to give over the dossier and search no more, that forces Johnson to his grand strategy of the universal and suggests to me that this strategy is a mask for his desperation, even as it may allow him (at least through the poem) to put that desperation aside.

Perhaps I can best justify my feeling that this is really a desperate poem by dealing with the assumption behind the strategy that insists upon the total mitigation of abstraction and generality, together with the universalizing rhetoric they permit. There is a single metaphorical assumption in the poem; and once again it is a metaphorical assumption that works both ways as it denies itself. All the subjects in the

[6] My language makes it clear that I see Johnson here as very close to Kierkegaard's knight of infinite resignation.

poem, we have seen, are abstractions, indeed even personifications—equally so, as Johnson works them out, whether they are abstract nouns or the names of historical personages. In using them this way, the poem is assuming (metaphorically) that such generalities are all that is, that they do contain all the particular realities which they absorb (or, perhaps, merely veil). The assumption is that personifications work, that they are adequate to reality, so that we merely have to focus upon them, our rationality thus retaining its sense of order, its dispassionate impersonality. There is, then, no need to study particulars.

But the cumbersome, disturbing data of the poem produce the nagging awareness that the personifications are not enough, that they do not work; not if we dared to specify, to make the precise extensions into the raw pain of the individual case as uniquely felt, instead of merging it into universals that obliterate the fearful, bloody realities now buried in unwritten footnotes. Still, the poem is proof that the personifications *are* enough after all—at least here and for now. They manage to account for the particular reality that evades them. So, in a way similar to what we noted about the double intentions of Johnson's criticism—at once wanting "the real state of sublunary nature" and wanting to set it morally straight for reason's sake—he uses his abstractions to hold off particularities and his personal involvement with them, even as he subtly acknowledges the continued unassimilated existence of all that he is using his abstractions to bypass. By thus working doubly, his abstractions make it possible for him not to be overcome by realities even as they remind him that those realities are there to be lived with. He may use abstractions to avoid confrontation, thus preserving sanity, though the strained persistence with which he clings to them is indicative of what lurks beyond and even within them.

Not only is this the eighteenth-century poem par excellence in its consistent manipulation of the period style, but it thereby becomes the necessary mechanism to allow the eighteenth-century period vision (which that style so excellently befits) with its idolatry of universals to stand unchallenged. Still, the poem itself, with its poet, indirectly proves to be the profound challenger of that vision through the very means used to preserve it.

An ultimately classic extension of one aspect of this vision may be seen in the late elegy, "On the Death of Mr. Robert Levet." It is as if Johnson is taking his treatment of that most modest wish—

> But grant, the virtues of a temp'rate prime
> Bless with an age exempt from scorn or crime;
> An age that melts with unperceiv'd decay,
> And glides in modest Innocence away—

and showing us its less grief-sticken possibilities. For this is precisely the nature of Levet's life and death as Johnson describes it—again with an unmatched exploitation of the universalizing possibilities which the rhetorical style of his period afforded him. The lyric possibilities of the elegy are rejected for a language of uncharged epithets and verbs, perhaps lyrically dead but invoked only in order to produce an even rarer sort of life. It is the life of the anti-extreme, the utter commonness of routinized man living the life of routine service, faithfully, reliably, incessantly performed—until the end when, almost automatically, without notice, there *is* cessation. And yet the poem forces us to see that there may be nothing rarer than just this persistent commonness. No wonder that the flatly generic language (e.g., "The busy day, the peaceful night"), far from disappointing us, should impress with its rightness, as just what is wanted.

We see Levet not as a single creature so much as the human possibility of routine process. Levet is one of "Our social comforts," undramatic, without discontinuity in his life, a totally unexceptional man. Camus to the contrary notwithstanding, Sisyphus-man is here made gently heroic, his life given a meaning by its very routineness of continuity. Johnson need not blink the fact that he was "Obscurely wise, and coarsely kind," with his "merit unrefin'd," possessed of the "single talent" (of course in both senses of "talent"). "The modest wants of ev'ry day" are met by equally modest "toil of ev'ry day." Cotidian man has only a "narrow round" for his virtues to pursue. But this confined circle of duty is remarkable for that unremarkable completeness, enemy to discontinuity. For these small virtues "Nor made a pause, nor left a void." Like the picture of blessed aging in "The Vanity of Human Wishes," "His frame was firm, his pow'rs were bright, / Though now his eightieth year was nigh."

The death itself is as gradual, as undramatic, as the life, with which it seems utterly continuous:

> *Then with no throbbing fiery pain,*
> *No cold gradations of decay,*
> *Death broke at once the vital chain,*
> *And freed his soul the nearest way.*

With Levet all change has always occurred "the nearest way," almost undetected ("The busy day, the peaceful night, / Unfelt, uncounted, glided by"). It is this view of his death as undramatized natural process, continuous with his life, that gives special strength to the sixth line of the poem: "See Levet to the grave descend." We see him before us moving downward into the earth, the active verb "descend" suggesting the routine and volitional nature of the act. Nowhere will we be closer to the vision of Tennyson's Tithonus, the communal vision of continuity and routine: "Man comes and tills the field and lies beneath." Here is a vision of the private death which might dispel the terrors from which Johnson suffered.

But if Levet is seen as the ideal classic existent, Johnson can never be more than the classic visionary. In his dramatic self-consciousness, revealed even in this poem, is his realization that he can never be a Levet. As soon as the poet sees Levet this completely in his modest routine, he is rendered incapable of being Levet, who would have to lose it all once he realized his pattern and meaning. In this way Levet serves Johnson's sanity here as the abstractions served him in the "Vanity." Levet provides the pattern of existence (indeed existence abstracted into pure pattern) which permits the self-consciousness, the dramatic discontinuities in all experience outside his own to be momentarily reduced to order.

Here, in a pre-Wordsworthian mood, Johnson uses Levet as his alternative way to the way of extremity, thus permitting acceptance of the capriciousness and the disorderly particularity of "the real state of sublunary nature." This mask of order does not demand the unnatural artifice that Pope's does. But it also works to keep at a distance the pain and anguish of "the man of flesh and bones." The poet can use his poem, so specially and scrupulously constructed, to prevent the private involvement of his self, for his artistic care has persuaded him to make his peace with even the worst of existence. But *not* through ignoring it is this peace made. Which is why the classic visionary, thanks to the self-consciousness which damns him never to be a classic existent, remains hopelessly (but hopefully, for art) in a state of dialogue. The desperate private case may be transfigured to the universal nature of things, but only as we recognize that the stoic description is also the indispensable stoic tactic, the one way of making oneself and keeping oneself resigned and acceptant, self-consciously almost self-deceived, but faithful.

The fusing of all these forces in the simple figure of Levet makes that character into something like Johnson's equivalent of Michael or the leech-gatherer, performing "the common routine" (in a key phrase used by T. S. Eliot) in the service of the human community. The bloodless abstractions have prepared the way for the return to man, for another consideration of all that is all too human and, once again, time-ridden.

II

The Retreat from Extremity

Through the Embrace of
the Natural Human Community

6

William Wordsworth and the *Felix Culpa*

There are those who would dispute Wordsworth's claim to admission to the classic vision as I am defining it. Not that his vision fails to have affirmative elements in it—far from it—nor that he fails to retreat from extremity. Indeed, many readers feel him to be in full flight from extremity at the best or, at the worst, never to have known of its existence, the very possibility of its existence, at all. From the start I have insisted on the awareness of the extremity one chooses not to confront as prerequisite to the classic vision. Mature reconciliation may be one thing, but mere blandness (or is it blindness?) is something else.

This suspicion of Wordsworth's visionary inadequacy was apparent, for example, even in that celebrated volume we might think of as a belated *Festschrift*, produced for the centennial of his death.[1] Even on an occasion of such ritualistic idolatry, two of the more exciting essays address themselves explicitly to Wordsworth's apparent or real failure to have a keen enough vision to be relevant to the darker awarenesses of the contemporary world. Lionel Trilling (in "Wordsworth and the Iron Time") may be less unhappy than Douglas Bush (in "Wordsworth: A Minority Report") with Wordsworth's evasions of the problem of evil and the crisis of despair, but the two seem equally concerned with—and uneasy about—what Wordsworth seems not to see. To Trilling the quietism of Wordsworth's "cheerful faith" may seem to promise a therapeutic alternative to the melodramatic tendencies, the drivenness, of the contemporary polar consciousness (which is what Trilling's idol, Arnold, spoke of as the "soothing

[1] *Wordsworth: Centenary Studies Presented at Cornell and Princeton Universities*, ed. Gilbert T. Dunklin (Princeton: Princeton University Press, 1951).

voice" of "Wordsworth's healing power"); but this entire defense of Wordsworth rests on the concession that there are moral and existential depths—so central to modern experience—which Wordsworth's sensibility was incapable of sounding, or even envisaging. Most moderns, possessed of a more illiberal imagination than Trilling's, are less patient than he with these incapacities.

It is probably our awareness of Wordsworth's governing limitations, the attention we pay to his untragic assumptions about man's relation to nature, that causes us to emphasize—as we commonly do —the monistic philosophic assumptions on which many of his poems rest. Indeed, even some dedicated Wordsworthians among us tend to reduce his poems and the claims that can be made about their greatness to the optimistic promise found in the simplism of his "philosophy of nature" as they find it embodied in what they think of as the most representative (most properly "Wordsworthian") of them. This limited reading of Wordsworth leads to the common rejection of the poet that Wordsworth later became and for some time remained: the simple Wordsworth who is "Nature's Priest"—Wordsworth the monist, believer in man's natural purity (or natural piety)—should not have matured (or decayed), with poetical elegances, into the austere, orthodox didact, at once properly Virgilian and properly Christian. Somehow the Wordsworthian pietist complains about the Laureate's sellout to Christian affirmation while he extols nostalgically the mild fervor of the early, unchurchly affirmation of nature's immediacy and transcendence. Our darker contemporary spirits, however, like Douglas Bush in his essay (which is really a majority rather than a minority report on Wordsworth), could very well view the later sellout to easy affirmation as but a slightly changed version of the earlier sellout to just as easy an affirmation.

But Wordsworth's assumptions are, of course, not so simplistic, nor is his view of man—either in his natural or in his humanly unnatural dimension—so oblivious to all that darkens our vision. He does see that the problem rests in man's humanness as well as his naturalness —that is, in the fact that man is cursed by that which he does not share with nature as well as being blessed by that which he shares with her. Even so early and unsophisticated a poem as "Lines Written in Early Spring"—in contrast to the more singleminded nature worship of poems like "The Tables Turned"—reveals a curious wavering between man's involvement with nature and his separation from her.

William Wordsworth and the *Felix Culpa*

The "thousand blended notes" the poet hears assures us of nature's harmony, the harmony that carries through the poem in its contrast to man's discord ("What man has made of man") which causes the poet to lament. Apparently just outside the poem, beckoning but rejected by the poet, is "the still, sad music of humanity" which was the cause of the major conversion in "Tintern Abbey." But the poet, though human, is—for the occasion—joined to nature.

> *To her fair works did Nature link*
> *The human soul that through me ran;*
> *And much it grieved my heart to think*
> *What man has made of man.*

Thanks to—or cursed by—his human soul, the poet is outside nature, but that soul is momentarily plugged into nature's harmonious network. Thus his very union with nature carries with it evidence of his normal separateness from her. Nevertheless, the poem issues from the moment and the perspective of his naturalization. He speaks, then, out of an awareness of both worlds. Momentarily a part of the natural community, he can comment sadly on the state of his human community. With his soul linked to nature's fair works, the poet must view man's disharmony with regret. With his soul so linked, he can also sense, from the inside, nature's blended joys. The next three quatrains treat three natural objects into which the poet, from his preferred position, reads the consciousness of joy.

But the poet, as the human who is momentarily naturalized, does not totally ignore the inhuman (or rather pre-human) character of nature. He refrains from claiming, uncritically, that these objects actually feel the pleasures that his mood attributes to them. He remains one crucial step short of the indulgence of the pathetic fallacy. He claims, not that "every flower / Enjoys the air it breathes," but only that " 'tis my faith that every flower / Enjoys the air it breathes." Similarly, he acknowledges that he "cannot measure" the birds' thoughts, though their every motion "seemed [to the poet] a thrill of pleasure." Finally, watching the twigs catching the breeze, "I must think, do all I can, / That there was pleasure there." The "must" and the "do all I can" may merely be padding in what is admittedly a weak poem; but they may also indicate the poet's common-sense resistance to the extravagant imputation of self-consciousness to natural objects ("mute insensate things" in the third *Lucy* poem) luckily deprived of it. For there is an enormous amount of poetic and human self-consciousness in the poem. The poet sees his human predicament and his more than human desire: he wants both the harmony of nature and the human capacity for self-consciousness which could experience the joy of such harmony. He does not, in the poem, deny the possibility that nature may have the harmony without being able to know it and feel it and that humanity may have the capacity to know and to feel though it brings only disharmony. The poet, his human soul momentarily linked to nature's fair work, can—for the occasion—both have the consciousness and feel the harmony. Even so, it can only lead him to the further sad awareness of the human disharmony that surrounds and, therefore, must follow this moment. This awareness is also his acknowledgment that man *is*, after all, outside nature and shut off from her harmony. Such is the price of his self-consciousness. So, moved by the dichotomy between man and nature, the poet is scrupulous not to impute joy to nature, but to see himself, in the faith to which his sadness has driven him ("I must think, do all I can"), as having to impute such joy, whether there is any objective basis for it or not. The poem is a subjective confession, not a metaphysical claim.

Only in the final quatrain, in the hypothetical "ifs" which are the consequences of his faith, does the poet dare suggest the possibility that perhaps what he has imputed to nature may really be there: perhaps nature *is* holy:

> If this belief from heaven be sent,
> If such be Nature's holy plan,
> Have I not reason to lament
> What man has made of man?

The last line is converted to refrain, now newly justified by the possibilities opened up by the hypothetical hope: "What if all that I have claimed for nature's inherent consciousness truly was there? Then we would have the sort of teleological construct that could insist upon harmony and consciousness (like mine, momentarily, in this poem)." The either/or of subject and object could be breached and human disharmony could be seen as a serious perversion of the natural order. For all distance between the natural and the human community would vanish. Domesticate the natural, make it one with us, and it can become our model instead of merely remaining that insensate "other" into which, via a pathetic fallacy admitted to be fallacious, we can read our wishful thoughts as we seek to convert an alien world into our natural home. Still, the poet, in his self-consciousness, nowhere allows his "faith" to move him beyond those final "ifs."

Clearly, we are still trapped within what, from my earlier discussions, I might call the Kantian question, that central dilemma of the earlier eighteenth century which produced the rich, added dimensions I claimed to find in Pope and Johnson. The dogmatic certainty of a rational, God-structured universe rested upon the anthropomorphic assurance that objective order truly existed out there as a comforting reflection of the rational order of the human mind, that God was as smart a rational architect as the best of us, as smart as Newton. And, ranged against such security, the unavoidable skepticism of the time-ridden "man of flesh and bones" prompts the Hume-like fear that our claims to objective order are just such projections of mental constructs upon the elusive, sliding, alien somethings out there, in order to reduce them to the shape and dimensions needed for our comfort as we seek to live among them. We have seen Pope and Johnson covertly concerned, in their different ways, about the possibility that the rationalist's claim to order was not really sustained in the nature of things but was a universalizing projection of his rage for order. As subject of perception, the rationalist named his world and attributed substance to his names, though in so doing he might have been telling us more about his mind than about the objects contemplated by that mind. What if the object resisted the dogmatic impositions by the subject, its substance remaining independent of his names for it? The Kantian alternative to eighteenth-century dogmatics acknowledges such resistance by the object but insists on the subject's power to impose its order even as it insists that such imposition not be confused with an objective, independently grounded structure. So we have seen our eighteenth-century writers attempt to persuade themselves of a universal order while they nourish the doubt that kills—or that would kill if the human imagination did not construct substitute ways of living with this doubt.

Insecurity about the cosmic architecture threatened man with exclusion from his world. If the world did not answer to his dream, if its shape did not reflect his own inward shapings, then—whatever it might be that lurked out there on its own—it held the threat of an indifference that would leave him alienated from it. The collapse of the eighteenth-century intellectual monolith left man homeless. For the anthropomorphic claim of the naïve Realist, by definition, assumed a universe that was the mirror of the human mind: mind and universe were made for one another, mind tailor-made for universe if one believed the metaphysical claim of the Realist or universe tailor-made for mind if one looked down critically as a skeptical Idealist. In either case it was a cozy arrangement which absorbed, one way or the other, the alienating antinomy between subject and object. But in the later eighteenth century, as the minor misgivings of a Pope or a Johnson became a major disruption, man found himself ejected from his universe. The subject, no longer certain of what forces truly ruled those alien objects around him, certain only of the false confidence into which he had been lulled, keenly felt the existential loneliness of his exile. It was not only an ejection; it was a Fall. The loss of union between self and other was indeed the loss of Eden and the beginning of solitary wanderings in search of that subjective creation which would be a justifiable substitute for all the substance of the objective which had slipped away.

The opening moments of Goethe's *Faust* are an allegory of the plight of man in the exile created for him by the train of thinkers of whom Goethe's philosophical colleague Kant was the final—if inevitable—instrument. Faust, weary of his knowledge, is anxious to forsake the empty word for the full spiritual flowing of action. Weary of himself, he wants to open outward. Aware—despite his unique triumphs —of his common limitations, he seeks unlimited creativity. So he contemplates the sign of the Macrocosm, envying the ever-creative, dynamic harmony of nature's organic proliferation. But, however he may wish to feel himself—his subjective self—in this movement, at once restless and satisfying, he remains helplessly outside, and inside himself alone. Then, less transcendentally, he turns to the sign of the Earth-Spirit, to the immanent source of the life force. He summons it and it appears. But it rejects him, denying his claim to be its peer, treats him with contempt, and disappears, insisting that it is beyond his comprehension. Faust, we recall, is discovered on the stage alone —alone and restless—restless with his aloneness. He is man in the wake of the eighteenth century—both its dogmatism and its insecurity created by the explosion of that dogmatism. He is, then, man who has been ejected from the comfortable home in nature that his imagination tried to create for himself, ejected and unable to get back in. That nature which, in his metaphysical dogmatism, he tried to make a reflection of himself—his peer—now is hopelessly and frighteningly other. It is totally outside him, unresponsive, answering only its own secret sources of being, whatever (so far as he can know) they may be. So man, isolated in his subjectivity, has no choice but to cultivate and master that subjectivity, to create within himself and from himself his own uniquely human world, now that rapport with the natural world is to be denied him. Faust, then, must roar through experience, living it in all its varieties, always creating himself anew, until finally he vies with nature and, at last creating outwardly, he wins from the sea the land which he can convert to a human future. A newly won harmony through the subjective man-god can become the happy and heroic replacement for the lost harmony in the objective that was thoroughly destroyed by Hume and Kant. Man's striving has made the Fall a fortunate one: we have lost nature but can surpass her.

If the plight of eighteenth-century man led Goethe to produce such an allegory, it also led to an analogous configuration in the philosophic work of Kant. Here too man must construct out of himself in the absence of a grounded universe, whose substructure he cannot know. Hence the opposed worlds of nature and of man, the world of determinate judgments and the world of freedom.

It is this opposition between nature and freedom that leads to the Kantian aesthetic of Goethe's fellow poet Schiller. Schiller's well-known distinction between the naïve and the sentimental clearly derives from the opposition between man in nature and man in competition with nature, from outside her. Again we have an analogy to the Fall, this time placed within the psychological history of cultures and literatures. Man begins as natural man, a part of nature, partaking of her harmonious, sensuous perfection. Since the nature which lies immanently within him is all of him, there is no surplus remaining to make him other than nature, to allow him to transcend or see himself as distinct from nature. The naïve poet, then, is neither aware of his self nor self-consciously aware of nature as other, for there is no differentiated self to be aware of since nature contains nothing which he does not share. When the civilizing process disintegrates the naïve poet's simple sensuous unity, there follow a separation of his faculties and the birth of a discrete moral consciousness. These raise the poet above nature and transform him from naïve to sentimental. He longs nostalgically for his lost unity, except that, now endowed with his human self-consciousness, he really wants, not the sensuous natural unity, but a higher and unattainable moral unity. And nature, the only unity available to his senses or his racial memory, must now serve as a symbol (but only a symbol) of the perfection for which he must strive in the world of ideas (rather than just in the world of senses). Thus, as Schiller says, either "the poet *is* nature or he *seeks* nature." No longer a part of nature, he tries to rediscover and return to her. But since he is now a self-conscious, moral being—human, and, as human, more than natural as well as other than natural—his return cannot be complete, so that he must rather use nature as a symbolic reflection of what he strives toward in the realm of ideas. Nature becomes mere metaphor, imbued with moral qualities which the human in him reads into it: we are ready for the "pathetic fallacy." So Schiller can say, "In proportion as nature ceases to be experienced as a subject—we see it dawn and increase in the poetical world in the guise of an *idea* and as an *object*."

Schiller could not have put it better for our purposes here. When Faust, modern Western man toward the end of the eighteenth century, recognizes his Fall, his ejection, his alienation from nature, the curse and blessing of his "dreadful freedom" as human, this is the consequence. Still, for the mighty humanism of *Stürm und Drang*, the Fall is fortunate and full of promise. After all, Schiller himself was ready to do without the "naïve" perfection of the Greeks and even Shakespeare, in order to allow for the "sentimental" strivings of Goethe.

Perhaps the philosophical and psychological revolutions in the eighteenth century opened the way for us to project the Fall onto man's sudden consciousness, at a given point in his cultural development, of his eviction from his home in nature. Whether it happened once for us all (as in the doctrinal Fall) or once in the development of each civilization or once in the lives of each of us, the Fall is always a fall out of nature into our sole human selves; now outside nature's order, we are left to develop our own, although we now have become sophisticated enough not to read that order back into nature. But what befell Western man, first in the Renaissance and then—with finality—after the valiant futilities of his Rationalist impositions, encouraged cultural mythologizing of Schiller's sort. Indeed, closer to our own day, we find much the same arrangement in T. S. Eliot's reading of the history of our poetry in terms of the "unity of sensibility" and the "dissociation of sensibility," creating the "intellectual" as opposed to the "reflective" poet. Of course, for Eliot there is a different disposition of values, Schiller's "sentimental" having for him become a far more unequivocal term of disparagement. But then Eliot is hardly, like Schiller, a humanistic progressive, even as his day had far less promising a future.

But whichever the attitude toward man's original unified consciousness (thought of as an un-self-consciousness), the sort of development of sensibility we see in Schiller or Eliot reflects their common attempt to translate the Fall into historical terms, to place it—or some traumatic movement analogous to it—within human history, or more precisely, within the development of Western culture. In such remarkable writers as William Blake, on the other hand, the Fall from Innocence to Experience is a continual part of the historical present. It is reenacted in every individual; it is the death-dealing force in the development of single consciousness. Here we are close to where we left Wordsworth. For him too the Fall is forever occurring, or recurring; but it occurs uniquely for each man in the act of reorienting his sensibility. As in Kierkegaard, the trauma of shock provokes the discontinuous movement we trace from the "aesthetic" to the "ethical" stage. All of these writers—whether they see the Fall as the organizing myth of our shared cultural history or as the central fact of the psychological coming of age of each of us—are profoundly aware of what it costs our sensibilities to be ejected from their natural and congenial home; they must face the bankruptcy of the factitiously secure world view, a bankruptcy that, as we have seen, terrorized even neoclassical temperaments.

In *his* response, however, Wordsworth seems to combine—or to muddle—lamentations for a most unfortunate Fall and hope for what fallen man can create out of a fortunate Fall. We have noted Schiller's pleasure in the gains won through the transformation from the naïve to the sentimental, as man, having fallen from natural grace, can raise himself to a thoroughly human and moral grace. But a more Blakean attitude sees in the Fall only a degeneration, a falling from grace that is redeemable only by a return, a regaining of the innocent sensibility. Wordsworth seems to fluctuate between both these attitudes, sometimes even seems—ambivalently—to want to hold both at once.

Should man attempt to force himself back into the harmonious perfection of his original absorption in nature, or should he attempt to
realize his own higher nature as man by going self-consciously beyond
his earlier state into the human, and thus the moral, realm? Has there
really been a Fall? How literally do we mean the Fall as our metaphor?
Wordsworth seems to want it both ways, at once affirming and denying the archetypal role of the Fall. He hesitates between the monistic
view which sees nature as inspirited, with God immanently within it,
and the more orthodox, dualistic view which sees an opposition between nature and the spiritual principle, with the latter outside and
beyond nature. Is a God-laden nature to be always available to man
as his proper home, or is man, a fallen creature now cut off from
nature, to bring himself toward a transcendent God who has ordered
a higher, more than natural destiny for him? Even the early Wordsworth is divided in his allegiance to nature as he contemplates his
awareness of man. What we may see as Wordsworth's philosophical
indecision serves him poetically, as he uses it to illuminate—by way
of a metaphor urged and withdrawn—the phenomenology of the Fall
and man's multiple awarenesses of its possible applicability.

It is his double awareness that justifies the many poems in which
Wordsworth, by double vision, views a single place from two perspectives in time. And it is the double vision, as well as his double awareness of man's role inside and outside nature, that supports the claim
with which I began this chapter: that there is in Wordsworth a far
less simple and cheerful faith than the one to which the modern mind,
obsessed with its own darkness and complexity, often restricts him.
So often, as we have already seen in "Lines Written in Early Spring,"
any suggestion of nature's conscious harmony is accompanied by the
poet's self-conscious acknowledgment of the possibility that his own
sadly human subjectivity is reading all this into an alien, "insensate"
object. So often, too, the nostalgic idyll of nature as man's lost home,
always beckoning him, is accompanied or followed by the poet's insistence on the compensatory features of man's new human possibilities. Again we find the Fall from nature man's curse and his blessing,
author of his woe as of his weal.

To his "Intimations" ode, a poem dedicated to just this balance—
the loss of the earlier sections balanced by the consoling prospects in
the sections added later—Wordsworth finally prefixed a note that
explicitly deals with his use of the Fall. It must be granted that the

older conservative Wordsworth, embarrassed by the heterodoxy of his suggestions about Platonic pre-existence, is attempting to reduce an apparent metaphysical claim to a metaphorical suggestion. He sees it as his mythic datum, invoked as a projection of psychological delusion. But under the apologetic note that undercuts the extravagance of the poem is his appeal to our common experience of the Fall. This appeal reveals an awareness that supports what I have been claiming here.

> *To that dream-like vividness and splendor which*
> *invest objects of sight in childhood, every one, I believe,*
> *if he would look back, could bear testimony, and I*
> *need not dwell upon it here: but having in the poem*
> *regarded it as presumptive evidence of a prior state*
> *of existence, I think it right to protest against a*
> *conclusion, which has given pain to some good and*
> *pious persons, that I meant to inculcate such a belief. It*
> *is far too shadowy a notion to be recommended to*
> *faith, as more than an element in our instincts of*
> *immortality. But let us bear in mind, that though the*
> *idea is not advanced in revelation, there is nothing*
> *there to contradict it, and the fall of Man presents*
> *an analogy in its favor.... Archimedes said that he*
> *could move the world if he had a point whereon to rest*
> *his machine.... I took hold of the notion of pre-*
> *existence as having sufficient foundation in humanity*
> *for authorizing me to make for my purpose the best*
> *use of it I could as a poet.*

What we have observed even as early as "Lines Written in Early Spring" indicates that Wordsworth's consciousness of the human aftermath of the Fall—his consciousness of the delusions about nature which it sponsored—was not restricted to his later years. The poet's humanity cannot afford *not* to read self-conscious harmony into nature—for his sake, not nature's. Here is man seeking nature, in the sense of Schiller, even as he is uncertain about his capacity ever again to *be* nature. And it is Wordsworth's capacity to create this double awareness that refutes those who underestimate the fullness of his vision. Sometimes, it must be said, his control wavers as he seeks to balance an imaginative indulgence and an intellectual restraint, the inward movement toward identity with the object and the hesitant withdrawal from it. He cannot always manage the representation that permits him both to yield and to observe himself as yielding. He senses not only his surrender but his need to surrender, though he cannot always with equal mastery persuade us of these companion, and yet opposing, pulls within him.

"I Wandered Lonely as a Cloud," a poem somewhat later than "Lines Written in Early Spring," is the sort of partial failure I am suggesting. It has the necessary ingredients: the isolation of solitary man from the natural community, the animation of nature to the point where it seems to be aware of its communal joys, and the vain attempt of man to rejoin the community in order to share those joys—together with his *imaginative* reunion with it and the consoling pleasures of that act. The poet is to the daffodils as the cloud is to the peopled earth: he is alone, floating without definite purpose, far above the gathered crowd below. "Crowd" and "host" emphasize the unindividuated, collective character of what can be seen from his (the cloud's) height. (This moment is not altogether unreminiscent of Johnson's lofty view of mankind "from China to Peru" at the outset of "The Vanity of Human Wishes.") But the daffodils constitute no imperfect society. The harmony of their collective movements is insisted upon in their "dance"; and some form of the word occurs four times in this brief poem. The poet moves quickly from the literally descriptive "fluttering" to the merest suggestion of animation in the barely metaphorical "dancing" ("Fluttering and dancing in the breeze"). But he presses onward to an explicitly conscious movement which fulfills the earlier possibility of consciousness: "Tossing their heads in sprightly dance." The waves next to them join in the dance, and nothing less than "glee" is attributed to them. They have indeed become a "jocund company," whose gaiety must infect the poet-observer, who now, apparently, joins them ("A poet could not but be gay, / In such a jocund company"). Perhaps Wordsworth is here saying that only the poet can be counted on to respond in this way: only he of the imaginative power can animate his objects, can transform them into an alive and gleeful company which he can join, thus enlightening himself through natural communion. But has the poet been taken in? Is there any awareness here of the subjective nature of his magical feat? Or is there actually a claim of an immanent spirit in nature into which man must feel himself? Is the poet claiming that the daffodils are independently gleeful, or that his human separateness has permitted him to read glee into them? Or has he not, by the end of the third stanza, forgotten how unalterably separate from the natural community his lonely, cloudlike singleness has left him?

The main suggestions here have been that the poet has forgotten himself, has permitted his movement toward identity with his object to put to rest the critical faculty that would lead to his withdrawal and continuing distinctness from his object. Thus he is led to the excess, the uncritical indulgence of the final line, when solitude breaks open and flows outward to a renewed identity with nature, so that the poet forgets to remember where he is and where, for all the momentary joys of imagination, he is fated to remain: "And then my heart with pleasure fills, / And dances with the daffodils." Is it they who have danced and still dance and who call him to them, or is it he who must have them dance so as to create a community into which his sole self can merge imaginatively? It is disappointing that there is so much less consciousness of his role and nature's in this poem. Where this is lacking, where the poet—from his couch—can unabashedly and without reservation dance with the daffodils, we find ourselves, with some embarrassment, faced with the pathetic fallacy, naked and unguarded. And we feel closer to the charges of thinness of vision and naïveté which this chapter began by recording.

In as successful a poem as "To the Cuckoo," on the other hand, we discover the poet's need both to indulge his delusion and to show himself as deluded, to represent himself within the broader framework of the poem's drama that contains him. He at once establishes his awareness of—indeed, his primary concern with—the difference between the bird as limited physical object and the bird as metaphorical source of the poet's imaginative projections. The poet freely acknowledges the trivial and finite object he has chosen to inflate; nor does he anywhere insist that the bird actually possesses the transcendent character he chooses to attribute to it. He begins by asking explicitly, "shall I call thee Bird, / Or but a wandering Voice?" It is his consciousness of both sides and of the need to choose that leads him to recognize the bird's voice as a "twofold shout." The doubleness of its voice makes it, metaphorically as well as literally, "At once far off, and near." Moving "from hill to hill," its voice echoing its presence in its absence, the bird also creates echoes within the poet's sense of time. The movement from hill to hill, at once far off and near, becomes the ideal action on which to base the movement in the poet's imagination from the fact of place to the dream of identity through time, from the here-and-now to the before-now-and-always.

The bird's voice, as I have noted elsewhere,[2] is a made-to-order vehicle for the willful operation of the poetic imagination. The here and the now can be blurred into the everywhere and the always by virtue of the happy—if lamented—fact that the poet cannot find the bird, so that he has the sound of its voice to hold onto as the only certain evidence of its existence. As in Keats's famous example, if this voice and earlier voices are the same, what proof is there that they all don't emanate from one bird? The romantic poet is thus permitted to move from identity of sound to identity of occasion, from the assumption of a mortal, fleshly creature (seeable even if not seen) to a transcendent, unseeable spirit whose oneness is evidenced by the oneness of his voice ("The voice I hear this passing night was heard / In ancient days," "the self-same song," "The same that"). Thus the operation of synecdoche—converting the voice into the thing itself, indeed into that which transcends the thing—allows the romantic bird-poet to use the elusiveness of the bird's body as his excuse for willful self-delusion, for lulling himself into an easy Platonism.

So it is here with Wordsworth, although no other of his rival bird-poets keeps us as explicitly aware of his awareness that he is slipping into self-delusion. The third quatrain leads us from the simultaneous sense of distance and nearness, absence and presence, to his open admission of his "twofold" sensing of meaninglessness and of the profoundest meanings of all. He knows that the physical bird is merely "babbling," even as, converted through the poet's Platonism, its voice brings to him "a tale / Of visionary hours." The transfer is ready to be made complete, as the mortal "babbling" creature is to be rejected for the voice and all that the imaginative freedom of the poet can make it mean for him. Until now he has responded to both of the "twofold" alternatives; now he turns wholly to the unnaturalistic one and grasps it, no longer with any common-sense qualms: "thou art to me / No bird, but an invisible thing, / A voice, a mystery." Like Keats's speaker in his "Nightingale," Wordsworth's can now move across time to insist that the voice is indeed "the same": "The same whom in my schoolboy days / I listened to." Of course, for Words-

---

[2] See *The Play and Place of Criticism*, pp. 73n., 120–21.

worth, unlike Keats, the sameness refers only to his own personal history rather than to the history of a culture. Thus this becomes one of the poems I spoke of earlier, in which Wordsworth's double vision permits him to collapse time by repeating an earlier experience at a later moment, converging upon the "spot of time" from a dual perspective. In Wordsworth as in Keats, the bird, in flying and in escaping human sight, soars beyond man and human time. By flying unseen through space, it somehow (thanks to metaphor) flies through time, passing years or centuries like hills. Thus the spatial subsumes the temporal, the bird's ubiquity in time reflecting its resistance to being seen in a single spot even as it is heard everywhere. The conceit is just what Wordsworth needs to merge his mature present with the "golden time" of his childhood past.

The charm of his recollection is that it centers on his inability as a child to find the bird and his untiring efforts to find her. So she was then, and has been able to remain, "a hope, a love; / Still longed for, never seen." The beginning of the next-to-last quatrain, "And I can listen to thee yet," follows through on his total commitment to delusion: the "thee yet" assumes the identical bird in a continuing action unbroken since the poet's childhood. But before the quatrain is done, something is added that does indicate a break from the "golden time" of his original experience. If the bird hasn't changed, he has. The poet now must actively work, under the spell of the bird's voice, to recreate the experience which comes automatically to the child as passive recipient. He must now "listen, till I do beget / That golden time again." The begetting is an act of imaginative creation: the golden time, an Eden of instinctive innocence, must now be worked for by the mature man who, having lost it, seeks the rediscovery and the re-entry. He will keep listening until finally he can make it come. But even his momentary achievement of it, though a brilliant imaginative triumph, is managed only as he acknowledges—through the "beget" —how artificial the merger is. Indeed, it is a tribute to the mature imagination rather than to the inspirited world of childhood; it is a tribute that is consecrated in the very act of writing this poem to that moment and as a result of it. The present tense of the poem, with the breathless joy of discovery and participation in its final quatrain, is itself the testimony and testament of that golden time recaptured. But it testifies also to the human, imaginative effort required to redeliver oneself to nature's primitive magic.

Still these final lines are spoken out of the trance, the magical land, which the poet has begotten for himself. We have witnessed the process of begetting: first the poet's skeptical common sense in opposition to the romantic impulse to animate nature, then the conscious choice of that impulse, and finally the avid seizing upon the ultimate, the most dreamy consequences of the choice. His final lines come to us from that golden world he has created out of his poetic temperament; they are his rewards for his effort and his achievement. As in "Lines Written in Early Spring," but so much more forcefully, the poet is revealed as linked to the natural harmonies while still enjoying—as a double advantage—the human self-consciousness that allows him now to savor the moment as well as to have it:

> *O blessèd Bird! the earth we pace*
> *Again appears to be*
> *An unsubstantial, faery place;*
> *That is fit home for Thee!*

There are judgments here that only the mature visionary, in contrast to an innocent existent, could make. The bird as he has created it can be termed "blessèd" out of his awareness of its sacred, other-than-natural virtues. Phrases like "the earth we pace" and "*appears* to be" suggest the still existing humdrum world of common sense that surrounds, in time and space, this timeless world of most un-common sense. And the word "unsubstantial" admits the price of his rapture. But his sensibility is now at the stage where the unworldly is a requirement for the enchanted bird. The bird cannot have its natural, substantial place, as in the poet's youth. If the "far off" is to be brought "near" and time is to be overcome, clearly substance itself must now be yielded up. Hence the poet's choice of the wandering voice over the bird, the visionary tale over the babble. For the mature poet, then, the only "fit home" for the bird—the only place where it can have existence as a bird transformed, as a transcendent union of bird and vision—is the "unsubstantial, faery place" into which he has transformed his world. But unlike Byzantium, Yeats's fit home for golden birds, Wordsworth's is, in effect, the world of his poem, one that reproduces the shimmering recollections of childhood magic that the older Wordsworth records in that prefatory note to the "Intimations" ode from which I quoted earlier: "I was often unable to think of external things as having external existence, and I communed with all that I saw as something not apart from, but inherent in, my own immaterial nature. Many times while going to school have I grasped at a wall or tree to recall myself from this abyss of idealism to the reality." In "To the Cuckoo," in the "unsubstantial, faery place" that poem finally arrives at, we find the self-conscious fabrication—the strenuous re-creation—of such a moment: its glory as well as its sadness results from the make-believe character of the imagination that creates it, though that creation bespeaks the fallen nature of the creation behind it.

How much less self-consciousness, how much less awareness of what the speaker is revealing about his mature and thus no longer spontaneous nature, we find in "To My Sister," a companion poem to "Lines Written in Early Spring." And how unfortunate an exposure the poem suffers through this uncritical self-delusion by the poet. The poem strains for spontaneity, for instant response, for a summoning of natural instinct—almost in the manner of (or trying to match the tone of) a poem like Herrick's "Corinna's Going a-Maying." But everything about it reveals that the poet is too stiffly arguing his sister (and himself) into the immediacies of feeling. He is working too hard for us to believe in his repeated desire to give himself to idleness. He summons his sister as Herrick summons Corinna, except that, next to Herrick's sweeping dynamics, Wordsworth's call is strained:

> My sister! ('tis a wish of mine)
> Now that our morning meal is done,
> Make haste, your morning task resign;
> Come forth and feel the sun.

The awkward parenthesis, the end-stopped lines, the inversion coupled with the unforceful Latinate verb ("resign") in the third line, all weaken the intended impatience of "Make haste." These difficulties are general ones throughout the poem. There is too much care here for the spirit of reckless indulgence he wants to impart to his sister.

Elsewhere also the poem is too thoughtful an expression of the anti-bookish ("And bring no book") call to instinct over thought. It is positively philosophic. Though this is a call to idleness, emphasized by the use of the refrain, the poet is imposing a weighty metaphysical task upon his listener. He is giving her a program for feeling herself into the soothing receptivity of nature. He summons her to "the hour of feeling" almost as if on a schedule. Rejecting the "toiling reason," he yet speaks of their "minds" as drinking "at every pore / The spirit of the season." Similarly, their hearts will make "silent laws" for their own obedience. Though unlike the "joyless forms" that "regulate" the lifeless calendar of man when he is not attuned to nature, even the "silent laws" still suggest a more-than-natural effort. This is a good deal more than the "wise passiveness" called for by the receiver of sensations in "Expostulation and Reply."

The poet and his sister are to use this hour of feeling as a means of returning to nature's bosom, as if they can, and without human interference. Love, we are told, moves "From earth to man, from man to earth." There is no concern here for the human community, for the movement from man to man, the very concern that introduced the complications of "Lines Written in Early Spring." The love is to return man, without intermediary, to the heart of things:

> And from the blessed power that rolls
> About, below, above,
> We'll frame the measure of our souls:
> They shall be tuned to love.

The return seems to require a surrender of their humanity, a hard-won loss of self that the very effort of the poem leads us to doubt. It is as if the poet has forgotten in this poem the irrevocability of the Fall that has elsewhere conditioned his nostalgic attempt to reverse his movement from nature to the self-consciously human.

The poem itself consists of the appeals of a denaturalized man insisting on the continuing availability to him of the instinctual life in nature's immediacy. But the poem everywhere reveals, in the strenuousness of those appeals, how factitious that insistence is, how more than natural his summons is, how much more he is calling for than a passive "idleness." Once the innocence of the "aesthetic" stage is lost, the immediacy of rapport with nature is lost with it, so that any return to nature must depend on the human conditions of maturity: Schiller's "sentimental" must replace his "naïve" for good. All this, Wordsworth's more successful earlier poems accept, and with a surprising self-awareness in view of the uncritical claims of an instant return to instinct in poems like "To My Sister," "Expostulation and Reply," and "The Tables Turned." Of such poems, "To My Sister" is especially valuable to us in its display—through rhetoric, language, and the argument itself—of the earnestness of man's high purpose. But if we see this display so clearly, its speaker apparently does not. He remains deceived by his own call for a return to instinct, one that would strip his sister and him of their human selves.

The Lucy poems, especially the third and fourth, spring from this awareness of the cost as well as the glory of man's pre-human absorption within the natural community. That is, they are obsessed by our need to fall from nature as well as by our need to know the instinctual harmony we must forgo. "Three years she grew in sun and shower" traces the process—and points to the consequences—of creating an eternal child of nature. The bulk of the poem is the carrying out of Nature's promise in the first stanza to make Lucy "A Lady of my own." And so well does Nature, as character, carry it out that Lucy is unfit to fall into being human: hence her premature death. As Nature describes the process, there is nothing in Lucy that does not come from nature as its reflection. Her response to the natural forces that form her is a passiveness neither "wise" nor even willed, but instinctive: "hers [are] the silence and the calm / Of mute insensate things." It is important to recognize the full force, indeed the shocking force, of the phrase "mute insensate things" applied to Lucy as a happy comparison. It is, after all, a rather extreme characterization of her passivity as a part of nature. She clearly is to have no more consciousness (to say nothing of self-consciousness) than the flowers, birds, and twigs into which the poet had to project pleasure in "Lines Written in Early Spring."

Most of the poem is taken up with the several stages of Nature's making of this lady of his own, stages constituted of successive displays of the ways in which Nature reflects himself in her and creates her being out of these reflections. She will borrow from Nature the simultaneous obedience to law and impulse, in her innocence feeling an identity between that which kindles and that which restrains—an identity which, for those of us fallen into experience, becomes polarized into opposition. Thus the springing sportiveness of the fawn joins with the calm hush of the mute insensate thing. The next three stanzas show her literally formed by the nature which she sees and of which she partakes as she lives intimately with it (him):

> "The floating clouds their state shall lend
> To her; for her the willow bend;
> Nor shall she fail to see

> *Even in the motions of the Storm*
> *Grace that shall mould the Maiden's form*
> *By silent sympathy."*

The blending of nature in her (as in her form's being molded "by silent sympathy") is beautifully created in Wordsworth's language. Similarly, in the next stanza, changing from eye to ear, she shall so sympathetically listen that "beauty born of murmuring sound / Shall pass into her face." But the metaphor that creates Nature (as a speaking, acting character) out of nature is made to work: he concludes, in the spirit of Marlowe's passionate shepherd in the "Come live with me" tradition,

> *"Such thoughts to Lucy I will give*
> *While she and I together live*
> *Here in this happy dell."*

Nature has made a lady of his own who has come and lived with him, and with him will stay. The speaker of the poem adds, "Thus Nature spake—The work was done—." For the speaker, being human, can see only that Lucy has died. There is a shocking but bitter irony in this final stanza as we are wrenched out of Nature's perspective and forced to view Lucy's fate from the uncomprehending perspective of man. This concluding comment is troublesome indeed and might be viewed ironically, except for the poet's failure to place the speaker and his lamentation within a dramatic context. So we must view it as the poet's loss of control. Clearly the "*my* Lucy" of the unfortunate second line ("How soon my Lucy's race was run!") refers to the speaker, who certainly is not Nature but is rather in opposition to Nature. The very line itself, so inappropriately worded, reveals the alien perspective out of which it issues. If the datum of the poem, its central metaphor, is to be taken seriously, then in what sense can Lucy be the speaker's? Only Nature, whom we have watched making Lucy a lady of his own, can call her "mine." Yet the speaker refers to her as "my Lucy" and to her death as his loss of her. And the poem closes with four self-pitying lines in which the speaker laments what has been left to him out of his loss. The lines are hopelessly human and, as such, are an inappropriate conclusion to what he has narrated. If we accept the terms of the poem, how can Lucy be lost to Nature?

Is Lucy dead, then, or is she somehow alive in nature, permanently Nature's bride? Perhaps Nature's refusal to permit her to grow from a natural to a human state, thus preserving her innocence and protecting her from the Fall, has the necessary consequence of making her dead in the eyes of man. So perhaps we could not expect the speaker of the last stanza (despite the fact that he has just related Nature's words to us) to understand whose Lucy she was and why he would have to see her as dead before she could ever truly become his—and ours. Though Wordsworth gives us no sense that he is aware of the violent incongruity of perspectives between the last stanza and all that precedes it, we still can find the meaning of the poem enriched by the final speaker's poverty of understanding. We now feel fully the price of Lucy's natural purity and perfect innocence. If these qualities are to continue forever, if she is never to fall into mere humanity, if the natural community is always to claim all of her, then clearly she must die before she grows and is inevitably transformed. This poem and the one which follows are early and powerful variations upon the theme Keats's speaker stumbles upon in "Ode to a Nightingale," when his hope for a timeless union with the bird leads to his shocked awareness that timelessness for man is not an ideal eternity but is the brute fact of death: "To thy high requiem become a sod."

It may be, however, that the poet—or even the speaker—is, after all, aware of his insensibility in that last stanza and aware of the total meaning of the blissful natural creation in the earlier ones. For however we may decide about the possible alternative meanings in the much-debated fourth Lucy poem ("A slumber did my spirit seal"), one thing seems certain: this is a profound confession following directly upon the speaker's blindness as revealed in the third Lucy poem and, especially, in its final stanza. It is as if shock was produced upon the speaker at the end, when he turned the poem around to serve his private human sorrow, a shock that brings about the very understanding that it tried to conceal. Thus he now sees the slumber that sealed his spirit; and he senses that he has collaborated with that force (Nature?) which would not permit Lucy to be humanized in that even he himself saw her as "a thing" (a "mute insensate thing"). If she seemed to be a thing not subject to human time ("earthly years"), she too—whatever she seems to his poet's fancy—in reality has turned into Keats's "sod." And the consequences of her thinghood, which the speaker's slumbering spirit has in part conferred upon her, are seen in the cold negation, the passivity, the deadness, of the overinterpreted second quatrain:

> *No motion has she now, no force;*
> *She neither hears nor sees;*
> *Rolled round in earth's diurnal course,*
> *With rocks, and stones, and trees.*[3]

Nowhere does the Wordsworth of the early poems seem more certain of the alienation between the natural and the human communities. Far from suggesting the possibility of the return of the human to the natural, Wordsworth seems ready to concede the impenetrability of nature once man has fallen out of it into his own realm.

It is, however, in other poems that Wordsworth dwells upon the cultivation of the human community by fallen man. Until now we have seen in his poems the uncertainty (or we can soften our criticism by terming it ambivalence) of his response to the fallen human state, alternating between his acceptance of it and his attempt to get back into the natural community as he refuses to accept the Fall as irrevocable. The subliminal metaphor of the Fall is both affirmed and retreated from in these poems. But even as early as "Tintern Abbey" we find Wordsworth pressing forward from the regrets over what maturing man must lose to the compensating union he can find with his fellow fallen creatures.

"Tintern Abbey" is perhaps Wordsworth's supreme poem of the double vision, that use (which we witnessed in "To the Cuckoo") of a single experience or a single place viewed from two points in time. Of course, in such poems he usually concentrates doubly on a spot rather than, as in "To the Cuckoo," on a happening. This specialness of place permits the spatial joining of "spots of time," as it evokes dual reactions separated in time but joined by the mature poet's bringing to the present the present-ness of the past. So the primary vision is that of maturity, with only an idyllic nostalgia operating to bring the past's golden time to illuminate the present. In "Tintern Abbey," however,

---

[3] The last word, "trees," in the dead company of rocks and stones, is, with its organic implications, either a monumental irony directed against nature or an unfortunate oversight by Wordsworth. The poet who tried to attribute pleasure to twigs either slipped here (in a way especially strange for him) or is emphasizing bitterly the gap between all nature and man, and not that between the inorganic and organic in nature.

the poet finds the advantage of representing both past and present responses to the scene as occurring together in the present. The presence of his sister, as a re-presenting of his own youth standing side by side with his own maturity, permits an incarnation of his original vision to be companion to his current one. And to complete the possibilities, the poet looks to the future, to his sister's return to this spot, to the second part of her own double vision, anticipated—or prefigured—by his own current companionship with her. The sister, then, not only links the poet to nature through being an embodiment of his own childhood attachment to it, but, in bringing the past into the present and projecting the future out of the present, she also affirms through her presence their kinship and their history, thereby linking the poet to the history of the human family, both in and out of nature, in their own natural relations to one another. This is no longer simply the history of one man's varying attachments to nature, for it is also the history of man's mixed attachments to nature and to man.

There are in this poem actually three, rather than just two, stages in the speaker's development, probably reflecting the often-imputed influence of Hartleyan psychology. The first two are both passive responses to nature, the first to nature present and the second to nature absent. Together they suggest the empiricist's inevitable distinction between sensations and ideas, together with the complete dependence of the second on the first. The first is the instinctual life in nature, life totally absorbed in nature. It is an animal response, not unlike Lucy's, the response of a being formed by his relation to nature. This response is "an appetite,"

> *a feeling and a love,*
> *That had no need of a remoter charm,*
> *By thought supplied, nor any interest*
> *Unborrowed from the eye.*

> (ll. 80–83)

But "through [the speaker's] long absence" in alien "towns and cities," nature has been removed from his eye. Still, if only in memory, he is passively subjected to

> *sensations sweet,*
> *Felt in the blood, and felt along the heart;*

171

II. Through the Embrace of the Natural Human Community

> *And passing even into my purer mind,*
> *With tranquil restoration. . . .*

(ll. 27–30)

The speaker is still united to nature as, led into a mystical trance, he is carried into the heart of the universe:

> *that blessed mood,*
> *In which the burthen of the mystery,*
> *In which the heavy and the weary weight*
> *Of all this unintelligible world,*
> *Is lightened . . .*
>
> .   .   .   .
>
> *Until, the breath of this corporeal frame*
> *And even the motion of our human blood*
> *Almost suspended, we are laid asleep*
> *In body, and become a living soul:*
> *While with an eye made quiet by the power*
> *Of harmony, and the deep power of joy,*
> *We see into the life of things.*

(ll. 37–49)

The harmony and the joy which the speaker in "Lines Written in Early Spring" tried to impose upon the natural objects of his sensations still move this poet to join with them, even in the absence of those objects. Indeed, his response is the more profound, the more metaphysical, as their absence prompts him to move beyond them to the essential harmony and joy out of which they come and function for him. This second stage, then, is really a development, or transposition, of the first stage: threatened by the curse of individuation, by the separation from nature induced by the Fall into human singleness, the poet yet manages to sustain his passivity as—with the loss of self —he is returned to the soul of nature, to the pool of being. All is immanence in nature; there is no transcendence, no surplus, in him or in nature.

But the third stage, which is the present tense of the poem, does spring from his separateness, his humanness, his awareness that his Fall from the oneness in nature is irrevocable. He clearly has surrendered the naïve for Schiller's sentimental state. Immanence yields to transcendence, passivity yields to creativity, the natural community yields to the human community. His looking upon nature is now severely modified by his "hearing oftentimes / The still, sad music of humanity," that which must "chasten and subdue." The lines which follow are difficult, and probably weak in their vagueness, but that they struggle toward a transcendent something beyond the indwelling soul of nature seems evident:

> *And I have felt*
> *A presence that disturbs me with the joy*
> *Of elevated thoughts; a sense sublime*
> *Of something far more deeply interfused,*
> *Whose dwelling is the light of setting suns,*
> *And the round ocean and the living air,*
> *And the blue sky, and in the mind of man.*
>
> (ll. 93–99)

The endless coordination of the "and" leads at last beyond nature to "the mind of man," generator of "the still, sad music." Perhaps this is the addition that permits the something to be "far more deeply interfused"—in that strangely incomplete comparative phrase—"more deeply" than the degree of interfusion in a universe that stops with nature short of man. The poet is awakened to this "presence," which incorporates the human into all that must be accounted for, because he—with his earlier sense of the self-sufficiency of nature—has been chastened and subdued by man's still, sad music. And man, no longer passively emptied into nature, is himself creative, self-generative. It is as if Wordsworth has incorporated Kant, as well as the sorrows of the French Revolution or his own private sorrows in France. For now nature, "all the mighty world / Of eye, and ear," is something these senses "half create" as well as perceive. The human world now lies somewhere between the receptivity of the empiricist's senses and the spontaneity of an active, constitutive mind. No wonder that, in proper Schiller-like language, nature can be humanly transformed to become the "soul / Of all my moral being." Man may no longer be enveloped in nature in the secure way that produced, in "To My Sister," the exhaustion of feeling "From earth to man, from man to earth." Alienated and fallen, he can attempt to achieve an imperfect, sad harmony among his fellow fallen creatures as he works to relate man to man.

Perhaps in no poem does Wordsworth more successfully combine the aloneness of man with his union with the race and its history than in "The Solitary Reaper," a somewhat later work. The reaper's isolation, though in nature, is emphasized from the start: "Behold her, single in the field," a line followed by "solitary," "by herself," and "alone" in succeeding lines. This aloneness is linked to the melancholy of her song. Such solitude and such melancholy occur despite her complete absorption in nature and in her natural duties as reaper. Clearly, in her stark isolation, she is not of nature, nor is her song, whose melancholy humanity overflows "the Vale profound." In this poem the human figure thus surpasses nature in its demands upon the attention of the poet-observer.

In the second stanza, the poet openly confronts the challenge of nature as an alternative subject for poetry. As if turning upon his earlier self and upon romantic poets generally, he rejects such obvious subjects drawn from nature as the nightingale and the cuckoo, even though they may be associated with far-off, exotic places. The voice of neither bird could so hold him as does this homely, human voice. Humanity, though in a natural setting and so existing almost as a part of the landscape, thus replaces nature as Wordsworth's subject.[4] For it is her humanness, her human sadness, as characterized by the song she sings, that confers upon her her preferred status. The "plaintive numbers flow" (like human tears or the stream of human history) either for sorrows distant in time and place ("old, unhappy, far-off things, / And battles long ago") or common and current ("some more humble lay, / Familiar matter of to-day"). It doesn't matter: the human story is one story, its history generating new versions of the same suffering. The final lines of the stanza join the past to the present evidence of "the still, sad music of humanity": "Some natural sorrow, loss, or pain, / That has been, and may be again." The word "natural" has an ironic ring for us here if we remind ourselves of the joy and harmony that, elsewhere in Wordsworth, accompany natural workings as a model for man. Here what is "natural" for man (but, alas, so unnatural to the Wordsworthian world), what is inevitable to

[4] A similar substitution of the human for the natural as his preferred subject occurs in the "Westminster Bridge" sonnet, where Wordsworth replaces nature with the "City": "Never did sun more beautifully steep / In his first splendour, valley, rock, or hill." London may be asleep, but it is its man-made structures ("Ships, towers, domes, theatres, and temples") that are items in the poet's landscape.

man's fallen state, is the "sorrow, loss, or pain" that is one with human history.

No wonder the girl sings whatever she sings as if it "could have no ending." The proof that her song is endless (like, but so unlike, the cuckoo's) is provided by the poet's sudden shift to the past tense, so that even now, in retrospect, it exists still, extending into the future as it comes out of the past. And it is well that her song's "theme" is no more precisely defined for, or by, the poet. Whatever it is, he knows what it must be, as he knows that it must go on forever, essentially unchanged, whatever the names and dates. In this final stanza, the girl takes on archetypal significance. The endless nature of her song is now fused with the endlessly seasonal nature of her work: "o'er the sickle bending." The lamentation over inevitable loss is echoed by her autumnal function as reaper, as—in accordance with the conventional image of time as reaper, wielder of the sickle—she seconds the work of nature. The implied comparison of nature's seasons and man's generations is accompanied by an awareness of the marked differences between them in producing joy or lamentation. Nature's cycle and man's are both natural, but man's, thanks to the Fall, has its sense of loss, as irrevocable, unaccompanied by the joys of incipient return. The "maiden," so alone, not only affirms her ties to humanity; she has become one with its entire history. For the poet, her song has converted her labor in nature's seasonal cycles to a metaphor relating to man's passing generations. Seen by the poet as alone (despite the flourishing of the natural community about her), she is now seen to join—indeed to become an embodiment of—the natural human community.

It is not surprising that the poem ends, as have others we have seen, with the poet recollecting the scene in tranquility and learning from it ever anew: "The music in my heart I bore, / Long after it was heard no more." As man has replaced nature as his subject, so the reaper functions for the poet, after the experience, in the way that—for example—the daffodils did at the close of "I wandered lonely as a cloud." She is there, she is always there, humanity singing still its endless, sad song. For, having fallen, humanity is involved with death; it is the grain cut by the reaper that will not grow again. Surely this awareness requires another consolation, a consolation more relevant to our sorrow than that held out by a metaphorical return, via pathetic fallacy, to a now alien nature. If man's Fall from the natural community is irrevocable and leaves him alone, then he can discover whether something may not be gained from a community of fallen, alienated creatures. It may un-alienate them, even if, in their union, they can do little more than make their sad music together.

Of course, as with the cuckoo or the daffodils, it is—admittedly—what the poetic sensibility has made of the solitary reaper, rather than the girl herself, that counts. She exists out there in the landscape, *as* the landscape, the human landscape, and as his subject. She, then, is the existent and he is the visionary who reads her as classic existent, even as this act transforms him into classic visionary. Her existence is naïve, un-self-conscious, and his placement of that existence within his vision charges it with a symbolism that grows to archetype. He is not an existent himself here, but a poet-observer only, though a poet with what Henry James called a sense for the subject. He chooses her as his subject and insists, as an imperative, that we see her this way too ("Behold her") and thus share his vision. This vision is earned through the ways by which she is related to and distinguished from nature and her song is related to and distinguished from other possible songs. And it is by way of this vision that—despite her own unawareness—her solitude and her reaping and singing are made to serve, as *subjects*, his (and our) need to make her the illuminating representative of man and human history. She can, of course, so serve only in her own sublime naïveté, just as her song can serve only so long as we do not understand its actual words. Thus the meaningless and the routine attain extraordinary meaning.

The leech-gatherer in "Resolution and Independence" does not serve very differently. Here too there is the isolated figure, far from any of his fellow creatures, appearing almost like a part of the landscape, yet—as seen by the poet for whom he functions crucially—utterly human in his close bonds to his kind. The poem is clearly the poet's and not the leech-gatherer's—which is why the change of title from "The Leech-Gatherer" was a wise one. The poet, as the developing protagonist-visionary, comes to the point where he has great need of a force beyond himself to bring him to make peace with his condition. As Wordsworth tells us in the well-known letter, the old man seemed to have been placed there for him, "almost as an interposition of Providence." But the poem itself tells this to us, in at least two places: in stanza 8 ("Now, whether it were by peculiar grace, / A leading from above, a something given"), and in stanza 16 ("Or like a man from some far region sent, / To give me human strength, by apt admonishment"). He is there, then, for what he can do for the poet, or rather for what the poet can make of him. And at first, before he speaks, he indeed seems to be a natural object, there to be seen:

> As a huge stone is sometimes seen to lie
> Couched on the bald top of an eminence;
> Wonder to all who do the same espy,
> By what means it could thither come, and whence;
> So that it seems a thing endued with sense:
> Like a sea-beast crawled forth, that on a shelf
> Of rock or sand reposeth, there to sun itself.
>
> (ll. 57–63)

The old man thus seems to be mere existence itself, although he will be pure human existence. We are reminded of Wordsworth's description in his letter: "A lonely place, 'a pond by which an old man *was*, far from all house or home:' not *stood*, nor *sat*, but *was*—the figure presented in the most naked simplicity possible." Here is an existent awaiting his visionary to articulate all that his existence can be made to mean.

And what has the development of the poet-protagonist been, that he needs the leech-gatherer? It is reminiscent of the movement from nature to man that we have been continually observing. The poem begins with the intensity of the present tense ("But now"), the first two stanzas describing with a sympathetic, even participatory, fervor the active joys of "all things that love the sun." The poet intrudes upon this world of nature's bliss in the third stanza; and his entrance signals the shift to the past tense, from the "now" to the "then" ("I was a Traveller then upon the moor"). For with the human subject of experience comes recollection, the transforming of the immediacy of experience into the seeds of contemplation. At first he describes himself as partaking of the joys of nature, with the instinctual carelessness of youth ("as happy as a boy"). This state requires his momentary turning away from his fallen, human state ("all the ways of men, so vain and melancholy").

But, as we have been witnessing in other poems, the attempt to abandon the human for the natural state is, for mature man, a momentary delusion. So "fears and fancies," "dim sadness," "blind thoughts," all come "thick" upon the poet. He berates himself for trying to live his life as "a happy Child of earth," as one of such "blissful creatures" as the "playful hare," walking "far from the world" "as if life's business were a summer mood." In effect, the poet is chiding himself for deserting the human community for the natural community, for choosing aloneness with nature (which alienates him from other men) instead of alienation from nature (which might unite him with his similarly alienated fellows). And he despairs over the degeneration of poets, perhaps awaiting him: those who "in our youth begin in gladness; / But thereof come in the end despondency and madness." No longer in youthful gladness, this poet surely has become despondent. But, thanks to the "peculiar grace" that provides him with the leech-gatherer, madness does not follow.

The man's immense age ("The oldest man he seemed that ever wore grey hairs") is what first strikes the speaker, whose anxieties were rooted in the poet's incapacity to sustain the process of aging. He is struck by the man's "extreme old age" *and* by his simple there-ness, his just being there, immovable and a fixed part of the landscape, like the huge stone or the sea-beast. But what counts is that this is a man, one who has carried and carries still a "more than human weight." When the old man speaks, his language—despite his feebleness—is "stately," "above the reach / Of ordinary men," reminiscent of "grave Livers" ("Religious men, who give to God and man their dues"). The poet is moved by his firmness and his dignity, his sense of purpose together with his awareness of the apparent futility which has dogged the fulfillment of that purpose. Or has it? Can anything inhibit his dedicated, daily pursuits? More than his speech is like the "grave Livers"; his very existence is defined by the routine of giving "to God and man their dues."

His first statement to the poet describes his "hazardous and wearisome" employment, pursued continually and systematically "from pond to pond," "from moor to moor," even as he endures "many hardships." Momentarily infused with "human strength" and feeling himself aptly admonished, the poet yet backslides into his former human fears and despair, though now these self-torturing feelings seek the comfort the old man has begun to provide. So the poet "eagerly" renews his question, in effect asking for a second and more lasting injection of strength, of admonishment. The old man obliges and tells his story again. The only direct quotation of his words we are given in the poem (the final three lines of stanza 18) adds to the indirect recitals an emphasis upon the futility of his task and the response of human faith to that futility:

> *"Once I could meet with them on every side;*
> *But they have dwindled long by slow decay;*
> *Yet still I persevere, and find them where I may."*

The almost redundant coupling of "yet" and "still" in the last line points up the constancy with which he must "persevere." The not very successful gathering of leeches, agents of healing, is what ties him—despite his apparent isolation—to the human community. Is he not, after all, a faint echo of Johnson's Dr. Levet? Thus mildly and routinely—but in his own way relentlessly—pursuing his peripheral (and hardly self-conscious) function in the alleviation of human suffering (why else leeches?), the old man indeed perseveres, gathering many or gathering few, or even fewer, so long as there are more than none.

This is the admonishment that provides a human response to the poet's anxieties about "Cold, pain, and labour, and all fleshly ills." And the old man perseveres in his talk—his narrative that carries, un-self-consciously, his self-justification—just as he perseveres in his task. Once more he "the same discourse renewed," while the poet's imagination is awakened "to see him pace / About the weary moors continually"—weary and continual, though unswervingly purposeful, even when the practical effects of that purpose are diminished almost to the vanishing point. The gesture, the ritual of service to man, the tie to his race, require his constancy. So the poet thanks God for the help he has sent in the old man and, like the Wordsworth we have seen indebted either to natural or to human experiences, promises to recall this moment—its strength and its admonishment—as it recedes into his past and he returns to moments of a poet's weakness and a man's strength. But, presumably, the momentary (present tense), careless, hare-like natural joys with which the youthful poet opened the poem are now behind him for good.

It is just such a ritual dedication to human fidelity, for its own sake, that enlightens the pathos of the earlier poem, "Michael." And it is another person "now old / Beyond the common life of man" who provides this dedication. The sense of the routine, of labor at once necessary and ceremonial, is provided by the poem's slow, greatly attenuated pace. Its lengthy indirections of description and action make it almost a poem of attrition, reflecting in its movement the wearying round of the shepherd's life on the land, as it moves toward the dissolution of the family title he has worked to preserve.

Yet, after an enormous number of lines is consumed in bringing us so painfully to Luke's departure, we should be shocked to find him dispatched to his degenerate fate in less than half a dozen lines. There must be a better justification for this gross disparity in pace than the difficulty, and irrelevance, of accounting for Luke's change. In a poem where everything is tedious process, suddenly there is no process at all—just a flat *fait accompli*. Luke falls upon evil ways in the "dissolute city" and is permanently removed to another continent. Clearly, however late this sad consequence is introduced, we are to accept it as an inevitable course, a given, in the prodigal son tradition. Whether it accords with what we know of Luke or expect of him after the life he has known is not at issue (although, as we remember from "Tintern Abbey," the city is an alien place where it is difficult even for the most sensitive of refugees from nature to hang on).

It is enough to say that Luke is dispensed with in this precipitate way in order to assure us that, finally, he and his fate do not count, that we are rather to concentrate on the faithful, unshakable, unchanging response of Michael to that fate. Though so deeply moved, he still cannot be moved from his resolution and his dedication. The fate of Luke serves to remove all normal, common-sense meaning, all practical consequence, from Michael's perseverance, his holding onto the bond between his son and him. It makes the conclusion and the final tribute to Michael's life and way of life all the more unqualified, even as it allows the pathos in us and in the poet to respond to its purest human object.

The poet, of course, is very much in this poem, entering at the start as our narrator in the role of a poet, a visionary now mature and removed from nature, though still aware of nature's special powers to purify human relations. And by repeating, from his mature and sophisticated position, this tale—remembered from childhood—of shepherds of old ("For the delight of a few natural hearts"), he establishes, below his own role of interpreter-visionary, the role of Michael as the un-self-conscious, the totally committed existent.

In this tale unlocked from the narrator's history, history itself is the major value—human history as it is consecrated in the land and in man's working of the land. Clearly, the value of Michael is intimately related to his own intimate relation to nature and his relative isolation from man (who, we must remember, creates his own crowd mainly in those "dissolute" cities). But we should not make the mistake of looking upon Michael simply as man *in* the natural community, as man before the Fall. For his fundamental ties, his primary motives, relate not to his obligations to nature as having claims of its own but to man's rights to work nature. He is, after all, alone in nature with his family; and there is a strong sense of the self-enclosure of that minimal natural *human* community represented by that family in its historical dimension.

It is the routine passage of the land from generation to generation that establishes a sacred law which guides Michael throughout and to which, even at the end, he must give at least a ritual obedience. And the land passes, carrying with it the burden of having to be worked. Wordsworth may call this "a pastoral poem," but it is far from idyllic. These are hard-working shepherds, tending a land that needs hard work when it comes to them and when it passes from them. Even at night, we are told, "their labour did not cease," thanks to their proverbial dedication to "endless industry." (Michael admits, "Our lot is a hard lot; the sun himself/Has scarcely been more diligent than I.") But the work is no more than Michael's discharging of his debt to the land, or rather to those who passed it down to him for him, in turn, to pass along. Thus the threat to the family's continued ownership of the land is the direst that could invade his existence. Only so dire a possibility could lead Michael to send Luke away despite all risks.

Indeed, Michael's attitude to the land, as it affects the passing generations who tend it, makes the magnificently simple and significant line I earlier quoted from Tennyson's "Tithonus" ("Man comes and tills the field and lies beneath") seem an echo of this poem. Michael speaks in much these terms to Isabel of what the sale of "his patrimonial fields" would mean to him:

> *"I have been toiling more than seventy years,*
> *And in the open sunshine of God's love*
> *Have we all lived; yet, if these fields of ours*

> *Should pass into a stranger's hand, I think*
> *That I could not lie quiet in my grave."*

(ll. 228–32)

Luke's departure is intended to lead to the ransom of the land, so that it may be passed to him with the family's title again secure: "He shall possess it, free as is the wind / That passes over it"—even as, we are to assume, Isabel and Michael and the older generations lie under it. The sacred bond between father and son in the poem is in part the result of just this sense of the ever-rejuvenated family, rejuvenated by the unbroken march of generations. Thus all of nature has its meaning renewed for Michael by the advent of Luke, so that with the boy "the old Man's heart seemed born again." Even so is the family ever renewed by each successive generation—which is why the dead stop at the end of the poem, symbolized by the Sheep-fold ever unfinished, reflects the profoundest dashing of Michael's hopes and of the meaning of his life.

Michael's speech to Luke in which he justifies sending him away even more clearly anticipates the tone and the meaning of the line from "Tithonus" that I have been using as a touchstone. As he speaks to his son, so he invokes the memory of his parents, extending the chain of lives backward as well as forward:

> *Both of them sleep together: here they lived,*
> *As all their Forefathers had done; and, when*
> *At length their time was come, they were not loth*
> *To give their bodies to the family mould.*
> *I wished that thou shouldst live the life they lived,*
> *But 'tis a long time to look back, my Son,*
> *And see so little gain from threescore years.*
> *These fields were burthened when they came to me;*
> *Till I was forty years of age, not more*
> *Than half of my inheritance was mine.*
> *I toiled and toiled; God blessed me in my work,*
> *And till these three weeks past the land was free.*
> *—It looks as if it never could endure*
> *Another Master.*

(ll. 367–80)

The past generations lie beneath the land they worked, the present generations work on the land until it is their turn to lie beneath, while the free wind, the unbound force of nature, passes freely over it now, as it has before and will again. By sending the boy away, Michael breaks the union in labor of the generations still alive. He will now do alone, as he had before Luke's arrival, the work they have been performing together. And Luke is to depart the fields, though he is to be protected from temptation in his absence by bearing "in mind the life [his] Fathers lived." He is to be protected also by remembering the Sheep-fold, which represents the bond between them. It had been originally proposed as a task to be performed jointly; but Michael is now to build it himself on the cornerstone laid by Luke before his departure. But the covenant between them, for work to be done separately before they are to come together again, involves a final provision—unexpected even from so austerely gentle a soul as Michael—that the father's love for the son be absolute, that it continue to the end in spite of anything the boy might do or become:

> "but, whatever fate
> Befall thee, I shall love thee to the last,
> And bear thy memory with me to the grave."
>
> (ll. 415–17)

Michael is called upon to make good this extravagant promise, and he is of course true to his word, as true as he is to his love for Luke, which remains an absolute, uncontingent value:

> There is a comfort in the strength of love;
> 'Twill make a thing endurable, which else
> Would overset the brain, or break the heart.
>
> (ll. 448–50)

It is just this strength of love that keeps Michael performing his hard, routine labors "for his sheep, / And for the land, his small inheritance," even though he must know that it is doomed, after all, to go "into a stranger's hand." However futile his efforts may be, now that all hopes for extending the patrimony to any additional generations are gone, he must perform what the land and the sheep demand. He proves his endless faithfulness to their covenant by working, "from time to time," on the Sheep-fold, however unlikely the chances of his finishing it alone before his death and however insignificant it would be if he did finish it, in view of what is to become of his land. By now the gesture is all, and he preserves the ritual of repairing to work at the Fold "from time to time." The furthest concession Wordsworth will make to his grief and his hopelessness, as impediments to his dedication, occurs in the lines,

> and 'tis believed by all
> That many and many a day he thither went,
> And never lifted up a single stone.
>
> (ll. 464–66)

For this old man, such a concession to despair is significant indeed. Yet, in withdrawing from the scene, the poet again emphasizes his persistence by repeating that

> from time to time,
> He at the building of this Sheep-fold wrought,
> And left the work unfinished when he died.

Since seven years have passed since Luke's departure, Michael must have been ninety-one, with no hope of finishing, so that the persistence—however intermittent—makes the Fold a remarkable testament of his faith, his tribute to the life he and his fathers lived.

Here, in so early a poem, is a magnificent expression of natural human piety. Close enough to nature to keep human relations purified, the life in "Michael" is yet contained within a thoroughly human rather than a natural community. Man lives in constant awareness of his mortal taint: both his history and his future emphasize death and the acceptance of death. It is the awareness of death that sophisticates the pastoral metaphor of man's relation to nature. In the innocent state suggested in some of Wordsworth's early poetry, the child shares nature's immediacy as if there were no death; and the man can will the passivity that allows him to return to nature's bosom. The pathetic fallacy is fallacious no longer, so that nature is alive and absorbs man as he shares that life. Here is the true and simple timeless metaphor of the pastoral, the naïve refusal to see human life as apart from nature, as having fallen out of nature. On the other hand, an awareness of the separateness of the human state must carry with it an emphasis upon the difference between the single human life and the leaf on the tree. Their wintry deaths and springtime rebirths are only analogies, alas, and not true metaphors at all. The leaf that buds next year is not the one that has just died; and if this is of little importance to those who see leaves as interchangeable, it matters greatly when we cross over to human life, where each is unique and irreplaceable—and thus irretrievably gone. The reality principle of our lost innocence reminds us to deny the magical transference of the natural metaphor and, consequently, to press the metaphor to the point of its own absurdity.[5] Each death in a fallen mankind produces an individuated sorrow within a human herd that knows its individual mortality, even as a collective sense of community presses it toward a belief in a collective, generational immortality. But, driven by time, man is not like the leaf on a tree filled with untimely joys; he is not without the individual and the special—though shared and common—sorrows he both suffers and produces in others. Fallen man, alienated from nature, can through his history create a crowd, though hardly like the crowd of daffodils—even when, like Michael, he remains close to nature still.

The fact that the history of Michael's generations is a collective *human* history accounts for the strength of his love and his fidelity. For his response to Luke's prodigality rests on his reverence for the familial tie and the covenant which binds it. There is no moral judgment in him. This is to say that the natural human community, as distinct as it is from the natural community, is distinct also from the ethical human community which rests on moral judgment. Human sin is not to be outlawed along with the sinful agent; rather, it is to be lived with as the very foundation of those limitations which create the human as merely human and create the history of those suffering generations. Their sad music is sung in unison for what is suffered singly and yet is endured because it has all been suffered before. The sacred bond persists despite all one may do: it exists as that which verifies mortality and the history that mortality at once permits and dooms.

---

[5] Here is an extension and transformation of the general metaphor of the Fall which, I earlier noted, Wordsworth treated both as real and as a will-o'-the-wisp, making it—in the manner of Archimedes—the "point whereon to rest his machine" in order to "move the world."

What remains despite all is one's historic role, what one owes and what—through the ritual of never-ending routine gestures—one never stops repaying.

It is this natural human community that sustains Michael and the rest—except for Luke, who is sent away from its sustaining powers. With its historical, generational sanctions, the natural human community holds its members within itself, preventing each of them from asserting his unique rights to what is owed him because he has suffered in singleness that which man commonly suffers. To demand special treatment, or the special right of private moral judgment, is to rebel against the natural human community in behalf of the other, more self-conscious and self-righteous community I have called (after Kierkegaard) the ethical. From the standpoint of the ethical, Luke would have been condemned and all fidelity to him terminated, since —ethically—that fidelity had to rest upon just cause in his behavior. Even his memory would be cast out into the exile (out-cast state) that he was forced into by life in the disinterested city, where there is no history to temper moral necessity. But not so Michael, whose gentle, humane, unlimited capacity for acceptance is evident as he lives "the life [his] Fathers lived." The "comfort in the strength of [his] love" makes everything—any action—"endurable." And, like the leech-gatherer, like the Dilsey-like creatures in Faulkner, Michael endures, making his gesture by toiling at the Sheep-fold "from time to time," even though there are moments of despair when he "never lifted up a single stone." Beyond this momentary lapse he cannot go, and he never fails to work yet again (though again only "from time to time") at what he can now never finish.

This relaxed catholicity of acceptance, this refraining from moral judgment, is a hard-won self-denial for the classic existent. It calls for an un-self-consciousness that comes hard to the visionary—which is why Michael only partly reflects Wordsworth, why the poet-narrator of the poem, now an outsider cut off by time and by temperament, nostalgically looks upon Michael's world as a blissful archaism. Still, the alienated visionary, learns from the less self-conscious existences from which he is cut off but which his poet's calling requires him to observe—here no less than in "The Solitary Reaper" and "Resolution and Independence." And he chronicles the "still sad music of humanity" which he hears and partly comes to understand.

The visionary, as a man trapped in dialogue, has been sophisticated by other commitments, most notably the ethical. And there is always for him the danger that he will confound the relaxed demands for natural human commonness in the herd with the hard insistences of ethical universality. The common need to endure what one suffers is beyond the ethical in that it requires a suspension of the very moral judgment upon which the ethical thrives. Yet, to the self-conscious sophistication of moral man, commonness translates into the universality under whose aegis judgment beckons (with what consequences *The Tragic Vision* was designed to point out). Thus it is that Wordsworth can slip into the ethical severity of a poem like his "Ode to Duty" almost interchangeably with the other sort of conservative restraint which we found in "The Solitary Reaper," which serves almost as a companion piece.

Using as his model a poem by Gray (the same Gray he complained about in the "Preface" to *Lyrical Ballads*), which in its turn was modeled on a poem by Horace, and using as his epigraph an aphorism from Seneca, Wordsworth clearly has established his conservative credentials both in the style and substance of "Ode to Duty." The first word of the poem in its opening apostrophe sets the tone: "Stern." There is explicit distrust—and rejection—of actions undertaken and justified by the immediacies of instinct, the claim of natural innocence, "the genial sense of youth." Instead, the poet invokes the dread interposition of the "Stern Lawgiver," the implacable ethical, and delivers himself to the service of "reason" and "truth." Rejecting freedom, he answers Duty's demand of "self-sacrifice" from her "Bondman." His freedom being "unchartered" and his "desires" springing from "chance," he feels—as a part of "frail humanity"—a weariness that longs only for rest and a fixed guidance. There is no doubting the unqualified nature of the ethical and propositional firmness of the poem's singleness of didactic intent. Wordsworth even felt obliged to omit from later editions of the poem a stanza he had earlier included after stanza 5 to introduce some note of compromise and thus to moderate his choice of the polar extreme of blind obedience in response to the extreme of blind impulse.[6]

[6] The stanza, which was omitted in editions after that of 1807, reads as follows:

> Yet not the less would I throughout
> Still act according to the voice
> Of my own wish; and feel past Doubt
> That my submissiveness was choice:
> Not seeking in the school of pride

It should be evident that Wordsworth, in this poem, sees the ethical rather than the classic as the alternative to the loss of the "aesthetic." Once innocence has abandoned the instinctual, after the Fall has occurred, only rational and universalistic repression is left to man. The kinds of endurance suggested in "The Solitary Reaper" or "Resolution and Independence" or "Michael" simply do not exist for the speaker in "Ode to Duty," perhaps because he has lost that other sort of innocence—human rather than natural innocence—required to be the Highland Lass or the leech-gatherer or the simple shepherd. Instead, he seems to trace the traumatic—and not altogether fortunate —leap from the aesthetic to the ethical as it is made by Kierkegaard's now universal man. Properly, the "Happy Warrior"—"he whose law is reason"—may follow.

The stern judgment which the poet joins "the just Gods" in delivering upon Laodamia also follows upon these convictions. Her crime derives from a refusal to surrender her private desires to the common need for human suffering. In "Laodamia" it is difficult to determine whether she has sinned against the ethical or against the classic. Clearly, through her love for Protesiláus, she claims a unique right, the right to have the law of nature and man suspended so that her dead husband can be returned to her. She is unwilling to accept the suffering that is decreed for her, even though her husband—in the spirit of the "Happy Warrior"—himself chose the role that brought forth such suffering. Knowing from the oracle that he would die if he were the first Greek to touch Trojan soil, he chooses to be first. "A self-devoted chief," he must elect to honor his obligation to his kind: "A generous cause a victim did demand" (l. 46). Laodamia cannot do as well, and misunderstands the temporary nature of his return as well as the spiritual nature of that which has temporarily returned.

> For "precepts over dignified,"
> Denial and restraint I prize
> No farther than they breed a second Will more wise.

There is a wavering, an uncertainty here—a desire to eat one's cake and have it too—that may have expressed Wordsworth's embarrassment at having come so far so fast from the spirit of many other of his poems. It seems clear that, as time went by and his conservatism hardened, he felt more embarrassment at the ambiguity of this stanza and so removed it. Whatever possible doubleness of intent the poem may have had (and, in view of what follows to conclude the poem, one must admit that there was little even at the start) was surely removed with this stanza.

No Platonist, she demands that the body come and that it stay with her. Rewarded by his brief and disembodied return to her as a considerable gesture from the gods for her profound fidelity, she shows her love to be as "ungovernable" as it is "fervent." She will not accept her role, even if all nature must alter its course to appease her desires. And she is punished: as his spirit departs, she dies and is condemned.

> *Thus, all in vain exhorted and reproved,*
> *She perished; and, as for a wilful crime,*
> *By the just Gods whom no weak pity moved,*
> *Was doomed to wear out her appointed time,*
> *Apart from happy Ghosts, that gather flowers*
> *Of blissful quiet 'mid unfading bowers.*
>
> (ll. 158–63)

Here again this later version of the poem finds Wordsworth far harsher in his judgment than he was earlier.[7] The early version

[7] Note how gently sympathetic, for example, the following early version of these lines is:

> *Ah, judge her gently who so deeply loved!*
> *Her, who, in reason's spite, yet without crime,*
> *Was in a trance of passion thus removed;*
> *Delivered from the galling yoke of time*
> *And these frail elements—to gather flowers*
> *Of blissful quiet 'mid unfading bowers.*

Or, somewhat later, there seems to be an intermediate phase, an uncertainty about her guilt and about the justness of the gods:

> *By no weak pity might the Gods be moved;*
> *She who thus perished not without the crime*
> *Of Lovers that in Reason's spite have loved,*
> *Was doomed to wander in a grosser clime,*
> *Apart from happy Ghosts, that gather flowers*
> *Of blissful quiet 'mid unfading bowers.*

Laodamia has been successively characterized as being "without crime," as being "not without the crime," and as committing "a wilful crime." From being judged gently and counted among the happy flower-gathering ghosts, she comes to be judged harshly by gods who are moved by "no weak pity" and is set apart from the happy ghosts. And the poet moves from asking us to judge her gently, to watching the gods judge her harshly, to judging her as harshly as the gods have (by referring to them as "just Gods").

(though already as late as 1814) seems closer to Wordsworth's classic moments than to his ethical ones. Whatever her failings, he seems to prefer not to judge them so much as to place them in the collection of the ways of human suffering—here the female as differentiated from the male—and their lamentable consequences.

It is for this reason that the final stanza of the poem seems far more in accord with the earlier, milder judgment—the call to pity instead of the approval of the gods for rejecting pity as "weak"—than with the stern verdict Wordsworth at the last leaves with us. Its first line puts Laodamia's story and its sad ending in its place: "Yet tears to human suffering are due." By now this is a familiar response in Wordsworth, although it is in keeping more with his classic than with his ethical moments. The Laodamia story, concerned as it is with the historic human roles of warrior and of wife and with the acceptance or rejection of those roles, somehow evokes Wordsworth's soft understanding of what leads one to demand a singularity of treatment as well as what leads another to make his peace with the common fate. The more he returned to the poem, the more he hardened toward the inflexibility of judgment that characterizes the ethical. But the humane retreat of the final stanza remains, in which man mourns with his tears the "mortal hopes defeated and o'erthrown." Man mourns rather than condemns, whatever the gods may command.

And more than man so mourns. In a moving reversal of those early poems, in which man moves only in response to nature's joy, here Wordsworth concludes by having nature shape itself in a mournful response to human suffering (or so, at least, human faith must have it):

> Upon the side
> Of Hellespont (such faith was entertained)
> A knot of spiry trees for ages grew
> From out the tomb of him for whom she died;
> And ever, when such stature they had gained
> That Ilium's walls were subject to their view,
> The trees' tall summits withered at the sight;
> A constant interchange of growth and blight!
>
> (ll. 167–74)

The chastening and subduing of mature, sophisticated man by the sorrows of human experience are difficult for Wordsworth to trace without falling into the ethical as the alternative to the naïvely aesthetic. If the trust in instinct is gone, then obedience to reason as instituted in law summons us. But the Wordsworth I have meant to show as possessing a special value for us is classic instead: he emphasizes the merger of one's suffering with man's common lot rather than the self-indulgence in judging others in order to preserve one's special privileges of lamentation. It is not often, from what we have seen, that Wordsworth succeeds in creating the classic alternative, except by inventing a naïve existent—a leech-gatherer, a Michael— with the poet the vicarious, but still alienated, onlooker who cannot quite join his subject.

A striking exception is one of Wordsworth's finest poems, the "Elegiac Stanzas" inspired by Sir George Beaumont's painting of Peele Castle in a storm. Perhaps more than any other of his poems, this one has its meaning contained in its language and its metaphor, with a tightness of structure and a manipulation of his poetic materials that are very rare in the kind of poetry he writes. The poem can serve also as a recapitulation and consummation of all that we have been observing about the several moments in Wordsworth's work. All this is achieved through the use of the poet-protagonist who needs no existential surrogate. He can be both visionary and existent because his action is symbolic only: his self-consciousness has thoroughly embedded the development of his awareness in the diffuse precision of metaphor.

The poem is dominated by the use of multiple reflections and what these imply about the illusory nature of the poet's reality. We feel ourselves almost in Plato's world. There are reflections within reflections as we follow the poet in his pursuit of a reality in which he can rest. There is the original castle of his memory, its image in the "glassy sea," the image of that experience in the picture the poet would have painted, and the present picture by Beaumont, which, in turn, is an image of the poet's present state of mind. Of course, his first experience of the castle, in its static and peaceful perfection, has precisely the character required for unmarred reflection. We have a cluster of the appropriate adjectives: "pure," "quiet," "perfect," "calm" (though here it is used as a substantive), "gentle," "tranquil," "peaceful," and again "quiet" (though this time as a substantive). But this language supports subtler elements that are at work. In the fourth line, as if to emphasize the Platonic quality of the secure world of peace, the poet speaks of the castle's "Form" "sleeping on a glassy sea." Of course, the utter sameness and stillness of the sleeping Form would require the utter peacefulness of the sea. The poet could look either at the castle or at its reflection in the water and see the one "Form." In so constant a world, he need not distinguish between reality and its image. All is sameness, apparently with no threat of change: "Whene'er I looked, thy Image still was there; / It trembled, but it never passed away."

There is no more than the slightest ruffle of the water, and that temporary, so that the "Image" is a dependable reflection of the "Form."[8] The lines themselves imitate the sameness of the world: "So pure the sky, so quiet was the air! / So like, so very like, was day to day!" We move from redundancy to repetition, as if the sameness of words can reproduce that constant sense of stasis. The second of the two quoted lines is a series of exactly reproductive mirrors: of the nine words there are fully three pairs ("so," "like," "day"). The like-ness of the days is demonstrated most simply but surely by the second, unvaried use of the word. The "like" to "like," the "day" to "day," these establish the timeless assurance of the next two lines that speak of the certainty of the "Image." No wonder the poet can speak of the "calm" as "perfect," the calm of the day, the calm of the sea, the calm of the castle's image. Thus it is that he can then create for us the verbal equivalent of the picture he would have painted of "the Poet's dream." It would have been a celebration of just this "lasting ease" or "Elysian quiet." The world of the picture would be one with "silent Nature's breathing life."

Here, then, is a vision of that joyous harmony before the Fall such as we have witnessed again and again in Wordsworth. The world of nature represented by the sea and the creation of man represented by the castle reflect one another to the point where they are beyond distinction. This "steadfast peace" is indeed "the Poet's dream," but— from the perspective of his present awareness—no more than a dream. It is now confessed to be only "the fond illusion of [his] heart." It has no more reality than the castle's image, which appeared so constant

---

[8] Or should the poet perceive in the trembling a threat that reminds him how fragile that "Image" is, and what slight disturbance of the water will be required for it to pass away altogether? But his assurance at this point would not permit him to acknowledge any warning of what nature must have in store for him.

but really could last only until the peace of the water was disrupted. Here is a further extension and realization of the conceit: the identity of "Form" and "Image" in the early dream world—an identity permitted by the use of the water as mirror—leads to the relegation of that entire world to mere unsubstantial illusion, no more real than a world without storms.

As the apparently real castle, trapped in the transience of a water image, first provoked his imaginary picture of the dream, so the actual picture provokes his awareness of the state of the real castle, now out of sight. The stormy sea in the painting, we remind ourselves, must have wiped the castle's image off the sea—and permanently, since Beaumont's picture, for all its dynamics, is a fixed object. The turbulence of the world is with us for good. Yet the poet himself seems almost to have painted the picture as a reflection of his own anguish. For the storm that has come to the poet is the death of his brother, destroying in him—also for good—the power to create "the Poet's dream." This is the power, now "gone, which nothing can restore." Time and change—the change that works destruction—have entered to transform his static world, although the speaker must answer the challenge with a newly earned peace of his own. Thus he has "submitted to a new control."[9]

The line "A deep distress hath humanised my Soul" must describe the process I have noted so often: the Fall from the joyous natural community to the sad human community. The word "humanised" says it all, suggesting—especially if we recall the Lucy poems—what is to be gained out of the loss that makes us human. So, though his loss will always be fresh, and the world's calm gone forever, he acknowledges this awareness "with mind serene." Like the castle that "labours in the deadly swell," amid "this pageantry of fear," he "braves" his storm with a calm that cannot be undone by the turbulence that surrounds him. Edmund Burke's awesome and dynamic "sublime" may have replaced the placid, static "beautiful" in the world, but a newly strengthened serenity can still be achieved by man. "Cased in the unfeeling armour of old time," the castle will not lose its constancy in the unconstancy, the utter fluidity, of the ocean; it will not submerge its reality in the images of a momentary mirror.

---

[9] If this "new control" refers to the "Ode to Duty," Wordsworth is doing himself an injustice, since the "control" in this poem goes far beyond the ethical in its classic profundity.

And the castle must be seen as man's creation and the embodiment of his history (his "old time"). In its steadfastness, like the poet's, it now stands in contrast to the natural elements with which it earlier existed in the harmony of like reflecting like.

It is to his early self, to man isolated from his fellows—however comfortably he may relate to nature—that the poet bids farewell: "Farewell, farewell the heart that lives alone, / Housed in a dream, at distance from the Kind!" The "heart" that is here being rejected is the same that earlier invented "the fond illusion," the idyllic picture, of the opening stanzas. It is the victim of its own creation, "the Poet's dream," "the light that never was, on sea or land." And it was this dream that kept the poet—like the poet who learns the lesson of "Resolution and Independence"—"at distance from the Kind." Sustained by the illusion of peace and timelessness, he could not hear "the still, sad music of humanity." The blindness to the lamentably dynamic truths of nature, as man is related to it and distinct from it, leads to a false joy.

The melodramatic turbulence of the sea in the painting—the death of his brother—becomes the challenge of extremity, the Kierkegaardian shock, to the naïve and isolated "aesthetic" state in which the poet has rested. He responds not with the self-generating fury of the "ethical" but with the calm of the classic. Not judgment, not the demand for unique treatment as one who has been wronged,

> But welcome fortitude, and patient cheer,
> And frequent sights of what is to be borne!
> And sights, or worse, as are before me here.—
> Not without hope we suffer and we mourn.

This is no pollyanna cheeriness. The speaker has in the final line transferred at last from the "I" to the "we," as a sign of his recognition of the need to submerge his sorrows into ours, those common to "the Kind," sorrows as violent as the ones pictured before him and the personal one he is now celebrating, "or worse." Our historic role is suffering, and our historic response—one that preserves us as human and as creatures in a continuum—is endurance, endurance "of what is to be borne." Here is "Wordsworth's healing power," of which Arnold wrote. All these poems of Wordsworth's mature classic vision cherish that natural human community in which we discover what is most natural to us as man: neither identity with nature nor—in our alienation from it—an inflation of the self-consciousness with which we are left, but an awareness of our historic dimension which helps lose us in the human whole. Attuned to the echoes of history, we hear the sounds of those about us which help us to "frame the measure" of our private voices.

7

Adam Bede and the Cushioned Fall:
The Extenuation of Extremity

George Eliot lets us know at once that *Adam Bede* takes place in Wordsworth's world, a world not unrelated to Michael's. We can note the date of 1799 in her first paragraph. But I am speaking of a more profound relevance than this. Indeed, we must start before the first paragraph, with her epigraph from Wordsworth. It is precisely the Wordsworth I have been concerned with, the Wordsworth who is aware of the Fall and who responds to it not with ethical judgment, but with the understanding warmth of the natural human community:

> *So that ye may have*
> *Clear images before your gladdened eyes*
> *Of nature's unambitious underwood*
> *And flowers that prosper in the shade. And when*
> *I speak of such among the flock as swerved*
> *Or fell, those only shall be singled out*
> *Upon whose lapse, or error, something more*
> *Than brotherly forgiveness may attend.*

The naturalness of this human community is revealed by the consistently pastoral language: "nature's unambitious underwood," "flowers that prosper in the shade," "such among the flock." The human actors are those who have been "singled out" of the herd. In their singleness they are no longer under the protection of the "canopy" that allows the natural community of flowers to "prosper in the shade." (We can recall the trees in Shakespeare's Sonnet 12 "which erst from heat did canopy the herd." Or the flowers are like Wordsworth's crowd of daffodils, from which the lonely, cloud-like poet was singled out.) Those who are singled out of the flock may be seen as having fallen ("such . . . as swerved / Or fell"). But theirs must be a fall upon which "something more / Than brotherly forgiveness may attend." Our response is not to be within the austere sphere of ethical judgment. Clearly, what is required is for them to be reabsorbed into the flock, to be returned to the shade, under the communal, protective canopy.

Of course, we have learned from Wordsworth that man, as a fallen creature, is not nature, although by making his community more natural than ethical he can survive as part of his crowd. At the opening of the fourth book of *Adam Bede* (chapter 27, "A Crisis"), Eliot exaggerates the contrast between a glorious, utterly fulfilled day in nature and the sorrows about to befall her characters on just such a day: "A merry day for the children, who ran and shouted to see if they could top the wind with their voices; and the grown-up people, too, were in good spirits, inclined to believe in yet finer days, when the wind had fallen." But the next sentence converts to a metaphor that is a presentiment of the bastard child to come; and as such it emphasizes the disparity between the amoral innocence of pre-fallen nature and its transfer to a moral—and morally imperfect—man: "If only the corn were not ripe enough to be blown out of the husk and scattered as untimely seed." Now she can make the contrast explicit: "And yet a day on which a blighting sorrow may fall upon a man. . . . There are so many of us, and our lots are so different: what wonder that Nature's mood is often in harsh contrast with the great crisis of our lives? We are children of a large family, and must learn, as such children do, not to expect that our hurts will be made much of—to be content with little nurture and caressing, and help each other the more."[1] Again the call to human sympathy, "something more / Than brotherly forgiveness," reminds us of the need to re-naturalize the human community that admittedly has lost its oneness with nature, to make that community classic rather than ethical.

Thus the mild, unassuming character of the human community within "nature's unambitious underwood" is the classic assumption of Eliot's Wordsworthian novel. This is the assumption she reminds us of in the introductory chapter (chapter 17) to the Second Book ("In Which the Story Pauses a Little"), in which she presents her "Dutch

[1] *Adam Bede*, Rinehart ed. (New York, 1948), p. 298. Other citations from this edition are given in the text. The textual discrepancies in the epigraph from *The Excursion* (bk. 6) are Eliot's.

painting" theory of the modestly realistic novel. Not only are her characters to be represented as imperfect as they are, but they are to be the commonplace, unheroic folk whose depiction Wordsworth defended in his preface to the *Lyrical Ballads*. Of course, Eliot's attitude toward their moral imperfections is to be characterized by sympathy rather than by the strictures of ethical righteousness: "I find a source of delicious sympathy in these faithful pictures of a monotonous homely existence, which has been the fate of so many more among my fellow-mortals than a life of pomp or of absolute indigence, of tragic suffering or of world-stirring actions" (p. 180). Eliot here turns explicitly from the tragic to an alternative arena of human behavior, what I have been calling the classic. Just as explicitly she rejects extremity for the less definitive richness of the center of experience: "In this world there are so many of these common coarse people, who have no picturesque sentimental wretchedness! It is so needful we should remember their existence, else we may happen to leave them quite out of our religion and philosophy, and frame lofty theories which only fit a world of extremes" (p. 182).

But Eliot's statements about the objects of her fictional imitation are obviously thematic as well as methodological in their consequences. Her relaxed alternative to "a world of extremes" eases man's moral burden of judgment, transforming the universal human ethical to private human sympathy. It is thus proper that we are led into and out of this digression concerning her fictional intentions by way of her apologetic discussion of Reverend Irwine and the easy, all-accepting warmth of his human response in turning aside from the stern priestly role of judgment, of firm ethical guidance. Her defense of Mr. Irwine makes necessary the defense of her sort of novel, one which would have him as a major voice within it. And as we move, in this candidly introspective chapter of self-conscious digression by the novelist, from the "pagan" Rector of Broxton to Eliot's modestly realistic objectives and then back again to Mr. Irwine with a newly charitable receptivity to his lack of zealousness, we discover that our charity toward him is to be a reflection of his charity toward his erring parishioners and of Eliot's charity to them all. The sort of tale we are being told is to arouse a relaxed moral acceptance as much in contrast with the moral fervor of the heroic novel devoted to "a world of extremes" as the "wholesome" Mr. Irwine is to his more austerely Protestant successor, "the zealous Mr. Ryde." There is, of course, this pastoral nostalgia in the novel—of time as well as of place—for the world of Hayslope in 1799, with the inevitable advent (after the time of the novel's ending) of Mr. Ryde, and, with him, the inevitable imposition of those ethical inhumanities that wipe out the classic as a possible mode of existence. The stern ethical alternative to be provided by time in Mr. Ryde is an echo of the equally zealous Mr. Roe, who already exists in the time of the novel as Irwine's more ethically conscious, ascetic alternative— even as the forbidding *Stony*shire exists as the geographical and moral alternative to the full-living ease of *Loam*shire. Is it not appropriate that, in her trouble, Hetty must forsake Loamshire for Stonyshire, and that she must have her trial and almost her execution in the harshness of Stoniton?

It is the quality of Loamshire living that makes Mr. Irwine its proper pastor and George Eliot its proper chronicler: 1799 and Loamshire, the time and place for a village of Michaels. Theirs *is* a natural human community, an "unambitious underwood," a "flock" with a mutually sustaining power that becomes the power to contain even its most errant member, provided he does not push his separateness from them too far, so far—that is—as to escape that sustaining, containing power which finally, through time's attrition, heals all private wounds. It is the human capacity to set oneself apart, together with the communal capacity to reabsorb the alien member through sympathy, that makes these creatures more than the flock or the crowd of daffodils. Such a community needs no spiritual guide more ethically zealous than Mr. Irwine, who properly secures his role as preserver of the healing power of its communal balm. His relaxed tolerance represents a flight from the ethical with its self-assertiveness, as an earlier passage describing him makes clear: "for his was one of those large-hearted, sweet-blooded natures that never know a narrow or a grudging thought; epicurean, if you will, with no enthusiasm, no self-scourging sense of duty; but yet, as you have seen, of a sufficiently subtle moral fibre to have an unwearying tenderness for obscure and monotonous suffering. . . . He held it no virtue to frown at irremediable faults" (pp. 66–67). Eliot joins his "subtle moral fibre" with her own, using a morality beyond what we have been seeing as the ethical and thus judging him humanly rather than with "the eyes of a critical neighbour who [like the zealous Mr. Roe] thinks of him as an embodied system or opinion rather than as a man" (p. 67). For it is precisely such a reduction of a man to "an embodied system" which, in the eyes of a classic visionary, the ethical persists in achieving. For his part, Mr. Irwine answers charges made against members of his flock by his more ethically earnest parishioners in a properly Loamshire manner: "We must 'live and let live,' Joshua, in religion as well as in other things. You go on doing your duty, as parish clerk and sexton, as well as you've always done it, and making those capital thick boots for your neighbours, and things won't go far wrong in Hayslope, depend upon it" (p. 58). Here is the ultimate in the minister as non-dissenter. Instead of judging, one need only fulfill his continuing function in this natural human community, trusting to that communal sustenance to keep within it and under its unassuming control whatever human failings occur, as they inevitably will. It is also true that such sentiments as those of Mr. Irwine recorded here accord—too closely for comfort—with the Victorian "doctrine of works." But we should not permit that shabby doctrine of youthful capitalism to detract from, or distort, the essentially communal direction of Mr. Irwine's call to perform one's duty, or play one's role, within a mutually sustaining, daffodil-like "crowd," in which the only unforgivable crime is one's claim to a separate, privileged destiny and, with it, to a superior position from which to make a moral judgment.

Nevertheless, we must not rest too easily in the bland moral comforts of the Reverend's vision, nor should we come too close to an identity with that vision. We can note that the timing of Eliot's digression, this pause in her story in which she apologizes for the nature of her Reverend and her novel, indicates its ironic function. After all, Eliot feels compelled to intervene because we have just witnessed a meeting between Irwine and Arthur Donnithorne—between the pastor-confidant and his young protégé—in which the minister has scrupulously refrained from intruding himself upon the young man's troubled spirits. He even resists the urge to press Arthur toward the confession the young man seems to want to make. Eliot is called upon to explain and excuse such niceties as springing from other causes than his un-Christian neglect of duty: hence her digressive chapter.

The fact is that Irwine's scrupulousness proves to be enormously costly: this occasion represents the last chance for Arthur to be pulled back from the action that causes the sorrows which threaten to tear the Loamshire community apart. Yet the occasion is one which Irwine fails to seize. Arthur has come to confess to his minister in order to dispel the temptation brought upon him by Hetty (see the explicit

statement of his intention at the close of chapter 13). But Irwine fails
to act upon the signs given him by Arthur, even as he appears to read
them correctly. Arthur asks a general question: ought not a man be
given some moral credit if he yields to temptations that spring upon
him unasked and in a surprising way that throws him off guard, and
if he yields only after a hard and sincere struggle? Irwine's answer is
prophetically precise and, especially for him, shows a stern awareness
of the irrevocable consequences that make an act itself irrevocable:
"A man can never do anything at variance with his own nature. He
carries within him the germ of his most exceptional action. . . . Consequences are unpitying. Our deeds carry their terrible consequences,
quite apart from any fluctuations that went before—consequences that
are hardly ever confined to ourselves" (p. 175). Irwine is ready to apply
his considerable moral insights to Arthur and wonders whether he
should. "He really suspected that Arthur wanted to tell him something." But Arthur backs off and Irwine, though he has shown us (and
Arthur) his keen awareness of bleak moral consequences, fails to press
on as even he feels perhaps he should: "The idea of Hetty had just
crossed Mr. Irwine's mind as he looked inquiringly at Arthur. . . . If
there had been anything special on Arthur's mind in the previous conversation, it was clear he was not inclined to enter into details, and
Mr. Irwine was too delicate to imply even a friendly curiosity. He
perceived a change of subject would be welcome" (pp. 176–77).

This ironic use of Irwine's lax pursuit of his role—as the enabling
action (or inaction) of the near-tragedy—should put us on our guard
against an uncritical acceptance of his other-than-ethical position.
Eliot herself suggests Irwine's ministerial failure: "The opportunity
was gone. While Arthur was hesitating, the rope to which he might
have clung had drifted away—he must trust now to his own swim-
ming." Nor does Irwine turn away from condemning himself later, in
retrospect:

> It was a bitter remembrance to him now—that
> morning when Arthur breakfasted with him, and seemed
> as if he were on the verge of a confession. It was
> plain enough now what he had wanted to confess.
> And if their words had taken another turn . . . if
> he himself had been less fastidious about intruding
> on another man's secrets . . . it was cruel to think how

> thin a film had shut out rescue from all this guilt and
> misery. He saw the whole history now by that terrible
> illumination which the present sheds back upon the past.
>
> (p. 416)

In the light of "all this guilt and misery" to come, caused in part—if indirectly—by Irwine's excessive fastidiousness, by his character as minister to a congregation of classic existents, Eliot must interrupt her story, at the very moment of his failure, in order to defend him and, along with him, the kind of novel that uses him as a major one of its voices. For Irwine's "live and let live" attitude, in contrast to ethical austerity, *is* the right one for Loamshire in its routine aspect. That is what makes it Loamy rather than Stony, of course. But this attitude is sadly wanting when the routine is disrupted through a character's "most exceptional action." All members of the flock, who fulfill their communal roles through performance of the common routine, then close round the threat of secession introduced by the singular and the exceptional. The routine community thus reabsorbs its errant member within its loamy richness of mutual sustenance. The evil created by the irrevocable consequences endangers the community since, by spreading to other members, it can isolate them as well. The need, then, is for the evil itself to be isolated until it can be reabsorbed into the still solvent whole, as the routine seeks to re-establish itself and its hegemony.

Clearly, secrecy is the enemy of the communal, which requires a continuing shared openness in its human relations, even though that openness does carry with it the menace of spreading the evil. But it is excessive secrecy that permits the nourishing of those private dreams that lead to exceptional acts which single out the perpetrators. What is open is healthily exposed to the air; what is secret can only fester by being closed in upon itself. Eliot reveals just this opposition in her use of earrings as the rather obvious symbol of an errant sexuality that leads one astray from a conscientious attitude toward one's rightful function. Both Hetty and Bessy Cranage have a weakness for these questionable ornaments. Bessy is discovered wearing her earrings by Dinah in the early preaching scene and, after being scourged in public for them, tears them from her ears and, crying aloud, throws them down. But, presumably, she is not without them for long: when we see her at the birthday games, we learn that she "had taken to her earrings again since Dinah's departure" (p. 281). It is at this point that Bessy is juxtaposed to Hetty: "Anyone who could have looked into poor Bessy's heart would have seen a striking resemblance between her little hopes and anxieties and Hetty's." And Hetty, we recall, also has an addiction to earrings, so that two passages are devoted to this addiction as well. In the first (p. 152) Hetty tries on the large, gaudy, glass earrings in the secrecy of her bedchamber while she dreams luxuriant dreams of gifts from her rich lover, Arthur. In the second (pp. 254–56), again in the secrecy of her bedchamber, she once more puts on her fancy earrings for a moment, but this time—her dreams having been realized—they are the jeweled gold earrings Arthur *has* bought her to gratify her desires. In both cases she can wear them only in secret, as she nourishes her forbidden, if petty, desires in secret, hiding the trinkets away before she shows herself to her community. Here, of course, is the difference between her and Bessy, despite their common love for earrings. Whatever "her little hopes and anxieties," as symbolized in the earrings she cannot resist wearing, Bessy displays them openly. She is in no danger, even if she reverts to them after having sworn off, for she is not struggling to change her role or her place. Rather, it is precisely her role to be the somewhat laughable, if openly culpable, village flirt. She is not likely to evade or escape that role. What Hetty nourishes in secret, on the other hand, is in sharp contrast to what the Poysers expect to make of her with her own apparent—if somewhat grudging—compliance. Thus she can fool the heavy, sober Adam, while Bessy fools no one. Eliot herself puts it best: "You would have been inclined to box Bessy's ears, and you would have longed to kiss Hetty" (p. 281).

Indeed, Dinah, who seemed to have so moving an effect upon Bessy, however temporarily, can move Hetty—or even reach her—not at all. Hetty's first scene with the earrings occurs in the chapter, "The Two Bed-Chambers," the very title of which emphasizes the separation between Hetty and Dinah as the latter tries to reach her. Dinah, sensing some trouble in Hetty, comes from the next room to try to make herself Hetty's confidante. But Hetty petulantly refuses to confide in her, wishes to return to secret dreams of Arthur, and drives Dinah from her, so that she is left alone to enjoy the solitude of her now sealed-off chamber. The relation between the two girls is precisely the reverse of that between Arthur and Irwine in the chapter which follows immediately—ironically entitled "Links"—and which contains the abortive interview we have already traced, for it is Dinah who is the aggressor and intruder, who presses an unyielding Hetty toward a confession Hetty's secretiveness prevents her from making. In the following chapter of another confidence that was not quite confided, Arthur's essentially "open, generous" nature (p. 312) seeks out just such an intruding spiritual adviser, only to find Irwine too reticent to receive his intended confession. Here, then, are two critical meetings that fail, when the success of either could have prevented the sorrows which follow. If Irwine played his role as Dinah played hers, or if Hetty played her role as Arthur played his, all might have been well. But instead, the combination of advisers and advisees is such that the necessary openness cannot be achieved, and the truth remains to be played out, at high cost, in the shadows—the shadows of secret bed-chambers and the shadows of the wood.

The portions of the novel which trace the deeds that activate the rest of it are marked by these dramatic shifts from communal openness to alienating secrecy. The warm, homey chapter "in the cottage" is followed by the chapters (that begin at the same time the cottage chapter does) between Arthur and Hetty "in the wood." These, in turn, are followed by "the return home" to the open world of the Poysers, now joined by Dinah. Evening leads to the next chapter, the separated "two bed-chambers," and then to the ironic attempt to find "links" between characters. Whether the alienating separateness is caused by the nourishing of secrecy or by meetings that fail, the destruction of members of the community is threatened by that isolation.

The fatal function of secrecy, and the role of the wood in fostering it, are enhanced when we recognize in *Adam Bede* echoes of *The Scarlet Letter*, published almost a decade earlier. Mere coincidence cannot account for even the superficial similarities. In both cases the ruined girl is named Hester (although we normally hear of Eliot's by her pet name, Hetty), and the agents of their illicit motherhood are Arthur Dimmesdale and Arthur Donnithorne. The names could hardly be closer, even if Eliot could not resist making her Arthur the giver of the thorn. The function of the wood and of sin as the isolating elements further illuminates the second work by way of the first. Of course, the two Hesters are far more unlike than are the two Arthurs, who share a strange compound of conscience and irresponsibility. Hester Prynne must with her own strength work her way toward community despite the alien Puritan world that surrounds her, while

II. Through the Embrace of the Natural Human Community

Hester Sorrel allows her petty, shallow weakness to lead her away from the sustaining world, the warmly human community, that surrounds *her*. The strength of a member to withstand, by a transcendent dedication, a harshly ethical community in the one case is replaced in the other by the community's strength, which fails, however, to rescue the self-severing member, who, through weakness, "swerved or fell."

It is the element of secrecy and isolation which defeats the healthy, if routine, efforts of the natural human community and which, consequently, makes Irwine no longer an adequate pastor to meet such exigencies. This is why Arthur, as Irwine's disciple, is endangered by the private license which only communal containment can prevent from becoming a threat to that community. Arthur's social role as above and outside the natural working community of Hayslope (symbolized by the position of his table at the birthday party) leaves him specially exposed. He even lives by the wrong time (what Mrs. Poyser calls "gentle-folks's time" [p. 147]), so that Hetty's difficulty is, in part, traceable to the fact that she has forgotten the difference between the two times, that of the working farm community and that of the leisurely "gentle-folks." Her turning away from the daylight-saving needs of the loamy community is a turning away from a reality in nature to the artifice of a society that does not have labor as its way of life. Thus Arthur, who does not work for a living, alone with his gentleman's time to waste, can—without serious or ill intent—corrupt the shallow Hetty, whose devotion to her own way of life and concept of time is inconstant.[2] Thus also he can resort to semi-deceptions, contrary to his "natural" candor, when his secret actions demand contrivances to keep them hidden.[3] If Arthur's position prevents him from finding and using his "link" to the community, Irwine's reticence to

[2] The value Eliot places on work is continually demonstrated in her admiration for Adam's sense of craft, as it is in Arthur's defenselessness without it: "if Adam loved a bit of good work, he loved also to think, 'I did it!' And I believe the only people who are free from that weakness are those who have no work to call their own" (p. 300). Again the intrusion of the Victorian doctrine of works (Carlyle's *"laborare est orare"*) is evident enough.

[3] "Arthur was in the wretched position of an open, generous man, who has committed an error which makes deception seem a necessity. The native impulse to give truth in return for truth, to meet trust with frank confession, must be suppressed, and duty was become a question of tactics" (pp. 312–13).

pry—grounded on a trustworthy communal morality—precludes the necessary "link" between them which could rescue the young disciple. The isolation of Arthur's position and his lack of dedication to work put him in need of a "stony" rather than a "loamy" morality, although Irwine makes only the latter available to him.

In the end, it is only through the opening possibilities afforded by "meetings" that the alienating tendencies, and their disruptive consequences, can be overcome. Indeed, there have been meetings all through, so that we may see the very fortunes of the characters in the novel as structured by them. The first meeting we witness between Adam and Arthur occurs early in the chapter "Links," while Arthur is on his way to Irwine to seek the advice that is never given. It is a preliminary attempt at linkage, coming as it does immediately after the scene between Dinah and Hetty in "the two bed-chambers." This first meeting is filled with unknowing, veiled forebodings of things to come and ironic failures to get certain crucial things said. It thus prepares for the next scene between them, which occurs when Adam has caught Arthur kissing Hetty. This one is a meeting as unfortunate as it was unexpected. It culminates in the fight between them in which Adam, after knocking Arthur down, still refuses to forgive or to allow their relationship to reestablish itself, despite Arthur's desperate, if partly disingenuous, attempts to persuade him to do so. The two can never be further apart. The third meeting between them, in the chapter appropriately entitled "Another Meeting in the Wood," occurs after the catastrophe, with Hetty imprisoned, with Arthur about to depart and Adam threatening to do so. Adam remains unyielding: he insists on the irrevocability of the irrevocable act and will not allow any amelioration of its consequences. But there is a slight softening as he shows his awareness of the inevitability of human imperfection, even to the point of agreeing to shake hands with Arthur and to work to make whatever is to follow—for him and the Poysers—less rather than more painful, for them and for Arthur. Finally, the epilogue of the novel, with its leap of the years to 1807, finds the family at the homestead awaiting Adam's return from his ultimate meeting with the returned, the restored Arthur. They have come together: the tear has been mended, or at least patched as well as can be managed, although its existence can never be erased. The ground for this final scene has been laid by another meeting, "The Meeting on the Hill," in which Adam and Dinah come together. Through its meetings the novel has moved from the secret no man's land of the wood to the open, highland promise of the hill.

So the novel closes with the openness, the mutually sustaining warmth, and the relaxed classic acceptance that are at the heart of Irwine's attitude and performance of his function. Arthur has been returned to a community that now, even through Adam, offers to reabsorb him. And he is returning to Irwine, we are told, who jokingly threatens to keep him under his "old tutor's thumb." Under the new conditions, and in view of what all have learned, Irwine can now be tutor enough, even for Arthur. But in spite of the now common acknowledgment of Adam's earlier insistence that things can never be as they were—that "there's a sort of wrong that can never be made up for"—things are considerably better than they might have been. We close, not by witnessing Arthur's meeting with Adam, but by overhearing the narration of that meeting as we witness Adam's homecoming, watching him being met by Dinah, Seth, the children, with the Poysers—symbols of the loamiest aspects of Loamshire— just "coming in at the yard gate" to complete the note of homey affirmation in the communal union.

Adam Bede ends, as it began, in gracious accord with Eliot's self-conscious intention to defend the propriety of the good Reverend Irwine, as she protects the possibility of an alternative to "a world of extremes." The rich celebration of commonplace solidarity, with its modest muddling acceptances, thus offers a moving alternative to the extremity-driven tragic vision, as I have presented it, even as Eliot's Hetty and Arthur—for all their woes—collide with a more yielding, less austere society than did Hawthorne's Hetty and Arthur. This is not to say, however, that Eliot doesn't freely open herself to the tragic possibilities of her tale, especially through the forbidding and intransigent figure of Adam.

There is, indeed, an obvious but instructive paradox at the heart of the novel: this work of classic acceptance has as its protagonist (sufficiently central for the book to wear his name as its title) a character whose austerity leads him toward the tragic. For all her admiration for him, the novelist and her work seem at war with their hero, struggling with him to dominate not only the tone of the story but the consequences of its central catastrophe. Adam's stony morality, planted in Loamshire, struggles to subvert Loamshire's (and Eliot's) insistence on using its classic continuity to convert even catastrophe into comedy.

But of course the paradox is seeming only: Eliot has well arranged matters to assure the conversion of Adam and his puritanical intent rather than his subversion of Loamshire's (and her) absorptive and restorative continuity.

Through Adam we observe, sometimes fearfully, potentially tragic ingredients in both character and plot. Thanks to him, we see the severe threat of the fractures of dis-continuity, with the confrontation of extremity that would ensue. The elements are there in the tale, and Adam does all he can to seize upon them at their sharpest and most painful, trying to sharpen their already thin edge so that they can cut most deeply. Against this dedication to extremity Loamshire tries to apply its blunting instruments and Eliot her extenuating devices. Thanks to the latter, the former succeed: extremity sufficiently extenuated is extremity blunted.

If we recall what I saw as the tragic model in *The Tragic Vision*, we may be strikingly reminded of it in Adam's actions and in the situation in which he feels called upon to so act. There is the self-righteous protagonist, ready to indict all who do not measure up to his inflexible moral standards; and there is the immoral act which increases his capacity to break the continuity of his moral universe. After Arthur's action with Hetty, which Adam has witnessed, things can never again be as they were: "But Adam could receive no amends; his suffering could not be cancelled" (p. 318). "He's not the same man to me, and I can't *feel* the same towards him. God help me! I don't know whether I feel the same towards anybody: I seem as if I'd been measuring my work from a false line, and had got it all to measure over again" (p. 324). So there has been a fall, as Adam's very name should have warned us to expect. But because he acts absolutely in behalf of the ethical, he is exposed to all the destructive risks of the demoniacal, even as he is exposed to the revelation of his own failings, which undercut his self-righteous pretensions. He discovers that he has himself fallen, and can only add to his self-indictment as he contemplates the judgment he has so freely made and acted upon. Could the tragic pattern be more typically adhered to?

Adam devotes all his moral energy to making Arthur's action absolutely traumatic. He insists on discontinuity, as we have seen, turning Arthur's act into the ethical shock that converts all his thoughts to punishment—punishment as a form of vengeance—as he must rethink all of his relations to others and to his community. All that he retains is his sense of the irrevocability of the irrevocable act; and he resists with resentment any argument for the amelioration of the consequences of that act, not only when it issues from the defensive Arthur or from Irwine (who may be seen as Arthur's protector) but even when it is made by his trusted schoolmaster friend, Bartle Massey, rock of Broxton. For any suggestion that life must still go on, and that since it must it would be better for it to go on less rather than more painfully, is to suggest a continuity from life before the act to life after it. And such a continuity the traumatized sensibility of Adam must not accept.

But George Eliot has been at work undermining the profundity of the shock so as to make possible Adam's partial recovery and return to a life and communal values disturbed but not, in the end, totally disrupted. Eliot's primary tactic to counter Adam's tragic impulse is her attenuation of the action. She is forever slowing the pace, pausing lovingly over details in the routine life, luxuriating in a leisure that she seems almost reluctant to interrupt in order to get her story told. True to the Wordsworthian note she has struck from the beginning, she blunts her melodrama with the rich, if unpointed, expansiveness of her lingering descriptions. Much in the way that "Michael" deserved to be called a poem of attrition, *Adam Bede* is a novel of attrition—and with many of the same effects. It is probably because of this anti-melodramatic, leisurely pace that we find the arrival of Arthur with a last-minute reprieve for Hetty—embarrassing at best— especially unforgivable.

There are also precise ways in which Eliot's "deliberate speed" works against Adam's reckless ardor. For example, how cunningly Eliot contrives it so that Adam's traumatic discovery about Arthur and Hetty is limited to his witnessing their kiss. Upset as Adam is, insistent as he is about re-evaluating all human relations, nevertheless he still has witnessed only a kiss and suspects only an annoying flirtation. It is not until much later, when so much of his capacity for dismay has already been spent, that he learns the full extent of Arthur's villainy. Had he learned the entire story at once—had he discovered Hetty's pregnancy when he first discovered anything amiss at all—he would have responded with a violence beyond the possibility of eventual reconciliation. Instead, as Eliot has it, angry as Adam is, he can try to return to his hopes of marrying Hetty, though doubts engendered by the scene he has witnessed already exist within him. What if he had been engaged to marry her, and was without suspicion, when the entire truth about Hetty and Arthur broke in upon him? What possible extenuation of his tragic response could then have been invented? Far more useful to Eliot's purposes is this two-step letdown, and far less likely to serve Adam's tendency to make a total rupture out of a single action, to make every fall into the Fall.

But, as I have suggested, Adam also—in accord with the tragic pattern—is not without guilt, a guilt that must affect his insistence on the purity of moral judgment. If Arthur falls, Adam himself—true to his name—has fallen in the course of the novel, indeed, even before Arthur does. But here too Eliot manages to diminish the intensity of Adam's awareness. And again it is by attenuating the process by which he becomes aware that Eliot blunts the consequences of that awareness.

It is very early in the novel that the resentfulness Adam feels toward his irresponsible father brings him close to wishing that father dead. Indeed, in retrospect he assumes the guilt of having done so. The act which later brings him remorse occurs while he is working on the coffin which his father had neglected to make before he went out drinking. His father has shirked—and, in his place, Adam must perform—a sacred task. There is in Loamshire a classic, ritual need to celebrate death as well as life and thus to bury the dead with propriety. So Adam insists that, despite his father's truancy, the coffin must be ready though he may have to work through the night: "What signifies how long it takes me? Isn't the coffin promised? Can they bury the man without a coffin?" (p. 39). While he works, Adam proceeds to make a self-pitying, self-righteous statement to himself about the burden his father is to him: "Nay, nay, I'll never slip my neck out o' the yoke, and leave the load to be drawn by the weak uns. Father's a sore cross to me, an's likely to be for many a long year to come" (p. 47). Just then the rap at the door ("as if with a willow wand") and the dog's strange howl in response give Adam the superstitious sign that someone is dying at the very moment when his complaint about his father's longevity was on his lips. As Adam comes upon his father's body the next day, on the return home after delivering the coffin, he recalls guiltily that moment of his grudging thoughts and the mysterious rap at the door: "This was what the omen meant, then! And the grey-haired father, of whom he had thought with a sort of hardness a few hours ago, as certain to live to be a thorn in his side, was perhaps even then struggling with that watery death! This was the first thought that flashed through Adam's conscience" (p. 51). It is as if, through the resentment he uttered the night before, it was his own father's coffin that he had been symbolically constructing.

From this point onward Adam should be disqualified from making any harsh and unyielding judgment of others, since for such judgment self-righteousness is a prerequisite. Yet this self-realization has occurred well before he comes upon Arthur and Hetty and allows himself to suffer an ethical shock. Nevertheless, though it does not prevent him from pressing his rigid claim, it does undercut his right to make that claim as absolutely as he does, so that Eliot can simply call upon him to disqualify himself as a righteous judge whenever she needs him to. And so Adam does, in his own good time. In this way Eliot again has provided herself with the means to soften the hard consequences of her tale of moral villainy derived from weakness: by softening the hardness of Adam's inflexible response. It is also true, however, that the shock and consequences of Adam's realization of his guilt are weakened by his not making self-conscious use of them until much later, when his inflexible response to Arthur's behavior has already been allowed to develop. Indeed, after Adam's first instinctive reaction to his father's death and to his sense of complicity in it, no effective use is made of this moment in what follows in the tale. Adam is no Ivan Karamazov, to convict himself of symbolic parricide. Indeed, he is permitted by Eliot to give full rein to his angriest reactions to what Arthur has done, while she keeps his self-knowledge in reserve to make use of when she has to soften him.

During the funeral service for his father, Adam does summarize his judgment of his own austerity in a way that Eliot can allow him to return to whenever she wants him to move toward flexibility. But once the occasion of the funeral has led him to make this judgment of himself, no use is made of it that might have prevented Adam from swinging so rudely and recklessly into recriminating action. Adam's confession to himself should condition his future actions, but even he sees that his hardness may be incurable:

> "Ah, I was always too hard," Adam said to himself.
> "It's a sore fault in me as I'm so hot and out o' patience
> with people when they do wrong, and my heart gets
> shut up against 'em, so as I can't bring myself to

> forgive 'em. I see clear enough there's more pride nor
> love in my soul, for I could sooner make a thousand
> strokes with th' hammer for my father than bring
> myself to say a kind word to him. And there went plenty
> o' pride and temper to the strokes, as the devil will
> be having his finger in what we call our duties as
> well as our sins. Mayhap the best thing I ever did in
> my life was only doing what was easiest for myself. It's
> allays been easier for me to work nor to sit still,
> but the real tough job for me 'ud be to master my own
> will and temper, and go right against my own pride.
> It seems to me now, if I was to find father at home
> to-night, I should behave different; but there's
> no knowing—perhaps nothing 'ud be a lesson to us if
> it didn't come too late. It's well we should feel as life's a
> reckoning we can't make twice over."
>
> (p. 205)

This, we are told, "was the key-note to which Adam's thoughts had perpetually returned since his father's death." But despite the pitiless introspection of this passage, in it we are warned not to expect any change in him as a result of what his excesses have led him to see in himself. And he is as good as his word: his reactions to Arthur will be as self-indulgent, as absolute, as if there were no questioning the absoluteness of his own self-righteousness.

Still, although it does not impede his actions as a would-be tragic existent, Adam's self-consciousness is there to be tapped when Eliot is ready to start him on the road toward his healing and, with that healing, toward a partial restoration. His third meeting with Arthur, discussed above, marks the first significant change in him. Hetty's trial is over; she has just (in the previous chapter) been saved from death by the absurdly melodramatic appearance of Arthur on his horse, reprieve in hand; and she is now painfully imprisoned for life, a state which serves as a continual and agonizing reminder of the irrevocability of the recent past. Consequently, in order to render a visible tribute to that irrevocability, the Poysers are to leave Hayslope, and Adam with them. Here is the way to make the disruption of the community permanent and most painful: by uprooting the most soundly rooted of the communal elements that gave Loamshire its meaning ("to leave the place where they have lived so many years—for generations" [p. 477]). It is this horrifying prospect, destructive of the entire world of the novel as the trauma of discontinuity is erected into a final cause, that Arthur is out to prevent when he meets Adam. And they meet at the very beech tree in the wood where their traumatic meeting had occurred eight months before. Even before Arthur appears, Adam thinks of him and the beech tree and of that prior meeting, but thinks of him in a way that confirms the utter discontinuity: "at this moment, there was a stirring of affection at the remembrance of that Arthur Donnithorne whom he had believed in before he had come up to this beech eight months ago. It was affection for the dead; *that* Arthur existed no longer" (p. 475).

The conversation that ensues between them seems a replay of quarrels that Adam has been having with Irwine, with his old teacher Bartle Massey, with anyone who tries to persuade him to lighten rather than darken the already catastrophic effects of recent events. Invariably, Adam sees such arguments as attempts to erase Arthur's villainy and pretend it had never occurred; and invariably his interlocutor insists that only an insatiable and irrational desire for vengeance would drain every ounce of bitterness out of the events and would turn away from even the slightest hope of sweetening the aftertaste of the admittedly poisonous draught. The same debate takes place between Adam and Arthur: the latter pleads that no one but him leave the community, that Adam not permit the Poysers and himself to be uprooted. At once Adam rejects the suggestion, seeing it as a way of deriving some slight comfort from this sorrow. As Arthur speaks, Adam sees in his words "that notion of compensation for irretrievable wrong, that self-soothing attempt to make evil bear the same fruits as good, which most of all roused his indignation" (p. 477). And Arthur responds, like the others, by accusing Adam of "trying to make the evil worse."

At this point something occurs which begins Adam's turn toward the possibility of amelioration. Arthur, unknowingly, hits at Adam's weak spot in a way that, at last, initiates the thaw: "Perhaps you've never done anything you've had bitterly to repent of in your life, Adam; if you had, you would be more generous" (p. 479). Out of Arthur's hopeless certainty about the strong Adam's moral perfection, he has accidentally spoken the very words needed to arouse Adam's awareness of his considerable imperfections. He has blundered into the sort of suggestion of common guilt that worked so successfully for the shrewdly machinating "Gentleman Brown" in his confrontation with Jim in Conrad's *Lord Jim*. And, though unintended, it works here too, as Adam's concession reveals: "It's true what you say, sir: I'm hard—it's in my nature. I was too hard with my father, for doing wrong. . . . I've known what it is in my life to repent and feel it's too late: I felt I'd been too harsh to my father when he was gone from me —I feel it now, when I think of him. I've no right to be hard towards them as have done wrong and repent" (p. 480). And Adam relents. There is nothing here that he has not known before; even the terms of his confession are similar to the words hundreds of pages earlier. But now, after the lapse of time during which he has done the things he has known he had no right to do, these words belatedly begin to affect his behavior. Once again the drawing-out of the action and the act of routine repetition have worked for Eliot and against Adam's tragic impulse. He now at last offers to shake Arthur's hand, and he acknowledges that the less painful way may after all be the more unselfish way. He is almost generous as he agrees to stay and persuade the Poysers to stay. "God forbid I should make things worse for you. I used to wish I could do it, in my passion;—but that was when I thought you didn't feel enough. I'll stay, sir: I'll do the best I can. It's all I've got to think of now—to do my work well, and make the world a bit better place for them as can enjoy it" (p. 482).

So he will allow Loamshire to work its healing powers upon him. Despite the self-pity of the passage in its suggestion that from now on his can only be the joyless service of others, Adam himself finally is one of those who can enjoy the world's improvement which he here promises to help undertake. This may perhaps be an ironic note in the conclusion (so often criticized for its saccharine flavor), since Adam, in ending up with Dinah and those splendid children they have together, is clearly far better off than he would have been with Hetty had none of the sordid events of the novel transpired. His turning toward amelioration for others certainly leads to an ultimate amelioration for himself. Of course, what makes it possible is the healing workings of Loamshire communal magic. And it works on Dinah too. Torn between her religious vocation and her desire to minister as wife to Adam, she chooses her historic role in the human community over her zealous missionary role. It can be said that she truly has moved from Stonyshire to Loamshire. It is in terms of these warmly human pressures to embrace all—from Dinah through Adam to Arthur—under the Loamshire canopy that the conclusion of the novel, despite our reservations, can be said to be earned.

When Adam acknowledges to Arthur his excessive desire for vengeance while he was in his "passion," he is confirming Irwine's earlier judgment, delivered in words of warning which, prior to the third meeting with Arthur, Adam had chosen to ignore—or, worse, to reject:

> *"you have no right to say that the guilt of her crime*
> *lies with him, and that he ought to bear the punishment.*
> *It is not for us men to apportion the shares of moral*
> *guilt and retribution. We find it impossible to avoid*
> *mistakes even in determining who has committed a*
> *single criminal act, and the problem how far a man is*
> *to be held responsible for the unforeseen consequences*
> *of his own deed, is one that might well make us*
> *tremble to look into it. . . . If you were to obey your*
> *passion—for it is passion, and you deceive yourself in*
> *calling it justice—it might be with you precisely*
> *as it has been with Arthur; nay, worse; your passion*
> *might lead you yourself into a horrible crime."*
>
> (p. 433)

It is precisely this possibility (so similar to those patterns I traced in *The Tragic Vision*) that leads Adam toward the edge of tragic existence—and away from the compromising middle of existence represented by Loamshire classicism. And Eliot throws her weight—the weight of the pacing and structure of her plot—in support of the attempts of Loamshire to contain the dangerous tendencies of Adam, and thus to gain Arthur into the bargain.

We can now retrace the ethical and anti-ethical modes, the tragic and anti-tragic poles, set loose and controlled in the novel. If man has fallen out of the "insensate" perfection of nature's community, he falls either into the ethical human community (Stonyshire) or the natural human community (Loamshire). The ethical human community sees man as opposed to nature (and to his own nature), as the moral principle in self-conscious, struggling opposition to the spontaneity of the natural principle. It is the veil of universals without the protective canopy. The human-as-ethical is thus the antagonistic alternative to the natural: man rejects the Fall. Such a community is exposed to the tragic as an inevitable outgrowth of ethical insufficiency. The natural human community, on the other hand, accepts all of nature in man, even his fallen nature. It is a *natural* human community also because it views man's destiny through the pastoral metaphor, seeing in the life of communal man the analogy to growth and death in nature's seasonal generations, in the manner of Ecclesiastes. Such a vision of continuity, classic or choral, can unite man with the flock, with the crowd of daffodils, without losing his special destiny as man, man who both creates and suffers his history. It is the canopy without the veil. In this way the community, in its historical depth, is at once natural and human, a community of Michaels: Loamshire.

Close to nature and responsive to nature's demands on man, Loamshire is still human and thus responsive also to man's demands upon man, primarily upon his sympathy, a sympathy that may require the suspension of ethical judgment. Nature as nature can be joyous, while man—though responding to nature's joys—may stumble into sorrows that require human sympathy since they occur within nature's indifference. For while nature as nature is perfect, man is fallen, with only his herd to sustain him and his fellows in their common fallenness. Human evil can be kept from spreading by the healing, sustaining action of the community that accepts it as necessary but works to lessen its consequences. It is only when man separates himself from that community and nurtures the consequences of the acts of fallen man that evil is compounded. There is, then, the state of nature, no longer available to man; there is the sympathetic bond of a commonly fallen human herd that minimizes the consequences of the Fall, mitigating the inevitable suffering caused by those who fail the community; and there is the isolated creature who secedes from the community in order to maximize those consequences. Thus it is the second fall, the fall from the community of fallen humanity, that creates the sorrows of history which the community must absorb.

We have seen that Irwine, Arthur, and Adam have all erred grievously. Irwine's failure to be an adequate minister to Arthur stems from his Loamshire nature and can be made up for so long as Loamshire is given time to do its healing work. On the other hand, both Arthur and Adam fail their fallen community by denying it, consciously or unconsciously, its historic rights. Arthur, insufficiently joined to it since he is not part of the community of labor, is free (since Irwine refrains from binding him) to secede from its obligations by claiming for himself unique privileges that deny his bond to his fellows. And Adam, instead of joining a communal effort to reabsorb Arthur, stands alone in claiming his own right—as the uniquely injured party—to set Arthur apart for special and unforgiving condemnation. Arthur's human frailty has permitted his fall; and the herd, understanding its commonly fallen nature, must seek to lessen the consequences of any single fall from it by preventing it from spreading among other members who can be singled out. Instead, it absorbs that fall communally. It therefore must reject ethical judgment, recognizing the ethical sense of justice to be a disguised form of the fury of vengeance. But Adam must insist on the ethical, thereby creating grave danger to the entire community as well as to himself. He is willing to secede to exercise his unique right to condemn, thus seconding Arthur's secession instead of counteracting it. Irwine is thus correct to warn that Adam is on the verge of committing a worse crime than Arthur's. It is the sort of crime that occurs repeatedly among the protagonists in *The Tragic Vision*.

So Adam's crime in the novel is not the half-spoken wish that coincides with his father's death. This only establishes him as part of a commonly fallen humanity, like the rest of us. But this act finally (and Eliot's purposes require that it take too long a time) works upon him to keep him from committing the more singular, the more egregious crime against the community in its effort to sustain itself. The secession from communal sympathy is invariably the greater fall, since a crime against a single man—always to be expected—can be suffered so long as the historically ordained agency for human sympathy remains intact. But the withdrawal from community to claim one's unique rights, even—or especially!—the unique right to judge and punish, can lead to those unique vices of which Plinlimmon warned Melville's Pierre. Such ethical austerity would harden Loamshire into Stonyshire, and freeze Hayslope into Snowfield, when Dinah, by the end of the novel, is to show us that the movement ought to be the other way. But perhaps we should add that the date and archaic rural flavor of the action of the novel suggest that Eliot is only too aware, nostalgically, that classic existence is becoming an anachronism.

Fortunately, Eliot has plotted to allow Adam to draw back just in time, although surely—in defeating and subduing Adam's tragic propensities—she has had the help of those Loamshire stalwarts the

Poysers, Bartle Massey, and of course the steadfast Irwine. Not, of course, that Adam simply reverts to what he would have been had the events of the novel never occurred. To absorb is not to erase. To the extent that an evil act is irrevocable, Adam's insistence on our ethical need to judge is itself justified. But to the extent that its consequences can be softened, Irwine's insistence on communal absorption through sympathy should prompt our resistance to judgment. Despite the sweet comforts of the conclusion, clearly we are to see the suffering as continuing, even if its form has changed and its pain is somewhat covered over. Perhaps our discomfort with that conclusion is our sense that the transformed pain is not evident enough. As Arthur tells us in almost the final lines, he never was able to do anything for Hetty, who has by now been put conveniently out of the way for good—neither he nor anyone else. Which is perhaps why there was nothing left for Eliot except to kill her off if the novel was to achieve as much reconciliation as she wanted it to. Still, the loss of Hetty is absolute, and remains naggingly present to the end—and beyond.

It is for this reason that Arthur in the end acknowledges the justness of Adam's insistence on the irrevocability of the act. But all that surrounds this final moment (especially, as we have seen, Adam's good fortune in Dinah) insists on the likelihood of its consequences being ameliorated. So, as Arthur acknowledges the justness of Adam's claim, Adam's entire story acknowledges the justness of Irwine's claim and, with it, Arthur's attempt to make things less rather than more painful. By the end, as detractors of the novel have claimed, things are too close to being downright pleasurable. George Eliot has certainly beaten off the tragic alternative with a vengeance. As for Adam himself, Eliot gives us the most authoritative word on him when she describes his return to his work and to the communal routine after Hetty's trial and Arthur's departure:

> For Adam, though you see him quite master of
> himself, working hard and delighting in his work after
> his inborn inalienable nature, had not outlived his
> sorrow—had not felt it slip from him as a temporary
> burthen, and leave him the same man again. Do any of
> us? God forbid. It would be a poor result of all our
> anguish and our wrestling, if we won nothing but our
> old selves at the end of it. . . . Let us rather be thankful
> that our sorrow lives in us as an indestructible force,

> *only changing its form, as forces do, and passing*
> *from pain into sympathy—the one poor word which*
> *includes all our best insight and our best love. Not that*
> *this transformation of pain into sympathy had*
> *completely taken place in Adam yet; there was still*
> *a great remnant of pain, and this he felt would subsist*
> *as long as her pain was not a memory, but an*
> *existing thing, which he must think of as renewed with*
> *the light of every new morning. But we get*
> *accustomed to mental as well as bodily pain, without,*
> *for all that, losing our sensibility to it: it becomes*
> *a habit of our lives, and we cease to imagine a condition*
> *of perfect ease as possible for us. Desire is chastened*
> *into submission; and we are contented with our day*
> *when we have been able to bear our grief in silence, and*
> *act as if we were not suffering.*

(pp. 497–98)

Of course, this is his state prior to Hetty's death (after which *her* pain will be a memory and no longer an existing thing) and prior to his marriage to Dinah and the semi-idyllic state of the epilogue. Perhaps Eliot's desire for Adam to move further, from pain to sympathy, accounts for her finishing Hetty off as well as allowing the marriage. Nevertheless, the quoted passage indicates that Eliot does not want us to ask too much of Adam's restoration or of Loamshire's capacity to re-found itself. And Arthur's final words as well as Arthur's precarious state of health reinforce our sense of the lingering sorrow. Of course, the persistence of regret is offset by those who surround Adam upon his return from his meeting with Arthur and by the proper Loamshire prediction that Arthur will "soon be set right in his own country air" (p. 550). The pains of the fall persist, though some of those who have fallen manage to get up again, even if they do not quite rise. We have, after all, come through catastrophe even as we have advanced with Adam to the very edge of that destructive, tragic chasm. George Eliot has revealed her awareness of all the urgent drives that lead toward it as well as the comforts of retreat. But it is a retreat that has its modest gains, providing we can convert ourselves into choral man, whose history has earned him the right to sing sad songs with a communal joy.

8

Postscript: The Naïve Classic and the Merely Comic

PRIDE AND PREJUDICE

Before turning from works that embrace the natural human community, I should deal briefly with an example or two that take this communal sense too much for granted, that assume it as a given, never essentially challenged. These should thus be seen as examples of a not-quite-classic vision. We have seen Wordsworth and Eliot earning their way to the dream of a communal home only as they retreat from an extremity whose presence is real and whose threat is both immediate and profound. But what follows in this discussion is a mere postscript to those awarenesses we have seen fully achieved, as we now witness communal attachments that are not seriously enough questioned. It is a blessing and an unfreighted joy to have the private world at once translated into communal values that are instantly available. But we can have such a joy only as we retain a naïveté which need not confront the dialogue that we have from the first seen as framing the fully aware classic vision. To retain this naïve unaware-ness of tragic as well as classic alternatives (as I have defined them, of course) is to retain the comic sense unimpeded by the darker concerns that force the comic to be shaded into the comic-as-classic. And it is the latter only that should be the proper business of this book. Never-theless, a glance just the other side of our boundary between the comic-as-classic and the merely comic, if only to establish it as our limiting case, may be more than a digression; it should indeed be helpful.

It is in a context thus qualified that I mean to introduce Jane Austen's *Pride and Prejudice*. I want to emphasize those aspects of the novel that inhibit any profound challenge to the acceptance of community and its values. And there are a variety of effective ways in which Austen prevents her game from being an open one, susceptible of going either way. Her cards are so wonderfully stacked that we either do not recognize that they are or prefer them that way. The hope, the expectation, and the thwarting or accomplishment of marriage are the most serious problems the novel deals with. They provide the obstacles to be overcome; they are the disturbers of tranquillity and the creators, in turn, of further tranquillity. And the moment we are persuaded to accept these as the world's major difficulties, we are affirming the primary values of Austen's middle-class society. This world, in which morals are largely reduced to manners and manners are the means for "making it"—by way of a desirable, or at least a suitable, marriage—is a world which precludes any serious challenge. The revolutionary impulse, momentarily alive in Wickham, is subdued before it can attain any vigor, as Wickham is revealed to be a fool as well as a cad. On the other side, the bitterness of an all-denying cynicism, keenly pointed up in Mr. Bennet, is sharply undercut by the more usefully applied intelligence of Elizabeth, who reveals the serious moral consequences (in this world of manners) of such unconstructive negativity.

The modesty of plot is echoed in the modesty of theme. The slightness of the obstacles to be overcome for Austen's characters to achieve their comic denouement is but another way of talking of the ease with which—for all the apparent difficulties—the desirable marriages can finally be accomplished and the intelligent and responsible continuance of this society assured. From the first page the major question to be resolved is whether Jane is to marry Bingley, and it shortly becomes clear that this resolution hinges on that other question which more warmly concerns us: whether Elizabeth is to marry Darcy. Very little, if anything, occurs in the novel which is not directed to these resolutions. We observe the multiple probabilities in favor of or opposed to the happy conclusion of our hopes (and the Bennets') and see the elimination—sometimes gradually, sometimes by pauses and leaps—of all the probabilities but those needed to tie matters up neatly and satisfactorily. There is also the almost too proper five-act structure, as we move several times from the Bennets' home to the visits away from home, where the two daughters can be displayed without the handicap of their undisplayable family. Austen needs to get them away from their home and she does, though they alternate travels with returns home, so that we can measure their gains and losses each time they re-establish their unhappy family routine. Thus Elizabeth, on whose fortunes Jane's fortunes clearly depend, ventures farther and farther from Longbourn: to Netherfield, to London, almost climactically to Rosings, and climactically to Pemberley. At each step obstacles of sentiment are cleared away and rivals are removed, each time only after affairs look darker than ever, so that the least likely becomes likely indeed. Of course, until Pemberley new obstacles and new rivals seem to arise, and even after Pemberley the short-range threat of the Lydia-Wickham affair looms over Elizabeth and Darcy, although that affairs turns out to expedite rather than prevent the desired conclusion. For a while, Pemberley seems to be another Rosings, with family ties turning a promising situation into one darker than it had been. But if Rosings turned out to be a false climax, Pemberley turns out to be a false anti-climax—and the proper climax, happily. In this careful way, Austen works her simple structural magic, bringing always closer to realization the marriages she works to manage, even as their probability appears to diminish.

There is a structural irony, close to the Aristotelian peripeteia, behind this procedure, although it here serves a comic rather than a tragic purpose. We have observed how Austen manages her incidents so that, while they seem to be moving in an unfortunate direction, they are actually preparing to veer around to the opposite and desired direction. This tendency is enhanced by the separate frustrations of the intentions of individual characters, so that what their actions bring about is precisely what it has been their purpose to avoid and what they fail to bring about is precisely what they have worked for. But it is to Austen's comic purpose to use these incongruous relations between expectations and fulfillment to get her people to perform their proper social roles. The reversals of intention work against whatever would isolate the individual and, instead, work to bring him into his place in the patterned social fabric. It is as if, for all his resistance, the individual is snapped into place by the concatenation of events. Neither intellectual cynicism nor rebellious or secessionistic tendencies can withstand the pull of that fabric which has the complicity of Austen's plot-engineering to ensure its intactness. The somewhat anti-social position of Mr. Bennet was caused by events prior to our story; and even the mock-sinister challenge of Wickham is turned to reinforcement as he too is snapped into place. Whether this fabric is but a flimsy veil fronting for an unstable psychological reality (which events in the novel might occasionally lead us to suspect to be the case) is, finally, not a possible question in the world of Austen's tale as she creates and disposes of it. There is nothing flimsy about this social fabric: it resists any tear that might reveal another, less manageable kind of reality behind or beneath it.

The story is dominated by a single major reversal: Elizabeth's desire to alienate Darcy prompts her to that behavior and those tactics which turn out to be the only way she could have won him. Similarly, her desire to escape her situation leads to those travels which are required to bring her into the midst of it and, in a way, to transform it. (We must remember that she consents to go to Pemberley, for example, only when she is assured that Darcy is not to be there.) The behavior of the comic villains follows a similar pattern. We can easily observe how each effort of Miss Bingley to discredit Elizabeth and to improve her own standing in Darcy's eyes ends by working in Elizabeth's favor. Or there is the final, ironically enabling act of Lady Catherine, who comes indignantly to Elizabeth with an imperious demand on behalf of her own daughter's chances; it is this demand that tells Elizabeth what she must know about Darcy's continuing intentions toward her in spite of the Lydia-Wickham affair. Further, Lady Catherine's report to Darcy of Elizabeth's attitude during their unhappy interview gives him the hope he needs. (Austen directs us to the reversal of intention: "unluckily for her ladyship, [her] effect had been exactly contrariwise" from what she intended; or, "Lady Catherine's unjustifiable endeavors to separate us were the means of removing all my doubts"; "Lady Catherine has been of infinite use.") Finally, we have seen how Lydia's escapade effects the final solidification of the marriage it seemed to threaten. Elizabeth regrets telling Darcy about the runaway couple, certain that this confidence has caused her to lose him, but this allows him to act in a way that not only saves Lydia and Wickham but permits a far more satisfactory union between the couple which is our central concern.

Nor are matters different when we observe the relation between the Elizabeth-Darcy match and the other central one between Jane and Bingley. The latter involves two docile creatures to whose union the only obstacles could be external, imposed by meddlesome or malevolent or misconstruing intruders, so that only external clarification—of the sort that could permit the Elizabeth-Darcy marriage—can remove the impediments. So the match between the simple folk depends on the internal resolution of that turbulent opposition between the complex couple. This dependence of the one match on the other is so managed that the forcing of Bingley away from Jane early in the story (which seems to doom any future for Elizabeth and Darcy as well) clears the way for the Elizabeth-Darcy relationship to mature so that it may blossom—in spite of both principals—into marriage, the very marriage required for the Jane-Bingley marriage to come to pass after all.

One could look at endless details and find that the pattern is consistent. Structural ironies are everywhere, and everywhere they appear to defy the very expectation they are really fulfilling: just the combination of the surprising and the probable which Aristotle originally prescribed. Austen's comic purpose turns everything to social advantage, so that the reversals seem both to disguise and to facilitate our subliminal awareness of a society that always claims its own in the end. There is in them a suggestion of teleological inevitability as the fabric is woven into a wholeness that permits no ripping away. So it is also that Austen's very concern with perfection of form—a small and modest form that arranges minor obstacles and minor victories over them—reflects her un-self-critical classic vision. It is as if she is, in my terms, a classic existent rather than the classic visionary who is trapped in—and exploits—his dialogue for all its multiple awarenesses. For any major challenge, or even any possibility of profound provocation, would threaten her entire structure, thematic as well as formal. It is in this sense that I have found her special use of reversal to be the device which enables her to ensure safe management of both theme and form. The individual is not permitted to produce a crisis: consequently there can be no "either/or" except as a romantic extravagance pursued by fools or frauds and exposed by events as misleading fancies. Events work to undo the minor frailties or follies of errant individuals, and to undo them in the interest of overriding social good sense. Thus works the comic reversal, the fortunate irony that insists on setting things straight by snapping even recalcitrant characters back into their soundly functioning roles.

It is the diminished sense of serious freedom in the individual, resulting from Austen's inexorable reliance on the action of the novel to put its characters into place, that predisposes her to deal with characters whose inner life is of limited complexity. It also exposes her to the difficulties of handling someone like Darcy. Thus the often-noted structural imperfections of *Pride and Prejudice*—next to works like *Emma*, for example—derive in large measure from Austen's problems with Darcy and are instructive enough to justify our dealing with this novel instead of her less flawed ones.

Darcy must appear to be prideful enough at the start to provoke Elizabeth's prejudice, so that she is prepared to believe the worst of him in his relations with Wickham; and he must be gentle enough— indeed, must be shy almost to the point of humility—for Elizabeth to warm to him from their meeting at Pemberley onward. Austen's difficulty in working this transformation stems in large part from her inability ever to take us inside Darcy's consciousness, as she freely takes us inside Elizabeth's. We cannot see him react from within, so that we find so radical a change hard to credit.

There is no question about the facts when Elizabeth learns at Rosings that she has morally misjudged Darcy by believing Wickham's lies concerning Darcy's treatment of him; but we never are sure of the facts concerning his pridefulness. Clearly, as we have already seen, the meetings at Rosings and Pemberley are the two peaks in the action, the first functioning as a false climax, while the second truly removes all the major obstacles between Elizabeth and Darcy, with only the minor seeming obstacle of the Lydia-Wickham escapade needed to resolve matters thoroughly. In the matter of Elizabeth's judgment of Darcy, it is at Rosings that she learns of the falseness of Wickham, which eliminates all moral charges against Darcy and establishes his decency in her eyes. But his insufferable pride of manner, revealed by the nature of his proposal and his admission that he was the principal cause of Bingley's defection from Jane, persists as a sufficient reason for Elizabeth to reject him. This objection is removed at Pemberley, but only in an unfortunately ambiguous way. At the crucial moment, *before* Elizabeth sees Darcy for the first time at Pemberley and in order to prepare her for the changed creature she is shortly to find greeting them, Elizabeth encounters the splendid housekeeper Mrs. Reynolds, whose testimonial concerning Darcy is to be persuasive. Suddenly, here on his own princely estate, the realities are changed: it is the estate of a prince charming, which is pretty much what he will be when he shows up. Mrs. Reynolds, "much less fine, and more civil" than Elizabeth had expected to find her, maintainer of Darcy's tasteful home ("neither gaudy nor uselessly fine"), denies that Darcy is proud or ever has been. Indeed, speaking for all his tenants and servants, she finds him ideal in all respects, even if he is occasionally diffident. Elizabeth confesses to herself that this "commendation" "was of no trifling nature. What praise is more valuable than the praise of an intelligent servant?"[1] At this very point along comes Darcy himself to match Mrs. Reynolds' description in all details of his behavior, however much he seems at odds with the earlier Darcy whom Elizabeth and we have seen. The magic holds from here on, as the fairy-tale hero, utterly receptive to the Gardiners (acting here as Elizabeth's parent-substitutes, a more acceptable variety of her family), even rescues the damsel in distress, gets Lydia married off and the Bennets off the hook, all for the love of his lady fair.

What, then, does Austen want us to make of Darcy? In the context of her attempt at middle-class social realism, how are we to accept this sudden transfiguration of the priggish snob into an archetypal romantic hero? Are we to believe in Mrs. Reynolds' Darcy and reinterpret everything we have seen about him, or are we to believe that the events of the novel have forced him to change radically his nature as well as his behavior? It is clear that Austen leaves ample evidence to support both hypotheses and does not herself seem to choose between them, even though they would appear to be mutually contradictory. Is it possible that Darcy has really been modest all along and that his actions have been misconstrued? We can point to other evidence besides Mrs. Reynolds' testimony. Darcy himself has spoken of his awkwardness and shyness with strangers (in his conversation with Elizabeth and Colonel Fitzwilliam in chapter 31), as if to help Austen account for the difference between his early behavior in a new and alien company and his later behavior on his home ground. Also, Elizabeth herself corroborates Darcy's claim that Jane did not openly show her feelings for Bingley, so that Darcy's pressure on Bingley to withdraw had more than only snobbish motives. She corroborates also the scandalous behavior of her family as coming close to deserving Darcy's scorn. And we have seen Darcy's equal willingness to feel shame when his highly placed aunt, Lady Catherine, reveals her "illbreeding." So his judgment is based on a keen and refined sensibility, not on a sense of class. Consequently, when Elizabeth shows up at Pemberley accompanied by the Gardiners, who live by trade (though

[1] *Pride and Prejudice* (Oxford: Oxford University Press, 1929), p. 239. All text quotations refer to this edition.

he is "well-bred and agreeable" and she is "an amiable, intelligent, elegant woman"), Darcy is cordial and responsive, thereby surprising Elizabeth, who had been convinced that he would treat them contemptuously. So again he seems to have reacted to the person rather than to the social position. The Gardiners, who have seen the Pemberley Darcy but not the Netherfield Darcy, of course sense no pride in him, and become trustworthy witnesses to Mrs. Reynolds' Darcy. Perhaps Austen is putting her seal on this interpretation of Darcy when she writes of Georgiana Darcy's behavior toward Elizabeth and Mrs. Gardiner that it was "attended with all that embarrassment which, though proceeding from shyness and the fear of doing wrong, would easily give to those who felt themselves inferior the belief of her being proud and reserved" (p. 256). Surely these words about the Miss Darcy whom we had been for so long expecting to be so forbidding are to rub off on our judgment of her brother as well.

But of course it is also true that Austen has done her job in the Netherfield portion of the novel too well for us to be able to accept Mrs. Reynolds' notion of an unchanging, never-proud Darcy. And she knows it. Though she has sought, in the ways noted, to support Mrs. Reynolds' version, she also permits herself to plant a chain of evidence supporting a Darcy who was indeed rather insufferable but who has changed, thanks to the power of love and Elizabeth. His own confession to Elizabeth at the end presupposes just this notion of his initial insufferability:

> "I have been a selfish being all my life, in practice,
> though not in principle. As a child I was taught what
> was right; but I was not taught to correct my
> temper. I was given good principles, but left to follow
> them in pride and conceit. Unfortunately an only
> son (for many years an only child), I was spoilt by my
> parents, who though good themselves . . . allowed,
> encouraged, almost taught me to be selfish and over-
> bearing, to care for none beyond my own family
> circle, to think meanly of all the rest of the world, to
> wish at least to think meanly of their sense and
> worth compared with my own. Such I was, from
> eight to eight and twenty; and such I might still have
> been but for you, dearest, loveliest Elizabeth! What do I

> *not owe you! You taught me a lesson, hard indeed*
> *at first, but most advantageous, By you, I was*
> *properly humbled."*
>
> (p. 357)

This confession describes just the fellow whom Elizabeth found innocent of wrongdoing but guilty of injurious pride at Rosings. So her
erroneous judgment concerned only his prior actions but not his current behavior, which, to satisfy her, would have to undergo the sea-
change we find taking place in the magic air of Pemberley when, with
Mrs. Reynolds' introduction, he is converted into the kindly fairy
prince. His confession, then, is Austen's safeguard in case, initiated
into a shrewd social realism by her steady eye and pen, we refuse to
buy the theory of Mrs. Reynolds despite the fact that Austen's own
weakness for Darcy has led her to build in occasional supporting evidence for that theory.

Still, her own uncertainty about Darcy leads Austen to undercut her
chain of evidence. I earlier cited the conversation among Darcy, Elizabeth, and Colonel Fitzwilliam—in which Darcy speaks of his diffi-
dence with strangers—as part of Austen's attempt to bolster what will
be Mrs. Reynolds' Darcy; it was also a preview of our first sight of
Georgiana Darcy, in whom shyness was mistaken for pride. But we
must also note in this conversation that, when Elizabeth asks why
Darcy, "a man of sense and education, and who has lived in the world,
is ill qualified to recommend himself to strangers," his cousin, the
honest Fitzwilliam, says, "It is because he will not give himself the
trouble" (p. 170). So Austen permits us to take the passage as we will:
we can see Darcy's words as preparation for the Pemberley Darcy
who has been there—though hidden—all along; or we can see Fitzwilliam's caustic addendum as that which converts those words into
an insincere rationalization for pride in a man greatly in need of being
changed.

Long before Darcy's confession to her, Elizabeth herself seems to
recognize a total change in Darcy with his first words to her at Pemberley, "his civil inquiries after her family": "Amazed at the alteration
of his manner since they last parted, every sentence that he uttered
was increasing her embarrassment. . . . when he spoke, his accent had
none of its usual sedateness" (p. 240). It has been just this "accent"
that characterized the early, stuffy Darcy. There originally was in it a

stilted quality that at moments almost seemed a reflection of Mr. Collins' laughable turgidity. Darcy himself implicitly defended the pompousness of his early "style of writing," characterized by the simple Bingley as one which finds him studying "too much for words of four syllables" (p. 44). But, from the time of his appearance at Pemberley, Austen does change Darcy's "accent" to a directness of expression that we suspect must have seemed a change even to Mrs. Reynolds, had she been listening to him before.

It seems clear the two possible Darcys—an unchanging one whose early shyness was mistaken for pride and a prideful one whom love causes to undergo a profound change to humility—are both left standing, each supported by some passages and disputed by others. Austen must choose to play it safe either way, though she is fully committed to neither. One might, sympathetically, claim a synthesis by asserting that, while Darcy has indeed changed as he has acknowledged, he had not really too far to come because even at the first he was less blameworthy than he appeared. But of course if this would not totally ignore either of the two Darcys, using each to qualify the other, it would not explain either of them or those elements in each which would seem to contradict the other. The passages involved rather suggest that we must choose one or the other and that Austen wishes to protect herself whichever way we choose. She needs Darcy to appear as he does at the start, but she also needs the Darcy described by Mrs. Reynolds so that the Pemberley magic can transform Elizabeth's concept of him. And she cannot quite trust either one or rework her materials to eliminate either one.

It is, as I began by suggesting, the unyielding complexity of Darcy that causes Austen her difficulties with him. Instead of using the reversals with which she snapped her other characters into place, she is confronted with the need to stage a character shift—even if she momentarily denies it is a shift. And a total turnabout by a character is very different from a reversal forced upon essentially static characters by the structure of the plot. Yet such a turnabout is by far the more likely interpretation of her intention, although she is clearly uncomfortable with the weak conviction her case carries, so that she is driven to lay out an alternative set of probabilities as well. Part of the cause of her discomfort and of her unconvincing rendition of a dynamic, changing Darcy stems from the sort of character he would have to have been and the doubts this sort of character would have cast on the communal security she values most. Thus this character shift tells us a good deal about Austen's visionary propensities and limitations.

I perhaps have oversimplified the issues by asking only whether Darcy was prideful before, or only diffident, or something of each. The questions really concern the early Darcy as a brooding, somewhat anti-social, internalized being, enough of an aristocrat to contemn the petty togetherness into which Bingley's company thrusts him—even if his loyalty to Bingley apparently persuades him to put up with it, he does so always grudgingly. It is this brooding internality that Austen must not put up with, lest it challenge dangerously the unquestioned security with which she presents her bourgeois world, for all its failings, which she so freely mocks. The cordial good humor we find in him at Pemberley is conditioned in part by his feelings for Elizabeth, which by now have convinced him to try to please her, in part by the superior behavior of the Gardiners, in part because—as Mrs. Reynolds has tipped us off—he is on his home ground. But mainly he changes in order to be worthy of Elizabeth, as she has changed to be worthy of him; and that means he changes in order to satisfy Austen's need to break through whatever is anti-social in him, to make him one—an acceptable and only partly exceptional one—of her many. So, through Elizabeth, Austen domesticates him and externalizes his being. Still, she has enough misgivings to leave the possibility that perhaps he has been misunderstood and has been a proper social being all along, so that we should never have had to worry about him.

Assuming that Austen has rescued Darcy for Elizabeth and for her own view of the public social order as revealed by social good sense, we must wonder how much this society is worth, with its values that she so pervasively satirizes. Are these superficial idols, having to do with petty worth and petty arrangements or attachments (which is to say attachments *as* arrangements), in their turn worth the sacrifice of that interiority—that consciousness of an isolated self—before which they would crumble? It is in the character of Elizabeth and the somewhat more moderate change *she* undergoes that we can best examine these questions. Elizabeth must also change to earn her right to Darcy, since her early failings need correction as much as his do. But her change is made more credible than his because we can trace it within her consciousness, inasmuch as Austen occasionally shifts her own perspective as objective observer to that of her favorite, Elizabeth. In other places too, despite what is mainly a neutral, dramatic point of view consisting of speeches and stage directions, from time to time we have an awareness of a narrating presence capable of a mockery close to Elizabeth's, even as Elizabeth's capacity for mockery is a reflection of her father's.

As her father's daughter, Liz[2] begins primarily as a humorist. As such, her success depends upon her wit and her judgment; and she clearly has a substantial supply of both. But both of these produce failings which suggest not only her imperfection but—in the light of this imperfection—her need to soften and humanize her responses and to temper them with a mature sense of social responsibility. Her judgment deserts her not merely in the matter of Charlotte's cold-blooded decision to marry Mr. Collins, but far more crucially, in her weighing the respective moral capacities for decency and villainy in Darcy and Wickham. Her instincts, because of her personal involvement, turn out to mislead her; and—thus misled—she even misreads considerable evidence which, as she recapitulates it too late, she should have judged differently. Such costly errors in judgment lead her to recognize the limits of her acuteness and, more than this, the limited value of mere acuteness self-indulged. This recognition leads in turn to her critique of both mere wit and the profession of the humorist which she has learned from her father. The social consequences of the detachment, the bemused disinvolvement required for the satisfaction of wit, are an irresponsibility that can produce social disaster.

Of course, this notion requires as its assumption that social disaster is to be avoided rather than laughed at after it occurs, that society as an ongoing mechanism is sufficiently acceptable for one to want to prevent disaster. This is the assumption which Liz learns to make, as her father does not. It leads to her moral rejection of her father's posture as well as of her own earlier posture. If she recognizes that her father has arrived at this posture as his only possible response to the misery of his unfortunate marriage, she sees also that one has the duty to try to prevent further miseries of this sort for others.

It is Darcy's letter to her at Rosings that reveals to her her own inadequacy and the inadequacy of her posture. Her confidence in both her wit and her judgment is undermined by his defense of himself. She explicitly tells herself that this is a moment of utter self-discovery:

[2] I feel more comfortable using the diminutive, Liz, when discussing Elizabeth as her father's whimsical daughter.

> *She grew absolutely ashamed of herself.—Of neither*
> *Darcy nor Wickham could she think, without feeling*
> *that she had been blind, partial, prejudiced, absurd.*
>
> *"How despicably have I acted!" she cried.—"I,*
> *who have prided myself on my discernment!—I, who*
> *have valued myself on my abilities! . . . How humiliating*
> *is this discovery!—Yet, how just a humiliation! . . .*
> *vanity, not love, has been my folly. . . . Till this*
> *moment, I never knew myself."*
>
> (p. 201)

Thus she condemns her judgment. But it is her free, unattached wittiness—like that of her father—and the dedication of them both to wit that are more severely condemned. The condemnation of this wittiness is more gradual, but its consequences are far-reaching. It begins with her painful acknowledgment to herself that Darcy's complaints in the letter about the unseemly behavior of her family (all but Jane's and her own, of course), however she resents his uttering them, are justified. But her responses here are not simply immediate and made once only; she reverts to this charge again and again, adjusting her own behavior to meet it. She shortly sees "the folly and indecorum of her own family" as depriving Jane of her deserved happiness, and she attributes "the unhappy defects of her family" in large measure to her father, who, "contented with laughing at them, would never exert himself to restrain the wild giddiness of his youngest daughters" (p. 206). He freely laughs too at the mother, who reveals no more sense or more decorous behavior than they do. Liz begins to see him— and, indirectly herself—as a fool of wit instead of the paragon of wittiness she thought them both earlier. If they were leagued together in their disdainful contempt before, they are guilty of its consequences now. And if her father cannot change, Liz can, and dedicates herself to do so.

Austen's own statement about Mr. Bennet's position and his bright daughter's attitude toward it, now undergoing a profound change, is a reflection of Elizabeth's—or, rather, suggests the extent to which Liz serves as Austen's mouthpiece. The exposition which opens chapter 42 brings us up to date on what is happening to Elizabeth's sense of her family's social appearance and her father's responsibility for it, in the light of Darcy's letter. In this exposition Austen corroborates the moral judgment that has just followed from Elizabeth's self-discovery.

II. Through the Embrace of the Natural Human Community

Austen sees Mr. Bennet's enormous mistake in his choice of a wife as the source of his irresponsibility, his role as a fool of wit: "To his wife he was very little otherwise indebted, than as her ignorance and folly had contributed to his amusement. This is not the sort of happiness which a man would in general wish to owe to his wife; but where other powers of entertainment are wanting, the true philosopher will derive benefit from such as are given." Austen slips from her own view to Elizabeth's without a break, describing her painful awareness of "the impropriety of her father's behavior as a husband" which she had preferred not to dwell upon, in part because of the sympathy of their temperaments. Darcy's note, however, has brought a critical component to her awareness: "But she had never felt so strongly as now, the disadvantages which must attend the children of so unsuitable a marriage, nor ever been so fully aware of the evils arising from so ill-judged a direction of talents; talents which rightly used, might at least have preserved the respectability of his daughters, even if incapable of enlarging the mind of his wife" (p. 228).

Elizabeth has already acted upon this new sense of responsibility. When she hears the inane "lamentations resounding perpetually through Longbourn-house" as the regiment prepares to leave Meryton, "Elizabeth tried to be diverted by them; but all sense of pleasure was lost in shame. She felt anew the justice of Mr. Darcy's objections" (p. 221). Further, she now undertakes to oppose her father's detached acquiescence when Lydia desires to go with the regiment to Brighton in the company of the Forsters ("Lydia will never be easy till she has exposed herself in some public place or other, and we can never expect her to do it with so little expense or inconvenience to her family as under the present circumstances"). Liz is clearly impatient with this by now familiar pattern of her father's mockery and willingly draws some of that mockery on herself and her new-found earnestness as she speaks (though only in general terms) of the unfortunate consequences of the sort of behavior Mr. Bennet's laxity indirectly condones. She even half-prophesies the imminent danger into which Lydia's freely permitted indulgence will place the family as well as Lydia herself:

> *Our importance, our respectability in the world, must be affected by the wild volatility, the assurance and disdain of all restraint which mark Lydia's character.*

234

> *Excuse me—for I must speak plainly. If you,*
> *my dear father, will not take the trouble of checking*
> *her exuberant spirits, and of teaching her that her*
> *present pursuits are not to be the business of her life,*
> *she will soon be beyond the reach of amendment.*
>
> (p. 223)

But Mr. Bennet, though more serious for a moment, persists in his permissiveness with Lydia, closing with another sardonic remark: "At any rate, she cannot grow many degrees worse, without authorizing us to lock her up for the rest of her life." Though "disappointed and sorry," Elizabeth is content with her sense "of having performed her duty" and lets it go at that. She will come to rue not being more intransigent with her father when the Brighton escapade later proves so costly.

It is clear that Elizabeth finds parts of the blame for these unhappy consequences in herself as the half-willing confederate of her father. After the news about Lydia and Wickham disperses the friendly gathering at Pemberley, Liz reacts by referring again to the family's role in Lydia's unfortunate act: "The mischief of neglect and mistaken indulgence towards such a girl—Oh! how acutely did she now feel it" (p. 268). Indeed, it is their mutual guilt, their shared responsibility for Lydia's plight, that helps bring Liz and Darcy together. What each has failed to do to prevent the impending domestic catastrophe results from their resistance to full social self-commitment. The embarrassing episode involving Wickham and Georgiana Darcy (which occurred long before the events of the novel) had given Darcy information about the potential dangers in Wickham, information which might have been used to protect Lydia from the similar fate Wickham creates for her. In the end, Darcy sees himself as having failed to have sufficient interest in affairs or people outside his immediate circle to forestall Wickham's further villainy. We are told that Darcy feels that it was

> *owing to himself that Wickham's worthlessness*
> *had not been so well known, as to make it impossible*
> *for any young woman of character, to love or*
> *confide in him. He generously imputed the whole to*
> *his mistaken pride, and confessed that he had before*

235

> *thought it beneath him, to lay his private actions*
> *open to the world. His character was to speak for*
> *itself. He called it, therefore, his duty to step forward,*
> *and endeavour to remedy an evil, which had been*
> *brought on by himself.*
>
> (pp. 309–10)

If Darcy's lack of social involvement has allowed Wickham the unblemished reputation that made him available to Lydia (or, earlier, to Liz herself!), Liz—as we have observed—failed to provide for Lydia those conditions that would have prevented her from being his willing victim. And Liz's failure is related to her own earlier resistance to personal involvement, which springs in her case from the objectivity and detachment that wit requires, as Mr. Bennet's example had taught her. We have noted that her failures of judgment occur when her personal concerns lead to a subjectivity that blurs her normal clarity of perception. It is this discovery of herself, of her imperfect humanity, that brings her down from the transcendent perch she used to share with her father; and she descends so that she may now work at making herself and those about her fitter for their social roles. She can from this time on indulge her solicitude and, in doing so, earns her right to Darcy, who in turn has earned his right to her by also taking up the responsibility of commitment. In this way the crisis over Lydia, in part attributed by each of them to his own failings, leads them to move from a mutual sense of guilt to a mutual responsibility for the helpful social role which, together in marriage, they can play. At the close, the suggested improvement of Kitty under their guidance ("by proper attention and management") is to serve as impressive evidence of their functioning within this new role.

But we must ask again about the value of that society and its niches, for the service of which Liz and Darcy feel so much responsibility that they undertake to shed the excess individuality, which can have anti-social consequences. Can the flimsy values which Austen so honestly —and often satirically—shows us sustain the allegiance of a serious intelligence? Can we ignore the obvious fact that, from the standpoint of what happens to Elizabeth, this is a novel about "making it"—much in the British novelistic tradition of *Pamela* and *Joseph Andrews*? But Wickham is not permitted to make it: it is as if, in *Tom Jones*, Blifil turned out to be the good guy. For it is Darcy, the wealthiest and most highly placed character in the novel, who is its hero and who gets the girl. The girl also gets *him* and in a bound vaults to the top of this social world. Wickham does not, like Tom Jones, make the discovery which makes him the worthy hero; rather, the discovery is made *about* him to make him the worthless villain. He stays poor, as befits his original low-born status, while Darcy retains his desirable status intact. And Austen, here a defender of her society, gives to each the character whose moral worth matches the worth attached to his social position. By not allowing Wickham to be her hero and choosing Darcy instead (rich boy makes good), Austen forgoes her opportunity for a satire truly directed against the appearances that dominate her society's petty structure. And by allowing Liz to "make it" with Darcy, Austen further supports that structure by allowing her most intelligent (and, finally, her most morally aware) character to achieve a hoped-for escalation within it, but only by underwriting it.

It must be noted that Austen shrewdly refuses to force Liz to choose between a marriage of convenience and a marriage of inclination. This stacking of the cards is in accordance with Austen's naïvely classic avoidance of the "either/or," as if there were no possibility except the "both/and." (Here is a further thematic reflection of her persistent use of the peripety in order to ensure the wholeness of the social fabric.) But what if it were Wickham rather than Darcy, the poor rather than the wealthy, whom Liz loved? Though Austen cannot permit this either/or, she is too honest not to let us see the difficulty of the problem, even if her dedication to her society precludes her seeing the problem as more than a hypothetical one. But she does allow it to become at least hypothetical by having Liz consider Wickham as a potential husband early in the novel. And in two dialogues between Liz and Mrs. Gardiner she freely exhibits the dilemma that even the most intelligent can feel when confronted by this society's values. By inserting these dialogues and permitting the hypothetical problem, she candidly opens herself and the values her best characters espouse to the most damaging casuistic assault, and by providing this assault herself, she disarms us.

In chapter 26 Mrs. Gardiner openly advises Liz not to become involved "in an affection which the want of fortune would make so very imprudent"—whatever Wickham's charms and however strong her feelings for him. In response, Liz acknowledges the imprudence of any serious relationship between them, so that it would be better for

Wickham not to become "attached" to her. Still, she cannot promise to be prudent, though she can promise "not to be in a hurry," even not to wish to have won him: "In short, I will do my best." But she cannot guarantee that her best will be good enough, that her affections might not force her to throw prudence to the winds. Her aunt seems satisfied, and Elizabeth is not resentful of this apparently cold-blooded intrusion. Her own response has been anything but irrationally hotblooded; she clearly has the good sense her aunt has attributed to her. Indeed, there is a large measure of agreement between them. Austen has been most shrewd to have given this role and these words to Mrs. Gardiner, whose intelligence and taste we are to respect and who is by no means a representative of the more objectionable features or values of this society.

In the next chapter, however, there is a second round to this discussion, one in which Elizabeth somewhat bitterly and sharply takes the offensive, getting a measure of revenge with a mock-worldliness of her own which is more extreme than her aunt's had been. Wickham has turned from Elizabeth to Miss King, who has recently become wealthy. In accordance with her conversation with her aunt, Elizabeth finds this a prudent and acceptable act on his part. Austen has warned us, however—in words that anticipate what Mrs. Gardiner's position will be—that in approving his act, Liz is being "less clear-sighted perhaps in this case than in Charlotte's" (since she had rejected Charlotte's marriage to Collins as a shabby compromise with convenience). When Mrs. Gardiner accuses Wickham of being mercenary, Elizabeth, recalling their prior conversation, asks, "Pray, my dear aunt, what is the difference in matrimonial affairs, between the mercenary and the prudent motive? Where does discretion end, and avarice begin? Last Christmas you were afraid of his marrying me, because it would be imprudent; and now, because he is trying to get a girl with only ten thousand pounds, you want to find out that he is mercenary" (p. 149). If her aunt thinks Liz has bettered her, she gives no sign of it. Rather, she proceeds to distinguish carefully among shades of indelicacy that move certain acts over the boundary separating the prudent from the mercenary, discretion from avarice. Clearly, this excellent woman is resorting to discriminations based, not on principle, but on a worldly though not amoral compromise with principle, on ad hoc considerations that—morally speaking—may seem shabby, pragmatic, mere trimming. But she presents them with a firmness that makes them

Austen's last and authoritative word. Neither Elizabeth nor we need to worry about testing them by means of our story, of course, since Wickham is removed from consideration by his author, who has arranged for him to have a villainous character and for Elizabeth soon to discover it. It is in conformity with her comic sense and her Mrs.-Gardiner-like worldliness that Austen prudently arranges for Elizabeth to join inclination and convenience in her marriage to Darcy. Any extremity that might arise from Liz having to make a choice between the two is neatly avoided. Again, as in her structure of reversals, Austen allies herself with those forces that work for social affirmation.

We have seen that the question of convenience is closely tied to the Charlotte-Collins marriage. What Elizabeth sees as Charlotte's sell-out of herself is to be distinguished from the prudence and caution Mrs. Gardiner urges upon Elizabeth in her relations with Wickham; but it is to be seen as similar to Wickham's sudden interest in the newly rich Miss King. So the marriage of convenience (without inclination) is to be avoided, as is the marriage of inclination (without convenience). How to choose, then? The answer, of course, is to be guided by an author like Jane Austen so as not to permit the dilemma to arise, to avoid the either/or by having convenience accompany inclination, as it does for Elizabeth with Darcy.

Out of these attitudes toward marriage emerges one's possible attitude toward the social structure: acceptance and submission, or rejection and rebellion, or a withdrawn satiric transcendence. Certainly total, uncritical submission is represented by Charlotte's marriage to Collins, a marriage which, first offered Elizabeth, she did not for a moment contemplate seriously and which she sadly, disappointedly condemns (seeing Charlotte as having "sacrificed every better feeling to worldly advantage" [pp. 123–24]). At the other end of the spectrum of attitudes, Wickham would seem to represent the extreme of rebellion, a reckless willingness to violate the most sacred taboos of the society (among other things, seeking twice to undo young virgins). But, as we have seen, he is a pseudo-romantic fraud: behind his dashing appearance of willful daring, he is a crass schemer who works to beat this money-ridden society at its own game, demonstrating as he goes his deep obeisance to its values. If Austen has arranged for Darcy to give up the internality that isolates him, she does not permit Wickham any inner life at all. He is no rebel, no dedicated outlaw, only a cheaply ambitious ne'er-do-well. He therefore presents no alternative but is just another less honest exemplar of the total subordination to this society's shabby values that we find in Charlotte. That's the way with would-be rebels in Austen's tight, circumscribed world. He may appear to be at the other end of the spectrum from Charlotte, but in Austen's world such apparent opposition is a deceptive mask for similarity. It is no accident that, as Austen herself intrusively reminds us, Wickham's pursuit of Miss King is reminiscent of Charlotte's acceptance of Collins, so that it is only Elizabeth's blindness which keeps her from making the comparison. No, a true rebellion against these values cannot take place within the context created by our shrewd, deck-stacking novelist.

But in Mr. Bennet we find that intelligence can provide an alternative response, an unwillingness to affirm and support society, to submit to values based on stupidities such as intelligence must scorn. But his alternative is no more than a hands-off satiric withdrawal from action, whether for or against the society, whether inside or outside society. Though hardly rebellion, it *is* a critical rejection of society, sponsored by the habit of derision, which is a costly luxury. Indeed, he seems to be rejecting the very possibilities of social life because of the folly it inevitably entails. But the costliness of this attitude leads to a clear condemnation of it, even on the part of Elizabeth, who has in part shared its spirit.

This notion of costliness assumes that there are consequences to be avoided; it assumes there is something to be lost which is worth trying to save; it assumes the need to preserve social values as a framework within which social relationships are to be made to serve the pleasures and satisfactions of man as a social animal. This is a great deal to assume, as her father seems to be reminding Liz when he sees her allegiance slipping away from him and her disapproval focusing on him. But Liz, like her aunt, puts aside the clean distinctions among positions in order to make life in society (and where else can it take place?) less rather than more painful and more rather than less honest; she must work for the ad hoc compromises that deny the purity of principle but affirm the possibility of improving human relations by improving the attitude of those who partake of them. Even marriages as unfortunate as that of the elder Bennets cannot be used to justify withdrawal or rejection. And those marriages which take place during the course of the novel between Charlotte and Collins or Lydia and Wickham are found at the end to be still part of the world within which Liz and Darcy operate helpfully. Of course, they also (together with Jane and Bingley) work with Kitty to try to prevent more such marriages from taking place. One does what one can with what one has.

The key to all this, of course, is the critical intelligence, intelligence used not to indulge the cruelly dissociated purposes of wit but to encourage the less unsatisfactory performance of the human function by persons forced to operate within a most deficient social structure—deficient, but the only one available at the moment and probably not much worse than most others, given the predominantly silly nature of man. But this acceptance is not to be confounded with an un-critical acceptance like Charlotte's, which is precisely the point of the two dialogues between Elizabeth and her aunt. For Elizabeth's is the highly critical acceptance of the mature intelligence. She does not totally forgo her wit, though human sympathy has softened it into a graceful humor. Intelligence like hers sees through to the silliest of society's follies, the most offensive of its absurdities, while continuing to accept it and its need to extend its domination into the future. This acceptance is dictated by the demands of social, human sympathy which, as subjective, exacts this price of intelligence: to see the truth about the social structure while still leaving that structure standing, even fortified. In this way, involvement forces intelligence to reject withdrawal for critical commitment, which is a sort of submission also, though a submission that has its hold-out sense of incompleteness. Still, intelligence is given its value by the human act of involvement and the mature responsibility that is its consequence; intelligence is thus converted into a social virtue, in Austen as later in Henry James.

The compliance with society by Jane and Bingley is yet another thing, different from the knowing, willfully uncritical submission of Charlotte and the knowing, willfully critical half-submission of Elizabeth. Jane's compliance grows out of her utter innocence, a lack of self-consciousness that has kept her from the first an inoffensive, because unwillful, almost automatic, part of the ongoing social structure. There may be in Jane or Bingley little intelligence (either to separate themselves from that structure or, having separated, to reunite themselves with it), but neither is there the unkindness that could turn them into those who pursue society's values selfishly, knowingly manipulating its worse public tendencies for private ends. The failure of someone as bright as Charlotte is not a failure of discernment but a failure to make an adequate moral assessment of the possibilities remaining for her to fulfill her social function. As a comic novelist, of course, Austen must take creatures like Jane and Bingley under her protection by weaving the pattern of their fortunes into her social fabric, of which they become such sturdy elements.

But Liz and Darcy remain her central and problematic concern. In them the problems of choice, of decision about one's personal and social destiny, present themselves to the rational and moral intelligence, which is to recognize that, in public structure and in private character, society will smile upon those who commit themselves— however critically—to it with the combined virtues of responsibility and involvement. Here too, then, the deck has been stacked in favor of the moderate victory of this hardly impressive set of social values, which Austen at once sees through and cherishes. Everything has been put into the service of this always managed, inevitable victory: plot with its comic pattern of reversals, the positioning of heroes and villains on appropriate levels in the social hierarchy, and even intelligence itself, which at first, in Mr. Bennet, was seen as the potential enemy—or at least as the *agent provocateur*—poised to thwart the realization of society's aims. Whatever the seeming obstacles, all comes out right-side-up for those who are on their way to a little bourgeois future.

There may be no challenge to the formality of this world, with every potential obstacle discovered to be an aid, every potential villain discovered to be either a hero or a more or less innocuous fool. It may not be a very natural community, but in its own way it is a human one. As if created by a classic existent rather than a classic visionary, Austen's is a precious world, preserved by the a priori exclusion of what she dares not allow to disturb it. It precludes, rather than rejects, extremity. Here is a tight little island of a book, formally and thematically, formally *because* thematically. The trim security of the little world's closed values[3] is joined to Austen's trimness of structure, in

---

[3] Austen shows us she is conscious of the narrow round of her concern. She explicitly limits herself to the bourgeois closet within which she has enclosed her interest. Thus, when her characters travel beyond their immediate ambience toward Pemberley, she is careful not to permit her novel and its concerns to open outward: "It is not the object of this work to give a description of Derbyshire, nor of any of the remarkable places through which their route thither lay; Oxford, Blenheim, Warwick, Kenelworth, Birmingham, &c. are sufficiently known. A small part of Derbyshire is all the present concern" (p. 232).

which all elements are manipulated so as to support this small, modest unity in a society (and a novel) whose form *is* its meaning as well as its value.

BARCHESTER TOWERS

From *Pride and Prejudice* we have learned the limitations upon the classic vision that are imposed by too hasty and uncritical an acceptance of the human community as a conventional human community. We see life only as life in society, without the challenge of private human presumption or even very much assumption that there is a private human realm. In my own terminology, I might say that the naïvely classic must prefer to see the veil as the canopy and thus to sense no distinction between a shabbily ethical community and a natural human community won through a retreat from that extremity which threatens to confront us once we have challenged the simplistic universality of the ethical. If he need not either confront or retreat from the threat of the vision yielded by a private awareness, the classic existent (insufficiently challenged by that which would convert him to visionary) must accept communal life as a good, as his major value, always to be asserted, always to be reimposed, whatever the weaknesses that sustain it in its social dimension. Thus it is that we have seen Austen's dominant metaphor to be one in which the overriding demands of society always are satisfied, in which everything and everyone—however they are thrown up into the air—find themselves resettled into the dominant patterns society requires of them. Their chance to stray permanently is precluded, even as extremity is.

Yet the utterly closed structure, as it is imposed upon this tight little closet of a world and a plot, need not be the only way to assure the dominance of the accepted—if admittedly imperfect—social order. Anthony Trollope shows us another way in *Barchester Towers*; it is enough of a variation within what I think of as the naïvely classic for me to pause briefly on it. Trollope's, by comparison with Austen's, is an open form, even though he too manages to stack the deck almost totally in favor of the victory of a relaxed communal consciousness. There is, let it be granted, more of what seems like a challenge to the reigning values of the novel's world than Austen permits, but here too the author has worked to undercut the seriousness of any threat that looms.

II. Through the Embrace of the Natural Human Community

The opposition raised by puritanical austerity to the modest relaxed-ness of the Church of England, Barchester-style, creates a conflict that is hardly new to the dominant English novelistic tradition. Indeed, we can recall it from the dawn of the English novel in Thomas Nashe's *The Unfortunate Traveller*, where Jack Wilton reserves his severest contempt and his best tricks for the moralistic puritan gravity that would undermine his essentially classic levity. Trollope himself con-fesses his inheritance from earlier English fiction when he traces the two names of his overly Protestant villain, Obadiah Slope, to two em-battled if ineffectual characters in *Tristram Shandy*, even suggesting that infamous malpractitioner Dr. Slop as an actual (though of course fictional) ancestor. This conflict between the ascetically moralistic (represented here, as so often in English fiction, by an "enthusiastic" Protestantism) and the relaxed classic (represented by the Church of England spirit of Barchester) is surely a more serious clash—threaten-ing the fortunes of all our favorites among the characters—than Austen allows; but Trollope remains as surely in control of the inevi-table happy resolution as Austen was.

His devices for ensuring the victory of Barchesterian values are, as I have noted, not those which grow out of a tightly manipulated structure of action, like Austen's. Trollope has an apparent openness of plot that would seem to be receptive to all possible threats. Yet this relaxed form echoes, as it secures, the dominant vision, equally relaxed, so that our anxieties are constantly allayed. Of course, here the author's persistent presence, his always reassuring tone, can accomplish what Austen leaves to her plot to do. Trollope is more willing than Austen to remind us of what his novel is *not*. While Austen will never permit a glance at any other sort of world or novel than what her tight social order and form enclose, Trollope can cozy us into a humorous aware-ness of the heroic and romantic world which he and the world of his novel deliberately eschew. Thus he continually—though gently—prods us with his mock-heroic or even downright anti-heroic re-minders, which reduce our sense of any threat either to the characters or to the values which their good fortune would reinforce and secure. Whether he is comparing Mrs. Quiverful to the lioness (chapter 25), Eleanor or Mr. Slope to figures within the scope of the "tragic muse" (chapters 29, 40, 51), or Mrs. Proudie to Medea (chapter 33), the mild and good-humored Trollope is reminding us of the relatively insignifi-cant consequences of actions undertaken in "the low-heeled buskin of modern fiction." When the author tries to deliver his proper Barchesterians from Slopean evils with a "melodramatic *dénouement*," he finds that Dr. Gwynne, his would-be *deus ex machina*, cannot come to Barchester as the "avenging god" because he is "laid up with the gout" (chapter 34).

There is a similar light-hearted mockery in the story itself, insofar as it is a constructed fable. With his easy openness of form, Trollope is anxious to speak for his story (and before his story) rather than allowing it to speak for him, as the manipulating Jane Austen did. The complications of his plot are false complications in that he wants us not to worry about them as he assures us that all will come out well. Announcing the arrival of Mr. Arabin on the scene with the promising chapter title "The New Champion" (chapter 14), Trollope follows with the chapter "The Widow's Suitors," in which he guarantees to keep the reader in his confidence and urges that "the gentle-hearted reader be under no apprehension whatsoever" because he will not permit Eleanor to marry either Slope or Bertie Stanhope. Thus, whatever misunderstandings follow are not to concern us, for we have the author's word for it that they are to be of no consequence.

Yet a good number of what might have been serious misunderstandings do follow, so that the complications of plot would seem to be intricate ones—they would seem to be, except that we have been guaranteed by our honest, cheerful author that they will, finally, be insignificant, that they are really make-believe complications. In this sense, unlike Austen's, this plot is explicitly paraded as a fake plot, not meant to work itself out but to be subjected to the author's willful offstage intrusions. Trollope's care to belittle any possibilities that would undermine the dominance of his Barchesterians and their values forces him to curtail the very appearance of a drama even momentarily unresolved. Such a drama would reveal itself by means of a brilliance of structure that would produce a thematic intensity out of key with the unshaken assurance his relaxed attitude would require. So, as the misunderstandings, cross-purposes, near-misses, and looming catastrophes occur, they do not alarm us, especially as they are accompanied by our author's constant and constantly soothing voice. Nothing can come of anything—except what we want to come and what we have been promised all along will come. In the meantime, the game that "befits the low-heeled buskin of modern fiction" is permitted to be played for our amusement. In the masquerades of feelings and mistaken identities of the long "middle" of the plot, we have partly a use and partly a mock-use of the Elizabethan formula for comedy. Finally, the conspiratorial comic villain—he who would gull others—is himself gulled and hooted off the stage. And, as we have noted, the pretext for his masquerade—his apparent motive—is an excessive sobriety, a fraudulent moralism which the good folk, in their less self-consciously moral way, unmask as fraudulent. As so often occurs in Renaissance literature too, in *Barchester Towers* the heartily classic English tradition rightly distrusts the self-righteousness which refuses to distrust itself.

A central feature of Trollope's mock-seriousness, whether of plot or of vision, is his invention of Slope as his villain. Nothing undercuts any possible melodramatic challenge more than the fact that Slope, for all his shrewdness, turns out to be half inept—and that the crucial half. Indeed, as a villain he is incomplete in every direction. He is clearly inadequate even in his apparent austerity of vision: because he uses his puritan guise only to serve his self-interest, he cannot represent a true challenge to Barchesterian values. He is equally inadequate as a threat to the fortunes of his antagonists because even his self-interest is undercut, undercut surprisingly, by his daring, almost admirable recklessness. This curious audacity tempts him to the pursuit of Signora Neroni, which must lead to the defeat of his hopes;[4] and it tempts him to the open defiance of Mrs. Proudie, which must destroy him utterly in Barchester. Hardly capable of a "deep agony of soul," he is also a creature of enormous resilience: he bobs up again, a successful, "eloquent" preacher and "pious" clergyman somewhere else ("it is well known that the family of the Slopes never starve: they always fall on their feet like cats").

This enrichment of Slope beyond what Trollope would appear to need or want to have in a spiritually impoverished villain actually serves his purposes well both structurally and thematically. Besides providing us additional assurances about how the story is to come out, Trollope's Slope also guarantees that we will not have to consider the possibility that Barchesterian values may be in need of correction, that Barchester's vision may be incomplete. For if Slope and Mrs. Proudie represent the major alternative to those values, then Barchester is not really being challenged at all. This is not another version of the con-

---

[4] A strange Machiavel this is, who, in his infatuation, "could not bring himself to be commonly prudent," as Trollope admits in chapter 32.

flict I have traced in *Adam Bede*. In that novel the moral position of Mr. Irwine betrayed its inadequacy when confronted by a dilemma to which a more austere ethic seemed appropriate: Irwine's very laxness opened him to the attack of Adam, opened Loamshire to the threat of Stonyshire. To this extent the classic vision, as it was achieved in *Adam Bede*, had to be profoundly earned. The world of Slope and Mrs. Proudie presents no such challenge to Messrs. Harding and Arabin. For Trollope, Slope represents a moralism which is inherently impossible because it makes too great demands upon man and encourages a self-righteousness which our actions—in our common weakness—can never justify. What easier device is there for the novelist who is anxious to preclude any serious challenge to Barchesterian values than to make his would-be puritans hypocrites? But the claim to righteousness must, for Trollope, be self-deceptive, thus opening the way to hypocrisy. And the most demandingly moral character turns out to be the most patently immoral, the most ruthlessly self-interested. Ethical severity, which would countenance none of the human failings that infect us all, is the cover for the basest worldly ambition, for money-grubbing and even lechery. By contrast, the more traditional Church of England spirit, which demands so little of man and understands so much about his incapacities, produces the good souls whose behavior belies their insistent acknowledgment of their imperfections.

The beneficent power of the church, of the spirit of Barchester, is shown at the very start of the novel as it operates upon the archdeacon, the younger Dr. Grantly. Here is a "proud, wishful, worldly man," indeed, a potential Slope. In the opening scene, one of the most delicate and sensitive in the novel, Grantly confronts the sinful consequence of his ambition: at his father's bedside during his final hours, Grantly finds himself, involuntarily, wishing that the old bishop's death can occur soon enough for the son to inherit his title. The father is dying "as he had lived, peaceably, slowly, without pain and without excitement. The breath ebbed from him almost imperceptibly, and for a month before his death, it was a question whether he were alive or dead." Here is a death like that of Dr. Johnson's Levet, or like the undramatic, routine death we have seen as the least vain of vain wishes ("An age that melts with unperceiv'd decay, / And glides in modest Innocence away"). Truly a Barchesterian death. But there is an urgency and timeliness to the younger Grantly's desire, since an impending change in the government could doom his chances for succeeding his father as bishop. Though the "proud, wishful, worldly man" is powerless to keep himself from wishing the death to occur in time, both Trollope and he are able to face and to accept his wishing it. We witness his embarrassment as he "at last dared to ask himself whether he really longed for his father's death," and we witness his confession as he falls to his knees "and taking the bishop's hand within his own, prayed eagerly that his sins might be forgiven him."

His father soon dies, and the son, not knowing it is already too late, engages in the comedy of haste with Mr. Harding, who in his innocence utters to Grantly the piety expressed for a peaceful death after a long illness, a piety that we must take ironically (and almost outrageously) once we hear it as Grantly must hear it: "You cannot but rejoice that it is over." Indeed the son can rejoice: "He had brought himself to pray for his father's life, but now that life was done, minutes were too precious to be lost." The crass worldliness of his futile connivings—even to his calculated misuse of the unknowing Harding—is more painful for Trollope to contemplate than it is for Grantly. But Trollope deals openly with the archdeacon's behavior, denies that such worldliness is "wicked" since it is inevitably human, and confesses that the *nolo episcopari* is "at variance with the tendency of all human wishes." "If we look to our clergymen to be more than men, we shall probably teach ourselves to think that they are less." Thus for Trollope (as it has been for Grantly) man can accept— by first acknowledging—what he is capable of. First there is the willingness *not* to rationalize one's actions but rather to confess the worst of one's human tendencies; then there is the prayerful hope that one may not be as wicked as one seems; finally there is the acceptance of what one is, as human, and this is the enabling act permitting one to carry on—about as before, if slightly chastened. So even the Grantlys of Barchester are tolerable so long as they remain within the churchly shelter of Barchester.

The habit of expecting and looking for the worst of secret motives in oneself characterizes even the utterly innocent Mr. Harding and the half-innocent half-warrior Mr. Arabin. They are full of self-distrust, always suspicious of a worldly, selfish motive for the best of their actions. They are, as Trollope admits, imperfect characters because of a weakness and indecisiveness that arise from a lack of moral self-confidence, a willingness "to look for impure motives" for their conduct. This is Barchesterian weakness, the reverse side of Barchesterian virtue, for they find such unworthy motives even where they clearly do not exist, so that they often cut themselves off from the firmness needed to be proper fighters for their "church militant." Surely this weakness is a less dangerous failing than others we see in the novel. Indeed, our author has arranged for such good people as these to be saved by the errors of their less self-distrustful enemies whose self-deceptions lead to fatal blunders. In this novel too much self-distrust is better—and more successful—than not enough. The religion of the Hardings and Arabins can thus be preserved in its humanness by the failures of any harsher religion to keep *its* defender from blunders of too much self-indulgence. The extreme Protestantism professed by Slope must leave him exposed to such failures.

> *And here the author must beg it to be remembered that Mr. Slope was not in all things a bad man. His motives, like those of most men, were mixed; and though his conduct was generally very different from that which we would wish to praise, it was actuated perhaps as often as that of the majority of the world by a desire to do his duty. He believed in the religion which he taught, harsh, unpalatable, uncharitable as that religion was. He believed those whom he wished to get under his hoof, the Grantlys and Gwynnes of the church, to be the enemies of that religion. He believed himself to be a pillar of strength, destined to do great things; and with that subtle, selfish, ambiguous sophistry to which the minds of all men are so subject, he had taught himself to think that in doing much for the promotion of his own interests he was doing much also for the promotion of religion.*

An incomplete religion produces an incomplete man, who makes use of it to mask his incompleteness. Slope turns out to be a not much more efficient villain than Wickham: in short, he too is only a comic villain, which is to say a semi-villain who is not allowed to pose a major threat to the comedy. True, in his proclaimed moralism he does seem to represent an alternative vision and way of life, as Wickham does not. So if the victory were to be Slope's, it would carry certain thematic consequences—especially in view of his tie with the half-awesome, half-comic Mrs. Proudie. But we have seen that Slope is a fraud, using moralism only to serve his private, most inhumane ends, so that his defeat is to be proof of the impossibility of upholding his self-righteous claim with honesty, without self-delusion. Thus, along with Mrs. Proudie, he turns out not to have been a challenge to the Barchesterian vision and way of life but a final demonstration of its justness, of the lack of any real alternative to it. For we finally have a conflict not between a relaxed Anglicanism and an ascetic puritanism (as we do have, for example, in *Adam Bede*), but—thanks to Trollope's preclusion of extremity—only between the one possible *human* religion, however modestly it imposes, and the immoral pursuit of self-interest that masquerades as moralism. But this is no serious conflict at all. Instead, Trollope's stacking of the deck allows him to keep himself from acknowledging the possibility of challenge from the purely ethical. So he can resort to his natural human community, like George Eliot's—matching Irwine with Arabin—but without seeing the moral danger in its laxness, as Eliot does.

It is nice that in Barchester the human community is what comes naturally, so that all alternatives seem somehow perverse. This community is what keeps its parishioners safe. We have seen how Dr. Grantly, the archdeacon, that confessedly worldly man, is contained by communal values and turned from a potential Slope into a proper Barchesterian. Indeed, one may say he is a Slope, but on the churchly side, which provides a human breadth and catholicity that preserve him as a means of support for the community, despite his private tendencies.

Even a creature as alien as Signora Neroni is made to function as a support for Barchesterian purposes. This is, perhaps, Trollope's most brilliant comic (and, in part, classic) stroke. Signora Neroni—indeed the entire Stanhope family, in their decadent cosmopolitanism—obviously seem uniquely out of place in the world of Barchester. That Trollope not only would allow them into his carefully protected world but would make use of her as the principal agent of his Barchesterian dénouement demonstrates how immune he means to make his world to even the most alien provocations. Having consciously become an ally of our favorites, Signora Neroni is able to accomplish what none of our favorites could bring themselves to do: she turns the gulling Slope into a gull. She is a necessary enabling force, then, since only she—in her transcendent amoralism—could work Slope as she does. Thus she can rescue those characters who, however righteous, are victimized by the weakness that is their virtue. If she is a diabolist, only the Slopes of the world are eligible to be overcome by her.

She is as clear-seeing as she is diabolical. In chapters 27 and 38 she has interviews with Slope and with Arabin, respectively, in which she sees through them so thoroughly that we must begin to believe that so unlikely a creature has, momentarily, become Trollope's mouthpiece. Seeing the puritan Slope panting after both worldly power and her crippled body, she can well accuse him of preaching a doctrine which he knows he does not believe, as she speaks her distrust of religious enthusiasm. And yet she leads him on, largely out of spite; she takes a special, almost obscene, pleasure in the fact that she can tell him the truth—about him and about her own heartless self—and yet lure him into a more helpless state. Treating Arabin more gently, she yet displays before him the weakness of his self-distrust, accusing him of worldly failures—of defeats by the Slopes—that his religion as well as his good sense should give him the courage to fight against. The goods of the world are good things worth struggling for: "You try to despise these good things, but you only try; you don't succeed." Arabin feels "as though he were being interrogated by some inner spirit of his own, to whom he could not refuse an answer, and to whom he did not dare to give a false reply." But she knows he must remain helpless, so that if he is to be helped she must help him. Thus she determines to do all in her "power to make up the match" between Eleanor and him.

So Signora Neroni turns matchmaker to bring about Trollope's comic victory, the victory of Barchester. How uncharacteristic of her, we ought to believe, despite the fact that her worldly anti-religious position furnishes Arabin an intellectual bolster for his Anglicanism. It is as if Slope had a point when he complained of the paganism embedded in the insufficiently Protestant versions of the English church. And Signora Neroni (doesn't the name, in the setting of Barchester, tell us enough?), perverse representative of a degraded family, *is* a diabolist. Trollope introduces her at his peril, since one slip of his pen could land us in a sick, deformed world, like that which Mann later projected onto *The Magic Mountain*. But though Trollope presents her generously, lets us see her head-on, and allows broad hints about her and her family's soft, decadent unhealthiness, his pen does not slip: rather, he makes her into his matchmaking comic agent. Even *she* serves Barchester, supporting its values intellectually, by argument, and supporting its fortunes diabolically, by action. If Dr. Gwynne is prevented by the gout from performing as *deus ex machina*, Signora Neroni insists on performing as *diabolus ex machina*, and most effectively. But once he has converted this threat to the ways of Barchester into a most essential support, Trollope withdraws her from the scene. And well he must, if our assurances about the happy ending are to be unqualified. Trollope himself says as much.

His final chapter, "Conclusion," is to tie everything up into a pretty package: "The end of a novel, like the end of a children's dinner-party, must be made up of sweetmeats and sugar-plums." Nothing is to mar the pleasantness of the wedding of Eleanor to Arabin and its aftermath. Trollope tells us of the promises each makes to the other during the ceremony. And he adds, with a wink and *almost* more candor than he can afford (but, of course, not quite), "We have no doubt that they will keep their promises; the more especially as the Signora Neroni has left Barchester before the ceremony was performed." Here is his acknowledgment of the potential danger within her, potential danger that he, as author, insisted on finding a use for, thus making her serve Barchester. How unswervingly he has precluded the extremity that seems indeed to be in her. Now that he has removed her, he can confess the unmaterialized threat that he, like Barchester, has contained and turned to good. But, he suggests with some relief, it is better for us all that she is out of the reach—even of Arabin! This concession that the potential for a moral fall lurks within any of us recalls us to Trollope's sense of the natural—and naturally imperfect—humanity that no community can afford to ignore. Let me recall an aphorism spoken by Trollope as he asks us, in chapter 43, to forgive a selfishly motivated prayer by Mr. Quiverful as something any of us might have uttered in his place. These, my last words from *Barchester Towers*, should perhaps rather have been my first words on Jonathan Swift, for they are in his spirit: "Till we can become divine we must be content to be human, lest in our hurry for a change we sink to something lower."

III

The Retreat from Extremity

Through the Acceptance of the Human Barnyard

9

The Human Inadequacy of Gulliver, Strephon, and Walter Shandy—and the Barnyard Alternative

The words of Trollope, with which I closed my preceding chapter, help shift our focus from the natural human community to the human barnyard as the social context for man's life. It is but a slight shift in emphasis, so that the groups will have considerable overlappings between them. For, from the first, the "natural" in the natural human community represents man as herded, as merged with the history that his race has generated and continues to generate. When we take the "herd" metaphor seriously, we enter the human barnyard—nor should the classic visionary be reluctant to countenance that metaphorical extension. His resistance to the arrogant pretensions of ethical vision stems precisely from his fear of the tragic consequences of trying to make man better than he can be. If we try to "become divine," Trollope has warned us, and are no longer "content to be human," "in our hurry for a change we [may] sink to something lower." As we saw in the kinds of motives and behavior Trollope was ready to put up with in the herd of Quiverfuls, the classic visionary must, then, be ready to comprehend the total lowliness of the human state—to accept and even embrace its barnyard propensities so long as that barnyard is a human barnyard, enclosing the warmth of a human community, though it smells of that humanity, and something worse.

Jonathan Swift

We are clearly moving in upon the concerns of Jonathan Swift and his critics, moving in upon those so often debated questions about Yahoo, Houyhnhnm, and man in *Gulliver's Travels*. These matters have been pursued so frequently and at such length that I refer to them here only briefly.[1] I confess that I am quite won over by the reading—revolutionary when it was suggested a couple of decades back—that sees Gulliver not as Swift's mouthpiece but as an object of his increasing satire as Gulliver's prideful misanthropy increases. So the misanthropy is to be attributed to the Gulliver of the fourth book, not to Swift. This by now common reading sees the fourth voyage not as a hymn of praise to reason but as a sad acknowledgment that man has to settle for something very different from (and probably less than) what the Houyhnhnms could lay claim to. Thus, for man to pretend to Houyhnhnm-hood is at least folly, and probably vice. Further, if man does not have the obligation to strive to be a Houyhnhnm, neither is he cursed with being a Yahoo.

The evidence that critics have accumulated seems convincing. There is the increasing villainy in the acts which, at the outset of each voyage, leave Gulliver isolated for the adventures which are to follow; and this downward path of human immorality seems calculated to darken his vision. By the time that the basest act of human faithlessness and treachery—mutiny—prepares him for the Houyhnhnms, his mind is so altered that he views all mankind (and judges them!) as Yahoos. Yet when Swift, toward the end of the voyage, introduces Pedro de Mendez as Gulliver's humane and gentlemanly savior, Gulliver—no longer capable of discrimination within the species—sees him as a Yahoo and is repelled by him. The decent values which de Mendez has been explicitly given by Swift (who thus proves to us that *he* still can discriminate among men) are essentially unappreciated by the maddened Gulliver. After all the horrors he has undergone at sea, a progression of evil which moved from accident to indifference to increasing malice, this single exemplary experience should have seemed all the more visible, and noteworthy, were Gulliver still a trustworthy moral observer. His paranoia now may lead us to remember that earlier, even in the most reprehensible acts against him

[1] Let me mention here, for those who wish to pursue the issues in detail, only the two treatments which I have found most persuasive among a great number of persuasive ones: Robert C. Elliott, "The Satirist Satirized: Studies of the Great Misanthropes," *The Power of Satire: Magic, Ritual, Art* (Princeton, N.J.: Princeton University Press, 1960), pp. 184–219; and Samuel Holt Monk, "The Pride of Lemuel Gulliver," in *Eighteenth-Century English Literature: Modern Essays in Criticism*, ed. James L. Clifford (New York: Oxford, 1959), pp. 112–29.

by pirates and mutineers, there was a saving human gesture that we —perhaps too Gulliver-like ourselves—did not notice.

We also become more alert, thanks to Swift, to signs of Gulliver's unbalanced, prideful excesses upon his return home. His prideful statement rejecting the pride of the lowly human-Yahoo is clear enough evidence. It is a very paradigm of the self-deception of self-righteously ethical man. In a more detailed way, the absurd disproportion between Gulliver's disdainful attitude toward his faithful, devoted family and his affection for his horses and his stableboy is made hilariously obvious by Swift, who, with a straight face, allows Gulliver to give himself away. Robert Elliott has reminded us[2] of the extent to which Gulliver's family represents "the common routine" (a phrase from T. S. Eliot which I have made much of already and will again, in the final chapter) from which he has repeatedly fled in his irresponsible restlessness. The wife and children are always there, ready to welcome their unresponsive traveler upon each of his returns, having forgiven his last desertion of them and, apparently, half-expecting his next. With a fidelity like Penelope's for Ulysses, his wife tends their unspectacular hearth, always waiting, always counted on by Gulliver to be unchanged: to supply a warm reception, to refrain from moral judgment of his errant behavior, and to allow him to make her "big with child" before he takes off again. These are the creatures he rejects as insufferable Yahoos, who repel him and drive him to his horses.

Gulliver, then, may be a creature driven by extremity, increasingly alienated from the center of all human experience—that which yields warmth as well as that which springs from cruelty—and incapable of distinguishing between the two. He seems beyond being able to return to the soft center from the hard edge of experience. Even after he begins to permit his wife to sit at dinner with him (though "at the farthest end of a long table" and with his "nose well stopped with rue, lavender, or tobacco leaves"), he closes his narration with a most extreme, pro-Houyhnhnm, anti-Yahoo diatribe. But if his extremity, as potentially tragic, would seem to keep him outside my interests in this volume, the work's vision which controls him within its maturest ironies would seem to be clearly classic. That vision is sustained by man's capacity to survive, despite his Yahoo nature, as a creature who

[2] *The Power of Satire*, p. 213.

holds his life together within a community that can manage but a small yield in response to low expectations. A Gulliver could never settle for so little, but man can expect little more—and he still must be brought to settle for it.

I am suggesting a receptiveness in *Gulliver's Travels* that is consistent with the calm, masterful blend of moods and attitudes and styles in Swift's mild city pastoral of many years earlier, "A Description of the Morning." Within the properly end-stopped heroic couplet, which encloses many satiric observations expressed through the juxtaposition of trivial details and mock-heroic elegance, this poem almost lovingly lingers over the minutiae of just another city morning. The speaker is a totally neutral observer, one who misses very little but who will not point out the moral consequences of what he sees so clearly. Indeed, he can mix matters of moral significance with merely routine observations without distinguishing between them. Unlike Dr. Johnson's, his "observation" has no "extensive view." All items are run serially, neutrally, before the moving camera-eye. Betty's secret sharing of her master's bed, and the Lord who cannot pay his bills, and the use of prisoners to steal in behalf of the law—all are interspersed without comment with the normal, if not very efficient, activities of the sweepers and cleaners and smallcoal-man and bailiffs and schoolboys. All are seen with an equal eye; none is judged. Morally significant or not, what they all have in common is their utterly routine nature. This is how it is, day after day, every day and this day, typically and uniquely. They also have in common with one another the fact that no one is carrying on quite as it appears he should: Betty, who has stolen from the bed in which she has been but did not belong to the bed in which she belongs but has not been; the apprentice, who is "slipshod"; Moll, whose "dext'rous airs" characterize her show of working rather than the work itself; the imprisoned thieves who are forced to steal legally; the "watchful bailiffs" who see nothing and say nothing ("their silent stands"); and even the schoolboys, who manage to "lag," delaying their arrival at where they are supposed to be in order to keep from doing what they are supposed to do.

In all these activities, or non-activities, the speaker maintains the same "watchful," benevolent neutrality as the bailiffs seem to. His ironic use of the adverb "duly" ("The Turnkey now his Flock returning sees, / Duly let out a Nights to Steal for Fees") emphasizes his awareness of the routine nature of this activity—one that is to be expected and is for that reason appropriate and acceptable, even if it is morally outrageous. The bailiffs react the same way: the poet introduces them immediately after the returning prisoner-thieves, and introduces them as "watchful," although, taking their "silent stands," they clearly accept, without judgment or reaction, the routine aspect of what they see.

But, just as the bailiffs do not react to the returning prisoners, none of the couplets interact with one another. This is an ongoing world of autonomous sights and sounds, but a world alive with the responses of a humanity expressing routinely its resistance to its assigned functions. Things and people barely move as they ought, but the city does get itself up and moving for another day. Yet the slowness of the day to get itself started once more in its common routine is reflected in the retarding movement of the final line with its simple, eternal observation: "And School-boys lag with Satchels in their Hands." Whatever elements of satire we may find in the discrete items of the poem or in its mock-heroic or mock-pastoral rhetorical moments, there is no hate or anger in it. Rather there is something close to affection, the affection of a familiarity, a closeness that yields understanding, as moral judgment—the capacity to condemn—is suspended. The speaker has seen no more than what he has expected to see, since he knows its routine nature and has seen it before. And though he sees it with a freshness, as if for the first time, there is throughout the poem the comfort of his not being disappointed and of his knowing that he will not be surprised.

It is the sense of knowing how things routinely are with people— watching and knowing—that leads to Swift's classic acceptance. It leads also to his need to reject the great expectations of a Gulliver as well as the violence which accompanies a Gulliver's disappointment. In Swift's well-known letter of 1725 to Pope and Bolingbroke, he makes clear his distrust of those (like those he is writing to) who ask too much of man, those who "would have them be reasonable animals, and are angry at being disappointed." Swift seems to be accusing his correspondents of being Gullivers in complaining that man is not a Houyhnhnm; he is protesting, in effect, that it is not the Swifts but the Popes, Bolingbrokes, and Gullivers, who—in their rational demands—are driven to hatred by the foibles of the individual person.

Swift, then, is ready—however unhappily—to settle for less, to acknowledge the sordid, barnyard propensities of man. We would not find him—as we found Pope in "The Rape of the Lock"—fabricating a purified, aesthetic abstraction of the fleshly world in order to evade Clarissa's homely truths. He not only would answer Pope with Clarissa but would go beyond her. We would find him embracing, with far more relish than Clarissa, the biological consequences of her picture of woman as the aging breeder. Thus we find Swift creating a "Lady's Dressing Room" far different from Belinda's. It is the difference between the worship of bloodless abstractions (in order to fend off an awareness of the human barnyard behind them) and the acceptance of the bloody reality of that barnyard. Here, in the dressing rooms of Pope and Swift, are two different modes of classic vision indeed.

The brute animal facts behind Celia's artful façade as "Goddess" are certainly dwelled upon—with an unhealthy thirst for scatological detail—in Swift's poem. But is that thirst the speaker's or poet's, or is it only Strephon's? Swift makes it clear that there is an obsession with the ugly reality behind "haughty Celia"; but it is Strephon who is obsessed, as our distressed narrator makes clear. The "swain" has stolen into the room to take "a strict Survey" of what the "Goddess" has left behind her. The more dreadful the things he sees, the further he searches: "No Object *Strephon's* Eye escapes" (l. 47). Like Celia's magnifying glass which he discovers, Strephon must enlarge upon all that has issued from her orifices and her pores: a veritable Gulliver investigating a Brobdingnagian. The speaker upbraids him for his persistence in exploring even the details of her chamber pot: "Why *Strephon* will you tell the rest? / And must you needs describe the Chest?" (ll. 69–70). By leaving it exposed in the corner, Celia, "that careless Wench," is allowing Strephon to "exercise [his] Spight" (l. 74).

Strephon is profoundly "disgusted," but he cherishes his disgust. So great is his shock at discovering that the biological facts of life apply also to his "Goddess" Celia that he must savor his foul-smelling disappointment obsessively, to its fullest. He madly pursues all its revolting consequences. When we get to the "Chest," the detailed description of Strephon's "strict Survey" breaks off. Instead, Swift inserts the one classical allusion that appears in the poem; and it is an extended one. This extraordinary intrusion would seem to be Swift's way of calling attention to the peculiar significance of this episode;

and it is significant. The allusion (ll. 83–94) is to the chamber pot as Pandora's box, with Strephon cast in the role of Epimetheus. The "sudden universal Crew / Of humane Evils" that Epimetheus released by opening the box here becomes the excremental vapors that fly up when Strephon lifts the lid.

But there is a crucial difference pointed out between Epimetheus and Strephon. After all of the "humane Evils" flew out of Pandora's box, we are told that Epimetheus "still was comforted to find / That *Hope* at last remain'd behind." Now, when Strephon "ventur'd to look in," he had "resolv'd to go thro' thick and thin." But, once the lid is open and he sees and smells the "humane Evils" (here, Celia's biological realities),

> *Strephon cautious never meant*
> *The Bottom of the Pan to grope,*
> *And foul his Hands in Search of* Hope.

It has been clear that Hope was never the objective of his resolution "to go thro' thick and thin." His desperate plumbing of the depths of Celia's animality was launched by a puritan fastidiousness that, deeply offended, has become insatiable in feeding its own despair. Once the facts on Celia are out, for Strephon there can never again be Hope, for Hope would require him to "go thro' thick and thin" to find Hope even there, at the bottom of the chamber pot, that all-too-human "vile Machine."

So for Strephon all appearance is seen as a fraud, beneath which all is really filth. Falsely enamored of Celia before, Strephon, "disgusted," has finished his "grand Survey" (which grew out of what began as a "strict Survey") and steals away as he began by stealing in (ll. 115–16, echoing l. 7). His traumatic experience has led him to a single grand conclusion: in his "amorous Fits," he can only repeat, "Oh! *Celia, Celia, Celia* shits!" (l. 118).[3] Was there ever a possibility that she didn't? What is significant here, of course, is the absurd naïveté

[3] On the authority of Harold Williams I use the Roberts editions of the poem rather than Faulkner's edition, also published in 1732, which omits the offensive couplet, ll. 117–18. Two couplets, ll. 115–18, standing apart from the longer strophes, are obviously meant to be the climactic conclusion of Strephon's visit. The first couplet by itself is far too weak, so that we must believe that, in the text which Faulkner printed, squeamishness led to the suppression of lines that properly belonged to the poem.

which could prompt such words as if they really represented a discovery. Only if one took Celia literally as the "Goddess," created by what Pope (in his dressing room scene) called "the sacred Rites of Pride," could there be any question about what biological functions she had to perform like the rest of us.

Strephon, like the most puritanical of Platonists, is decrying art as a liar. Seeing Celia "array'd in Lace, Brocades and Tissues," he was taken in by the aesthetic illusion (created by five hours of her labors) that she was a Goddess; and now that he thinks he knows the reality beneath, he abandons all Hope and, Gulliver-fashion, sees her as unadulterated Yahoo. Either Goddess or Yahoo—there is for the Strephons and the Gullivers no possibility for humanity or Hope in between the two. For Strephon the chamber pot has become the symbol for Celia: in his eyes she has become her pot. Like her, the pot also is decorated on the outside in a way that attempts to disguise its true nature and function:

> In vain, the Workmen shew'd his Wit
> With Rings and Hinges counterfeit
> To make it seem in this Disguise,
> A Cabinet to vulgar Eyes.

> (ll. 75–87)

Strephon's zeal in pursuing anti-aesthetic honesty leads him to strip the ornamental cabinet until it dwindles into a chamber pot, and to strip the brocaded Goddess until she dwindles into the smelly Yahoo beast. His enemy is the ambition of human artifice, which makes things appear as they are not. That ambition has led Celia to disguise that which exists for foul biological functions so that it appears to be a transcendent object of beauty. The true Celia, the Celia inside the brocades, is the functioning organism whose leavings fill the dressing room, just as the true chamber pot is characterized by what fills it rather than by the unfunctioning ornaments on the outside, the counterfeit "Rings and Hinges." Strephon is overwhelmed by this fact: that the true Celia is the Celia of the dressing room rather than the Celia of the drawing room. And from now on, we are told, he is fated to reduce—in his "foul Imagination"—every goddess-like drawing-room creature to the stinking Yahoo of the dressing room. It is as if he is condemning the artful dishonesty of every creature who refuses to make evident in her public appearance the base facts of her private toilet. How would he prefer Celia, poor Yahoo underneath, to look and to smell?

But is it not a considerable accomplishment to create the goddess-like illusion out of such unpromising materials? And is it not a considerable feat of an un-foul imagination for man to dream of such divine creations? The speaker seems to justify the punishment of Strephon, his being forever fated to link "Each Dame he sees with all her Stinks," so that he must indiscriminately reject all ladies as Yahoos. Unlike Strephon, the speaker—as aware as Strephon is of the "pocky," "smelly" underworld—accepts the miraculous gift of what woman can make of woman. He knows whence she comes ("Should I the Queen of Love refuse, / Because she rose from stinking Ooze?"); but he also knows how far she has come (his "ravisht Sight" sees "Such Order from Confusion sprung, / Such gaudy Tulips rais'd from Dung"). This is hardly a great compliment, as the speaker becomes only slightly less scatological than Strephon was. But however scornful and condescending, the speaker also admits that his sight is "ravisht" by this fantastic transformation to "Order" from "Confusion," to "Tulips" from "Dung." His willingness—nay, anxiousness —to accept the lady as she appears without questioning (or smelling for) the source of that appearance is perhaps the sign that he has not abandoned Hope for the human animal even though he knows what muck one must go through to retain that Hope. We must remember that it was the speaker, and not Strephon, who introduced the allusion to Pandora's box into the chamber pot interlude. And it was thus the speaker who marked the difference between Epimetheus and Strephon as the loss of Hope by the latter. Does not the Pandora reference, as the speaker manipulates it, suggest that Hope is always there for him who will "foul his hands" to get to it, as man normally will not? By the end, the speaker has restored Hope to the poem—in his still minimal concession to human possibilities.

There *is* something humanly noble—though at the same time false and showy, perhaps vainglorious rather than glorious—in raising gaudy tulips from dung, in our refusal to parade around in our excrement as if that was all we were or all we were capable of dreaming of. We exceed the animal in us when we express an imagination (no longer "foul") that would have us better than we are. And, however base our matter, when we raise confusion to order, though the product be trivial, we *are* on our way to the gods. All this is suggested by the voice of the speaker, who sees beyond the limited fanaticism of Strephon even as he sees all that Strephon sees. He will have his "Goddess" yet, though he knows as well as Strephon does all else she is that denies her divinity.

It is more difficult to free the poet from the naked assault on the raw underworld in a poem like Swift's "A Beautiful Young Nymph Going to Bed," written at much the same time. For this poem has no Strephon in it, so that we see Corinna directly through the speaker. Of course, Corinna is no Celia: she is hardly more divine outside her dressing room ("her Bow'r" four stories up) than she is in it. There is little that is deceptive in her outward appearance, this "batter'd, strolling Toast." When the speaker refers to her as "the lovely Goddess" (l. 23), the irony is direct and singlemindedly bitter, with no suggestion of the complex attitude which the word expressed when applied to Celia early in "The Lady's Dressing Room" ("The Goddess from her Chamber issues, / Array'd in Lace, Brocades and Tissues").[4] In "A Beautiful Young Nymph" it is too late: Corinna's dressing-room arts are woefully inadequate to transform a loathsome reality into a deceptively winning appearance. There can be no disappointment here— which, perhaps, is why no Strephon is needed. If there are no surprises, no stark contrasts, here where the ugliness is so persistent, if there are no ravished sights and no amorous fits, there is in the speaker's tone—beneath the straight recital of disgusting details—a constant pathos which only the shock of unrelieved revulsion keeps from turning sentimental.

The speaker's covert sympathy for his "batter'd, strolling Toast" undercuts the ferocity of his dispassionate descriptions. There is Corinna's weariness, beginning with her climb four stories up to her "Bow'r"; there are the disfigured and disintegrated parts of her body, so superficially and inefficiently patched together, together with her chancres and sores—all of these "Effects of many a sad Disaster" (l. 31). Even more forcefully, the speaker traces at some length (ll. 40–56), in her pill-induced sleep, the awesome variety of her nightmares, each of them rooted in the frightful reality of her life. She awakens to

[4] In "A Beautiful Young Nymph" we also find the single-minded irony of simple inversion in the title of the poem, in the name (Corinna) given to the "Nymph," and in such mock-pastoral touches as the use of the word "Bow'r" for the "Nymph" 's dismal room.

the even greater nightmare of the day to come amid the "dreadful Sight" bequeathed her by "the Ruins of the Night," those realities that occurred during her futile attempt to escape to some peace in sleep.

In the lines that follow, the narrator reveals, despite the horror, the sort of grudging admiration I have observed elsewhere for the human persistence in trying—even without hope—to turn confusion into order, even when it is too late to turn dung into tulips:

> The Nymph, tho' in this mangled Plight,
> Must ev'ry Morn her Limbs unite.
> But how shall I describe her Arts
> To recollect the scatter'd Parts?
> Or shew the Anguish, Toil, and Pain,
> Of gath'ring up herself again?
>
> (ll. 65–70)

Her efforts do not slacken, though we cannot understand what purpose moves her to these efforts. What reason can there be for her to go through the entire business again? Why yet another day go through the motions as if she were successfully transformed by the pretended, dressed-up finery in which she goes about in the world between her first and last moments of disarray in the bed? It is even beyond the Muse to relate what transpires during Corinna's desperate effort to unite her limbs yet one more time, to recollect her scattered parts: to gather up herself again. And this is *her* common routine, what she must do "ev'ry Morn." In view of her recent past, her present, and her unquestionable future—all of these reinforced by her nightmares of this and every night—why does she bother and how can she do it? Even the Muse is silent, we are told. Out of horror surely; but also, perhaps, because it is beyond the modest capacity of the "bashful Muse" to describe or understand. All of Corinna's labor and her exhausted life leave, at the end, only the horror: "*Corinna* in the Morning dizen'd, / Who sees, will spew; who smells, be poison'd." But, though her case is hopeless, we, who have gone through thick and thin with her, can find in her a humanity, rising above even her circumstances, that leaves Hope for us all—for us who, from our unalterable, disorderly place in the cosmos, must recollect our scattered parts, gathering up ourselves again to face every morn. Even without the presence of Strephon, the speaker, with his implicit sympathy, seems to have gone beyond the Strephon in himself. The Celia of Swift's "The Lady's Dressing Room" is now doubly justified—and Strephon doubly answered—if humanity's impulse to artifice, to cultivate order and tulips, is revealed not only in Celia's still hopefully duplicitous circumstances but in Corinna's single, day-and-night nightmare of street and dressing room alike.

In Swift's varied use of the word "Goddess" we see the ironic alternative he provides for Pope's goddess, decked out by "the sacred Rites of Pride." This alternative, in turn, reveals the major difference between the two ways of retreating from extremity, the worship of bloodless abstractions and the acceptance of the human barnyard, of man's natural inheritance as a stinking animal (and a more-than-animal) of flesh and blood. This difference affects not only our conception of man's realities but also our hopes for the arts of the human imagination and, with these, our hopes for a more-than-animal humanity itself.

But, to summarize, let me recapitulate four alternative attitudes toward woman as goddess and as animal—two that are compromises and two that we have seen represent the extremes. Only one of the four seems to me properly classic. At the extremes, of course, we have Pope's vision of Belinda's dressing room and Strephon's vision of Celia's. We must remember that Pope's dressing-room scene does indeed involve the creating of a goddess: the priestess (Belinda) who "adores" "the Cosmetic Pow'rs" and the inferior priestess (Betty) are decking out the "heav'nly Image" (the reflection of Belinda in the mirror). So the goddess-Belinda who dominates the poem (unlike the flesh-and-blood Belinda to whom Clarissa points) is a disembodied creature, possessor of the "purer" blush, whose lock alone can be raped since she has—in effect—no body. That lock achieves an eternal place in the heavens, in contrast to the fair "Tresses" of the mere woman, which are "laid in Dust." A total work of art related only to the "Beau-monde," the goddess-Belinda bears no relation to the organic world of flesh and blood, from which her art-world is in full flight (and, as Swift reveals, for good reasons). As I argue in Chapter 4 above, the poem is dedicated to this deification of appearance, of aesthetic artifact constructed without substance.

At the other extreme is Strephon's desperate reduction of all goddess-like qualities to the stinking animal that belies the claim to divinity. For him Celia is pure Yahoo, beyond elevation. Once Strephon has grasped her physiological reality, he presses it to its extreme consequences, refusing to see her as anything but an excreting body. Consequently, he rejects all art that might dress up that body and sweeten its odors so as to permit it to transcend itself. Having found what he deems to be reality, he insists on confronting it, turning aside from all that he deems to be aesthetic delusion. If he can no longer fool himself into accepting the make-believe world controlled by Belinda-like goddesses, he insists on the wholly fleshly animal. Either Goddess or Yahoo, either tulip or dung—these are seen as mutually exclusive alternatives.

Although Clarissa also is a sworn enemy to the goddess-Belinda's bodiless, toyshop being, her vision is by no means Strephon's. She moves from Pope's art-world toward Strephon's world of biological realities but stops far short of pressing it to its logical extreme. Clarissa is rather a common-sense supporter of the compromising demands of practical life and argues for the sort of woman which that life requires. She is, in effect, an ethical visionary who will accept the artifice of appearance, but solely as an instrument serving proper social objectives conceived for man as a conventional social being. Thus must "good Sense preserve what Beauty gains." Divinity is precluded for Clarissa by the fact that beauty ("curl'd or uncurl'd," "painted or not painted") is subject to time's destruction.[5] But while she reduces the goddess-Belinda to a breeding, aging animal, she will not—like Strephon—follow this reduction to its extremity. She may wish to replace the "purer" cosmetic blush with the blush of desire produced by real blood (so that the lady may not scorn the man and "die a Maid"); but it is clear that the goddess is to dwindle not into the bloody animal but only into the trim and proper wife. What Clarissa offers, then, is a serious justification and an unquestioning acceptance of the universalized moral function of man in his society. In her lack of authenticity, in the ethical rather than the classic alternative she provides, she deserves the impatient scorn which the artificial company visits upon her. The "Moral of the Poem" which she presents is, alas, far too "moral."

Although Swift's narrator in "The Lady's Dressing Room" also

---

[5] We have noted that Pope himself has it both ways at the end of the poem, since he at once sees the time when Belinda's "Tresses shall be laid in Dust" and places the immortalized lock in the heavens.

draws back from Strephon's self-impelled indulgence in extremity, this narrator is far too consciously aware of what has driven Strephon to such a state for him to entertain the crass compromises suggested by Clarissa. Swift's speaker is also a creature of compromise since he conceives of man as only *in part* Yahoo. But his compromises are less crass, founded as they are on the in-partness of the in-part Yahoo nature of man. Here and elsewhere, as we have seen, Swift in the end clings to the human capacity to create and maintain a modest routine order, to bind together days that man's largely Yahoo nature makes it barely possible to live out with dignity. So his is the classic alternative. Thanks to his protagonists, Swift sees and smells it all; nor does he hide anything from us. Indeed, it is his lack of restraint that leads to our attributing scatological obsessions to him. If he is at last impatient with his Gulliver-Strephons after standing at their side without inhibiting the fullness of their discoveries about the human barnyard, it is probably because too much of them is in him for his own comfort. But his dialogistic task as artist and visionary carries him back from their extremity after all, even while he too is haunted by what haunts them.

As we have come to Celia's dressing room by way of Belinda's, we have seen the extent to which the classic vision darkens as we move from the existential evasions of bloodless abstractions to the desperate acknowledgment of the human barnyard. We seem to be moving ever downward on the path leading toward the naked confrontation of extremity that we find with a Gulliver or a Strephon as protagonist. And only as delicately balanced a counter-voice and counter-vision as Swift's can keep us only on the verge, still this side of extremity, still able to retreat within the liberal confines of the classic. But I must confess that with Swift we are indeed on the verge of a realm in which the lines that divide the classic from the tragic dissolve under the pressures of the ironic.

Nevertheless, I would maintain that, although Swift may be our case of the minimal classic, he is securely that. At the end of my treatment of Franz Kafka in *The Tragic Vision* I spoke of Kafka as my example of the minimal tragic.[6] The ironic vision can put the tragic and classic into a new and close relationship with one another. It appears

---

[6] *The Tragic Vision*, p. 144: "he makes it to the state of the tragic visionary, however reduced a version. His vision, through diminution, is almost stopped at the boundary of the ironic, the merely pathetic and not quite comic."

to me now that, as Kafka is just inside the tragic side of the boundary line between the tragic and ironic visions, so Swift is just inside the classic side of its border with the ironic. By way of the ironic, Swift brings us as close to the tragic as the classic can come, even as Kafka brings us as close to the comic as the tragic can come. Somehow, despite my original inadequate diagram, the classic, like the tragic, descends toward a fusion in the ironic.[7] It may be that both writers would be more accurately described as ironic visionaries, although I do believe that, for the purposes of the discussion here, it is the classic quality of Swift's profoundest vision that finally characterizes it. As for the ironic vision and its relation to the tragic and the classic, this would require another volume, since it is a vision that cuts a different thematic path, moving through both, if not quite uniting them.

TRISTRAM SHANDY

> *True* Shandeism, *think what you will against it,*
> *opens the heart and lungs, and like all those affections*
> *which partake of its nature, it forces the blood and*
> *other vital fluids of the body to run freely through its*
> *channels, and makes the wheel of life run long*
> *and cheerfully round.*
>
> (vol. 4, chap. 32)

This incomparable masterpiece bears all over itself and within itself evidence that there can be almost unmitigated joy in the defense of the human barnyard, that the downward movement of the classic toward the near-tragic irony of a Swift can regain its buoyancy in the delightful earthiness of a Sterne. Our fictive author, Tristram, repeatedly affirms his objective of using the humors of his Shandean system to undo the ravages to our physiological systems (another set of humors) which life visits upon us:

> *If 'tis wrote against any thing,—'tis wrote, an'*
> *please your worships, against the spleen; in order,*

[7] I borrow this notion of a descent into the ironic from Northrop Frye's *Anatomy of Criticism* (Princeton, N.J.: Princeton University Press, 1957), especially pp. 40–49: "Irony descends from the low mimetic" (p. 42). It is true, however, that for Frye the ironic mode, at the bottom of the circle, also starts the movement back upward toward the undisguised gods.

> *by a more frequent and more convulsive eleva-*
> *tion and depression of the diaphragm, and the*
> *succussations of the intercostal and abdominal muscles*
> *in laughter, to drive the* gall *and other* bitter juices
> *from the gall bladder, liver and sweet-bread of*
> *his majesty's subjects, with all the inimicitious passions*
> *which belong to them, down into their duodenums.*
>
> (vol. 4, chap. 22)

There is all of life in this novel, of life's real and its absurd mock sorrows, together with man's constant and dedicated struggle to overcome life, to manage somehow to keep its wheel running "long and cheerfully round." All the pages of the book, though not all its characters, tacitly acknowledge the pain of the brute facts of life as well as the means by which humanity asserts itself by transforming those facts into metaphors one can live with. The novel itself thus becomes Tristram's metaphor, which we all are free to use to keep our organs and our blood from succumbing to the troubles brought on by life and the time along which it rolls.

In the language of the novel we consistently find a doubleness, magnificently exploited, which exaggerates the split between the literalness of things and the figurativeness of man's verbal substitutions for them. This in turn is an echo of the split between the chronological fact of time and the subjective dislocations of *human* time. In each case there is a reflection of the conflict between an objective fact-icity that enslaves us and our futures and our subjective transformation of fact-icity into that which we can live with, smilingly, in freedom. The objective-subjective dualism, so central to the philosophic world Locke inherits from Descartes, receives the richly human benefit of Sterne's balanced awareness. Nowhere in literature are necessary fictions more celebrated than they are here; but nowhere is the sad fact that they are fictions more keenly acknowledged. With Tristram's help, we must keep the wheel of our lives running long and cheerfully around, though, as we do so, he reminds us also that it is running out. Time, which we try to keep circular, has a habit of proving its simple linearity. Similarly, we may try to build our worlds out of the figurativeness of our language, though we are doggedly reminded by a naïve realism that things have their own existence, to which our language is intended, literally, to refer. And the linearity of time, like the literalness of language, carries with it the natural course within which our biological realities expend themselves.

Walter Shandy is, of course, our purest representation of the Shandean system. He functions only through his use of language, which, for him, becomes the world. Words forgo their usual nominal nature to become the only substance he can recognize. Though all he speaks may seem metaphorical, for him there is no metaphor because the figurative is taken to be literal, the only literalness he knows. In discussing Walter Shandy, it is not enough to bring in Locke to account for the association of his ideas as subjective entities; one must rather look ahead to a philosopher like Ernst Cassirer to account for the way in which Walter's entire universe is a symbolic construct fashioned according to the dimensions of his language. His words, in their syntactical dispositions, limit the number of things that can encroach upon his horizon and define what those things can be: these are all the substantive things that can exist for his consciousness. His language, with all its pedantic diversions, is his consciousness; and for him, as for the other characters in the novel, consciousness is the world.

The final frustration Walter must bear in the events surrounding Tristram's birth is the fact that he is named "Tristram" instead of "Trismegistus." It was, after all, to be the name that, because of its inherent power, would undo those other frustrations that Walter's system required him to see as an accumulation of catastrophes (see his summary of them in vol. 4, chap. 19). The decline of "animal spirits" in Walter's old age, the faulty transmission of these spirits because of the interruption of the act of conception, a gestation impeded by Mrs. Shandy's mental state, a head-first birth,[8] and a nose crushed in delivery—all five are blows to Shandean hypotheses when a naïve, common-sense realism would hardly find any of them catastrophic.[9] But all of these, crushing as they are, were to be overcome by the

---

[8] I cannot resist quoting, from Walter's enunciation of this theory, an excellent and immediately obvious sample of his figurative language becoming literal, becoming his substantive world. The fact of head-first birth is made to account "for the eldest son being the greatest blockhead in the family.—Poor Devil, he would say,—he made way for the capacity of his younger brothers" (vol. 2, chap. 19).

[9] By contrast, the one potentially dangerous occurrence that befalls Tristram, his accidental circumcision, is taken quite calmly by Walter (thanks to his discovery of favorable antique precedents).

word-magic of "Trismegistus." This attribution of substantive power to a name is the major symbolic instance of Walter's sense of language's substantive reality. For him, only language—that is, the word in its naming function—has substance; the world outside words has none.

The idiosyncratic worlds constructed out of the eccentric symbols of the several characters create the "hobby-horsical" realities in which they live. There are literal and figurative horses, literal and figurative rides throughout the novel. (For example, "my uncle *Toby* dismounted immediately. —I did not apprehend your uncle *Toby* was o' horseback." On the other hand, Yorick's actual horse is itself expressive of *his* hobby-horse. And both Toby and Yorick ride continually.) One after another abstract notion—like Walter Shandy's auxiliary verbs, which become Uncle Toby's auxiliaries—takes on materiality, the corporeal existence of a hobby-horse, on which a character mounts up and canters away, each in his own direction. Tristram himself, clearly his father's son, uses his book as *his* hobby-horse and accumulates a large number of code words—some his father's, some his own—which recur again and again with hobby-horsical resonance that transforms their meanings from the simple metaphorical clichés with which he began. Thus we follow through the book his modulations of terms and phrases like the hobby-horse itself, buttonholes and crevices, curtain, knots, hinges, Aunt Dinah, the right and wrong end of a woman. These and many others have hobby-horsical edges with which to prod us as we continually meet them.

For example, we have the long "affair of the hinge" in the Shandy household, in which nothing is well hung, we are told. The literal hinges of doors, the figurative hinges on which the management of life turns, the differently figurative hinges of a writer's subject, all lead to the accidental circumcision caused by the poorly hung window sash, as well as the poorly hung Tristram. Further, this train of associations is connected to the special distorting properties of Uncle Toby's hobby-horse when we learn the weights from the window had been removed by Corporal Trim in response to Toby's need for field weapons in his make-believe battlefield. So the sash, deprived of its two weights, came down on the young Tristram, persuaded by Susannah to use the window instead of a chamber pot, and Yorick can accuse Trim of cutting off "spouts enow" (vol. 5, chap. 23).

Or there is the ubiquitous curtain. Our narrator drops and raises curtains as he pleases, to begin, shift, or close a scene; he uses trousers with their apertures (thus connecting this train with a train of button-holes), just as he speaks of the groin (Toby's or Trim's) as "the very *curtain* of the *place*" (vol. 9, chap. 31). This use of "curtain" leads us down into the barnyard roots of these evasive pseudo-metaphors which Tristram (after his father) pursues so literally. The "place" which is curtained is the connecting link between Uncle Toby's wound as it relates to Widow Wadman and Corporal Trim's earlier wound as it related to the young Beguine. There is an echo of the latter affair in Trim's successful campaign with Bridget that accompanies Mrs. Wad-man's futile campaign for Toby. It is the notion of the "place" and the "curtain" that controls the hilarious manipulation of the widow's desire to learn, to see, and to place her finger upon "where" Toby received his wound. Her notion of the "where" (as physiological) and Toby's notion of the "where" (as geographical) create another major symbolic instance of Sterne's comic struggles with the problematics of language. The ambiguity of the "where" is the conflict of the two insulated hobby-horses. For Toby, the map—as a sign language—is the reality itself, not just an insubstantial representation of a reality in Flanders. In the same way, the miniature battlefield reproduction on the green is the Flemish reality itself. Once on his hobby-horse, he sees no signs, but only equally real realities. In his own way, as a proper Shandean, Toby is as blind to man's barnyard demands as is Walter; and he is as willing as Walter is to use his hobby-horse to preclude his seeing them. The widow, of course, requires a more earthy reality and must read the "where" with an equal singlemined-ness as a place on Toby's body. So it becomes clear that Tristram's modulations of his hobby-horsical language continually point to their substantive basis in our barnyard realities.

We have already seen that Tristram's concern with buttonholes seems to become involved with his concern with curtains in the affair in which the coal drops into the open trousers of Phutatorius, "which, in all good societies, the laws of decorum do strictly require, like the temple of *Janus* (in peace at least) to be universally shut up" (vol. 4, chap. 27).[10] And we see from Walter (for example, vol. 4, chap. 14)

[10] By implication, the hinge motive, as well as the curtain, is also sug-gested at this point: "The neglect of this punctilio in *Phutatorius* (which by the bye should be a warning to all mankind) had opened a door to this accident."

that in the Shandy family, alas, nothing is well buttoned any more than it is well hung (to mention again the matter of the hinges). There is also a metaphorical extension of buttonholes that accounts for the curative function of the hobby-horse as it acts upon our inevitable worldly sorrows, which are beyond all hobby-horses. We have seen that, for Walter, evil seems to have followed upon evil in the pre- and postnatal history of Tristram. Each time his hobby-horsical sense invents a device to overcome the evils already done, a further frustration defeats his intention. Finally, we have seen, the magic of the name Trismegistus was to undo all the profound handicaps visited upon the boy. Walter justifies his recourse to the name as an example of man's power to overcome his troubles by counterbalancing them with the good which his mind can invent:

> When I reflect, brother Toby, upon Man; and
> take a view of that dark side of him which represents
> his life as open to so many causes of trouble—when
> I consider, brother Toby, how oft we eat the bread of
> affliction, and that we are born to it, as to the
> portion of our inheritance . . . when one runs over
> the catalogue of all the cross reckonings and sorrowful
> items with which the heart of man is overcharged,
> 'tis wonderful by what hidden resources the mind is
> enabled to stand it out, and bear itself up as it does
> against the impositions laid upon our nature. . . .
> Though man is of all others the most curious vehicle,
> said my father, yet at the same time 'tis of so slight
> a frame and so totteringly put together, that the sudden
> jerks and hard jostlings it unavoidably meets with
> in this rugged journey, would overset and tear
> it to pieces a dozen times a day—was it not, brother
> Toby, that there is a secret spring within us. . . .
> the spring I am speaking of, is that great and elastic
> power within us of counterbalancing evil.
>
> (vol. 4, chaps. 7 and 8)

But of course the counterbalancing is by means of a hobby-horsical invention, so that man's worldly sorrows are hardly done away with in reality, although by its wonderful "hidden resources the mind is enabled to stand it out, and bear itself up." This is the function of the hobby-horse: to create a private reality in freedom that appears to melt away those enslaving deprivations of our extra-hobby-horsical reality. We can hobby-horse away our sufferings, though not even the hobby-horse can eliminate them. For, whatever our attempts, evil is succeeded only by evil rather than being obliterated by man's imposition of his own good. So the mix-up of names leading to Tristram instead of Trismegistus follows the other misfortunes which it was to ameliorate. The learned conference convened about the naming error has its pleasurable Shandean compensations for Walter, but it does not resolve the problem. Upon returning home, he is at once diverted by the letter which opens the two conflicting possibilities of developing the Ox-moor and sending Bobby abroad.[11] The need to choose between the two becomes a new form of suffering, except that a new sorrow settles matters:

> My father had certainly sunk under this evil,
> as certainly as he had done under that of my Christian
> name—had he not been rescued out of it, as he was
> out of that, by a fresh evil—the misfortune of my
> brother Bobby's death.
> What is the life of man! Is it not to shift from
> side to side?—from sorrow to sorrow?—to button up
> one cause of vexation!—and unbutton another!
>
> (vol. 4, chap. 31)

It is to be expected that Walter is unable to distinguish among his afflictions the truly consequential from the merely hobby-horsical, the death of one son from the misnaming of another. His response to Bobby's death is another pedantically inspired, allusion-filled divertissement such as we have had from him on several objectively less serious occasions. On this occasion, Tristram himself, as narrator, shares and enjoys his father's tactic. Still, this tactic performs its task

[11] Or, in Tristram's language of delightful barnyard ambiguity, "It had ever been the custom of the family, and by length of time was almost become a matter of common right, that the eldest son of it should have free ingress, egress, and regress into foreign parts before marriage—not only for the sake of bettering his own private parts, by the benefit of exercise and change of so much air—but simply for the mere delectation of his fancy, by the feather put into his cap, of having been abroad" (vol. 4, chap. 31).

of allowing Walter to live with this incurable loss—and of allowing
Tristram to comment appropriately upon it:

> 'Tis either Plato, or Plutarch, or Seneca, or
> Xenophon, or Epictetus, or Theophrastus, or Lucian
> —or some one perhaps of later date ... who affirms
> that it is an irresistible and natural passion to
> weep for the loss of our friends or children ...
> [this is followed, of course, by examples].
>   My father managed his affliction otherwise; and
> indeed differently from most men either ancient
> or modern; for he neither wept it away, as the Hebrews
> and the Romans—or slept it off, as the Laplanders
> —or hanged it, as the English, or drowned it, as the
> Germans—nor did he curse it, or damn it, or
> excommunicate it, or rhyme it, or lillabullero it.—
>   He got rid of it, however.

$$\text{(vol. 5, chap. 3)}$$

Of course, he had to hobby-horse it his own way, even though his
tactic is no more closely related to the world which prompts it than is
Toby's whistling of *Lillabullero*.

"True *Shandeism*," through its hobby-horsicality, would seem to be
dedicated to cultivating its own consciousness of time and things (that
is, words as things) while bypassing all in the world that is external to
itself: the world's inevitable sorrows, its physiological basis, its linear
temporality, in short, its involvement in death. So the hobby-horse
thrives on the realities it precludes, even as it adapts them to its own
insulated, escapist nature. But Tristram, as our fictive author, encom-
passes his characters. While we have seen how much of his father is
in him who is creating his hobby-horse of a book, he is also more
than, or other than, Walter. There is Yorick in him as well, that unworldly creature of the earth, for the book has in it that which reveals
the world before and outside words and maps, the actual horse of
Yorick's which rides along with so many of the book's hobby-horses.
The earthy alternative Yorick provides for Walter, Trim provides for
Toby. Trim's use of gesture, his simple un-self-conscious involvement
with things and flesh, set him apart among the characters in the book,
especially when we view him—by way of contrast—as Toby's col-

league in love as well as in mock-war. Trim's gesture of freedom with his stick, his dropping of his hat to mark Bobby's death, his panto-mime narration of Tristram's circumcision with his forefinger of one hand and the edge of the other—all separate him from the world of words and relate him to the world of things, just as his "amours" with the young Beguine and Bridget relate him to the barnyard realities, in contrast to Toby's misadventures with Widow Wadman. For Toby shares his brother's hobby-horsical flight from the insistent demands of that human barnyard which Trim can un-self-consciously inhabit.

Walter and Toby share a Shandean intensity about their hobby-horses, a total preoccupation by them. Though their hobby-horses are continually at odds with one another, they are united in their function of precluding their riders' awareness of the world of sorrows and sex. Walter, of course, is explicit about his disdain for the barnyard in man. He detests the dependence on animal nature for propagating so splendid a creature as man, with his spiritual capacity for hobby-horsing. Thus, in the novel's final chapter, Walter—goaded by Toby's romance—bitterly laments the fact that "continuing the race of so great, so exalted and godlike a Being as man ... should be done by means of a passion which bends down the faculties, and turns all the wisdom, contemplations, and operations of the soul backwards ... which couples and equals wise men with fools, and makes us come out of our caverns and hiding-places more like satyrs and four-footed beasts than men." The shame behind this subhuman indulgence is indicated by our putting out the candle "when we go about to make and plant a man." Nor can we hobby-horse away that "unruly appe-tite," lust, the cause of "every evil and disorder in the world of what kind or nature soever, from the first fall of Adam, down to my uncle Toby's (inclusive)." All that has to do with copulation can "be con-veyed to a cleanly mind by no language, translation, or periphrasis whatever"; and if it is beyond the power of speech, then it can exist for Walter only to be attacked. Even the act of destroying a man he finds susceptible of hobby-horsical glorification, as Toby's example has shown him these many years. As for the weapons of killing, "We march with them upon our shoulders—We strut with them by our sides—We gild them—We carve them—We in-lay them—We enrich them—Nay, if it be but a *scoundrel* cannon, we cast an ornament upon the breach of it." This is hardly what we do with the private weapon with which we create a man.

III. Through the Acceptance of the Human Barnyard

It is, undoubtedly, the nagging presence of the urgings of lust, a presence beyond the power of hobby-horsing, that has aroused Walter's primary wrath over the years because he is incapable of doing anything about it except to attack it. And this is very different from hobby-horsing it, as, for example, Toby does with war and its death. Different, and far less satisfying.

Walter's one hobby-horsical sally against sex is his symbolic reduction of all that has to do with our sensual reality to the word "ass." He borrows from Hilarion the hermit the characterization of his ascetic practices as "the means he used, to make his *ass* (meaning his body) leave off kicking" (vol. 8, chap. 31). This becomes Walter's way "of libelling . . . the desires and appetites of the lower part of us." Thus "ass" must refer to that part of our body (as Toby's error in the following chapter makes clear), as well as to the kicking beast. It is also Walter's pet substitution for the word "passions," as the abbreviation becomes the metonymic emblem in typical Shandean fashion. The "ass," as our "lower part," becomes the seat of the passions ("the desires and appetites of the lower part of us"). So when Walter asks his brother, "how goes it with your ASS?" he is asking about his passion for Widow Wadman, but Toby thinks he is asking about the posterior, and both are really correct.

But the "ass," as a kicking beast, is also a competitor of the hobby-horse: man is either a hobby-horse rider or an ass rider, although in the latter case he really is being ridden by his ass because only his hobby-horse allows him to control his world instead of being controlled (kicked) by it. Tristram makes the distinction for us, and in so doing also makes a noble defense of the classic necessity of the hobby-horse.

> *I must here observe to you, the difference betwixt*
> *My father's ass*
> *and my hobby-horse—in order to keep characters*
> *as separate as may be, in our fancies as we go*
> *along.*
> *For my hobby-horse, if you recollect a little, is*
> *no way a vicious beast; he has scarce one hair or*
> *lineament of the ass about him—'Tis the sporting little*
> *filly-folly which carries you out for the present*
> *hour—a maggot, a butterfly, a picture, a fiddle-stick—*

> an uncle Toby's siege—or an any thing, *which a man*
> *makes a shift to get a-stride on, to canter it away from*
> *the cares and solicitudes of life*—'Tis as useful a
> *beast as is in the whole creation—nor do I really see*
> *how the world could do without it—*
> —But for my father's ass—oh! mount him—
> mount him—mount him—(that's three times, is it not?)
> —mount him not:—'tis a beast concupiscent—and
> foul befall the man, who does not hinder him
> from kicking.

Walter's commitment to ride his hobby-horse rather than his ass is constant from the first page of the book. This commitment in part is the cause of the first of Tristram's misfortunes—this one prenatal—with which the novel begins (since it begins, we are told, *ab ovo*). The dispersion of his father's animal spirits at conception occurs because he is interrupted at the climactic moment by his wife's asking whether he has wound the clock. Now copulation and the winding of the clock are, in Mrs. Shandy's mind, items in a Lockean train of associations, thanks to Walter's unvarying joint practice of winding up the clock and having intercourse with his wife on the first Sunday night of every month. His reason for doing so stems from his commitment to ride his hobby-horse rather than his ass: he performs these twin functions at this time in order "to get them out of the way at one time, and be no more plagued and pestered with them the rest of the month" (vol. 1, chap. 4). Thus it happens "at length, that my poor mother could never hear the said clock wound up,—but the thoughts of some other things unavoidably popped into her head—and *vice versa.*" So at the instant of conception that one night, her sexual awareness popped the clock into her mind, whence her interrupting question and the dispersion of the animal spirits. It is important to note that clock time and sexual activity are linked in Mrs. Shandy's mind because they are linked in the mind and behavior of Walter, both of them disagreeable intrusions from the external world and both of them to be summarily dispensed with so that he can be free to hobby-horse his world for the rest of the month.

From this point on, clock time is the enemy—of Tristram as well as of his father. We have seen that it is the enemy of the hobby-horse as a free-ranging animal, since the hobby-horsical world depends on subjective notions of time as duration rather than any linear notion of clock time. When Walter is trying to explain duration and the association of ideas to Toby, he remarks parenthetically, "I wish there was not a clock in the kingdom" (vol. 3, chap. 18). He is here cursing not only what the clock did to inhibit Tristram's conception, but what the linear progression of time marked by the clock does to inhibit the hobby-horsical operation of Lockean duration. Indeed, it was that general annoyance caused by his chronological time consciousness that caused Walter to treat the clock-winding as he did, thereby bringing on Tristram's initial misfortune. The measuring of sexual activity by the externally imposed, mechanistic divisions of the clock ties man's barnyard nature to time's objective reality, which leads the aging body down the road to death. External clock time brings us beyond the realm where the hobby-horse can help us.

In the hobby-horsical subjectivity of duration, however, consciousness can transform time from linear to circular. And this is essentially what Tristram does in his hobby-horse of a book. He starts, as he tells us, *ab ovo*. But if his beginning from the fertilization of the egg leads us to expect linear progression toward some end, we are of course mistaken. Like the wheel of life, which, we are told, true Shandeism makes "run long and cheerfully round," the novel is joyfully circular. It runs round and round its incidents and its time sequences, shuffling and reshuffling their order and ending up long before the time at which it began. So the *ab ovo* is illusory; it is just as surely *ad ovum*. Moving from egg to egg, we pass death but do not stop at it.

We find that the final chapter deals with conception and birth, just as the first one did. It is immediately after Walter's lament about the barnyard indignities of procreation that Sterne brilliantly introduces the closing story, termed by Yorick (Walter's antagonist in this debate) the story about "a Cock and a Bull." In it, as a final taunt to Walter, human procreation becomes the measure for animal procreation (with the latter apparently the more precious!). Obadiah has brought his cow to be serviced by Walter's bull on the very day that he and the housemaid were married: "so one was a reckoning to the other. Therefore when Obadiah's wife was brought to bed—Obadiah thanked God—Now, said Obadiah, I shall have a calf." When the calf is not born shortly after Obadiah's child, Obadiah suspects the bull's potency. Walter defends his bull, favoring him because, despite the excessive demands made upon him by cows, he carries off his barnyard obligations "with a grave face" (reminiscent of Walter himself). Thus the question of the cock and the bull constitutes, in effect, Yorick's earthy answer to Walter's anti-barnyard priggishness.

This final chapter echoes the first in another way. We might remember that the actions of Walter which opened the book reduced human sexuality to the external measure of chronological time. How different is the reduction of human procreation to the measure of animal procreation in the final chapter? It is not very different at all if we use the two reductions as further evidence of Sterne's equation of clock-time reality and barnyard reality, two modes of death that—as the brute reality that cannot be wished away—resist, equally, the joyous evasions of the hobby-horse.

Tristram himself, in the very writing of his book, furnishes the prime example of the attempt to escape death on a hobby-horse. I have now claimed several times that the book was his hobby-horse, his own way of coming to terms with fact-icity—more precisely, the fact of death, of his death. He himself provides the figure of the hobby-horse rider using his mount to run away from the pursuit of unrelenting facts:

> What a rate have I gone on at, curvetting and
> frisking it away, two up and two down for four volumes
> together, without looking once behind, or even on
> one side of me, to see whom I trod upon!—I'll tread
> upon no one,—quoth I to myself when I mounted
> —I'll take a good rattling gallop, but I'll not hurt
> the poorest jack-ass upon the road—So off I set—up
> one lane—down another, through this turn-pike—over
> that, as if the arch-jockey of jockeys had got
> behind me.
>
> (vol. 4, chap. 20)

The entire seventh volume is an extension of this metaphor. Tristram has been writing his book, in accordance with its Shandean function (as defined in the quotation which introduced this treatment of the novel): despite earthly cares, his spirits have carried him forward on his hobby-horsical project, oblivious to the burdens of ill health that weigh upon the aging, decaying animal. But clock time is still his enemy, threatening his death as it had inhibited the conception that preceded his birth. His project is threatened, despite all that his spirits can perform, when "Death" himself knocks at his door: "But there is no *living*, Eugenius, replied I, at this rate; for as this son of a whore has found out my lodgings" (vol. 7, chap. 1). With what "few scattered spirits" are left to him, he must flee death on horseback (as he has been fleeing it on hobby-horseback): "had I not better, Eugenius, fly for my life? 'tis my advice, my dear Tristram, said Eugenius—then by heaven! I will lead him a dance he little thinks of—for I will gallop, quoth I, without looking once behind me, to the banks of the Garonne; and if I hear him clattering at my heels—I'll scamper away to mount Vesuvius—from thence to Joppa, and from Joppa to the world's end." Here, then, the literal horse and the actual world as geographical space take up the role played by the figurative hobby-horse and the Shandean world of "interior distance" (to borrow Poulet's phrase). These two, in a similar way, "canter it away from the cares and solicitudes of life" (life as gateway to death). The transformation from figurative to literal confers a further literal sense to the hobby-horse in its functions, just as it relates the several worlds of the novels to one another.

The sliding metaphor of the circle—of many circles, microcosmic and macrocosmic—conveys the union of these worlds to us. Tristram's hobby-horse has been traversing the circle of his world from the start of the novel. In speaking of the midwife (vol. 1, chap. 7), he refers to her considerable "reputation in the world"; "by which word *world*, need I in this place inform your worship, that I would be understood to mean no more of it, than a small circle described upon the circle of the great world, of four *English* miles diameter, or thereabouts, of which the cottage where the good old woman lived, is supposed to be the centre." Tristram's actual ride out into the geographical world throughout volume 7 thus acts to solidify the figurative rides which he, like his Shandean creatures, has been taking from the first—and for the same purpose, subjective flight from the objective facts of time and space: "but where am I? and into what a delicious riot of things am I rushing? I—I who must be cut short in the midst of my days, and taste no more of 'em than what I borrow from my imagination—peace to thee, generous fool! and let me go on" (vol. 7, chap. 14). The circular, imaginative structure of Tristram's book (from egg to egg) is thus continually modified by his awareness of linear time (from birth to death), even as mental space is modified by his awareness of physical space.

It is these awarenesses that prompted me to see Tristram as modifying his father's hobby-horsicality with Yorick's common-sense realism. He somehow combines within him a transcendent awareness that can indulge the hobby-horse without losing sight of the deadly actual, that can play among circles while marking the devastating finality of the line segment. As consummate author, he can toy with the several realities of the map of Flanders, the mock battlefield, and the actual place where wounds and deaths were inflicted; he can add to these the other place (on the body) where wounds are inflicted and can thus move to yet another battlefield—the body as the battlefield of love. In his European travels of volume 7, he can mingle several "times"— that of his original tour with Walter and Toby, that of his current flight from death, and that of his current writing about both (chap. 28) —as he can mingle matters hobby-horsical and real-horsical, internally spatial and externally spatial.

The lingering fact of death haunts the novel, giving to it a sense of time and the body—the barnyard realities of us all as decaying animals—that should threaten to dismount any rider from his hobby-horse. But it is just this sense that creates the human need for an imagination that can carry us away from confronting such inexorables. So Tristram stays mounted, still fleeing, though—more than Shande-ism permits—he has profound knowledge of the realities beyond the control of him and his horse. There is another rider, an "arch-jockey of jockeys," who drives us all. It is perhaps to emphasize his Yorick-like modesty that Tristram, in his travels through Volume VII, does much of his riding upon an ass, in a passage which foreshadows the discourse between horses and asses in the final volume. Further, Tristram reminds us of Yorick's differences with Walter when he objects to the phrase man "falls in love": "for to say a man is *fallen* in love,—or that he is *deeply* in love,—or up to the ears in love,—and sometimes even *over head and ears in it*,—carries an idiomatical kind of implication, that love is a thing *below* a man" (vol. 6, chap. 37). He will not restrict love to the act which man must stoop to perform. Here is Tristram seeing beyond his father, as Swift sees beyond Strephon: he sees man's barnyard propensities as facts, though man can think himself beyond those facts even if he cannot think them away. Tristram can hobby-horse the fact without destroying it or denying its hold on him. In riding from death, he can even substitute an ass for a horse.

Early in the book Tristram confesses that his multiple awarenesses, circular and linear, create the peculiarities of his method of organization:

> *the machinery of my work is of a species by itself;*
> *two contrary motions are introduced into it, and*
> *reconciled, which were thought to be at variance with*
> *each other. In a word, my work is digressive, and it is*
> *progressive too,—and at the same time. . . . I have*
> *constructed the main work and the adventitious*
> *parts of it with intersections, and have so complicated*
> *and involved the digressive and progressive movements,*
> *one wheel within another, that the whole machine,*
> *in general, has been kept a-going;—and, what's*
> *more, it shall be kept a-going these forty years, if it*
> *pleases the fountain of health to bless me so long with*
> *life and good spirits.*
>
> (vol. 1, chap. 22)

In this reconciliation of contrary motions is the heart of true Shandeism, thanks to whose good spirits "the wheel of life [can] run long and cheerfully round." This reconciliation is key to both Sterne's method and his vision; and I know of no work in which the two are more thoroughly one. When the digressive is reconciled with the progressive, the internal world of subjective duration is reconciled with the chronology of clock time, hobby-horsical reality with brute fact. The latter allows man to see himself both as hobby-horse rider and as ridden by his ass; that is, he is permitted to see himself as imaginatively beyond the earthy world and yet as enslaved by it. In his self-ordained freedom he hobby-horses death away, and in his conscious acceptance he wills his indulgence of his material basis. Finally, there is also a reconciliation of the active tendency to expand the word to be one's world (the word becoming flesh since there is no independent flesh) with the passive recognition—in accord with naïve realism—of the solid substantiality of the world and its furniture, those heavy things outside us, outside our language and its metaphors. Are distinctions among words and between words and things to be preserved, or are they to be blurred in an illusion of micro-macrocosmic union? For Tristram it clearly must be both, and both at once. The concentric circles of meaning—like outward-moving ripples in water—are at once totally cut off from each other, concentric, and yet lead into and out of each other through our multiplication of the levels of meanings, whether of words, of words as things, or of just plain things. The several hobby-horses create the possibility of an endless variety of mutually exclusive microcosms, except that (1) the reality of language, as multidimensional, enlarges them into one, leading into and out of one another, and (2) the objective reality of the world's demands emphasizes the mere *hobby* in the hobby-horse, even if Tristram, like the others, refuses to dismount.

Thus the novel can serve as an allegory for the general method in this book. Tristram's method and his vision have shown us two things at once: his commitment to the hobby-horsical imposition upon reality, together with his acknowledgment of the facts that cannot be hobby-horsed away. These in turn can be seen as a symbolic precedent for my own original double concern: for the contextualist's commitment to the substantive metaphor which is a visionary reduction of the world, together with his awareness of the prosy, worldly actualities which deny that the metaphor exists as more than a play on words. We are to be utterly inside the extreme, metaphorical reduction and yet aware that it is untenable from the common-sense perspective, just as Tristram rides his hobby-horse—and watches Walter and Toby ride theirs—and yet knows the underlying barnyard facts that no ride can escape, the facts that end by riding the rider. In dwelling on the need to manage the impossible union between metaphor and anti-metaphor, between word and fact, as a way of vision as well as a literary method, I am in my turn making the book I am writing *my* hobby-horse. Would that I had the classic breadth to close my circle by reopening it: such is the classic good humor that concludes, as Tristram does, with a story of "a Cock and a Bull."

10

The Assumption of the "Burden" of History in *All the King's Men*

> *I said, "But suppose there isn't anything to find?"*
> *And the Boss said, "There is always something."*
> *And I said, "Maybe not on the Judge."*
> *And he said, "Man is conceived in sin and born in corruption and he passeth from the stink of the didie to the stench of the shroud. There is always something."*[1]

It is a great leap in time and kind from Swift and Sterne to Robert Penn Warren's *All the King's Men*, perhaps too great for the reader, or for me, to manage. But I hope to show that this novel reveals the human barnyard—the relation between the classic visionary and the classic existent within the barnyard—in a way that I find in no other work. For my purposes, this way, and thus this novel, are indispensable.

The barnyard concern that is at the center of *All the King's Men* is at once evident from Willie Stark's judgment, quoted above. It is a theodicy that he persuades our narrator, Jack Burden, to share with him. Nor is it a difficult persuasion, since it is but a logical extension of Burden's own philosophical and existential development. The very first scene establishes the barnyard metaphor that dominates the novel. Willie, now "the Boss," the all-dominating governor, is visiting his old farm home. He comments on the pig trough he and Jack are looking at:

[1] Robert Penn Warren, *All the King's Men* (New York: Random House, 1953), p. 54. Page numbers of other references are found in the text.

III. Through the Acceptance of the Human Barnyard

> *"I bet I dumped ten thousand gallons of swill*
> *into that trough," he said, "one time and another."*
> *He let another glob of spit fall into the trough. "I*
> *bet I slopped five hundred head of hogs out of*
> *this trough," he said. "And," he said, "by God, I'm still*
> *doing it. Pouring swill."*
> *"Well," I said, "swill is what they live on, isn't it?"*
>
> (p. 34)

We see Jack adopt Willie's terminology and Willie's metaphor here, as well as his philosophy of man as a political animal: from here on both of them see the political life and the moral life as dominated by everyone's desire to control the pouring of the swill and to get into the trough himself, shoving aside any who stand in the way. Whatever can be done with man and for man must be done in recognition of the reality of this basic metaphor. So the language is recurrent in Jack's speech as well as in Willie's.

As we see from the tone of the opening quotation, Willie's barnyard doctrine derives from his Presbyterianism, which he tells us he has learned to make good use of to justify his ways to man. There are two major tenets which are not challenged—at least not until the very end of the novel. Man's nature is inherently and incorrigibly corrupt, indeed piggish; and man is predestined rather than free, so that he seeks only to fulfill his nature. This inevitability explains why you can dig up "dirt" about any man, even the Judge.[2] It also explains why no one who wishes to "do business" can ignore our dirty, piggish nature; for, if he *is* to do business, he must do it by providing the opportunity for that nature to fulfill itself. Thus, like God, such a man makes use of our dirt, which one can hardly do by denying its existence as a part of us, as our essence.

Such predestined human depravity makes man ripe for positivistic manipulation, like the pig in search of the swill in his trough. And the man-god who can do the manipulating, in accordance with his special knowledge, at once wins the gift bestowed by his grateful fellows: absolute power and abject worship of that power. And their need for

---

[2] There is a typically Stark-ish discourse on dirt on p. 50: "Dirt's a funny thing. . . . Come to think of it, there ain't a thing but dirt on this green God's globe except what's under water, and that's dirt too. It's dirt makes the grass grow. A diamond ain't a thing in the world but a piece of dirt that got awful hot. And God-a-Mighty picked up a handful of dirt and blew on it and made you and me and George Washington and mankind blessed in faculty and apprehension. It all depends on what you do with the dirt."

him is absolute. The process is much like that seen by the Grand Inquisitor projected by Ivan Karamazov: one must provide man not with freedom, but with miracle, mystery, and authority—combined with bread. Willie's commitment to action, his willingness to mess in the dirt (his own and that of others) which is the raw material of action, gives him control of the barnyard. He now can pour the swill to those who follow him, excluding "all those people who got pushed out of the trough" (p. 221). And he pours full and well. By allowing all the broad spectrum of men who come under his dominance to fulfill their natures in their various ways, he becomes irresistibly attractive to all: to corrupt men and to men of thought and even of puritanical moral conviction. Those ethical purists who distrust action because of the sour aftertaste of immoral necessities can act for Willie in a self-deceived purity of action, fulfilling their natures while he keeps hidden from them the dirty accompaniments which he is able to take on himself, for he knows the truth which their idealism cannot afford to confront. Of course, if what has been hidden should become apparent, then their purity will lead them to a shocked disavowal of political action once more. As Jack puts it, "Politics is action and all action is but a flaw in the perfection of inaction, which is peace" (p. 215). But Jack, our uncommitted, cynical narrator, can accept Willie's truth and the consequences of his worst action.

Jack's supposed father, "the Scholarly Attorney," is immune to all temptation of action, even Willie's sort that promises high results: "I will not touch the world of foulness again . . . that my hand shall come away with the stink on my fingers" (p. 215). These words remind us of Strephon's repulsion by foulness and Celia. Only a bit less insulated is Hugh Miller, who wants to lay about him with a baseball bat[3] without defiling his hands with the accompanying moral filth, leaving it to Willie to keep it out of sight. So he must "welch" on the role he is committed to enact and must desert when his purity cannot put up with what Willie forces it to confront. The latter pattern is pretty much that of the clean surgeon, Adam Stanton, as well; he also will not face the moral (or rather immoral) consequences of what Willie's actions can accomplish in the incidental service of Adam's

---

[3] "The man was Hugh Miller, Harvard Law School, Lafayette Escadrille, Croix de Guerre, clean hands, pure heart, and no political past. He was a fellow who had sat still for years, and then somebody (Willie Stark) handed him a baseball bat and he felt his fingers close on the tape. He was a man and was Attorney General" (p. 104).

III. Through the Acceptance of the Human Barnyard

ethical objectives. All these hold-outs and hold-backs refuse to partake of this grand barnyard scheme, which is both the political extension of a total pragmatic positivism and the perverse projection of Calvinist fundamentalism. Such is not the case with Jack, who—in his cynicism —neither holds out from Willie nor holds back from the moral consequences once he joins him.[4]

Insofar as Willie's Calvinist doctrine—so convenient to his program of action—rests upon a conception of man as an easily fed stimulus-response mechanism, it accords fully with the philosophical movement of Jack Burden, historian, from "Idealism" to the "Great Sleep" to the "Great Twitch." The reduction from the moral to the crudely factual, together with the acceptance of the latter in its most unelevated reality, is as much an assumption of Jack s positivism as it is of Willie's authoritarian benevolence, cynically based, as it is, on his perversion of Calvinist theology. This dedication to the crudest of our subhuman facts does not contradict Jack's early affiliation with the doctrine he terms his Idealism ("life as motion"), despite the fact that this Idealism persuades him not only of the unreality of all that is beyond the reach of his vision but even of the essential unreality of what he sees, inasmuch as it all depends upon his consciousness. From here it is a small step for him to doubt that he himself is real, except as a bundle of sensory receptacles. No wonder that he is ready to see all human values reduced to empirical fact—indeed, in the end, to neurological fact (whatever the ontological status of these "facts").

Jack's Idealism makes him ready for "The Great Sleep" which deadens so much of his life. He fails Anne early, disappointing her young hopes by his lack of commitment to any future, or even any serious interest in it. True to the "Scholarly Attorney" he supposes to be his father, he has an aimlessness in his youth that is already a kind of sleep. As we recall the recurrent image of purity represented in his mind by the young Anne in the water on the day of that idyllic picnic,[5] we see Anne playing the unavailable mermaid to Jack's Prufrock,

[4] It must be conceded that Willie has his own sporadic, if inconsistent and incomplete, purism, even if it contradicts his dark "theological" knowledge. It is this momentary purism, as in his zig-zaggings in the matter of the hospital, that leads to his own destruction—and to his deathbed plea to Jack that it all might have been different. The idealistic "Cousin Willie" is never altogether replaced by Willie the Boss, and helps to kill him.
[5] "The image I got in my head that day was the image of her face lying in the water, very smooth, with the eyes closed, under the dark greenish-purple sky, with the white gull passing over" (p. 126).

290

a young but already played-out Prufrock of the twilight world of the Old Dominion. Having sleepily failed Anne, he fails the dead Cass Mastern with a more complete indulgence in the "Great Sleep." He can momentarily emerge long enough to substitute—like a careless Meursault—Lois' sensualism for his more mysterious "sea-girl." This act (his marriage to Lois) is an extension and a proof of his Idealism, with its reduction of reality (only half believed in) to what the senses receive. Only momentarily revived, he lapses into sleep again. Jack is ready for Willie, whose activism makes him insistently real. Willie answers Jack's need, as he answers the needs of all those about him whom he implicates in his willful destiny—a destiny that is, as we shall see, founded on the reduction of others to a will-less response itself produced by the power of his will. Willie thus comes to be the medium of Jack's expression, the shaper of his language, and—as activist—the logical realization of Jack's negativism, his cynical sense of reality.

When his service to this reality, under Willie's godlike tutelage, results in Anne's becoming Willie's mistress, Jack is ready for the ultimate realization that human value is reducible to involuntary neurological response: the "Great Sleep" has become the "Great Twitch." He now feels that it was foolish for him to substitute Lois for Anne, since Lois and Anne were really the same after all. All distinctions among patterns and values of human behavior are now collapsed into the identity of the Twitch. How, then, could he have been so scrupulous about Anne and what he thought was her love for her "Jackie-Bird"?

> she hadn't loved him, but had merely had a
> mysterious itch in the blood and he was handy and
> the word love was a word for the mysterious
> itch. [Her] withholdments and hesitations were no
> better or worse than the hottest surrender nor better or
> worse than those withholdments practiced by
> Lois for other ends. And in the end you could not tell
> Anne Stanton from Lois Seager, for they were
> alike, and though the mad poet William Blake wrote
> a poem to tell the Adversary who is Prince of This
> World that He could not ever change Kate into Nan, the
> mad poet was quite wrong, for anybody could change
> Kate into Nan, or if indeed the Prince couldn't

> change Kate into Nan it was only because Kate and
> Nan were exactly alike to begin with and were, in fact,
> the same with only the illusory difference of name,
> which meant nothing, for names meant nothing and
> all the words we speak meant nothing and there
> was only the pulse in the blood and the twitch of the
> nerve, like a dead frog's leg in the experiment when the
> electric current goes through.
>
> (pp. 327–28)

So "The Great Twitch" becomes Jack's ultimate vision, the end of the historian's history: "So I fled west from the fact, and in the West, at the end of History, the Last Man on that Last Coast, on my hotel bed, I had discovered the dream. That dream was the dream that all life is but the dark heave of blood and the twitch of the nerve" (p. 329).

Here, at the end of his flight from history, Jack finds freedom from his responsibility, from guilt. "The words *Anne Stanton* were simply a name for a peculiarly complicated piece of mechanism which should mean nothing whatsoever to Jack Burden, who himself was simply another rather complicated piece of mechanism." Under the sublime indifference of fact, Jack discovers an innocence not very different from Meursault's: "nothing was your fault or anybody's fault, for things are always as they are" (p. 330). Unlike Ivan Karamazov sitting in judgment of himself, Jack can assert that "you are never guilty of a crime which you did not commit. So there is innocence and a new start in the West, after all."[6] On his ride back East Jack's confidence in his neurological reduction is confirmed for him by the twitch in the cheek of his elderly companion, the independent twitch with a life of its own, livelier than the face which bears it. So, Jack concludes, the twitch is all; and, more mysteriously, the twitch itself comes to know that it is all there really is. In this way, Jack, who like everything else is "all twitch," can come to "the secret knowledge" that this is so. Thus "the twitch can know that the twitch is all" (p. 334).

The utter reduction of man, of himself, is complete, the lower-than-barnyard gift that confers freedom. Jack is ripe to become the involved

---

[6] For the relation between Camus and Dostoevsky on this matter of innocence and guilt—especially as it affects Meursault and Ivan—see *The Tragic Vision*, pp. 144–53. For Meursault also the dissolution of distinctions into an egalitarian indifference is the enabling act of innocence—and freedom.

—almost obsessed—witness to the prefrontal lobectomy shortly to be performed by Adam Stanton. What better confirmation of man's twitching essence than the fact that brain-burning can transform personality and even remove moral awareness? Jack forces himself to witness the operation, allows himself a last disturbance over the fact "that the burning brain had a smell like the burning horses" (p. 338). When it is over, with enough of the brain burned away, "the little pieces of brain which had been cut out were put away to think their little thoughts quietly somewhere among the garbage, and what was left inside the split-open skull of the gaunt individual was sealed back up and left to think up an entirely new personality." And Jack suggests a baptism: "for he is born again and not of woman. I baptize thee in the name of the Big Twitch, the Little Twitch, and the Holy Ghost. Who, no doubt, is a Twitch, too" (p. 338).

Cass Mastern, Jack's elusive historical subject, possessed of a profound moral conscience, long before found himself on the path toward something like Jack's notion of the Twitch. As he observes the ease with which he is drawn to an adulterous relationship with Annabelle Trice, wife of his friend, Cass questions the basis of his previous morality: "Therefore what virtue and honor I had known in the past had been an accident of habit and not the fruit of the will" (p. 180). But, unlike Jack, Cass cannot accept this dreadful freedom from guilt. It is, rather, his nature to move on, through extremity, to re-earn his belief in the moral capacity of man. For him there can be no resting in the Great Twitch of neurological habit. This is what prevents Jack from understanding Cass well enough to complete his work on him. Jack gives up the task and enters the Great Sleep "because he was afraid to understand for what might be understood there was a reproach to him" (p. 201). It is a failure of his moral imagination. In contrast to Cass, who "learned that the world is all of one piece,"[7]

---

[7] There is an extended metaphor that speaks of the interrelations and spreading of evil, reminiscent of what we have seen in George Eliot: "it was as though the vibration set up in the whole fabric of the world by my act had spread infinitely and with ever increasing power and no man could know the end" (p. 189). On p. 200 the metaphor becomes more precise as Jack takes it up. It begins: "He learned that the world is like an enormous spider web and if you touch it, however lightly, at any point, the vibration ripples to the remotest perimeter and the drowsy spider feels the tingle and is drowsy no more but springs out to fling the gossamer coils about you who have touched the web and then inject the black, numbing poison under your hide."

Jack saw the world only as "an accumulation of items, odds and ends of things like the broken and misused and dust-shrouded things gathered in a garret. Or it was a flux of things before his eyes (or behind his eyes) and one thing had nothing to do, in the end, with anything else" (p. 201).

The story of Cass Mastern, then, makes demands upon Jack beyond what his historian's role has expected or can handle. And he fails in this first of his researches. Facts are not enough to reach to the moral imagination of a Cass Mastern; and Jack—both Idealist and positivist —is restricted to morally insignificant, uninterrelated facts. Jack's painful development in the novel—and his earlier resistance to that development—are alike centered in his relation both to history and to *his* history (and Cass, as at once forebear *and* historical subject, represents both to him). How is Jack to relate himself to the past and to *his* past when he cannot find a moral relationship among facts and cannot move beyond facts? Nor can he move beyond the determinism of fact to the free act of will. So, inheritor of the world of Cass Mastern and (as he wrongly believes) of the "Scholarly Attorney," he is Burden-ed by a history he cannot undo, even if he will not undertake the moral responsibility of accepting it.

Jack's second research is of another sort, concerned as it is with fact alone. How, then, can he—with the commitments we know him to have—be other than successful? Indeed, he is a smashing success: little is left standing in the wake of that success. Having come out of his Great Sleep to join Willie and having committed himself (though in his essentially uncommitted way) to Willie, Jack the factual historian is given his assignment. He is to dig up some dirt on Judge Irwin, his boyhood idol and (almost) foster-father. And when he questions whether there is anything to dig up on the Judge, Willie answers with the adaptation of Presbyterianism ("from the stink of the didie to the stench of the shroud") which furnished the opening quotation for this chapter. Thus Jack enters upon his second job of historical research, the "Case of the Upright Judge." This one is tailored to Willie's coldly political objectives, as it is cut to the dimensions of Willie's theology; thus it is limited by the factual requirements of Jack's Idealism-positivism. So Jack becomes the paragon of objective "historical researchers" ("we love truth" [p. 242]) as he proceeds to teach Anne and Adam—and himself a history lesson.

His historian's love for "truth," for the unmitigated fact that invariably turns out ugly, is a match for Willie's. We must remember that Willie never asked him to frame the Judge with untruths or half-truths: Willie only asked him to dig up the dirty truth that was surely there, hidden (and discoverable) somewhere. "You don't ever have to frame anybody, because the truth is always sufficient," Willie tells Jack (p. 358).[8] Having dug up a truth that turns out to dirty the memory of former Governor Stanton as well as his friend, the upright Judge, Jack puts it to work on Adam as well as on Anne: "I had found the truth, I had dug the truth up out of the ash pile, the garbage heap, the kitchen midden, the bone yard, and had sent that little piece of truth to Adam Stanton. I couldn't cut the truth to match his ideas. Well, he'd have to make his ideas match the truth. That is what all of us historical researchers believe. The truth shall make you free" (pp. 275–76).

Though Adam and Anne do not go quite as far as that Meursault-like conclusion, they both do cave in, Adam by forgoing his scruples to go to work for Willie and Anne by becoming Willie's mistress. The truth has worked to put everything in the order required to bring about the catastrophe of Willie's assassination (with, of course, Adam's subsequent death). And the catastrophe, in turn, accumulates in Jack a burden of guilt that even he can no longer evade. For whatever the sneaky Duffy may have done to put the gun in Adam's hand, Jack must come to know how thoroughly the responsibility for it is his own, as the value-free, positivistic "historical researcher." He will come to see what there had been in the Cass Mastern research to reproach him as he learns what there was in the Judge Irwin research that had to destroy morally the very success which its presuppositions guaranteed. Like Cass but unlike himself under the rule of the Great Twitch (see p. 330), Jack learns that one *can* be guilty of a crime which he did not commit.

We can see, then, that the dehumanized history of Judge Irwin, as Jack discovers it—in almost detective-story fashion—becomes the primary action for the fictional structure that is this novel (presumably written as fact by Jack). It is worth noting in some detail the ways in

[8] It is here that Willie acknowledges the austere theological basis for his handy political tactic, as he responds to Jack's ironic charge: "You sure take a high view of human nature." " 'Boy,' he said, 'I went to a Presbyterian Sunday school back in the days when they still had some theology, and that much of it stuck. And—' he grinned suddenly, 'I have found it very valuable.' "

which Warren (or rather Jack, his fictive narrator) transforms factual history into human history, that is, transforms biography into novel, the chronological chain of events into Aristotelian fable. The primary justification for what is included and the order of its inclusion is its place in the action rather than its role in the unfolding of Willie Stark's life and career. Indeed, we can ask to what extent this is Willie's story and to what extent Jack permits himself to move from his merely visionary role to usurp the place of protagonist.

It is perhaps appropriate, as we treat such matters, to note that the real Huey Long has been often seen as the historical basis for Willie Stark, so that Warren has been seen as writing a political pseudo-novel about the real Louisiana from his outpost at the state university. Those who read the work carefully should be persuaded by it to accept the author's disclaimers of such an intention, even as we recognize the biographical and political realities in the "germ" of the novel. But Warren has overcome the biographical and political realities of the Huey Long epoch and its cataclysmic end; he has overcome them as Jack Burden, in his story, overcomes the biographical and political pseudo-realities of the Willie Stark epoch and its cataclysmic end. If this were only Governor Stark's story, a make-believe biography, then Willie could be a stand-in for Governor Long. But, as an Aristotelian action, it is the story of neither.

At the very opening we must note the care with which Warren (or must we not say Jack?) begins at the beginning of the action rather than at the beginning of the career. We are not to confuse the beginning, middle, and end of Willie's story with the beginning, middle, and end of the story which is the structural whole that concerns us. The novel starts on the day that culminates in the unsatisfactory visit to Judge Irwin and Willie's consequent order to Jack to start digging for the inevitable dirt. All the major developments in the plot have their beginnings here. It is only after he, in chapter 1, has launched the action on that day in 1936 (*in medias res*) that our narrator can turn back, in chapter 2, to the chronological beginnings of Willie's story in 1922. First things first; and our narrator makes clear what comes first with him, just as he must carry his story to an end well beyond the end of Willie's story. Further, before he feels free to fill us in on the background, the biographical beginnings, he must also make it clear (in the final words of chapter 1 and the first words of chapter 2) that he is writing in 1939—three years after that day—and that most of the characters who figured in the opening of the tale (Masters, Adam Stanton, Judge Irwin, and Willie himself) are dead. So the tale is in a specially definitive sense finished by this time, before we enter upon its chronological beginning, whose subordinate place has now been assured. And there is a suggestion of catastrophe in its being finished, a catastrophe that, as is intimated by the final words of chapter 1 ("Little Jackie made it stick, all right"), grows out of the plot elements unleashed in that first chapter.

Almost everything does grow out of Jack's research on the "upright judge," which Willie, at the end of the first chapter, charges him to undertake so that Willie may have the potential blackmail to influence the Judge's future political behavior. His research produces the facts about Judge Irwin's acceptance of a bribe and about Governor Stanton's complicity in protecting his guilty friend and political side-kick. Jack first uses these facts to persuade Adam to take Willie's hospital position. Without meaning to, he has also helped persuade Anne to become Willie's mistress. When, at a propitious moment, Duffy sees to it that Adam learns what his sister has become, Adam assassinates Willie and is killed himself. In the meantime Jack has also tried to use the facts in order to blackmail the Judge, but Irwin kills himself. Yet strangely, ironically, the success of Jack's research, with all these dreadful consequences, can lead to *his* salvation. The "bright, beautiful, silvery soprano scream" of Jack's mother when she learns of the suicide (p. 370) turns the book around by giving Jack a new fact—the actual identity of Irwin as his father—and a new sense of the sort of humanity she has been capable of during the many years of his contempt for her.

So the fable has an Aristotelian completeness to it,[9] although it must be seen as casting Jack, rather than Willie, in the role of protagonist. Indeed, so far are we from mere history or biography that we can note the traditional form which the fable has been given: the search for identity takes on the literalness of the search for one's par-

---

[9] I have allowed the plot to appear more perfect than it is, although I *have* acknowledged that only *almost* everything grows out of Jack's research. The great structural flaw is Warren's need to introduce Tom Stark—first his involvement with Sibyl Frey's child and then the *deux ex machina* of his fatal injury—in order to work his way to the assassination. The Irwin investigation proves, after all, to be not quite enough to see the story through, so that Warren must make this one ad hoc addition to the elements he has set to work.

entage. Like many of literature's oldest heroes, Jack must discover who his father really is—a man crucially different from his apparent father—and who his mother really is (although this is a discovery of internal rather than external facts about her identity). And this discovery is central to his discovery of who *he* can really be. So much of what Jack has been seems to be a reflection of the "Scholarly Attorney," his supposed father, and his superficially flighty mother that his sense of his own identity must be profoundly changed by the twin discoveries which the "silvery soprano scream" forces him to make.[10] It is this internal development, this self-discovery, that enables Jack, instead of one of the more fixed characters who surround him, to become the protagonist of the tale.

But Jack is narrator as well as protagonist. In tracing the origin and development of the novel, Warren tells us that it began as a play and that, with its transformation into a novel, there arose the "necessity for a character of a higher degree of self-consciousness than my politician, a character to serve as a kind of commentator and *raisonneur* and chorus."[11] He also acknowledges what I have pointed out, that "the story, in a sense, became the story of Jack Burden, the teller of the tale." Warren's "desire to avoid writing a straight naturalistic novel, the kind of novel that the material so readily invited"—his desire, in other words, to be more than historian—led to his need for the perspective that the mock-historian, Burden, could give him as he proceeded to free himself from the historian's factual confines. As Jack frees himself from factual historicity, so the novel frees itself of its biographical encumbrance. But Jack's freeing of himself is a story in itself—*the* story—which has him as its protagonist.

If, in his desire to transform the play into a work that was truly novelistic, Warren invented a narrator who was at least a semi-protagonist even as he was "commentator and *raisonneur* and chorus," he had, in that invention, venerable literary precedent. Jack Burden is,

---

[10] "There was a kind of relief in knowing that that man was not my father. I had always felt some curse of his weakness upon me. . . . And he had been good. . . . My new father, however, had not been good. He had cuckolded a friend, betrayed a wife, taken a bride, driven a man, though unwittingly, to death. But he had done good. He had been a just judge. And he had carried his head high. . . . Well, I had swapped the good, weak father for the evil, strong one. I didn't feel bad about it" (p. 375).

[11] See Warren's introduction to the Modern Library (1953) edition of the novel, especially p. iv.

in effect, playing Marlow to Willie Stark's Mr. Kurtz. Nor is it inappropriate for us to look for Conradian parallels in Warren, who in more than one way seems technically indebted to the novelist about whom he has written so sensitively. I have noted, in Warren's disposition of his first two chapters, the extent to which he permits Jack to manipulate—at times to jumble—the time sequence of events in order to make it his tale rather than history's. The darting back and leaping ahead in time, seemingly at will but actually for good fictional purposes, continue throughout Jack's recital, and in ways similar to Marlow's manipulation of the chronology of events in *Lord Jim*.[12] In both works, mere events are worked about in order to make certain that human form and meaning predominate over the accidental, "straight naturalistic" facts in their accidental, "straight naturalistic" order. Both novels are also quite ready to reveal in advance how the affair turns out—Jack tells us in his first chapter who is to be dead by the time of his writing three short years later—so that the factual suspense that asks "What happened?" can be subordinated to the more profound, and less easily settled, human issues that they wish to concentrate upon. Such arranging indicates how far Jack-as-narrator, like Marlow, has moved from the bald historicity of his second research (into Judge Irwin), from his subservience to the bald inhumanity of raw fact. For we must not forget that it is the latest Jack, the Jack who emerges at the end of the book, who has written the book we have by then concluded.

If by the conclusion Jack, as protagonist, has changed from the earlier Jack, it must be that he has moved beyond the Great Twitch, despite everything in his positivism and in his devotion to the positivistic sort of history he can understand that seems to point to that final secret knowledge he called the Great Twitch. For him it is not to be final after all. Yet it is not what he seems at first to have done to Anne and to Adam by revealing the freedom-giving truths of factual history that turns him from the Twitch. Quite the contrary: it is during his flight to California, after Anne admits she has become Willie's mistress, that he first discovers the final liberating truth bestowed by the Twitch. Anne's confession allows him—by absolving himself of com-

[12] For elements in Conrad that I find reflected in Warren, see *The Tragic Vision*, pp. 154–79, especially pp. 170–72, and "From *Youth* to *Lord Jim*: the Formal-Thematic Use of Marlow," in *The Play and Place of Criticism*, pp. 91–104.

plicity—to equate her with Lois. Even the suicide of Irwin might not have turned him from liberation to a sense of his own guilt—though he might have recognized the parallel between his responsibility for Irwin's suicide and Irwin's responsibility for Mortimer Littlepaugh's suicide (which helps cause Irwin's own) or Cass Mastern's responsibility for Duncan Trice's (which precipitates Cass's own abandonment to extremity). But, as I have already noted, Jack begins to be turned around at the moment of Aristotelian discovery and peripety, the "bright, beautiful, silvery soprano scream" followed by the revelation of his parentage by his mother. Further, to his responsibility for Irwin's suicide one must soon add his responsibility—only slightly more indirect—for the killings of Willie and Adam. These responsibilities, now far more extensive than those of Cass or Irwin, might well carry him beyond the capacity of the Great Twitch to keep him innocent, might well defy its principle that "you are never guilty of a crime which you did not commit."

Jack finally refuses to act upon this principle when he turns away from his chance to take revenge upon Duffy as the arranger of Willie's death. As he learns the truth from Sadie Burke and threatens the new Governor Duffy with his knowledge, he admits to us, "I felt like a million because I thought it let me out. Duffy was the villain and I was the avenging hero" (pp. 441–42). But each time he feels like "St. George and the dragon" or "Jesus Christ with the horsewhip in the temple," he feels sick from an acid taste in the back of his mouth. For he recognizes his fellowship with Duffy: "It was as though in the midst of the scene Tiny Duffy had slowly and like a brother winked at me with his oyster eye and I had known he knew the nightmare truth, which was that we were twins bound together. . . . We were bound together forever and I could never hate him without hating myself or love myself without loving him. We were bound together under the unwinking eye of Eternity and by the Holy Grace of the Great Twitch whom we must all adore" (p. 442). Only one more step is required. Sugar-Boy's appearance gives Jack the chance to have Duffy killed as Duffy had Willie killed: by the merest whisper of a name to a desperate man with a loaded gun. But the thought of the resemblance between the act he contemplates and Duffy's act makes Jack's awareness of their fellowship complete. About to name him to Sugar-Boy as Willie's killer, again he envisions the wink of that fellowship passing between them: "I saw Duffy's face, large and lunar and sebaceous, nodding at me as at the covert and brotherly appreciation of a joke, and even as I opened my lips to speak the syllables of his name, he winked. He winked right at me like a brother" (p. 445). It is much like Ivan Karamazov's discovery of his feelings about Smerdyakov, from whose basest act he cannot separate himself. Jack can deny the Great Twitch, the power that denies all distinctions, only by insisting upon distinguishing himself from Duffy. So at the last moment he draws back: at an enormous risk to his own life—now exposed to Sugar-Boy's fury as he knows it will be—Jack names no one and treats the entire affair as a joke. But Sugar-Boy, almost miraculously, spares Jack: " 'I-I-I durn near d-d-done it.' I ran my tongue over my dry lips. 'I know it,' I said" (p. 446). Jack has run a moral risk because he would rather die for Duffy than remain his brother.

So Jack is not Duffy, and he has proved it. Not only has he refused to authorize Duffy's murder, but he has refused in the one way most dangerous to his own safety. Like the captain at the end of Conrad's *Secret Sharer* who steers his ship closer to the shore than good seamanship would permit—and closer than his "double," Leggatt, requires—Jack's reckless withdrawal is in part a gratuitous gesture that bears courageous testimony to moral strength.[13] None of what he has done before is changed by this act; indeed, he is now capable of feeling his guilt in all that has transpired. But, free of the Great Twitch, free to face the responsibility of his part in the universal complicity, he is obliged to make distinctions once again, distinctions between himself and Duffy, between Anne and Lois, between Adam and Willie.[14] With respect to man's capacity for evil, the all-or-none alternative of a puritanism turned sour has now given way to an infinite variety of possible degrees of goodness or badness. Jack need not deny the barnyard claims about man—Willie's, like Gulliver's—for him, like Swift, to acknowledge that in the herd we may find some surpris-

[13] We might also find a parallel in the risk Lord Jim runs (and loses) on behalf of the criminal Brown, as Jim seeks to triumph over their identity-in-guilt, to which Brown points.

[14] Just before the thaw in the frozen mass of his amorality, Jack struggles with the egalitarianism of the Twitch. But it still has not broken up: "And I heaved and writhed like the ox or the cat, and the acid burned my gullet and that was all there was to it and I hated everything and everybody and myself and Tiny Duffy and Willie Stark and Adam Stanton. To hell with them all, I said impartially under the stars. They all looked alike to me then. And I looked like them" (p. 442).

ing and gratifying actions. And these must be noted too. It is, after all, what Cass Mastern had discovered before him. No wonder that Jack shortly declares himself ready to return to the story of Cass.

We have seen that the extravagance of Jack's gesture in preventing Duffy from being killed is just such a surprising and gratifying action. Clearly Jack is getting ready to return to the herd, while preserving his distinction-making power, as he helps the herd to write its history. But now, of course, his will be a different sort of history, with a different hierarchy of values. Even factual truth may have to go. Because Jack has been an historian so faithful to fact, his lies will be believed. We have seen Sugar-Boy accept his lie that he had no further information about Willie's killer. In addition, the final words we see him speak to his mother represent a major untruth, although it helps to preserve the sort of being she has come to be for Jack since the moment of her "silvery soprano scream." It is a lie about Judge Irwin's last moments, a lie reminiscent of the earth-shaking one Marlow speaks to Kurtz's "intended" at the end of *Heart of Darkness*. While Kurtz's final words were "The horror! The horror!" Marlow tells the bereaved woman that his final words were her name; while Irwin's suicide stems from the newly resurrected facts about the evils of his political past, Jack tells his mother it was caused by nothing more damning than the depression related to failing health. He expressly denies any lingering history of wrongdoing on Irwin's part and, when there is some suggestion of doubts in her, he can even—little-boy style—"swear to God" that he speaks the truth. Marlow's profound abhorrence of lies gave his lie a special significance; Jack's ruthless fidelity to the cruelty of fact here guarantees that he will be believed. It also makes clear his new attitude to the truth, and makes clear the rejection of the Twitch, a rejection which this new attitude requires.

The truth of the Great Twitch, then, might set one morally free by equating all men as brothers in their automatic neurological responses. But it is not this truth which can allow one to rest with others' eyes upon him in mute condemnation, even the condemnation that proceeds out of brotherhood. Only the return to distinctions in degree, to crucial differences of more or less among human actions, can allow one to accept the consequences of behavior, including the consequence of being looked at by one's fellows. It may lead to an awareness of guilt, but one can accept the possibility of being more or less guilty once he admits that, even if everyone is doomed to be guilty, everyone is also free—under "the agony of will"—to be guilty in different ways.[15] We have seen that Jack's need to deprive Duffy of the right to bestow upon him the wink of brotherhood led him to play a dangerous game with Sugar-Boy rather than to play Duffy's game against Duffy.[16]

Earlier, we remember, it was just such a wink of fellowship that initially sealed the bond between Willie and Jack as they launched the political career founded on notions of the barnyard and on the Twitch that, theoretically, accounted for the equal and constant lowly state of the barnyard members. From Willie to Duffy: the wink binds Jack to those serving, with him, "the Holy Grace of the Great Twitch whom we must all adore." But the wink he welcomed from Willie he must reject from Duffy. Now he will be able to bear Duffy's eyes upon him and not feel them winking, now that he has acted to deny the truth of the Twitch. He will be able to assert, not only his own moral superiority to Duffy, but Willie's. This permits Jack the belief which he must maintain: that Willie was a great man, whatever else he may also have been. Similarly, we have seen, he can maintain that Judge Irwin was a just judge and a strong man—an admirable man—whatever evil he may have committed. The abandonment of all-or-none, the acceptance of human imperfection and the variety of degrees with which it expresses itself or is modified, encourages the beginning of a moral life that permits men to look upon one another without fearing the knowing smirk that disguises itself as a wink. Yet the relaxed acceptance of the looks of men—so far from the realm of austere judgment that looks *at* men—is well beyond the ethical and into the classic.

Other characters are also troubled by eyes turned upon them. The long trail of Cass Mastern's tragedy is largely impelled by the fact that his partner in adultery, Annabelle Trice, cannot tolerate the accusation in the eyes of her slave, Phebe, and, in desperation, sells her.

---

[15] "But at the same time Jack Burden came to see that his friends had been doomed, he saw that though doomed they had nothing to do with any doom under the godhead of the Great Twitch. They were doomed, but they lived in the agony of will" (p. 462).

[16] I again call attention to this struggle against the community—and transference—of guilt as an echo of Ivan and Smerdyakov in *The Brothers Karamazov*, Jim and Brown in *Lord Jim*, and the captain and Leggatt in *The Secret Sharer*. There is, on the contrary, no danger of Marlow's losing himself in an identity with Kurtz in *Heart of Darkness*, thanks to his fidelity to the ethical, to a "fixed standard of conduct."

III. Through the Acceptance of the Human Barnyard

Cass, who like Jack must prove that virtue is possible and is not merely a euphemism for habit, requires himself to follow her path in order to buy and free her. When he fails, he sets his own slaves free, though he is troubled by the further sorrows into which he feels he is sending them. Though he can take no moral credit for what he has done, still it is better than living with his sense of their eyes upon him:

> They had kissed my hands and wept for joy, but
> I could take no part in their rejoicing. I had not flattered
> myself that I had done anything for them. What I
> had done I had done for myself, to relieve my spirit of
> a burden, the burden of their misery and their
> eyes upon me. The wife of my dead friend had found
> the eyes of the girl Phebe upon her and had gone
> wild and had ceased to be herself and had sold the girl
> into misery. I had found their eyes upon me and
> had freed them into misery, lest I should do worse.
> For many cannot bear their eyes upon them, and enter
> into evil and cruel ways in their desperation.

(pp. 194–95)

Gilbert Mastern, successful and worldly brother of Cass, scorns the young man's impracticality as absurd and is offended at the thought of a fallow plantation, one which Cass will not sell, though he has no one to work it. Gilbert's reaction is a classic one: "My God, man, it is land, don't you understand, it is land, and land cries out for man's hand" (p. 196). Cass himself sees Gilbert as having a specially endowed worldliness which even permitted him to be a beneficent slaveowner: "Perhaps only a man like my brother Gilbert can in the midst of evil retain enough of innocence and strength to bear their eyes upon him and to do a little justice in the terms of the great injustice" (pp. 195–96).

If he sounds a bit like Judge Irwin, it is probably because he is meant to. In the final paragraphs of the novel, Jack describes himself turning once more to the life of Cass Mastern in hopes of having been granted a new understanding that will allow him to re-create himself as a historian. And he comments upon the strange juxtaposition of Cass Mastern and Judge Irwin: "I suppose that there is some humor

in the fact that while I write about Cass Mastern I live in the house of
Judge Irwin and eat bread bought with his money. For Judge Irwin
and Cass Mastern do not resemble each other very closely. (If Judge
Irwin resembles any Mastern it is Gilbert, the granite-headed brother
of Cass)" (pp. 463–64). It is rather the Scholarly Attorney, Ellis
Burden, who resembles Cass, while Jack, who thought himself the
inheritor of the weakness of his supposed father, has acted in ways
analogous to Cass. But now Jack emerges morally in a way that is
even more positive and surely less tragic than Cass's. Indeed it is
altogether untragic. But the juxtaposition of Cass and Irwin which
Jack notes here at the end, as he writes the story of Cass in the house
of Irwin, marks the joining of the two widely differing subjects of
Jack's previous historical researchers. And the Jack who now emerges
into the world, like the book now being completed under his pen,
unites them by extending their history into the metahistorical human
world of freedom.

As we see from Jack's unconscious search for his parentage, his history is bound up with his surname. Although Warren never explicitly
plays with Jack's name, I should like to for a moment, for it plays a
symbolic role in his position at the end. What has happened is that he
comes to accept that name and its meaning at the point where he no
longer has to. Much of what he has gone through in his earlier "stages
along life's way" he has gone through as a result of his being a
Burden: he thinks himself Ellis Burden's son, and Cass Mastern, as
well as being his historical subject, is an uncle of that supposed father.
But now that Jack has discovered that Ellis Burden is not his father,
now that he can be free of the historical burden of being a Burden, he
assumes that burden (Burden). He even brings Ellis Burden to live
with him, as he never could have done before. In his own words, but
without explicit reference to his name (though surely the pun is
there), he justifies his present attitude to Anne: "I tried to tell her how
if you could not accept the past and its burden there was no future,
for without one there cannot be the other, and how if you could
accept the past you might hope for the future, for only out of the past
can you make the future" (p. 461).

Jack has come to terms with history—and with *his* history—freeing
himself from it in order, as a free man, to accept it. "History is blind,
but man is not," he approvingly quotes Hugh Miller as saying (p.
462). However, doomed man must live "in the agony of will," for

the irreversibility of past facts does not make the future irreversible until it has happened. Man is not free of guilt, as under the Great Twitch, but he *is* free to be guilty (and not *only* guilty) and free to learn to live with *that* freedom. This double sense of being free of history only by being bound to it is what permits the final words of the novel, which describe the future of Jack and Anne: "soon now we shall go out of the house and go into the convulsion of the world, out of history into history and the awful responsibility of Time" (p. 464). With Anne, who by marrying him has also assumed the surname that she need not have assumed, he takes on Burden just as he is free to allow it to fall from him.

Jack Burden is for me a unique narrator (and *All the King's Men* a uniquely useful novel) because the existential development he undergoes permits me to see him as running the gamut of my categories. He first goes through what I have seen as the general pattern of apparently similar narrators. Like Marlow with his Kurtz or his Jim, or Ishmael with his Ahab, or Zeitblom with his Leverkühn, Jack appears to be the fictive narrator who creates and aesthetically sustains for us the self-destructive career of the tragic existent, here Willie Stark. Of course, Jack is less morally dedicated a narrator than the others: he is not a representative of ethical existence as is a Marlow or a Leverkühn. Still, like his counterparts, Jack is to be a tragic visionary rather than a tragic existent himself. Although the fictive narrator must assimilate his creature aesthetically, he does not dare replace him existentially. The narrator may threaten to become the protagonist himself, as in *Heart of Darkness*; but it is precisely as the tragic visionary who pulls back from the unmitigated indulgence in tragic existence that he does so. It is in this sense that we saw Jack choose Willie out of his need, his lack, so that Willie can be his existential agent, acting out his cynical principles. But when, on that bed in Long Beach, California, Jack commits himself to the utter nihilism of the Great Twitch, no longer flinching from its deadening consequences, he is ready to move—almost with less reservation than even Willie— to the state of being a tragic existent himself.

When Jack draws back from the ultimate act of having Duffy killed precisely in the way Duffy had Willie killed—merely by allowing himself to speak a word, a reflex action that would produce another, deadly reflex action—and when he discovers the reason for his drawing back, he is, in effect, rejecting the Great Twitch. He finally can see the Great Twitch as only a reduction, a metaphor for our barnyard behavior, but a metaphor which our humanity must struggle to elude if it is to assert, however sporadically, its freedom. And he must measure our humanity by its capacity to engage its messy, unpredictable reality, a reality that overruns our neat, metaphorical boundaries and thus demonstrates the insufficiency of the metaphor, although not quite to the point of denying its cogency.

So Jack has moved beyond the tragic, now as a classic visionary. He understands anew the role of history and man's responsibility to himself and to it: he understands the subtle dimensions of the historical community and its demands, as forces springing from solid reality. At last he may be able to make sense of a scene he once witnessed (early in the novel) which moved him deeply enough for him to recall it, poignantly, much later. From the window of a train moving through empty country, in which some insubstantial houses seem very temporarily to have been dropped, Jack sees the figure of a faceless woman come to the back door of a house, fling some water from a pan she is carrying, and go back into the house. Jack feels that she has gone back where "she is going to stay," back to "the secret" that is inside (p. 81). This is her place: it is not she or her house that is temporary but Jack, who is running away with no place to "stay." "And all at once you feel like crying. But the train is going fast, and almost immediately whatever you felt is taken away from you, too" (p. 82). Even the feeling of aimless desperation cannot stay. Jack the Idealist, with his exclusive claim about "life as motion," is thus confronted by this solid chunk of immovable reality. Later, at an important moment, he recalls the woman who "deliberately" entered the house, who was "not going to run away," who was "going into the house to some secret which is there, some knowledge" (p. 332). When he first witnessed the scene from the moving train, he did not comprehend its appeal to him; and when he thought about it during the later train ride returning him from California and his discovery of the Great Twitch, he rejected its significance, since he claimed a "secret knowledge" all his own (of the dominance of the Great Twitch) that superseded the woman's "secret knowledge." But if, after the final Duffy episode, he can come closer to this other secret knowledge—to the woman's sense of place, of solid reality—he still does so only from the outside, as a visionary, though he is clearly in the realm of the classic. It is the woman—or her counterpart in the story, Lucy Stark—who is the classic existent.

But when Jack returns at the end and permits himself to live in

Judge Irwin's house, when he takes Ellis Burden to live with him in that house, when he marries Anne, when he prepares to enter politics once more to work for a similarly rejuvenated Hugh Miller,[17] when he declares himself ready to return to the Cass Mastern materials in order at last to master them, when Anne and he, having lived in the Irwin house, now feel themselves free also to decide to leave it ("out of history into history")—all these decisions find him entering classic existence itself. I know of no other work in which so sophisticated, so self-conscious a life-scarred creature—especially a narrator-creator of a monumentally tragic figure—wills himself into such a simplicity of final commitments and comes close to getting away with it. Jack the narrator records, with a considerable sense of identity, Jack and his Anne walking off—but hardly idyllically, in view of all they know and accept about themselves and the world—into the future, into the history to come (which is partially free) out of the darkly bound history behind them. Certainly they do enter as existents themselves, as agents. It is a daring stroke, this walking off into the sunset (sunrise?); but, in view of what we know of Jack Burden, what we know he knows, it is—I believe—more daring than sentimental.

After all, it is this Jack who is presumably finishing the book we have been reading in the little time remaining before he is to leave the Irwin house with Anne. The writing of this book, like the writing of his Cass Mastern study, is his farewell to his status as classic visionary and the preparation for his departure as classic existent. This book, a mock-biography that turns confessional and autobiographical, has been written by the most recent Jack Burden, the Jack Burden of its last pages. So the events of the book have been the education that permitted his writing the book. This education has permitted him to triumph over the fact-icity of history. It has permitted him to find human vindication even in the disastrous results of his heartless research on Judge Irwin, which is the basic action of his fable. This action thus becomes the enabling act for him to write the Cass Mastern story, as the Cass Mastern story will be the enabling act for

[17] It is as if Hugh Miller, who earlier rejected (indeed "welched" on) the life of action when he learned of its inevitable involvement in evil, has learned Jack's lesson with him, although we do not know how. Perhaps this insertion about Miller has created too positive a note for some readers to accept: too many characters, who show no evidence of having earned the right, seem to be climbing onto the classic bandwagon.

him to leave the historian's visionary role for the actor's existential role. In this way the technical point of view upon action merges with action, aesthetics merges with thematics, history merges with a free present: in short, vision merges with existence. So far can the modest classic vision try to reach toward union when the barnyard is most richly conscious of itself.

IV

The Retreat from Extremity

Through an Alternative to Sainthood

11

The Light-ening of the "Burden" of History:
Light in August

*"A man will talk about how he'd like to escape
from living folks. But it's the dead folks that do him
the damage. It's the dead ones that lay quiet in
one place and dont try to hold him, that he cant escape
from."*[1]

These thoughts of Byron Bunch about the Reverend
Hightower are an immediate indication that, in *Light in August*, we
are still[2] tracing man's struggles with the oppressive burdens of history. The words are as true of Joanna Burden and Joe Christmas as
they are of Hightower. None of them can escape the familial past that
controls them; and their deaths, the three major deaths in the novel,
are all visited upon them as much by their ancestors as by those about
them. Indeed, each has a grandfather who seems to control the curse
under which he suffers and is finally destroyed.

Hightower is the character most explicitly merged into his grandfather's being: his total life is exhausted in the moment of his grandfather's mock-heroic death while raiding a henhouse during the Civil
War: Hightower was born, we are told, "about thirty years after the
only day he seemed to have ever lived in—that day when his grandfather was shot from the galloping horse" (p. 53). This is what has

[1] William Faulkner, *Light in August* (New York: Random House, 1950),
p. 65. Other citations appear in the text.
[2] I say "still" though of course *Light in August* appeared a decade and a
half earlier (1932) than *All the King's Men* (1946). I am speaking here not
of the chronological relation between the two novels but of the movement
of my own discourse.

driven him to the seminary and from the seminary to Jefferson: "Listen. God must call me to Jefferson because my life died there, was shot from the saddle of a galloping horse in a Jefferson street one night twenty years [*sic*] before it was ever born" (pp. 418–19). And at the moment of his own death, he makes judgments as if he is, simultaneously, his "dead grandfather on the instant of his death," seeing himself as "debaucher and murderer of my grandson's wife, since I could neither let my grandson live or die" (p. 430). So his end is in his beginning, according to the peculiarly unprogressive progress made by the wheel of history. The wheel is history's, though it is also man's rack. While man suffers under the burden of its turning, he tries desperately to hold it back:

> *Progress now is still progress, yet it is now*
> *indistinguishable from the recent past like the already*
> *traversed inches of sand which cling to the turning*
> *wheel, raining back with a dry hiss that before*
> *this should have warned him. . . . As he sits in the*
> *window, leaning forward above his motionless hands,*
> *sweat begins to pour from him, springing out like*
> *blood, and pouring. Out of the instant the*
> *sandclutched wheel of thinking turns on with the*
> *slow implacability of a mediaeval torture instrument,*
> *beneath the wrenched and broken sockets of his*
> *spirit, his life. . . .*
>
> *The wheel, released, seems to rush on with a*
> *long sighing sound. He sits motionless in its aftermath,*
> *in his cooling sweat, while the sweat pours and*
> *pours. The wheel whirls on. It is going fast and smooth*
> *now, because it is freed now of burden, of vehicle,*
> *axle, all. In the lambent suspension of August into*
> *which night is about to fully come, it seems to*
> *engender and surround itself with a faint glow like a*
> *halo.*
>
> (pp. 429–30)

For Hightower, the wheel can be "released" and "freed now of burden" only in those frozen moments prior to death ("the lambent suspension of August into which night is about to fully come"), which wins man his release from history altogether.

In this novel, as in *All the King's Men*, the burdens that history imposes upon its characters are epitomized by a person with that name, Burden. Joanna is the most profoundly victimized by history, by the exaggerated form of history that produces fanaticism, if we define fanaticism—as Faulkner seems to—as the final perversion of what begins as false historical traditions. She is the most heavily burdened by her history and her name. It is a name her grandfather, Calvin (originally Burrington), takes on, as if he wants to be sure he has a Burden to pass along to his heirs. He does have. And Joanna receives it most heavily, as her father predicted would be the case:

> "Your grandfather and brother are lying there,
> murdered not by one white man but by the curse which
> God put on a whole race before your grandfather or
> your brother or me or you were even thought of.
> A race doomed and cursed to be forever and ever a
> part of the white race's doom and curse for its
> sins. Remember that. His doom and his curse. Forever
> and ever. Mine. Your mother's. Yours, even though you
> are a child. The curse of every white child that ever
> was born and that ever will be born. None can
> escape it." And I said, "Not even me?" And he said,
> "Not even you. Least of all, you."
>
> (p. 221)

It is the consequences of this perverse abolitionism, just the reverse side of the insane racism of Eupheus Hines, that must doom Joanna Burden in her collision with Joe Christmas, who is at once in flight from and in pursuit of his black blood.

Eupheus Hines, unlike the other two grandfathers, is still alive to haunt his grandson, Joe Christmas, actively, so as to play a literal rather than a figurative role in Joe's destruction. He is responsible for the death of Joe's mother, for Joe's unhappy awareness from the first of the Negro within him, and, consequently, for his entering and never leaving "the street which ran for thirty years. It had been a paved street, where going should be fast. It had made a circle and he is still inside of it" (p. 296). Finally, of course, "old Doc Hines" tries to be responsible for spreading a spirit of lynching, although the different fanaticism of Percy Grimm can more effectively activate its own destructive power. Hines has accepted these responsibilities from the time his daughter first conceived Joe. He accepts them as a surrogate of God (indeed there are even moments when he allows himself to be thought of as God Himself): "and God said, 'You wait and see. Do you think it is just chanceso that I sent that young doctor to be the one that found My abomination laying wrapped in that blanket on that doorstep that Christmas night? Do you think it was just chanceso that the Madam should have been away that night and give them young sluts the chance and call to name him Christmas in sacrilege of My Son? So I am gone now, because I have set My will a-working and I can leave you here to watch it' " (p. 335). Under the aegis of such divinely demoniacal planning, how could the street run by the proclaimed Antichrist have any but one end? The ambiguity which surrounds Joe's role as Christ or parody of Christ, which has never stopped troubling commentators upon the novel, is reflected in the castration-crucifixion which is the inevitable conclusion of his prescribed story.

The intended ambiguities in the role of Joe Christmas are clues to the extremity which hounds his historically burdened world, as well as the worlds of Hightower and Joanna Burden. From the start of *The Tragic Vision*, I have defined extremity by its capacity to blur its antagonistic poles, so that opposition and identity become indistinguishable. Nowhere is this truer than in the world of Joe Christmas, who must serve as both demon and saint. We have learned from Kierkegaard that the "teleological suspension of the ethical" (even by an Abraham) rests upon a transgression against the ethical which involves profound moral and societal risks. Dostoevsky and Mann have taught us how dearly bought is salvation purchased by blood. Thus my earlier volume dwelt again and again upon tales of imitations of Christ carried on by merely human agents who were doomed to be no more than parodies of Christ. But the absurd claim to sainthood still clung to them (after the analogy to Abraham) here in this world of extremity, where sainthood can have no other source but an apparent demonism.

Joe Christmas is perhaps our least self-conscious imitator of Christ, although Faulkner takes considerable pains to work his character into such a "figure."[3] It is, as I have suggested, his desire to maintain Christmas' relation to Christ as a problematic one that prompts Faulkner to baffle his critics by offering parallels with one hand that he half-withdraws with the other. However un-self-conscious, Christmas becomes the living projection of his world's extremity as the "tragic mulatto," in Faulkner's adaptation of that common theme in Southern writing. (And are we not to see the mixture of black and white blood in Christmas as analogous to the mixture of divine and human blood in Christ?)

The several judgments in the novel upon black blood—often specifically the black blood in Christmas—make clear its place in the world of extremity. The insane ravings of Doc Hines, who can even bully masses of frightened Negroes to view him as the white God (p. 301), are based on the puritanical claim that would purge the sinful morality of the white race by putting all evil into the blackness of the Negro. The strategy of the scapegoat is sustained only by the surface metaphor that takes as substantive the superficial locution that equates black with evil and white with purity. But is this not how the puritanical mind, in its perverseness, must work? The depraved, sin-ridden white can maintain that he is pure only by unloading his evil so as to make it the exclusive property of black. The latter he must then destroy. Faulkner thus diagnoses the sick mentality of racism in the South by finding its source in the equally sick divisions of mind in New England puritanism. Thus we find the equation-in-ambivalence of the racial terror of Eupheus Hines and the abolitionism

---

[3] There are many potentially parabolic details to suggest that the story of Joe Christmas is a passion play. Just a few of the possible parallels to the Christ story which critics have either noted or squabbled over are the age of Christmas at his death and the details of his birth, his cleansing of the temple, and his being betrayed for a thousand dollars. I omit many other less obvious ones. Perhaps the most persuasive parallel occurs during that week of his passion (his flight after the murder). We see him repeatedly asking what day it is and then, when he learns it is Friday, at once turning back toward Jefferson to greet his fate: "his direction is straight as a surveyor's line, disregarding hill and valley and bog. Yet he is not hurrying. He is like a man who knows where he is and where he wants to go and how much time to the exact minute he has to get there in" (p. 295). This resoluteness is a surprising turn: it is as close as Christmas comes to being a conscious Christ.

of Joanna Burden. In each the cravings of debauchery and purity meet and end in violent hysteria. Both may be described in the way in which Faulkner, adapting the Petrarchan paradox of ice and fire, describes the desperation of Joanna Burden: "the abject fury of the New England glacier exposed suddenly to the fire of the New England biblical hell" (p. 225).[4]

Since it is Eupheus Hines, as the ubiquitous and controlling god, who has thrust Christmas into that street of his life—at once linear and circular—from which he never escapes, Joe instinctively accepts the white puritanical judgment of his black taint. Like Christ, he accepts—indeed seeks—the role of scapegoat, taking on the sins of others and being destroyed for them: allowing the whites to get rid of their sinfulness by projecting it and embodying it in him. For Hines, the black taint and sinful "womanfilth" are synonymous, since his daughter Milly accepted both together when she illicitly conceived Joe. Joe's life carries out this coupling. His enclosure within the street which runs for years without going anywhere traps him within "womanfilth" and his black heritage, which are confounded in his mind as much as they are in his grandfather's: "And always, sooner or later, the street ran through cities, through an identical and well-nigh interchangeable section of cities without remembered names, where beneath the dark and equivocal and symbolical archways of midnight he bedded with the women and paid them when he had the

---

[4] The perverse abolitionism of Joanna Burden, it might be pointed out, may foreshadow the anti-Negro violence in the Cass Mastern story of *All the King's Men*. Thinking of himself and Annabelle Trice, with the eyes of Negroes upon them, Cass recalls the wealthy

> *lady of position from Boston. This lady Caroline Turner*
> *. . . who had been nurtured in sentiments opposed to*
> *the institution of human servitude, quickly became notorious*
> *for her abominable cruelties performed in her fits of*
> *passion. All persons of the community reprehended her*
> *floggings, which she performed with her own hands, uttering*
> *meanwhile little cries in her throat, according to report. . . .*
> *To protect her from the process of law and the wrath of*
> *the community, Judge Turner committed her to a lunatic*
> *asylum. But later the physicians said her to be of sound*
> *mind and released her.*
>
> (p. 195)

She returns to her merciless floggings until one of her victims turns upon her and kills her.

money, and when he did not have it he bedded anyway and then told them that he was a Negro" (p. 196).[5]

From his earliest memory of the dietitian at the orphanage, it is Joe's fate to be smothered softly in the secret, smelly folds of all that belongs to womanliness. The many unwholesome elements that accompany him all stem from that moment behind the curtain which hides the child from the sexual activities he hears but does not understand, the moment which combines the sickly sweetness of the emptying tube of toothpaste with the smell of her clothes with the vomiting with his being discovered and with his sense of punishment deferred and then turned into secret reward. Add to this a later but still early experience: the failure—and the violence that accompanies it—of his first attempt at sexual intercourse: "There was something in him trying to get out, like when he had used to think of toothpaste. But he could not move at once, standing there, smelling the woman, smelling the Negro all at once; enclosed by the womanshenegro" (p. 137). There is, too, his discovery of menstruation (which he thinks of as "periodical filth" [p. 161]), which leads to his killing of the sheep and the washing of his hands in its blood.[6]

These sexual symbols determine the framework of his behavior and his fate. He will look for the open honesty of ruthless punishment from the hard masculine world, but will find himself enveloped by the clinging secrecy of the woman's world which seeks to rescue and protect him. His relations to his foster-parents, the McEacherns, are representative: the lean, undisguised cruelty which he can accept from the male and the soft, solicitous concealments which he must reject from the female.[7]

[5] In its unprogressiveness, the street may remind us of the wheels I have observed in Hightower's history, which can freely turn only when he is ready to be freed from history by death.

[6] This symbolism, at once sexual and Christian, blends the two sources of Joe's revulsion.

[7] Two typical passages will serve to make these relations explicit. "He believed that it was to go on for the rest of his life. . . . The dishes she would prepare for him in secret and then insist on his accepting and eating them in secret, when he did not want them . . . the times when, like tonight, she would try to get herself between him and the punishment which, deserved or not, just or unjust, was impersonal, both the man and the boy accepting it as a natural and inescapable fact until she, getting in the way, must give it an odor, an attenuation, and aftertaste" (p. 146). "It was not the hard work which he hated, nor the punishment and injustice. . . . It was the woman: that soft kindness which he believed himself doomed to be forever

The pattern is set which carries him to Bobby Allen, and beyond, to the other women on the street along which and within which his life runs, and finally to Joanna Burden. The course of his relation to Joanna Burden finds her playing, in succession, the role of the two sexes. She first goes to bed with him with a "hard, untearful and unselfpitying and almost manlike yielding" (p. 205): " 'My God,' he thought, 'it was like I was the woman and she was the man' " (p. 206). Next to this "first hard and manlike surrender," the "second phase . . . was as though he had fallen into a sewer" (p. 224). Now "living not alone in sin but in filth" (p. 226), with a corrupting frenzy erotically obsessed with both his body and his being Negro, she joins and outstrips the others and becomes the final representation of the "womanfilth" that has trapped him. The end is near: he will have to free her and himself from the wild extremity of their maddened histories. This is the final stage in Joe's struggle against his envelopment by the smells of secrecy, the secrecy of woman-sex like the secrecy of his being part black. Unconsciously following his grandfather's example, he confuses the two, his sense of "womanshenegro" blurring "womanfilth" with his own filth, his taint—and all filth hidden. No wonder he must seek to end all secrecy, at last destroying the woman just as he has constantly confessed his Negro blood.

He again turns to the frank, persecuting frenzy of the white, cruelly masculine world which will punish him—which, finally in the absurd person of Percy Grimm, destroys and mutilates him. He has attained the end sought by his masochism and the latent homosexuality that has fed it. From the toothpaste episode at the start of his life to the mocking charges toward the end that Brown is married to *him* and that he has seduced Hightower,[8] Faulkner prompts our questions about Joe's latent perversities. But it is in what he seeks and what he finds in men and women that his ambivalences are made clear and become literally, as well as figuratively, instrumental in the culminat-

---

victim of and which he hated worse than he did the dark and ruthless justice of men" (p. 147).

[8] The passage on Brown and Christmas is spoken by the Sheriff about Brown: "I aint interested in the wives he left in Alabama, or anywhere else. What I am interested in is the husband he seems to have had since he come to Jefferson" (p. 281). The passage on Hightower and Christmas is spoken by Grimm after Hightower, at the last moment, has tried to defend Christmas by saying the two of them were together the night of the murder: "Has every preacher and old maid in Jefferson taken their pants down to the yellowbellied son of a bitch?" (p. 406).

ing, as well as the terminating, act of his extremity. That the insanely cruel masculine world castrates him, as if in answer to his half-felt lifelong quest, may seem a fitting conclusion to his story.

Yet the final murder and mutilation of Joe Christmas by Percy Grimm have about them intimations of the Crucifixion that give validity to Faulkner's sporadic parallels with Christ. We have witnessed, well before the end, forebodings of crucifixion in the minds of both Miss Burden and Hightower, our other two characters driven by extremity, crushed like Joe by the burden of their histories, of their grandfathers. Joanna, recalling her father's words about the doom of the white race because of the curse put on the black, recalls also the image which her young girl's mind formed:

> *I seemed to see them [Negroes] for the first time*
> *not as people, but as a thing, a shadow in which I lived,*
> *we lived, all white people, all other people. I thought*
> *of all the children coming forever and ever into the*
> *world, white, with the black shadow already falling*
> *upon them before they drew breath. And I seemed to*
> *see the black shadow in the shape of a cross. And it*
> *seemed like the white babies were struggling,*
> *even before they drew breath, to escape from the*
> *shadow that was not only upon them but beneath*
> *them too, flung out like their arms were flung out, as if*
> *they were nailed to the cross. I saw all the little babies*
> *that would ever be in the world, the ones not yet*
> *even born—a long line of them with their arms spread,*
> *on the black crosses.*
>
> (pp. 221–22)

Here is a special turn given to the puritan's vision of infant damnation and permanent crucifixion. The need to separate white from black as absolute moral qualities, the need of the white to purge itself of the black clinging to it, the need to segregate the black on its cross in order to free and thus save the white—all these needs are implied in this image, and all can be traced to Joe's function in his society and to his end.

Hightower has his own vision of crucifixion, related not to black and white but to the austere Protestantism that cherishes crucifixion, and finally related to Joe Christmas himself:

> *The organ strains come rich and resonant through*
> *the summer night, blended, sonorous, with that quality*
> *of abjectness and sublimation, as if the freed voices*
> *themselves were assuming the shapes and attitudes of*
> *crucifixions, ecstatic, solemn, and profound in*
> *gathering volume. Yet even then the music has still*
> *a quality stern and implacable, deliberate and*
> *without passion so much as immolation, pleading,*
> *asking, for not love, not life, forbidding it to others,*
> *demanding in sonorous tones death as though death*
> *were the boon, like all Protestant music. . . . Listening,*
> *he seems to hear within it the apotheosis of his own*
> *history, his own land, his own environed blood. . . .*
> *Pleasure, ecstasy, they cannot seem to bear: their*
> *escape from it is in violence, in drinking and fighting*
> *and praying; catastrophe too, the violence identical*
> *and apparently inescapable* And so why should not their
> religion drive them to crucifixion of themselves and
> one another? *he thinks. It seems to him that he can*
> *hear within the music the declaration and dedication of*
> *that which they know that on the morrow they will have*
> *to do. . . . now on the brink of cataract the stream*
> *has raised a single blended and sonorous and austere*
> *cry . . . not to any god but to the doomed man in*
> *the barred cell within hearing of them and of the two*
> *other churches, and in whose crucifixion they too will*
> *raise a cross.*
>
> (pp. 321–22)

He further notes, half terrified at the discovery, that "they will do it gladly" in order to preserve their lack of "selfdoubt" by keeping all evil apart from themselves as they slaughter it.

So Joe Christmas must be transformed from being only slightly and unnoticeably Negro[9] to being all the blackness that the white man

---

[9] It must be kept in mind, now and earlier in my discussion, that Faulkner is careful never to answer definitely the question of whether or not Joe's father was really part Negro. We only have mad Doc Hines's judgment and the circus owner's questionable word that he was not indeed a Mexican, as was claimed. It clearly is important to Faulkner to show that it is totally *un*important to know whether Joe's mulatto status is fact or fiction, even if it initiates the absurd morality fiction. Christ's semi-divinity baffles us too.

must purge, as the silly morality play, which equates the presence or absence of color with the presence or absence of sin, moves to its dénouement. As the circle of his lifelong street closes in upon him, as on that final Friday he rides into Mottstown, so does the blackness overcome him: " 'But I have never got outside that circle. I have never broken out of the ring of what I have already done and cannot ever undo,' he thinks quietly, sitting on the seat, with planted on the dashboard before him the shoes, the black shoes smelling of Negro: that mark on his ankles the gauge definite and ineradicable of the black tide creeping up his legs, moving from his feet upward as death moves" (pp. 296–97). Only death can release his black blood now, and it does, for him and for us all. To the Crucifixion must be added the Resurrection:

> For a long moment he looked up at them with
> peaceful and unfathomable and unbearable eyes.
> Then his face, body, all, seemed to collapse, to fall in
> upon itself, and from out the slashed garments
> about his hips and loins the pent black blood seemed to
> rush like a released breath. It seemed to rush out of
> his pale body like the rush of sparks from a rising
> rocket; upon that black blast the man seemed to rise
> soaring into their memories forever and ever. They
> are not to lose it, in whatever peaceful valleys,
> beside whatever placid and reassuring streams of old
> age, in the mirroring faces of whatever children they
> will contemplate old disasters and newer hopes. It will
> be there, musing, quiet, steadfast, not fading and not
> particularly threatful, but of itself alone serene, of itself
> alone triumphant.
>
> (p. 407)

It is as if the spending of Joe's blood, now all black, is the purgative that brings to an end the extremity that an ugly history has continually provided for all its victims. In their violence they have made Joe the repository of all their evil: as the embodiment of all that he has inherited, as the unconscious agent of all that they have made him, Joe becomes their and their history's living, dying end: "But there was too much running with him, stride for stride with him. Not pursuers: but himself: years, acts, deeds omitted and committed, keeping pace with him, stride for stride, breath for breath, thud for thud of the heart, using a single heart. It was not alone all those thirty years . . . but all those successions of thirty years before that which had put that stain either on his white blood or his black blood, whichever you will, and which killed him" (p. 393).

It is in this function of taking their sins upon himself,[10] and of dying for them, that Joe seems closest to Christ. The questionable mulatto has become *the* Negro and then, the last Negro. A sick historical-sociological fact in the Southern community has moved through the psychosis of fanaticism to eschatology. After the soaring triumph which the author's voice attributes to Joe Christmas, only the steadfast and the peaceful can follow. All passion spent and all guilts shed in an apocalyptic fury, history is at an end and we are open to a new dispensation. This Christ has done his work and we are ready for a different sort of Christ altogether, a Christ mothered by one such as Lena Grove.

To be candid, one can only with severe qualifications speak of Joe Christmas as Christ. This loveless, driven, hate-filled creature of violence seems more of an Antichrist, of course. We need only remember the wild blasphemies he shrieks from the pulpit in the Negro church to see how far Faulkner means to go in this direction. But, as I have indicated about Joe's relation to his history and his society as their embodiment or projection, he is the only sort of Christ this world can produce. What else but a creature of extremity could he be? What, except a demon, can the people of such a world have as their saint, though all that is saint-like about him is his function of eliminating the need for any like him to appear again? He removes all history with him as he rises. What is to follow is a world which, in its serenity, has a Christ who need be no Christ, but just one of the herd which, in its removal from extremity, needs no saints. But this is to bring us out of history and its extremity into the barnyard—and to Lena Grove once again.

There is a clear similarity between the circumstances surrounding the conception of Lena's child and the conception of Joe Christmas by Milly, daughter of Eupheus Hines. Faulkner emphasizes the parallel roles of the two children not only by having Doc Hines and his wife present at Lena's delivery of her child, but by having Mrs. Hines totally confound the two occasions and the two infants. The presence

---

[10] Of course, I mean that he does so unconsciously, since really it is they who have unloaded their sins upon him.

of Christmas, waiting to be lynched (with the encouragement of Doc Hines), at the same time that Lena's child waits to be born (with the watchful participation of Mrs. Hines, who thinks it is Joe Christmas being born) enfolds the one story in the other. Though Faulkner makes sure that Lena and Christmas never meet or relate to one another directly, he also makes sure that it is in the cabin of Joe Christmas that Lena's child is born. Although critics who prefer a superficial unity have complained that the Lena story is too disengaged from the Christmas story, they miss the fact that Faulkner requires that Lena have no immediate contact with the world of extremity. It is enough that Hightower can be an intercessor in both stories, that in a sense Brown can cohabit with both so that she has the right to end up in the cabin of Christmas, and that the Hineses in their madness can yoke the two births together.

Lena herself must wander free, untouched by the world of Christmas, although Faulkner conspires to relate her story to Milly's as parallel lines that never meet. Indeed, one might shift the lines a bit by noting that the life of Lena's child can begin only when the life of Milly's child has ended. Figuratively, Lena's child is a product of the crucifixion and resurrection which I have discussed before: in effect he represents a Second Coming heralding a common world of innocence. This is the comic world of the final chapter, in which the coy, directedly aimless wanderings of Lena and Byron and the child—and the certain uncertainties of their relationship to one another—can withstand our amused condescension. For they have broken clear, as we—and the furniture dealer who is the shrewd narrator of this final chapter—have not. The new babe has made possible a classic existence, beyond extremity.

No matter how convinced Mrs. Hines is about the identity between Lena and Milly, her child of more than thirty years before, there is an important difference between them. Even at the beginning, Lena could conceive her illegitimate child without having any history to carry along with her. Faulkner has earlier arranged for the death of both her parents, so that she has no Doc Hines to kill her and haunt her child to death. She is free to travel in her indomitable, automatic, patient way, in search of the child's father—not out of moral compunction or personal outrage, but because "when a man and a woman are going to have a child . . . the Lord will see that they are all together when the right time comes" (p. 264). "Her face is calm as stone, but not hard. Its doggedness has a soft quality, an inwardlighted quality of tranquil and calm unreason and detachment" (p. 16). Cut off from history and from its morally induced urgency, only Lena can allow the circular character of life's unprogression to move freely and carry her along with it. She is neither trapped in the circle, as we saw Joe Christmas was, nor tortured by the turning wheel, as Hightower was:

> This road? It goes to Pocahontas. He might be
> there. It's possible. Here's a wagon that's going a piece
> of the way. It will take you that far; *backrolling*
> *now behind her a long monotonous succession of*
> *peaceful and undeviating changes from day to dark and*
> *dark to day again, through which she advanced in*
> *identical and anonymous and deliberate wagons as*
> *though through a succession of creakwheeled and*
> *limpeared avatars,*[11] *like something moving forever and*
> *without progress across an urn.*
>
> (p. 6)

How she has converted her extraordinary crisis, resulting from an unfeeling abandonment, into matter for a seamless common routine! Here is a classic consciousness—or rather a classic un-self-consciousness. She proves to be a singular, formidable example of those classic creatures whom, in the next chapter, Eliot's Becket will describe as being turned round on time's wheel.

Without struggle and without flight, Lena, we are told, represents the still movement of a figure on an urn. If, in the archetypal perfection of her unconscious movement, she is—like a frieze—part of our narrator's aesthetic vision, Joe Christmas has a vision of his own most unaesthetic urns. His vision follows the scene in which Bobby Allen

---

[11] I remind the reader of my discussion of volume 7 of *Tristram Shandy*, in which our fictive author must keep moving across Europe to escape death. In chapter 13 of that volume, he has a discourse on wheels. He disagrees with those who hate wheels, who wish their enemies "no worse luck than always to be rolling about." " '*Make them like unto a wheel*,' is a bitter sarcasm ... against the *grand tour*," he unsympathetically reports. Nor will he permit the wheel to be seen as "an Ixion's wheel." "Now I ... think differently; and that so much of motion, is so much of life, and so much of joy—and that to stand still, or get on but slowly, is death and the devil." "Now the wheel we are talking of," he goes on, "should certainly be a postchaise wheel." Here is a classic temperament that would understand Lena's movements.

forces upon him a further awareness of the facts of menstruation. The urns then become a symbol of the female sexual vessel, which he by now views solely as a receptacle of filth: "In the notseeing and the hardknowing as though in a cave he seemed to see a diminishing row of suavely shaped urns in moonlight, blanched. And not one was perfect. Each one was cracked and from each crack there issued something liquid, deathcolored, and foul. He touched a tree, leaning his propped arms against it, seeing the ranked and moonlit urns. He vomited" (p. 165). So while Lena is on the urn herself, Christmas sees the urns. But the urns he sees are utterly different from the one she moves across.[12] Hers is an unquestioning acceptance of human reality as barnyard reality seen as a mode of innocence; his is a Strephon-like revulsion against the barnyard and its secret and secretion-filled biological facts. For her there is no "womanfilth"; for him there is nothing else. It should not be surprising that he moves, by way of continual indulgence that increases his disgust, toward castration by the male.

Hightower, too, sees a receptacle, but he sees himself *in* it, protected by it from either Lena's commitment to life or Joe's commitment to death:

> *When he believed that he had heard the call it*
> *seemed to him that he could see his future, his life,*
> *intact and on all sides complete and inviolable,*
> *like a classic and serene vase, where the spirit could*
> *be born anew sheltered from the harsh gale of living and*
> *die so, peacefully, with only the far sound of the*
> *circumvented wind with scarce even a handful of*
> *rotting dust to be disposed of. That was what the word*
> *seminary meant: quiet and safe walls within which*
> *the hampered and garmentworried spirit could*
> *learn anew serenity to contemplate without horror or*
> *alarm its own nakedness.*
>
> (p. 419)

[12] C. Hugh Holman points out these passages about various vessels and their mutual illumination in his essay "The Unity of Faulkner's *Light in August*," *PMLA* 73 (March 1958):155–66, especially pp. 159, 161, and 164. I am indebted to this rich and full essay (and review of research) for any insights that have helped to shape this chapter.

But this is *not* what, at its root, the word "seminary" means, although Hightower's temperament cannot confront this fact. The protective walls should be the walls of the seed out of which life grows. So it is ironic that Hightower should seek succor in "seminary"—the impotent Hightower, whose "seed which his grandfather had transmitted to him had been on the horse too that night and had been killed too and time had stopped there and then for the seed and nothing had happened in time since, not even him" (p. 55). As "a classic and serene vase," Hightower's seminary is to be, not a seed, receptacle of life, but a coffin, receptacle of his living-dying ashes. It is an urn for after death, not an urn that is the source of life. It denies the possibility of Lena's urn, and it goes beyond Joe's urns, as if it had foreseen them and had to protect itself from them in advance. In this way —with his grandfather's killing of his seed—has history ended Hightower's life before it began. This is the irony behind Joe's running to Hightower at the end, not just to save his life, but to find an immunity to history with him—with Hightower, of all people! "Somewhere, somehow, in the shape or presence or whatever of that old outcast minister was a sanctuary which would be inviolable not only to officers and mobs, but to the very irrevocable past" (p. 392). But Christmas is as wrong as Hightower had been. For Christmas, Hightower's house is no more a sanctuary from the past than the seminary, and the assignment in Jefferson which had followed it, had originally been for "that old outcast minister."

No, Hightower's vase represents history's smothering triumph over the chances for a present. It requires an abdication from life before life has a chance to begin; and the abdication produces—in his wife and in his ministry at Jefferson—horrors which reinforce and extend his withdrawal through consequences that seem to justify it. With Hightower beyond life and death, as if he had foreseen (and forelived) both, his story—with the vase as its emblem—is a sort of *Purgatorio*. As such, it stands between the living *Inferno* of the Christmas story and the *Paradiso* to which the Lena story is, half-mockingly, converted in the final chapter. This middle position accords with Hightower's role in the plot, where he serves to connect the other two parallel actions. Joe's living hell is the product of the perversions of history which we see (in him and acting upon him) as fanaticism. Its domain is absolute in that he cannot escape it while he lives. (Perhaps the insistence upon his being irrevocably enclosed by the "circle" is significant in suggesting a Dantean place for him among the infernally damned.) But since he is, sacrilegiously, Christ also, he can be released —indeed resurrected—by death. But his death releases the others too in its wake. We have the final two chapters, following that death, devoted, one each, to a final view of Hightower and of Lena. Hightower, in his chapter, attains his own release from purgatory through the realization that Joe's death (together with the birth of Lena's child, Joe's successor) produces in him. But by this time it can be for him only a release for death. And Lena, having borne within her all along the possibility for a world beyond the historically ordained *Inferno* of Christmas and *Purgatorio* of Hightower, can now—with her child— enter her paradise. She is now free even of Brown (or Burch)—the last dregs of her history—and in turn has freed Byron, who had, though with less self-conscious commitment, been trapped in the purgatory of Hightower. So now, with Byron and the child of the new dispensation, she is free to pursue (really too strong a verb) her undemarcated future.

Thus, like *All the King's Men*, this novel ends with its most promising characters walking "out of history into history." But, unlike *All the King's Men*, those who finally depart from history (Christmas and Hightower) are not those who enter it (Lena, Byron, and the child). Nor, of course, is it the same history that is being departed from and entered. It is precisely "the awful responsibility of time" from which the second history, with its remarkably *ir*responsible agents, has freed itself. I have claimed that Joe Christmas, by his death and metaphorical resurrection, was to have had an eschatological effect upon the history whose ultimate embodiment embedded itself in him and his fate. *That* history is to have been finished by the purge of his black blood and his triumphant soaring into a permanent memory among the peaceful valleys and placid streams of the world. This world, initiating a new history now that it is unburdened of the old, initiates it with Lena and the coming of *her* child. This history-to-come can now be free of fanaticism or even the possibility of fanaticism. All that has been purged with Christmas. In keeping with Lena's own nature,[13] the new world she mothers will be characterized by the auto-

[13] In the essay cited C. Hugh Holman quotes from Faulkner's wonderful characterization of Lena in the *Paris Review* interview (4 [Spring 1956]: 50): "It was her destiny to have a husband and children, and she knew it and so she went out and attended to it without asking help from anyone."

matic acceptance of the natural-human barnyard. There will be no moral repugnance about "womanfilth," no revulsion that "gives it an odor," no damning consciousness (like Christmas' or Strephon's) of what smells that barnyard does naturally have.

It is the unburdening effect of this new dispensation that gives a special meaning to the "light" in the title of the novel; this is the meaning played upon in the title of this chapter. The surface meanings of "light" in *Light in August* are several: it probably refers to the fire which is the beacon first seen by the wandering Lena and which is the background against which she first meets Byron when she arrives in Jefferson; as the fire, it also marks the end of Joanna Burden and the impending end of Joe Christmas; and, as light, it probably suggests the brightening of the quality of life after the deaths and the birth, when the trio go on their way. But, as others have noted, things become "light" in weight as well as color. It is in this sense that I have spoken of the "light-ening" of the burden of history. If we took upon the two violent deaths as the ending of one sort of history, then we can think of the fire apocalyptically, as a purifying ritual, a purgation that lightens us all, and in two senses. And we can see the fire as followed by an even more brilliant light, a metaphorical illumination: the "sparks" of the "rising rocket" that releases Christmas and unburdens his world. The "rising" is the result of the lightening. It is also true that Lena is lightened as she is unburdened of the child she has been carrying,[14] just as the world's burden is lightened by Joe's soaring release and as Lena's child is to unburden, lighten, the world.

I have suggested that *Light in August* differs from *All the King's Men* in that it separates those who end the history that exists under extremity from those who initiate a new and relaxed history. This difference points to a significant structural feature of *Light in August*. This is the lack of direct contact, which I have spoken of, between Lena and Christmas: their stories are kept perceptibly distinct in order to permit the special discontinuity which Faulkner must maintain between the two dispensations. This, in turn, establishes the three-part polyphonic structure among the Christmas, Hightower, and Lena stories which—in terms of the Aristotelian fable—exist, primarily, in

[14] We should remember the special reading that others have suggested: that the pregnant woman who is due to give birth in August will be "light" in August.

parallel, despite some superficial points of contact made especially through the mediating role of Hightower, who is prodded into it by his half-disciple, Byron. It is this three-part polyphony that prompted my attempt to see the Dantean alternatives of *Inferno*, *Purgatorio*, and *Paradiso* among them. At the same time, as in any Christian "figural" scheme, there is also some element of succession present, of the sort we have observed in the temporal relations between the first and second Christs. Nevertheless, in the parallel, alternative movements back and forth in time among the three major plot elements, we have a structural process essentially different from the more classically Aristotelian development we have seen in *All the King's Men*, for example.

This difference has crucial thematic consequences. What I found remarkable in Warren's novel was its attempt (after having converted its narrator into protagonist) to carry him, by means of a single action, through the several stages of vision and existence until he could claim to be a classic existent himself. This univocal method requires each earlier stage to be denied as the later is attained. But what is remarkable in *Light in August* is that its structure allows it to sustain the entire spectrum of tragic and classic, of modes of vision and of existence, with the simultaneity that its parallel and coordinate parts permit. It provides us with sainthood (by the saint who appears as an inverted saint, in the pattern of Kierkegaard), and it provides us with the classic alternative to sainthood. As the stories coexist (though they are also curiously bound to one another and even—at the last— succeed one another), so the visions coexist in equal authenticity (though they also are curiously bound to one another and even—at the last—succeed one another). This peculiar blend of free and yet interrelated stories and visions reflects the extent to which its characters are inescapably bound to history and yet, finally, free of it. It is this half-independence of stories and visions that creates the epic (what I have thought of as the Dantean) completeness provided by *Light in August*. It moves from the tragic (infernal) to the classic (paradisiacal) by way of the purgatorial Hightower, who, like Moses, ends with a vision which he will not be able to verify by seeing it projected into actual existence, even though he has made that existence possible by delivering Lena's child. His existential resistance at the end, despite what he thinks he is coming to realize, marks the continuing hold of the tragic, despite what Lena and Byron are to show us. Similarly, though Christmas has been superseded, the complete sway of the tragic within and under the being of its demoniacal saint has not been denied. So once, out of the explosion of the tragic world (through the person of Joe Christmas) the classic (which has also been there all along) is free to emerge, it does so only by means of a negation by fiat of the dominion of the tragic.

The negation of the tragic by the classic—the appearance that there is a succession of Christs, of ways to exist—is arbitrary in that it is sustained only by those passages of metaphorical straining that I have noted. After all, those symbolic notions (which until now I have anxiously accepted) of the single embodiment in a representative man, of crucifixion, of resurrection, of first and second comings and dispensations—they all create a "figural" structure that the common-sense reader must admit imposes considerable (and perhaps too much) pressure upon what actually appears to be going on. What we have, "objectively," are a common, violently driven psychopath, a common bastard born to a too simple, now homeless girl, and an absurd minister whose style and mind have long been obsessed by the galloping of horses. The point is that, though Faulkner does so much—by language and the use of analogous action—to transform them to serve him figurally, he also means them to satisfy these unelevated descriptions as well. His humor is meant to sustain our disbelief in his highfalutin metaphors, as it seems to sustain his own. It also sustains our sense that these are sometimes simultaneous and sometimes consecutive events taking place among essentially unconnected personages, so that one set (like Lena's) does not succeed or invalidate another (like Christmas'). Still, our disbelief (prompted by humor and by common sense) is accompanied by our awe (prompted by metaphor and by analogous actions) as we see the pattern played out and by our relief as we see the imprint of that pattern lightened.

In these varied ways, sometimes mutually supporting and sometimes at cross-purposes with one another, the novel manages to keep its several modes of vision and existence in the air together, despite its metaphorical illusion of progression. The novel rolls on unprogressing wheels not unlike those that have carried Lena. This accounts for its remarkable fullness, its catholicity, perhaps unique in modern writing; this characteristic makes it, in parts, as eligible for a book on the tragic vision as for this one on the classic. Of course it seems finally classic, thanks to Faulkner's utterly classic, comic withdrawal at the end. But, unless we allow the figural reading of a new Christ to wipe our sensibilities clean, the tragic persists, in the many ways and for the several reasons I have suggested. This strange power of *Light in August* explains why, at the end of *The Tragic Vision*, in pointing to the need for the complementary study that has emerged as the present work, I made my exit by means of this novel. That exit was a confession of incompleteness, so that it also became the prospectus for work yet to be done.

It was by way of Byron Bunch and his capacity to bear the very worst in his own and in others' actions that I used *Light in August* to mitigate the consequences which extremity imposes upon action and inaction alike in works of the tragic vision. Byron is a disciple of Hightower's in that, without (as far as we know) having undergone a history like Hightower's, he has come to share Hightower's need to remain disengaged from action out of the fear that to act is to act immorally.[15] But Byron's meeting with Lena marks the end of his withdrawal from human and moral responsibility. Not that he does not put every barrier between himself and the possibility of such involvement: "It was a strange thing. I thought that if there ever was a place where a man would be where the chance to do harm could not have found him, it would have been out there at the mill on a Saturday evening" (p. 67). But without Hightower's history, Bunch cannot be expected to have as many defenses, so that he can be but an imperfect agent of the Hightower philosophy. He also comes to us in the novel as if he were a person without a history. So, strongly influenced as he may be by Hightower, he may also be part way on the road to Lena. For, despite his training, he certainly is quick enough to involve himself in her fate totally and irrevocably, much to Hightower's consternation.

Hightower rightly sees that, once Byron has committed himself to Lena and to hope, he has exposed himself to the self-interest that is the father of all lies, especially the lies that deceive oneself about one's good intentions. It is as if Hightower views Byron as a version of Melville's Pierre. As far as Hightower can tell, Byron is in the service of the devil. Whatever Byron claims to be doing for Lena, or for

---

[15] This fear of Hightower's, which in *The Tragic Vision* was compared to Heyst's similar reticence in Conrad's *Victory*, should be familiar from the several forms we have seen it take (most strongly, of course, in the Scholarly Attorney) in *All the King's Men*.

Brown, can be seen as a surreptitious attempt to advance his own hopes. His own persistence in intruding himself to work in behalf of the two is open to the reading—the reading given it by Hightower—that he is really making a place for himself at Lena's side by replacing Brown. Nor is Byron in a position to deny the charges. By involving himself in action and hope, he necessarily runs the moral risk of doing what he does out of self-interest, whatever the disinterested service in behalf of which he may claim, or even appear, to be doing what he does. All this Hightower had told him earlier, while they both were following the morally secure strategy of withdrawal, and all this Hightower forcefully tells him now, although it is clear that Byron will persist in his defection.

There are two moments that almost deflect him from his path. First, there is the shock of hearing the newborn child cry for the first time, as if proving to Byron that it exists. The fact of the child, what it forces him to acknowledge about its conception, about Lena's history with Brown, almost brings him to (what Hightower would think of as) his senses. Not until the moment after the birth does it really sink in "that she is not a virgin" (p. 352); in other words, not until then do the past biological realities about Lena and Brown sink in. Consequently, for now Byron is reconciled to giving her up. But this child must bring with it the acceptance of man's barnyard truths, so that Byron must not revert to accusations about "womanfilth" to account for Lena's behavior. It is not what he overlooks so much as what he learns to "bear" about the costs of living and the common innocence of those who must pay: "It seems like a man can just about bear anything. He can even bear what he never done. He can even bear the thinking how some things is just more than he can bear. He can even bear it that if he could just give down and cry, he wouldn't do it. He can even bear it to not look back, even when he knows that looking back or not looking back wont do him any good" (p. 371).

This is the second moment that almost turns Byron aside. He is ready to leave Lena to her Brown, though without resentment, and is walking away from it all, certain that looking back or not looking back is not going to make any difference. But it will make a difference. When he determines that he would suffer more by looking back, he decides he "might as well have the pleasure of not being able to bear looking back too" (p. 372). And when he does look back, he sees Brown in flight from Lena. He wins the right to return to her by fighting and losing in the attempt to keep Brown from running. And Lena, who accepts all, half-accepts him, in her own strange way. It is just as Hightower had predicted and what he said Byron was conspiring to bring about: Brown flees and Byron is there to take his place. But Byron, with the assurance that his fight was a moral gesture, will have to "bear" also the likelihood that Hightower was right. The relaxed terms of the barnyard turn out to be warmly human terms, except that the burden of original sin has been eased.

Actually, Hightower has not been left so far behind, it turns out. Though he has resented Byron's involvement and though he has resisted Byron's attempt to involve him, yet once he is trapped into delivering Lena's child, he comes close to being rejuvenated, or at least restored to the living, almost in spite of himself. Before it is all over, he even—now that it is too late—tries to intercede to save Christmas. This is precisely what Byron had earlier asked of him and what he angrily refused to do, questioning Byron's true motives. And in his final scene, which issues—in the penultimate chapter—out of the death of Christmas in Hightower's house and the resurrection metaphor that accompanies it, Hightower comes to understand and accept the failures of his life as *his* failures. He sees now that he failed his wife as a husband, driving her to her extremity of depravity, and failed his parish as their minister because of the mad privacy of his personal needs that drove him into the church and to Jefferson. He acknowledges now the moral cowardice behind his refusal to commit himself to the living, though he still feels the hold on him of that moment out of history which doomed him to that refusal. And he dies to the imagined thunder of the still-galloping horses.

Of course, what has turned Hightower from the negative contentment of his abstinence was his delivery of the babe. He makes possible the new "light" for Lena and Byron by the very act that brings "light" to him. The birth occurs, an emergency to which he responds splendidly, just after his angry rejection of Byron's request that he lend a helping hand to Christmas. He returns home after the delivery feeling "triumph and pride" (p. 355) and acknowledging this feeling without apology. Suddenly purposeful and vigorous, he turns away from his customary Tennyson, choosing instead *Henry IV*, "food for a man." Thinking ahead the next day to his return to Lena in the cabin, he admits, though not at all ruefully, "I have surrendered too. And I will permit myself" (p. 356).

As he prepares to go to the cabin, he has a vision of a classic future, a warm barnyard future of the natural human community, all descending from Lena and the child he has delivered. It is as if the second Christ were the second Adam, with Lena the earth mother who, with Hightower's help, has borne him to start things going: "*She will have to have others, more* remembering the young strong body from out whose travail even there shone something tranquil and unafraid. *More of them. Many more. That will be her life, her destiny. The good stock peopling in tranquil obedience to it the good earth; from these hearty loins without hurry or haste descending mother and daughter. But by Byron engendered next*" (p. 356). His vision permits him now to accept even this last. No longer feeling so old, Hightower enjoys the walk to the cabin. " 'I must do this more often,' he thinks, feeling the intermittent sun, the heat, smelling the savage and fecund odor of the earth, the woods, the loud silence" (p. 356). How different an attitude to the odor of fecundity this is from others we have had in this novel! Indeed, his vision of the "good stock" descending from Lena has given this sterile old man an obsession with fecundity. He feels sorry for Joanna Burden for dying just when fecundity was to return to her fallow ground: " 'Poor, barren woman. To have not lived only a week longer, until luck returned to this place. Under luck and life returned to these barren and ruined acres.' It seems to him that he can see, feel, about him the ghosts of rich fields, and of the rich fecund black life of the quarters, the mellow shouts, the presence of fecund women, the prolific naked children in the dust before the doors; and the big house again, noisy, loud with the treble shouts of the generations" (p. 357). Here is life under the "canopy" and free of the "veil." How different a history this is from the one Hightower has known! It is rather reminiscent of Hans Castorp's snow-dream of the children of the sun, of the golden world of barnyard innocence. So the novel's foremost tragic visionary now dreams a classic vision of the fecund generations of a primitive past and of an unburdened future, although—as we see in our final glimpse of him in the act of dying—he himself remains too trapped by a repressive history to enter such an existence. But what he points toward, what he opens us to, is what we find in the relaxed comic modesty of the epilogue-like final chapter. Whether we retain or disregard the ambitious reaches of the figural level of the novel, whether we are in a new, post-millennial Eden or with three common wayfarers, we find ourselves in the wandering and capacious freedom of a world no longer looking for extremity's sainthood, with its necessary accompaniment of satanism.

12

Murder in the Cathedral: The Limits of Drama and the Freedom of Vision

The question of authentic sainthood clearly brings us to the outer limits of the tragic and classic visions and almost beyond them into the religious—if the religious is a vision to which the fully functioning literary work can earn its way. Yet I must remember that my first chapter dealt negatively with the possibility of religious affirmation through literature. It would, then, be a challenge for me to take—as my limiting case—a work seemingly dedicated to establishing the case for sainthood, but to find in that work an alternative to sainthood that is classic rather than religious. I could not put my study to rest without testing this attempt to get beyond the earthiness of the classic vision, this attempt—despite all the divine-human paradoxes—to get back, where the Greek version of Western culture began, to a transcendence that overcomes and transforms all sublunary tensions. To ask whether a modern work, characterized by an aesthetic and visionary self-consciousness, can bring us there or must settle for the earthly alternative is, in effect, to formulate the problematic of T. S. Eliot's Murder in the Cathedral.

It is difficult to speak, except problematically, about Murder in the Cathedral; and this is the way the play's most useful commentators of three decades have invariably spoken. For one thing, its character as an enclosed, self-sufficient work must be reconciled with its extenuating relations to the works of Eliot which follow upon it. Obviously, one can make claims about the thematic relation of a single work of any writer to his total corpus; but the case is special with Murder in the Cathedral. I am thinking, of course, of the Four Quartets generally, but especially of "Burnt Norton," since this fine poem—opening the way to the later *Quartets*—is so largely a gleaning of leftovers from the play. Thus we can expect from the two not only mutually illuminating thematic returns but elaborations within a pattern of common imagery, again mutually explicative. It is conceivable also that the larger, less restrictive domain of the poem can provide the ground for a freeing of the vision, trapped but struggling to the end in the drama. And it may prove rewarding for the fullest understanding of the play to read that visionary freedom back into the limitations of the stricter form, for while it is true that Eliot took the demands of the stage rather lightly and was anxious not to permit them to impose upon his material, the limitations of drama still make themselves felt.

All this is to turn our attention from these other problems to the single issue treated here, one that is thoroughly thematic, involving the cluster of paradoxes surrounding the claims of sainthood and the claims of dramatic character in the play. I want to trace once more the crucial paradoxes that thrust the charges of the Fourth Tempter and the Fourth Knight (charges which we are to reject as Becket does) against the unquestionably sympathetic presentation of Becket's claim to sainthood. I must try to move beyond the flat acknowledgment of the fact that the charges of willful pride are never answered in drama or dialectic but are merely rejected out of hand, by postulation. Yet there is nothing ambiguous about the fact that the charges *are* rejected and Becket's claim to sainthood is held to be authentic. The problem of will and of resignation—of the possible rationalization that permits us to read the former as the latter—remains to haunt us after we have witnessed the reassurances of Becket and his play. This problem carries with it the generic problem of sainthood for man, the generic problem of the imitation of Christ for him who is less than Christ, who is the Son of Man only. And lurking just behind is fear of the demonism that prompts the false claim to sainthood, these two extremes now becoming masks for one another once the safety of life at the center, in the common routine, is forsaken.

If we are reassured by the daringly affirmative vision behind the play, can we accept it within the dramatic terms created *in* the play *as* the play? Or do we accept—indeed, reach for—the vision despite the play and the evidence earned by its dramatic totality? What is at issue here is the strange intertwining within and beyond the play of the visions that have been my concern. First, in Becket's daring transcendence of the ethical, his confrontation of his more-than-moral risk of demonism, he seems to be leading us into what I have treated as the tragic vision. But second, the presence of the Women of Canterbury as Chorus, the "small folk," "living and partly living," whose "pattern of fate" entwines them with Becket's fate, brings us beyond the tragic and its extremity to the classic vision. Finally, in Becket's pretentious claim to have crossed over, without final doubt or qualification, from the tragic to the religious, we have a Christian vision, the Christ story anew that overwhelms human tragedy. It is this vision—with the leap that is its enabling motion—that I have elsewhere denied the power of being "earned" dramatically, of having access to dramatic categories.[1] Not even the persuasions, the amazing transcendence, of *Murder in the Cathedral* lead me to a different conclusion here. Yet we must account for the power and seeming authenticity of this play.

To the extent, then, that *Murder in the Cathedral* is seen as both a reflection and an evasion of these three visions, it comes to be seen as either the outermost limit of each of them or the threshold to a transcendent union among them. It could lead us to recognize the inadequacy of our discursive demarcations, as we respond to a literary (and existential) experience that makes our categories break down. I believe that Eliot intends both the transcending and the mutual denial of what I have been calling the tragic, the classic, and the Christian; yet this self-conscious evasiveness, as exhibited in the play, can help to make visionary definition possible, despite the fact that, when a single great work can produce such a collapse of categories, it forces us to question the value of such limited entities as we are trying to define. This emergence out of vision and merger of visions thus can help us— eschatologically, as it were—to make our definitions of our limited visions just as the end of history can help to define all that history has been. All this is a great deal to ask of a single work, however ambitiously affirmative its thematic pretensions. Still, we must look into the firmness of its answers.

BECKET AND THE LIMITS OF THE TRAGIC VISION

The endlessly teasing problem of sainthood—how to choose martyrdom without its being a willful and prideful choice—has an emphasis here that retains the Kierkegaardian blurring of demon and saint ("true knight of faith"). It is thus proper, if not inevitable, that Eliot

---

[1] In *The Tragic Vision*, pp. 209–10, 260, 263–64.

should choose this as the issue with which to expose the blind arrogance of the modern secularism that must declare the saint mad with arrogance and sainthood impossible. Yet he freely gives skepticism its voice. I recall being shocked at my *not* feeling shocked upon learning that Eliot had found an occasion to make the Fourth Tempter's lines his own. Then I discovered there had been no reason to be shocked, but rather assured by the sense of the rightness of his choice of that role for himself. Certainly there was no one else in the play whose lines I would have preferred Eliot to have assigned himself. Of course, the Fourth Tempter is not just or right; but where do we find the play *showing* him wrong? This has from the first been the central problem for audiences struggling with the theme of this work and perhaps also for Eliot, as both orthodox writer and critical witness of his own writing.

Clearly, it is only the Fourth Temptation ("To do the right deed for the wrong reason") to which Becket can feel any vulnerability. The first three were expected and are easily dispensed with. Properly, the fourth is the only Tempter Becket had not expected. But the Fourth Tempter claims always to precede expectation, to be already known to Becket, and to tell Becket only what is already known by him. For the prideful seeking of the saint's glory, so claims this Tempter, has been steadily at work in Becket's unconscious, an unsought-for rationalization conditioning his decisions. The Tempter mockingly urges him to carry forth his arrogant quest consistently, in conscious and purposeful awareness of his sinful objective: "Seek the way of martyrdom, make yourself the lowest / On earth, to be high in heaven." The "to be" clearly has the force of "in order to be"—in order to be high in heaven—introducing the sense of conscious purpose in what has been proposed. Thus the very presumptuous action ("make yourself") has in it the willfulness that must contradict its supposed intention— saintly lowliness.

How is Becket to refute such charges convincingly? It is not possible once one submits to the rational procedure that sets them in motion and gives them their force. Every self-justifying claim conceals the taunting wink that suggests a further bit of self-deception. How can one become a saint without willing to be one? When all acts appear to be willed, how does one maintain that the will he is setting in motion is not his but God's, that what he does is not a temporal means to a more-than-temporal end but reflects a will and an act taken totally "out of time"? Of course, what the Tempter beckons him to is the seeking of martyrdom as an utter act of will, insisting there is no other way. Becket recognizes in the Tempter's words the echo of his own desires ("Who are you, tempting with my own desires?"), words and desires equally "dreams to damnation," "damnation in pride." The Tempters together end by seeing him in terms befitting what I have elsewhere termed the tragic existent, the creature of Kierkegaardian despair who has desperately "willed to be himself":

> This man is obstinate, blind, intent
> On self-destruction,
> Passing from deception to deception,
> From grandeur to grandeur to final illusion,
> Lost in the wonder of his own greatness,
> The enemy of society, enemy of himself.

How closely these words foreshadow those of the Four Knights (false knights without faith) in part 2, especially the Fourth Knight's crude verdict on Becket's death as "Suicide while of Unsound Mind." The anti-ethical tendency of Becket's apparent obsession is indicated by the pleas of Chorus, who entwine their fate with his: "O Thomas Archbishop, save us, save us, save yourself that we may be saved; / Destroy yourself and we are destroyed." His next words show his obliviousness to their common desperation in his own drivenness: "Now is my way clear, now is the meaning plain." Of course, he (through his action) is to become their partial savior, as Christ was. But he here acknowledges the justness (from their point of view) of the harsher, skeptic's judgment:

> What yet remains to show you of my history
> Will seem to most of you at best futility,
> Senseless self-slaughter of a lunatic,
> Arrogant passion of a fanatic.

Nevertheless, from his own new and transcendent resolve, such a judgment, though fit for the tragic visionary, is seen to have the visionary limitations—and the consequent blindness—of the fallen, empirical, Manichaean world that spawns it. And the Interlude, together with the second part to which it leads, rejecting such a vision and such a judgment, projects and extends the higher vision and the higher judgment which it justifies and celebrates. If, tragic visionaries ourselves, we choose not to be convinced, then we must accept as our alternative the lowly skeptical judgment that is reduced in stature and seriousness from the fearful, austere brilliance of the Fourth Tempter to the shabbily pragmatic superficiality of the Fourth Knight.

BECKET AND THE LIMITS OF THE CLASSIC VISION

For a while it seems that Becket has failed the Chorus ethically because he has, willfully and waywardly, consulted only his sense of his private destiny. This apparent failure points to the awesome gap between the common, communal role and the extraordinary requirements of the individuated creature chosen to be separated from the herd, between the way of the little people of history and the way of the single great persons, each way with its appropriate blessings and curses. The gap between the "two ways" was Eliot's constant concern, with the special prerogatives and risks of the saint's way an inherited existentialist problem for modern tragic and Christian visionaries, most dramatically posed for them by Kierkegaard. Eliot's conservative institutional allegiances do not make him less radical in his exploration of the alternatives. They are most explicitly formulated in the well-known speeches of Harcourt-Reilly to Celia in *The Cocktail Party*:

> *I can reconcile you to the human condition,*
> *The condition to which some who have gone as far as you*
> *Have succeeded in returning. They may remember*
> *The vision they have had, but they cease to regret it,*
> *Maintain themselves by the common routine,*
> *Learn to avoid excessive expectation,*
> *Become tolerant of themselves and others,*
> *Giving and taking, in the usual actions*
> *What there is to give and take. They do not repine;*
> *Are contented with the morning that separates*
> *And with the evening that brings together*
> *For casual talk before the fire*
> *Two people who know they do not understand each other,*
> *Breeding children whom they do not understand*
> *And who will never understand them.*

. . . .

> *It is a good life. Though you will not know how good*
> *Till you come to the end. But you will want nothing else,*
> *And the other life will be only like a book*
> *You have read once, and lost. In a world of lunacy,*
> *Violence, stupidity, greed . . . it is a good life.*
>
> . . . .
>
> *There is another way, if you have the courage.*
> *The first I could describe in familiar terms*
> *Because you have seen it, as we all have seen it,*
> *Illustrated, more or less, in lives of those about us.*
> *The second is unknown, and so requires faith—*
> *The kind of faith that issues from despair.*
> *The destination cannot be described;*
> *You will know very little until you get there;*
> *You will journey blind. But the way leads towards*
>   *possession*
> *Of what you have sought for in the wrong place.*

Of course Celia, unable like others in the play to settle for "the common routine," ends, though absurdly, in a Christ-like martyrdom of
her own, "crucified very near an ant-hill."

If the embracing of extremity, whether with demoniacal or saintly
frenzy—the product of despair or of transcendent bliss—leads either
into the tragic or beyond the tragic to the religious, so the homely
retreat from extremity found in the uncomprehending simplicities of
"the common routine" leads to what I term the classic. Instead of the
imitation of Christ, undertaken in pride or in submission, there is the
rejection of all that would distinguish a man and his destiny from
the common destiny of the race. The routine march of history is not
to be disrupted, turned into a series of discontinuous crises, by untimely intrusions from a non-temporal order through a temporal
agent. The piety induced by the single fact of Christ need not justify
His intrusion upon history as a precedent for the discomfort of further
eschatalogical punctuations. The quiet, routine continuity of history,
even with its routine sufferings, provides the common comfort of
expectations, for better or worse, being met:

> *We do not wish anything to happen.*
> *Seven years we have lived quietly,*
> *Succeeded in avoiding notice,*

> *Living and partly living.*
> *There have been oppression and luxury,*
> *There have been poverty and license,*
> *There has been minor injustice.*
> *Yet we have gone on living,*
> *Living and partly living.*
> *Sometimes the corn has failed us,*
> *Sometimes the harvest is good,*
> *One year is a year of rain,*
> *Another a year of dryness,*
> *One year the apples are abundant,*
> *Another year the plums are lacking.*
> *Yet we have gone on living,*
> *Living and partly living.*

So it has always been and, so far as the small folk of history can know or want, ought always to be. It is the unique act, the isolated intrusion upon history's universal sequence, that surpasses their understanding, coming as it does from "out of time."

> *But now a great fear is upon us, a fear not of one but*
> *   of many,*
> *A fear like birth and death, when we see birth and death*
> *   alone*
> *In a void apart. We*
> *Are afraid in a fear which we cannot know, which we*
> *   cannot face, which none understands,*
> *And our hearts are torn from us, our brains unskinned*
> *   like the layers of an onion, our selves are lost lost*
> *In a final fear which none understands.*

It is the fear of the separateness and alienation, and of the consequent loss of the clustered comforts shared by the historical human community. Their negative response to the imitator of Christ who threatens their continuity is suspiciously similar to that of Dostoevsky's Grand Inquisitor (and the people he protects and represents) to the return of Christ to history (in order to supersede history). So they reject the role of the exceptional man who tears at the fabric of history's common march, reject it for themselves and others, as they seek to keep that fabric whole and intact—and to cover themselves over with it.

The play is a kind of Christmas oratorio, if the musical metaphor can be applied, though of course far more tentatively than in *Four Quartets*. In the oratorio Becket is the only truly solo voice. All the characters are members of groups except Becket. Even others who sing singly—Priests, Tempters, Knights—are one among colleagues. And there is the central classic voice of the Chorus of Women of Canterbury. In this play in verse, the classic vision, through its passive endurance, its resistance to action and even to firm moral commitment, is really a choral vision. But the choral harmony usually sings sad songs, emerging out of their historical adjustment to the periodic infliction of history's sorrows.[2] Their poetry constitutes the finest passages in the play, but however authentic the resonance of their lines, the play cannot rest in them, must try to move beyond the communal emptiness of their sorrows.

The choral vision, for all its mutual security, feels itself utterly separated from God, even as Becket—in his persistent separateness from the Chorus and their destiny—can claim a union with God as an instrument in His cosmic harmony. But their human fears, as classic rather than tragic existents, lead them to choose their frightening separateness from God rather than to pay the price of separating any one of themselves from the human herd. But toward the end, just before Becket's reckless embracing of his fate, the Chorus fearfully acknowledges the religious consequences of their human togetherness: the fading away into nothingness of the mundane objects that bind communal life to itself. Deprived of the homely rewards of the community that has turned them from Becket in his chosen isolation, they now shrink from the awesome chasm that human consolations have created to keep them from the union with God available to God's lonely man, His saint:

> *Emptiness, absence, separation from God;*
> *The horror of the effortless journey, to the empty land*
> *Which is no land, only emptiness, absence, the Void,*
> *Where those who were men can no longer turn the mind*
> *To distraction, delusion, escape into dream, pretence,*

[2] I speak of sadness rather than despair inasmuch as the latter, at least since Kierkegaard, has been reserved for the singular extremity and intensity of the tragic rather than the routine resignation of the classic.

Where the soul is no longer deceived, for there are no
objects, no tones,
No colours, no forms to distract, to divert the soul
From seeing itself, foully united forever, nothing with
nothing,
Not what we call death, but what beyond death is not
death,
We fear, we fear.

Thus sing the small folk, the uncommitted ones of history, in consequence of their smallness and lack of commitment. How do these passive souls relate themselves to those foul deeds which are part of history's routine march? History's continuity can flow only in accord
with the choral complicity that refuses to see such deeds as creating
discontinuity, that allows human misdeeds to be subsumed within the
sequence of the natural order. How, then, to comprehend guilt within
the need of the classic existent to retain his catholic receptivity to
whatever comes?

How can the problem of guilt exist for those who, like the Chorus,
the small folk, can only look on, who—in their early words—"are
forced to bear witness"? Here, at the start of the action, with the wast-
ing and revitalizing routine calendar of autumn and winter threatened
with disruption by the advent of another Christ, "For us, the poor,
there is no action, / But only to wait and to witness." Still, the repeated language of soiling and cleansing indicates how even the witnesses are forced to become morally involved, are involuntary partici-
pants. The natural order, which is the order of the calendar that makes
up their common routine in its historical march, is itself morally indifferent, countenancing human ill and human good alike. And choral
man, in his "humble and tarnished frame of existence," appears to
cooperate with this natural order and its moral consequences by moving in response to each season, answering with his needs to its
demands.

Yet human evil, the terror of the singular malevolent act that can
shock man out of the complacency wrought by continuity, *is* embedded in the very historical march that tries to pass it by. It shrieks
for a special awareness of itself as a discrete entity, provocative of discontinuity, shrieks for the moral judgment which choral man must try
to resist:

346

> *And war among men defiles this world, but death in the*
>   *Lord renews it,*
> *And the world must be cleaned in the winter, or we shall*
>   *have only*
> *A sour spring, a parched summer, an empty harvest.*
> *Between Christmas and Easter what work shall be done?*
> *The ploughman shall go out in March and turn the same*
>   *earth*
> *He has turned before, the bird shall sing the same song.*
> *When the leaf is out on the tree, when the elder and may*
> *Burst over the stream, and the air is clear and high,*
> *And voices trill at windows, and children tumble in front*
>   *of the door,*
> *What work shall have been done, what wrong*
> *Shall the bird's song cover, the green tree cover, what*
>   *wrong*
> *Shall the fresh earth cover? We wait, and the time is*
>   *short*
> *But waiting is long.*

Man and nature (ploughman and bird) are here united in the other-than-moral circularity of eternal recurrence, as if natural and human evil were the same. But here, by the start of part 2, man has an other-than-natural, a Christian consciousness as well. And he waits, must wait again, wait to witness, and as a witness who is morally a part of it all. These lines have shown us, after all, that the major Christian moments (Christmas and Easter) do become superimposed—as transcendent interruptions—on the circular continuity of the uninterruptable seasonal calendar. (Here, in the two times and the two calendars, is an echo of the simultaneity of "instant" and "instance" that concerned me at the outset of this book.) Choral man must find himself moved beyond the natural, historical calendar to the Christian one, with what I have called its eschatological punctuations. The natural cleansing of the winter may be reflected in the hopes of what began on Christmas; but the wrong covered by bird's song, green tree, and fresh earth—joyous signs of the new year—may have to remain uncovered and still-happening in the Christian consciousness as chronological time turns static. Not unlike the blood sacrifice, the dismembering of the child quietly sanctioned by the "children of the sun" in

Thomas Mann's *The Magic Mountain*, or the single tear of another dismembered child that taunts Ivan Karamazov in his rebellion against the earthly paradise, here too the unique "wrong" can never be finally covered by "fresh earth" for man—not even for choral man, who, by thus allowing his history to be arrested, moves toward the gap between himself and Becket, his next Christian saint. And this is to close the gap between the classic and the Christian visions by announcing the insufficiency of the former. Human evil superimposes itself upon natural evil in a way that requires the discontinuity of special recognition, requires the interruption of the classic march of humanity that imitates the seasonal march of nature.

The human, then, must use its saints to respond more than naturally to the wrongs absorbed by the natural cycle, to force itself to the recognition that it too is "soiled" by each "new terror." Otherwise, in their natural uncommitment, the Chorus can see "the young man mutilated, / The torn girl trembling" (further dismemberment), and still go on living,

> *Living and partly living,*
> *Picking together the pieces,*
> *Gathering faggots at nightfall,*
> *Building a partial shelter,*
> *For sleeping, and eating and drinking and laughter.*

History and their classic historical role bring the Chorus, as the willing witnesses (willing in their acquiescence in history's march in order to preserve the comforts of the common routine), to complicity in history's sins. The play traces their increasing awareness of this complicity, enabling them, just before the murder, to confess the moral implications of their passivity:

> *I have smelt them, the death-bringers; now is too late*
> *For action, too soon for contrition.*
> *Nothing is possible but the shamed swoon*
> *Of those consenting to the last humiliation.*
> *I have consented, Lord Archbishop, have consented.*

Having partaken empathically in the death-dealings of nature, both killer and victim, they *have* known "What was coming to be":

> *What is woven on the loom of fate*
> *What is woven in the councils of princes*
> *Is woven also in our veins, our brains,*
> *Is woven like a pattern of living worms*
> *In the guts of the women of Canterbury.*

Becket attempts to exonerate them in their own eyes ("These things had to come to you and you to accept them") and promises that after the deed ("When the figure of God's purpose is made complete") a "sudden painful joy" shall lighten their return to their household routine. But the murder itself seems to lift them out of history and its common routine for good. All the world is incurably tainted with the complicity of a Lady Macbeth; the natural cleansing power of time's circle is abrogated; time indeed must have a stop: stop the world, I want to get off!

> *How how can I ever return, to the soft quiet seasons?*
> *Night stay with us, stop sun, hold season, let the day not*
> *come, let the spring not come.*
> *Can I look again at the day and its common things, and*
> *see them all smeared with blood, through a curtain*
> *of falling blood?*
> *We did not wish anything to happen.*
> *We understood the private catastrophe,*
> *The personal loss, the general misery,*
> *Living and partly living;*
> *The terror by night that ends in daily action,*
> *The terror by day that ends in sleep;*
> *But the talk in the market-place, the hand on the broom,*
> *The nighttime heaping of the ashes,*
> *The fuel laid on the fire at daybreak,*
> *These acts marked a limit to our suffering.*
> *Every horror had its definition,*
> *Every sorrow had a kind of end:*
> *In life there is not time to grieve long.*
> *But this, this is out of life, this is out of time,*
> *An instant eternity of evil and wrong.*

Nevertheless, the play closes with the hallelujah chorus—though finally it is a modest hallelujah—addressed to God, and at the last to

Christ and to Becket as newly risen: in the Christian time scheme Easter is already present in Christmas. The promise of Becket is ful-filled as the small folk, those who try vainly to clean ("the scrubbers and sweepers of Canterbury") and to accept history ("the men and women who shut the door and sit by the fire"), at once acknowledge their guilt, present and past, ask forgiveness together with the power to return to their role with its further guilts. Their commonness, and the limitation of role which it permits, still must prevent even the most momentary union with God or Christ or even Becket. But the polar relation to Becket with which we began has been appreciably closed, although the gap that remains is all-important and the closure cannot proceed further. Hence the separateness and emptiness are not even momentarily dispelled; but Becket, as resurrected, has become their divine intercessor. Their final lines call upon God and Christ to have mercy and upon Becket to pray for them. The imitation of Christ has worked and leads to divine consequences, even if their effects on "the common man" are limited by his continuing role as common man.

What we have been witnessing is the attempt to lighten the classic through the religious without that classic losing its essentially choral, routine, circular pattern. The play has moved from distance between Chorus and Becket to closeness with some crucial distance retained, as Becket's function turns out to serve, not only *his* service of God's pat-tern, but the needs of the Chorus and their self-awareness. They begin with a dedication only to history's amoral pattern and a resist-ance to all disruption of it; they move to an awareness of guilt and then to a total assumption of guilt, as they forgo history's pattern for the Christian pattern, the soothing passage of time for the apoca-lyptic stoppage of time; and they close with a most uncommonly justi-fied and uncommonly self-aware return to the common routine, together with a dedication to both time patterns at once. Becket is the agent of this reconciliation of the two patterns, his action "out of time" taken by this man of his time. The pattern of his agency and his saint's role before Christ and God establish him as intercessor for the common man as he adopts the pattern of the risen Christ, the arche-typal saint. The doubleness within the divine-human paradox clearly marks the pagan inadequacies of choral man, patterned only by the natural community in its common routine. The historical absorption of extremity denies the exceptional because of the terror produced by its risks. The greatest of such risks is the demoniacal probability lurk-ing beneath the impossible self-assignment of sainthood. This is the fear we have observed: that the Christian is the deceiving mask for the tragic. We must return to grapple with Becket's dismissal of such fear.

Becket and the Improbable Possibility of Christian Vision

In almost his very first words in the play, Becket instructs the Priests and the Women of Canterbury about the passive condition in which we discover the Chorus. He uses the metaphor of the wheel to characterize the circular time they aimlessly travel. It is this passage that establishes the terms for the problematics of will in this play:

> They know and do not know, what it is to act or suffer.
> They know and do not know, that acting is suffering
> And suffering is action. Neither does the actor suffer
> Nor the patient act. But both are fixed
> In an eternal action, an eternal patience
> To which all must consent that it may be willed
> And which all must suffer that they may will it,
> That the pattern may subsist, for the pattern is the
>   action
> And the suffering, that the wheel may turn and still
> Be forever still.

The Aristotelian opposition between action and the suffering of action, between actor (or agent) and patient, is central. This terminology gives Eliot the opportunity for effective puns on "suffering" and "patient" in characterizing the receptive passivity of the "small folk." As patients, those acted upon rather than acting, their only virtue is their capacity to be patient; they must suffer the acts visited upon them by history as they must suffer from them. Aristotelian patience, then, breeds the classic need for patience as Aristotelian suffering breeds the routinely accepted suffering of the classic existent. It was in this double sense that I referred earlier to the line "These acts marked a limit to our suffering," suggesting the crucial function of the common events of good and ill in keeping suffering finite ("Every horror had its definition") and in making possible the small folk's acceptance (suffering) of all that they must endure (suffer). Aristotelian and human patience, then, becomes both the motive and the consequence of human suffering as it becomes the equivalent of Aristotelian suffering. How many dimensions of meaning are thus locked in the paradoxical notion that "acting is suffering / And suffering is action." In this enigmatic relation between the mover and the moved is found the further puzzle of movement itself and its relation to stillness, to pattern. In effect it is the puzzle of the divine scheme and its relation to the endless motions of human history, as we are returned to the two kinds of calendars we have been concerned with, the serial and the Christian, which is to say the historical and the eschatological: "that the wheel may turn and still / Be forever still." These words send us to "Burnt Norton," that repository of unused lines from the play, where there is an important elaboration of the wheel image and its indispensable metaphorizing of movement and non-movement:

> At the still point of the turning world. Neither flesh nor
>   fleshless;
> Neither from nor towards; at the still point, there the
>   dance is,
> But neither arrest nor movement. And do not call it
>   fixity,
> Where past and future are gathered. Neither movement
>   from nor towards,
> Neither ascent nor decline. Except for the point, the still
>   point,
> There would be no dance, and there is only the dance.
> I can only say, there we have been: but I cannot say
>   where.
> And I cannot say, how long, for that is to place it in
>   time.

In all these words, in play and poem, is enclosed the problem of the will—the very determination of the possibility of will—of acting and/ or suffering action (and suffering *from* action). To return to the passage in the play, the endlessly repetitive movement along the rim would seem to produce the suffering patient who neither knows nor wills his being turned on the wheel. We recall Becket's early words,

> We do not know very much of the future
> Except that from generation to generation
> The same things happen again and again.

.   .   .   .

> *. . . Only*
> *The fool, fixed in his folly, may think*
> *He can turn the wheel on which he turns.*

Those on the rim, then, may know their historical role but not the significance of it, since that would call for metahistorical knowledge, a true knowing of the pattern, the dance—a knowledge reserved for the hub. So, by contrast to the passively turning world along the rim, the source of all movement at the hub is the sublime agent, the knowing, willing, turning agent. The hub, as both the still point and the source of movement, is not mere fixity but is rather that which transforms movement into dance, transforms action and suffering into "the pattern" of action and suffering, agent and patient becoming "fixed / In an eternal action, an eternal patience" which can unite the suffering with the willing of the suffering. Thus we come to the role of the saint as the spoke to run between rim and hub and thus to reconcile the two times: to reconcile the endless movement among unmarked moments with the movement as pattern, as dance, as tied to the sublime stillness of the wheel's hub.

In terms of the distinction between hub and rim, it would appear that no one who is subject to human time along the rim can safely take on the risks of the agent: acting, knowing, willing, turning the wheel. For, far from stillness and the origin of the pattern that is dance, he is by definition the patient: suffering and, neither knowing nor willing, being turned on the wheel. It is in this sense that the small folk are correct in their assessment of their historical role and that Becket is correct in his words about them. And that central problem of sainthood with which we began finally concerns itself with the possibility of the *active* existence of that connecting rod, the spoke, between that timeless first cause at the hub and the endless chronological effects along the rim. These are the risks that Becket, or Eliot behind him, assumes when he rejects the tragic and the classic (or the demoniacal and the choral) as his only alternative ways of action and elects the assurance and authenticity of the Christian.

The metaphor of the wheel would seem normally to leave two mutually exclusive ways of action: on the one hand, the abject resignation to fate of the small folk, which is in effect a surrender of will and of an individuated sense of special destiny (perhaps akin to Kierkegaard's "not willing to be oneself" or, less, "not willing to be a self"), or, on the other hand, the attempt to create one's private fate, to turn the wheel, which is the arrogant celebration of will (perhaps akin to Kierkegaard's defiant "willing despairingly to be oneself"). Becket's movement from part 1 through the Interlude of the Christmas sermon to part 2, as well as what we have seen him do for the Chorus as he moves them to their *Te Deum*, is clearly intended to reflect his miraculous discovery of the third way, the synthesis of agent and patient: the losing of his will in the will of God and his new capacity to act (or to suffer action) safely, in accordance with what he has found as a consequence of what he has willingly lost. The blessed resignation to the turning wheel allows him to will to have it turn as it does. The radiance is upon him, the power of radiating from hub to rim, the divine-human intermediary for the Chorus: their saint.

How persuasive can Eliot make this miracle, without which our skepticism will force us back once more to the fearsomeness of the tragic on the one hand or the selfless passivity of the classic on the other? The Fourth Tempter had urged Becket willfully to turn the wheel, at one point transposing the circular imagery to thread and skein: "You hold the skein: wind, Thomas, wind / The thread of eternal life and death." This call to prideful self-will, disdained by Becket, is echoed by contrast in lines we have looked at before in another connection: a different manipulation of the image expresses the selfless passivity with which the Chorus later feels its union with the common horrors of the historical process:

> What is woven on the loom of fate
> What is woven in the councils of princes
> Is woven also in our veins, our brains,
> Is woven like a pattern of living worms
> In the guts of the women of Canterbury.

How successful can Eliot be in assuring us that Becket neither does what the Tempter urges in the first of these passages nor shares the fated quality of the Chorus in the second?

Most of the assurances come from Becket himself, first in his response to the Fourth Tempter, more firmly in his Christmas sermon, and absolutely as he faces his death. The most explicit statement is, of course, the statement in prose, the flat assertion in the Christmas sermon, in which all the doubts of part 1 have, at least in Becket, been dispelled:

> *A Christian martyrdom is no accident. Saints are*
> *not made by accident. Still less is a Christian martyrdom*
> *the effect of a man's will to become a Saint, as a man*
> *by willing and contriving may become a ruler of*
> *men. . . . A martyrdom is never the design of man;*
> *for the true martyr is he who has become the instrument*
> *of God, who has lost his will in the will of God,*
> *not lost it but found it, for he has found freedom in*
> *submission to God. The martyr no longer desires*
> *anything for himself, not even the glory of martyrdom.*

Eliot clearly has made good use of the date of Becket's murder, the closeness with which it follows upon Christmas. This allows him to emphasize Becket as saintly imitator of Christ. Of course, the Christmas sermon prepares us for Becket's Easter, thus allowing Eliot also to unite the moment of martyrdom with the moment and promise of birth: to unite Easter with Christmas, mourning with rejoicing, end with beginning, all within a divine plan that enfolds the one in the other. Yet can we feel totally secure, after the words of Becket given above, when he concludes his sermon by confessing his own confidence that his own martyrdom may be at hand? "I have spoken to you today . . . of the martyrs of the past . . . because . . . I do not think I shall ever preach to you again; and because it is possible that in a short time you may have yet another martyr."

Once he is this confident that his will has been re-formed in accordance with a higher destiny, Becket can act, in part 2, in ways that make him seem amazingly anxious for martyrdom. And these acts also shake our confidence in his freedom from the prideful pursuit of sainthood. The challenges he repeatedly flings at the Knights may seem really too provocative. Thus, among his less antagonistic responses, "At whatsoever time you are ready to come, / You will find me still more ready for martyrdom." A bit later, as the Priests plead with him to retreat from the Knights, who have returned armed for the kill,

> *All my life they have been coming, these feet. All my*
> *life*
> *I have waited. Death will come only when I am worthy,*
> *And if I am worthy, there is no danger.*

IV. Through an Alternative to Sainthood

> *I have therefore only to make perfect my will.*

Or,

> *No life here is sought for but mine,*
> *And I am not in danger: only near to death.*

When the Priests ask about the consequences upon themselves ("What shall become of us, my Lord, if you are killed?"), Becket's answer reveals a sublime, if maddeningly anti-ethical, indifference:

> *That again is another theme*
> *To be developed and resolved in the pattern of time.*

His ecstatic longing knows no bounds:

> *I have had a tremor of bliss, a wink of heaven, a*
> *   whisper,*
> *And I would no longer be denied; all things*
> *Proceed to a joyful consummation.*

When the Priests, having barred the door, rejoice in their safety, Becket's reaction, in words he admits they will find "reckless, desperate, mad," is that they "unbar the doors! throw open the doors!" For he has "only to conquer / Now, by suffering. This is the easier victory."

Can we help worrying that it is too easy? With the Fourth Tempter behind us and so exaggeratedly extreme a performance before us, can we help retaining some of our skepticism? But then, as if to show us how thoroughly we have allowed our fallen, secular selves to be tricked, Eliot puts on stage the *reductio* of that secular skepticism in the argument of the Knights, especially the Fourth. His coarseness and shallowness of mind and temperament are simply the extension of our own ironic attitude toward the action. If we accept our reasonable doubts, we have to accept him. And we discover that this is precisely why he is addressing us this way, that between him and us there is also the wink of fellowship. But against his sophomoric rationalism there are only those firm assertions of the frenzied Archbishop, heaven-bent (or hell-bent?) for fellowship with Christ—

> *His blood given to buy my life,*
> *My blood given to pay for His death,*
> *My death for His death.*

Those assertions, as ungrounded in action or argument as they are in their appeal to miracle, leave us free to believe or not to believe, in which latter case we must accept fellowship with the Knights. Having allowed us our smugness of unbelief, Eliot now uses the Knights as a mirror for our shame.

The fact is that Eliot has reinforced the inspired Becket's confident assertions by the ways in which he has allowed his play to develop. There is an upward movement in Becket and the Chorus that confirms his victory, matched by a downward movement in the dignity of opposing arguments that damns the skeptical denial of that victory. Becket moves from doubts to the absolving of doubts to absolute certainty; similarly, the Chorus moves from total alienation from Becket to a partial identity of goals with him, so that they find a new relation to him and, through him, to God and Christ. Thus there is for the Chorus incompleteness even at the end, with the modesty of the choral vision never altogether abandoned; but there is considerable advance toward momentary union also, even if there is retreat as well. But for Becket the closure with heaven is absolute, even as the meaning of this closure for the Chorus remains relative. In the meantime, the force of the skeptic's counterargument weakens significantly as we move from the dignity, the poetic brilliance, the awesome Mephistophelian mockery of the Fourth Tempter's lines downward to the offensive prosaic vulgarity of the several Knights. The daring lines of the Fourth Tempter seem to have tempted Eliot himself to mouth them, while our embarrassment at the end is occasioned by the leering inference that we ought to be mouthing the lines of prose with the Knights. So Eliot has strategically ordered the progression of the opposed lines of possibility, fashioning them as a rhetorical support for the desperate claims of Becket which we are to accept.

Yet what evidence do we have, after all, besides the explicit and more subtle manipulations of rhetoric? Since it is all presumably a matter of faith, however, what more dare we possibly expect to have? Nevertheless, whatever Becket may or may not be in terms of the metaphor of the wheel, as acting patient or patient actor, he is after all—on stage and in this play—the central agent, carrying on before our eyes causes that have cataclysmic effects. And it is when we must judge him as dramatic character, basing that judgment upon dramatic evidence, upon what seems probable, that we find our willingness to share Becket's faith in his special destiny sorely tried. Becket (like Eliot behind him) well knows it will be, as he acknowledges again and again the privateness of his sense of his vindication, his private sense of the sureness with which he has evaded the traps of demoniacal temptations. He can give us no more certainty, can no more communicate the authenticity of his vision—in defense against the charge that it is a self-deceptive, corrupting illusion—than could Kierkegaard's Abraham, who was ready to sacrifice Isaac.

No one is more aware than Becket (unless it is the Eliot behind him) of the difficulty, if not the impossibility, of his movement, and of the obvious danger that it will be confounded with the willful pursuit of martyrdom. In my own terms, this difficulty results from the skeptic's claim that only the tragic or demoniacal and the classic or choral are authentic visions, and that the would-be Christian is a self-deceptive version of the first. Eliot shows us his awareness of this difficulty throughout the play, from the persuasiveness—never reasonably dispensed with—of the Fourth Tempter to the *reductio* of the Knights. Theirs is the appropriate response of the secular, rational-empirical mind to the evidence. It is, after all, Eliot himself who indulges the irony of putting into the mouth of the Fourth Tempter, in his final speech to Becket, the very words on acting and suffering, actor and patient, that we have heard Becket speak at the beginning about the Chorus ("You know and do not know," etc.). It is a savage mockery, reducing Becket to one of the small folk—the only kind there are—and reminding him that these words can also be used to justify the ways of human will: that acting willfully is also a way of existing that humankind must suffer. For the Tempter hurls these words of Becket's back into his teeth in response to the still-doubting Becket's desperate questions:

> *Is there no way, in my soul's sickness,*
> *Does not lead to damnation in pride?*
> *I well know that these temptations*
> *Mean present vanity and future torment.*
> *Can sinful pride be driven out*
> *Only by more sinful? Can I neither act nor suffer*
> *Without perdition?*

The Tempter is shrewd to answer by echoing Becket's words, telling him to suffer his need to act pridefully, to suffer this much perdition while using the small folk's excuse that removes moral responsibility. Yet Becket is shortly to resolve these doubts, whether or not we join him.

"Can sinful pride be driven out / Only by more sinful?" Becket has asked. Such circularity suggests an infinite regress as the charge of self-deceptive rationalization confronts and is confronted by Becket's ambitious postulation of the union of his will with God's. Each new claim of victory over the earthbound temptation is made only to face the leering face of doubt again. An earlier Tempter, suggesting the hidden nature of Becket's collaboration, has said, "a nod is as good as a wink." And the sense of the wink persists long after Becket achieves his certainty until it becomes the downright smirk of the Knights.[3] Thus the possibility of a new rationalization lurks behind each unrationalized rationalization to challenge the possibility of sainthood. Only the irrational leap beyond the evidence of human drama can dissolve the last and lasting doubt.[4]

These dangers in our response, and in our proper response, Eliot well knows, as he knows that he has put the Fourth Tempter into the play, and Becket's words into the Fourth Tempter's mouth, at his peril. It is his way of precluding our skepticism by himself explicitly providing the basis for it. The Fourth Tempter, after all, has foreseen our skeptical response as well as that of the Fourth Knight when, speaking cynically about the anti-miraculous role of "historical fact" in future judgments, he warns Becket of the time "When men shall declare that there was no mystery / About this man who played a certain part in history." Similarly, Eliot warns us by having Becket warn first the Chorus and later the Priests that they (and we) will not be able to distinguish, through what they (and we) see, between the behavior of

---

[3] The reader should recall the "wink" as an instrument that produces moral self-condemnation from the discussion of *All the King's Men* in Chapter 10 above.

[4] In its way, this infinite regress is a reverse of the similarly maddening one in Thomas Mann's *Doctor Faustus*, in which the sinner's self-conscious awareness of the challenge made to God by his depraved unrepentance must compete endlessly with the everlastingness of God's goodness (see the discussion of this infinite regress of diabolical competition in *The Tragic Vision*, pp. 100–102). Such an inversion of competitions between Leverkühn and Becket is appropriate to the difference in their intended pretensions; Leverkühn's Christ-like imitation of the Antichrist and Becket's Christ-like imitation of Christ.

IV. Through an Alternative to Sainthood

Becket as incipient saint and the behavior of Becket as willful demon, between his claim of acting outside time and the dramatic reality of his action as a part of "history" (the word that is brilliantly rhymed here with "mystery," the force opposed to "history"). That is, the actions of Becket are identical with what they would be if the Fourth Tempter were correct. The worst sin, Becket has told us, is "to do the right deed for the wrong reason." But how can reason show us his reason to be right or wrong? We have already seen him tell the Chorus, at the end of part 1,

> What yet remains to show you of my history
> Will seem to most of you at best futility,
> Senseless self-slaughter of a lunatic,
> Arrogant passion of a fanatic.

And I have remarked that later, in answer to the Priests' sensible plea that he should not pursue death so perversely as to refuse to bar the door, Becket is himself aware that he is removed from all sensible argument:

> Unbar the door!
> You think me reckless, desperate and mad.
> You argue by results, as this world does,
> To settle if an act be good or bad.
> You defer to the fact.

Surely this is also addressed to the beholder of the spectacle, the necessarily empiricist audience bound by the facts that pass before it.

Eliot thus *is* our Fourth Tempter, as through Becket he insists that nothing his drama can show us can remove our doubts about this desperate mode of Christian affirmation. Yet if we retain our doubts, we must suffer our fellowship with the Fourth Knight. We cannot quarrel with the factual accuracy of the Fourth Knight's claim that Becket "used every means of provocation; from his conduct, step by step, there can be no inference except that he had determined upon a death by martyrdom." But we are struck by the doubleness revealed by the possible significance of these words. Does the Knight really know all he is saying, or is he merely saying all he knows?

What Eliot has shown us is that his work must fail (is *intended* to fail) dramatically in order to succeed theologically; and its success as poem can still be realized because it is a more-than-dramatic work, if not indeed an anti-drama. We know somehow that Becket's vision as authentic *does* take shape here, that Eliot *has* worked it, although we must await the totality of *Four Quartets* to find that vision earned in a way that is not at war with itself. It can come to us in *Four Quartets* because, musical rather than dramatic, there is no action there to cultivate extremity and its ultimate dilemma, so that purely metaphorical resolutions of the paradoxes leave us less divided.

At war with the fact and with what facts allow, Eliot presses the uncompromising, seemingly anti-ethical extremity of Becket at the end in order to urge the phenomenal identity between Becket and the self-slaughtering "lunatic." The play's facts cannot *show* that we have one rather than the other. Yet the final hallelujah of the Chorus proves that they have been moved beyond dull empiricism and that his moving of them is a major part of Becket's gift: it is what the saint, in his intrusion upon history, does to lighten its common routine. Having failed dramatically to demonstrate his miracle, Eliot has managed to produce it in us after all.

It is as if the end of the play finds us sitting on the frame of our picture, looking both ways and noting its limits. The metadramatic leap of faith that affirms Becket's saintliness reveals the limits of the narrowly aesthetic by reducing the play to the secular skepticism, the brute empiricism, behind the Aristotelian doctrine of probability. For we must, despite Aristotle, open ourselves to the improbable possibility, however it violates our aesthetic convictions. As Christian visionary, Eliot becomes a denier of his own drama, of what he has—with tactical shrewdness—shown us. He can do no better and no more, if we refuse to join the final Chorus, except to leave us the absurd negations in the Knights' reductions—although, alas, these are not without justification in the action. We can say, then, that while "The Mortal No" (as chronicled—after Wallace Stevens—by Frederick Hoffman[5]) is sustained by the limiting structure of Eliot's drama, the metadramatic vision yet can see beyond to an everlasting yea. Dare we say that this visionary thrust occurs *because* of the drama and not in spite of it, that the miracle succeeds even as it fails, that we are persuaded of it even as our skepticism reduces it? I believe we

[5] *The Mortal No: Death and the Modern Imagination* (Princeton, N.J.: Princeton University Press, 1964).

must. I believe that negation has worked a strange and special magic: that here, at the fringes of what literature can allow, the play, by pretending to earn a most ambitious vision it cannot earn, has earned it after all.

But this is to soar too high for this volume. For finally, I must maintain, as I have warned, that whatever has been earned beyond drama has also been earned beyond the classic vision, which, in its modesty, stays within human history. It will not, even at the end, move beyond the fate of the ploughman: it will share the vision of human destiny of Tithonus ("Man comes and tills the field and lies beneath") so that it need not share his fate. Like the force attributed by Zeitblom to the end of Leverkühn's *Lamentation of Doctor Faustus* ("It changes its meaning; it abides as a light in the night"), my treatment of *Murder in the Cathedral* is to abide as the light in the night of this book. There *is* a moving, if modest, alternative to sainthood, so that nothing within the book is changed. Yet, in the reflection of Becket, all *seems* changed. The classic may never be able to move beyond where we have left it, but we can never see it as being quite the same—quite so modest—again.

Epilogue

We have enlarged our authors' metaphors into extravagant contextual systems and have allowed ourselves to become trapped in them. But in each case—with the author's guidance—we have had the steadfast common sense required to unmask the entire operation as no more than verbal play, as we retreated to the pre-aesthetic reality of objects in the world, of things rather than words. The aesthetic purist, like the moral purist, is a creature of extremity. Like the moral purist in his commitments, the aesthetic purist—in his contextual commitments to metaphor—must claim a nothing-left-out-ness for that metaphor. But *everything* is left out, according to the voice of anti-extremity: the whole organic world outside language. Still, the hold of the metaphor upon us persists, if anything the more magically, because of the firm worldly skepticism which we have allowed free play.

So the metaphors have held and they haven't. In each case the total yielding to the metaphor, as an extreme reduction, risks producing the unmitigated tragic, while total resistance to it can produce merely the dull ethical; only a willingness at once to engage and disengage characterizes the most richly and maturely classic. Thus the total commitment to metaphor is a puritanical commitment, as the retreat to the inconsistent and the sloppily human represents the unyielding living organism, with its hold-out capacity that resists even language. It resists language for the sake of the rich life outside, to which, at the last, it requires the language—in its anti-metaphorical mode—to point. Together with the commitment to metaphor, there is a commitment to the representation of a common reality such as will be familiar to readers of Erich Auerbach. Here is the source of the anti-puritanism of so many of these works.

It should be worth reviewing—even in too simplified a form—this aspect of the several examples of the "richly and maturely classic" which I have treated. In each of them there has been a reductive metaphor which has created a context that seemed all-controlling, and in each there somehow comes to be a counter-metaphorical assertion. I do not mean to use "somehow" as a cover-all to mask a mystique. Rather I mean it—here and in what follows—to stand for the many, often surreptitious or half-seen ways we have observed in which the classic-visionary author forces life's stubborn, unpredictable contingencies to rebound within the exclusiveness, the wrought-ness, of his art (that is, his metaphor, his context). If I have done my job, the "somehow" is what the preceding chapters have, for the most part, been about.

Here, then, is an admittedly crude summary of my chapters as they relate to the reductive metaphor.

The Renaissance poets whom I classified as an early variety of classic visionary oppose the "monistic poets" by pressing the metaphor that reduces earthly activity to a lowly status, untouchable by any higher realm or hope. It similarly reduces language to a nominalism of discrete entities that cannot be enlarged or transformed into a substantive union. But the poets' willingness to create modest joys within such lowliness and such limitations "somehow" asserts itself so as to make an unelevatable life worth pursuing.

In the works of Pope which I treated, the master-metaphor reduces the weighty, fleshly reality to the abstract, airy purity of aesthetic form. But the elementary requirements of bodily existence somehow assert themselves, heavily but unavoidably.

In the works of Johnson the master-metaphor reduces worldly sorrow, by way of aesthetic and moral distance, to the undifferentiated universals which cool contemplation prevails upon us to bear without pain. But the frustration and agony of the private vanity (in both senses) somehow assert themselves to keep life painfully warm.

In the works of Wordsworth the master-metaphor reduces the imperfection of man's position in nature and of his behavior to the Fall of Man and the sense of absolute and irrecoverable loss that accompanies it. But the camaraderie of sorrow and the mutuality of human need somehow assert themselves to permit some recovery from what should have been a Fall beyond recovery.

In *Adam Bede* the master-metaphor reduces all acts to their final, extreme, and irreversible consequences, so that discontinuity strikes and life cannot go on. But life, as ongoing, somehow asserts itself, ameliorating the consequences of the trauma which seemed beyond amelioration.

I do not treat *Pride and Prejudice* or *Barchester Towers* in these terms since I classify them as "naïve." They are not, in the manner of the others, doubled in voice, lacking as they do the existential and metaphorical risk, the now-you-see-it-now-you-don't breadth and receptiveness of the well-orchestrated choral vision.

In the works of Swift the master-metaphor reduces man to unmitigated Yahoo, except that man's clumsy assembling of his routine life as human somehow does mitigate his role as creature.

In *Tristram Shandy* the master-metaphor reduces all of our living reality to the dimensions of mentally created hobby-horses, except that time and the bodily demands somehow assert themselves to keep objective, chronological life moving.

In *All the King's Men* the master-metaphor reduces moral decisions to the neutral accidents of our neurological twitches. But man manages somehow to assert his claim to find differences of moral value among his decisions as he asserts his responsibility for making his history.

In *Light in August* the master-metaphor reduces our sinful history to its incarnation in a single "figure," except that the empirical variety of our commonly separate existences somehow asserts itself, in guilt and innocence.

In *Murder in the Cathedral* the master-metaphor reduces the claim to sainthood to the demonism of a self-conscious act of will that destroys oneself and others. But humanity's choral capacity to absorb and suffer consequences—to do more than witness—somehow gives the exemplary life a beneficent (and saintly?) historical power.

So now, as Rosalie Colie puts it, our metaphors have been "unmetaphored."[1] But (to borrow a notion and some words from Prospero) are poetry's charms all o'erthrown? Or are they not rather reinforced? The metaphors may have been unmetaphored, but they remain forms of imagination that constitute a reality, though it is now seen as imperfect. As such forms, the metaphors sustain us still. And that is perhaps the most classic notion of all.

[1] This notion of "unmetaphoring" is the seat of the power of her remarkable book, *"My Ecchoing Song": Andrew Marvell's Poetry of Criticism* (Princeton, N.J.: Princeton University Press, 1970).

Index

Index

Index